THE PURSUIT OF PERFECTION

BOOKS BY GARRY O'CONNOR

The Pursuit of Perfection
A Life of Maggie Teyte   1979

French Theatre Today   1976

Maggie Teyte at nineteen, making her début at the Opéra-Comique, Paris, as Glycère in *Circé*.

THE PURSUIT OF PERFECTION
A Life of Maggie Teyte

by

GARRY O'CONNOR

But the singer must still have one thing: the universal ground of
all mood, the ability to apply imagination to the voice, the
ability to sing with imagination.

SÖREN KIERKEGAARD, from "A
Passing Comment on a Detail
in *Don Giovanni*", 1845

ATHENEUM

NEW YORK

1979

To
Laurie with love,
and in memoriam
Bill Meredith-Owens

Contents

Illustrations

As Antonia in Offenbach's *Les Contes d'Hoffmann*

As Cherubino in *Le Nozze di Figaro*

In the title role of *Mignon* by Ambroise Thomas

As Mimi in *La Bohème*

In costume for a recital of old French songs (Matzene, Chicago)

In California, 1915, with Charles Wakefield Cadman and Indian Princess Redfeather (courtesy of Elma R. Marvin and the Riverside, California, Municipal Museum)

following page 160

Teyte as the Little Dutch Girl, 1920

Woolley Hall, home of the Cottinghams near Maidenhead, Berkshire (courtesy of Southern Electricity Board)

Sherwin Cottingham, Maggie Teyte's second husband (courtesy of Mrs Howlett)

Sherwin's father, Walter C. Cottingham, at Woolley

Maggie exercising her dogs in the grounds at Woolley

Woolley Grange (courtesy of Southern Electricity Board)

Sherwin Cottingham in the late 1920s

Sherwin and Vera Owen at their wedding in 1931

Vera Cottingham with her daughter Patricia

Programme for the 1930 production of *Pelléas* at Covent Garden

Teyte in the 1930s

Sir Thomas Beecham (courtesy of Shirley, Lady Beecham)

Teyte as Madama Butterfly in the 1930s

As Hänsel, in Humperdinck's *Hänsel und Gretel*

Rita Odoli-Tate, Maggie Teyte's niece, with the Tate family nurse

Rita in the 1920s, before her marriage to Cavan O'Connor

Cavan O'Connor, in a 1963 drawing by his son John

Maggie's friend Grace Vernon, with Michael O'Connor

Maggie in New York in the 1930s, with Joe Brogan

"Mélisande's tower", where Maggie lived in New York

following page 224

On board the *Queen Elizabeth I* in 1946 (PA-Reuters)

Rehearsing for *Pelléas* at the New York City Center, 1948 (Ben Greenhaus)

With Stephen Spender at Stockbridge, Massachusetts, 1949

following page 256

Teyte with Maria Callas in the Crush Bar at Covent Garden (Barratts Photo Press)

After receiving her DBE, 1958 (N.S. Rota-PA-Reuters)

Maggie Teyte in her seventies, with the score of *Pelléas et Mélisande* (photograph by Garry O'Connor)

ILLUSTRATIONS IN THE TEXT

Preface

DAME MAGGIE TEYTE, DBE, who died on 27 May 1976 aged eighty-eight, was the most famous English singer of her generation, an international celebrity in Edwardian times, outstanding as a soprano in opera and in musical comedy; also supreme as an interpreter of French art song. Her long professional life divides into three almost distinct careers: in the first, success as a prima donna came early, with her famous interpretation of Debussy's Mélisande, as well as with her part in the rise to popularity of Mozart in France and England during the first decade of this century; the second produced a set of French song recordings of such subtlety and profound appeal as to guarantee immortality; her third career, begun at the age of fifty-seven, took on, as one commentator has written, a "fairy-tale" quality when she made a triumphant return to the United States, finally achieving, at the age of sixty, her ambition to sing Mélisande in New York. "What enabled her to hold her own beside . . . Melba and Eames and Calvé was her special interpretive gift," wrote Desmond Shawe-Taylor on the Festival Hall concert given in 1955 to mark her forty-ninth anniversary as a singer, "her peculiar insight into the new poetic world of Debussy, Duparc, Fauré and Hahn, and her power of communicating that insight in terms of an uncommon and captivating personality." Debussy summed up his admiration for her voice, writing from Russia to his beloved daughter Chouchou, some forty-five years earlier, of a bird "which sang almost as well as Miss Teyte".

My own interest in Maggie Teyte began at an early age, for she was a great-aunt, and I saw much of her. She was, as well as my mother's aunt, her guardian, and as both my parents were singers, they shared a professional interest. Maggie Teyte's unusually vivid character, her physical toughness and remarkable strength of will, made a deep and lasting impression on me, and I became fascinated by the interplay between character and fortune, both on the professional and private plane, in a life devoted ruthlessly to the pursuit of perfection in the art of singing. For the intimate details of her life, my mother, Rita O'Connor, has been the main, but by no means the only, source: to her my gratitude is due not only for authorizing this book, but for invaluable help in many other ways. Other sources I must acknowledge with thanks are my father and brothers, while Teyte's own reminiscences, directly recorded by myself, her memorable indiscretions to friends and pupils, tape-recordings, interviews, broadcasts, articles, and her own book *Star on the Door*, have proved enlightening. From a combination of these I have pieced together an often shadowy past, as well as the fugitive world of her two marriages and other personal relationships—though out of consideration for the living I have had to exercise a certain restraint in the use of some of the more vivid details from her own and others' recollections. The professional side of her life is more clearly documented, both in the press and in music criticism and biography covering the period. I need only add that the interpretation I place on personalities and events represents my own views, not those of my sources.

G. O'C.

OXFORD
JULY 1978

Acknowledgements

I MUST RECORD my thanks to Richard Bebb for lending me the sole collection of Teyte's letters which remain—passed to him by Grace Vernon before she died—and for being an inspiring source of information. To him, and to Felix Aprahamian, Nigel Bryant, Ronald Crichton, and Theodore Purdy, I must record my gratitude for reading through the typescript, and for other valuable advice.

I must also record my thanks to Patrick Mahony, of Hollywood, who focused Teyte's early American career for me through his knowledge of some of her former associates; to Josephine Inslee, of Santa Ana, California, who valorously sought material on my behalf; otherwise to those numerous American admirers, friends, and former colleagues of Teyte who generously sent material.

My indebtedness to the following, with whom I discussed Maggie Teyte, or who communicated recollections, or who gave other help, must also be placed on record: Joan Anton, Dennis Arundell, Betty Bannerman, Lady Barbirolli, Pierre Bernac, Louis Biancolli, David Bicknell, Harry Blech, Jean-Loup Bourget, Lady Bramall, Rupert Bruce Lockhart, Ruth Miller Chamlee, Mrs G. W. Chapman, the *Chicago Tribune*, Professor Richard Cobb, Mrs E. M. Coleman, Bernard Constable, Lady Diana Cooper, Joan Cross, Constance M. Danks, Martha Deatherage, Clara Evelyn, Barbara Fischer-Williams, Megan Foster, Miron Grindea, Barrie Hall, Thelma Halverson, the Revd B. J. Hartnell, Professor Francis Haskell, Jack Henderson, Imogen Holst, Mrs Howlett, Mrs K. E. Hudson, Dr J. Janvrin, Estelle Johnstone, Freda Kennedy, J. W. Lambert, Josephine Lee, Walter Legge, Adèle Leigh, David Leitch, François Lesure, the *Liverpool Post*, Christopher Lloyd, Roger Lubbock, Yves Mabin, the *Maidenhead Advertiser*, Colleen Margetson, Stella Margetson, Elma R. Marvin, Tony Mayer, Barbara McClure, William Miles, Gerald Moore, Dr Gayer Morgan, Angus Morrison, Boyd Neel, Ivor Newton, the late Benedict Nicolson, Nigel Nicolson, J. W. Perman, Andrew Porter, Winifred Radford, Harold Rosenthal, Alec Robertson, Marguerite Ross, Don Ross, Linda Rowley, Margaret Royle, Catherine Salkeld, Patrick Saul and the British Institute of Recorded Sound, Desmond Shawe-Taylor, Boris Skidelsky, Leonard Smith, Sydney F. Smith, Stephen

Spender, Dr Morris Springer, Madeau Stewart, Irene Taylor, David Tron, Dame Eva Turner, John Tydeman, Lois West-Russell, Robert Tuggle, Theodore Uppman, R. Wheeler, Lady Margaret Wilson, the *Wolverhampton Star and Express*, Sister M. Xavier, B. A. Young.

I wish to thank Peter Wadland for making available tape-recordings of informal conversations he held with Teyte; Bryan Crimp, for access to material relating to the Gramophone Company; the editors, John Robson and Michael Madden, of the *Southern Electricity Board Magazine* for access to material they printed, and the Director of the Board for allowing me to visit Woolley Hall; the BBC, for access to, and permission to quote from, material in their Archives, both Sound and Written. I am also indebted, too, to Livia Gollancz and to Catharine Carver, of Victor Gollancz.

My thanks are due to the French Government for a grant covering part of my research in Paris, and the Institut Francophone and Michael Fleury for providing me with accommodation during several visits there.

Finally I wish to acknowledge the assistance of the Arts Council of Great Britain.

G. O'C.

PART ONE

John Bowen: Did your love of music make you less able to love, in the ordinary human sense, a human being?
Maggie Teyte: Yes . . . Yes, sir . . . Yes, Mr Bowen.

BBC broadcast, 1959

I've never had a gramophone; I never had a picture of myself in my life.

ibid.

CHAPTER ONE

Good God, Why Wolverhampton?
(1888–1900)

Then—in my childhood, in the dawn
Of a most stormy life—was drawn
From every depth and good and ill
The mystery which binds me still.
                        EDGAR ALLAN POE

ONE WINTER'S DAY in darkest '43, Ivor Newton the accompanist asked
Maggie Teyte if she would like to go on a tour of the factory towns. He
outlined the arrangements to her. In Wolverhampton she would stay at
the Victoria Hotel. The manager when pressed if the room had a private
bath had told him he didn't care for people who wanted private baths.
Wolverhampton? The name was like a red rag to a bull. "Good God,"
she exploded, "Why Wolverhampton?" Newton looked amazed.
"Didn't you know," she went on in the dark cutting tone which once
heard could never be mistaken for anyone else, "that I was *born* in
Wolverhampton?" And with that, she cancelled the tour.

But her memory went back to a different kind of Wolverhampton
altogether. When she was a child of three or four, living in a rectory-
style mansion in the decaying grounds of a manor house, she was playing
(as she wrote in some unfinished verses) one autumn morning in the grey
light when, suddenly and without warning, she "came upon a silent
pool". The pool was guarded all around by ancient trees, trees that were
now dead or dying, their boughs broken or torn; by a ruin too, of a stone
tower, its crumbling wall covered in ivy: only bats and birds lived there.
By contrast the life of the pool was vivid, with water-lilies, their large
fanlike leaves joined to weed, spreading a carpet over the surface of the
water. Bright little green frogs squatted on the leaves; dragon-flies,
flitting from flower to flower, darted their eyes to and fro.

After painting this fey picture, much at odds with her more usual tough and dismissive humour, she recalled taking a step down, reaching out perhaps for a lily, but then slipping, falling, crying out for her nurse. Then, she said, beneath the close, mysterious surface of the pool she passed out of sight. She was saved by the nurse, who seized her by the scruff of the neck and pulled her out. She little thought then that fate might one day lead her into a similar situation, in a role she would be called on to sing.

The imagination of a child chooses memories in obedience to its own laws, and it is curious that the memory of being alone by the pool's edge, trying to reach for a lily, should stay with Teyte for ever as almost her sole memory of childhood. What made her, the first time she had a sense of her own identity, see herself as Mélisande, the Mélisande of Maeterlinck's and Debussy's music drama *Pelléas et Mélisande*, the Mélisande who reaches down into the water, trying to retrieve her lost crown? "I would like to see to the bottom of the water" are Mélisande's own words.

Maggie was born plain Margaret Tate in Wolverhampton, in the English Midlands, on 17 April 1888. Her sign is fiery and tough, that of Aries the Ram, whose nature is reckless, given to falling in love like a thunderbolt. "I believe in the stars," she said eighty-four years later to the very day; "I'm a fighting person, I butt everybody."[1]* She was one of a family of ten children born to two mothers and one father over a quarter-century span. The eldest was Jacob, named after his father, Jacob James Tate. He and his brother Frederick were the sons of the first wife, Hannah. After she died in childbirth—her third son was stillborn—Jacob James married again, this time a talented and gently sensuous lady of Irish blood, Maria Doughty, who was twenty years his junior. The eldest child of this marriage was Arthur, known as Jack, then Bernard, then James William, or Jas. W. as he later became known. The last two boys were Sidney and— youngest of all the family—Howard. Dividing this last brace of boys, after Sidney, were born in quick succession three daughters, Gertrude, Marie, and finally Margaret, known as Maggie.

Jacob James Tate was Scottish by birth and Maggie always singled out Scots blood as her ancestral quality, preferring it to Irish, which also ran in her veins. Yet the name Tate is not especially Scottish, it seems, and the Tates could further back have had a French origin, for there were

* Numbered references are to the Notes at p. 267.

Huguenot families called Tate who fled persecution in France and settled in the more northern Protestant parts of a Catholic England. The French spelling of their name was of course Tête, meaning "head", and from one of these Têtes could well have sprung the Scottish Presbyterian who was Maggie's grandfather. If this is not just a romantic supposition then some of the distinctly non-Celtic traits of both Maggie and her father could be accounted for: the stature shorter than is usual in Scots, the prominent, thin, yet almost hooked nose—also a Gallic characteristic. This becomes the more plausible when we remember that for much of her life Maggie Teyte was believed to be French.* From the start she had an innate sympathy with French sounds, which led to her easy mastery of the French language, perhaps the most striking evidence of distant Huguenot blood.

Grandfather Tate, the Scots Presbyterian, was converted to Roman Catholicism out of a design to marry an Irishwoman he loved. He was very strict and his only son, Jacob James, was raised a staunch Catholic. Maggie's mother, herself Catholic, thus married into a devout family, but Maggie quickly lapsed from practice as she grew up and art became her sole religion. Once when teasingly accused of suffragette leanings she answered hotly, "The only railings I'm chained to are those of art": this was true, though she became quite the reverse of a martyr.

Her father spent a large part of his life in Wolverhampton, some forty out of his seventy years. He prospered as a wine and spirits merchant, owning several public houses, among them the well-known Chequer Ball, the Old Still Inn in King Street, and even, according to one report, a butcher's stall. Not only a man of commerce, he was also a dedicated amateur musician, a pianist. In pursuit of his enthusiasm, he once journeyed to Leipzig where he took lessons with Theodor Leschetizky, the greatest piano teacher of his day.

Jacob Tate was much enamoured of Leschetizky, a fearsome-looking man, white-haired and white-bearded, who had been a student of Czerny, himself an intimate friend and pupil of Beethoven. Jacob Tate told his children many stories about this hero of his. The Polish pianist's great virtue was that he encouraged modesty in his students, showing a marked preference for narrower and more perfect compositions, as opposed to unfinished work on a grand scale. One day he was composing something at the piano in Vienna, when Brahms walked in and peered

* See p. 68. She began spelling her name in the French manner in 1907.

over his shoulder to see what he was doing. "Ha, what sort of things are you writing this morning? I see—quite *little* things, *little* things, of course, yes." "*Little* things," replied Leschetizky. "Yes, they are, but they are ten times more amusing than yours, I can tell you."

Maggie's father found qualities in Leschetizky that she herself could not but recognize later in her own teacher, another Pole, the famous tenor Jean de Reszke. For Leschetizky's "method" consisted in having no rules, and caring more for what was done than for what was said. He saw teaching as akin to the work of a doctor to whom patients came to be cured of their musical ailments, with the remedy varying in each case. So dedicated was he that he had started taking pupils when he was a mere fourteen years of age and went on till he was seventy-five, when he was still filled with the same heartiness and zeal to impart his experience, still swept along on the stream of ardent young natures. But he was no lover of England: he told Jacob Tate that the solidity of the English atmosphere, musical and climatic, brought him down, and that he was always glad to be off again to sunnier lands. The same longing to escape her own philistine shores later came upon Jacob's daughter.

Leschetizky observed his pupils acutely, assessing national traits of character from their playing in a way which it is hard to improve on. "The English are good musicians," he wrote,

good workers, and bad executants, doing by work what the Slavs do by instinct; their heads serving them better than their hearts. Russians have passion, dramatic power, elemental force and extraordinary vitality. Turbulent natures, difficult to keep within bounds but making wonderful players when they have the patience to endure to the end. Poles, less strong and rugged than the Russians, lean more to the poetical side of music; originality is to be found in all they do; refinement, an exquisite tenderness and instinctive rhythm. The French are like birds of passage, flying lightly up in the clouds, unconscious of what lies below. They are dainty, crisp, clear-cut in their playing and they phrase well. The Germans possess earnestness, patient devotion to detail, orderliness and intense and humble love of their art, but their outlook is a little grey. . . . I love the Italians because they are Italians, though they cannot, as a rule, play the pianoforte in the very least.[2]

As a Pole, Leschetizky brought out the peculiar eminence in music then held by his countrymen, among them Paderewski, his most famous pupil.*

Maria Tate was also an amateur musician, hardly less gifted than her husband. She sang prettily, though not nearly as well as her sister, Rose Doughty, who was chosen by the noted English baritone, Charles Santley, to go on a world tour with him. Sadly the sister never began the tour, for her departure was vetoed by her husband. A jealous man, he would hardly allow her to appear in public in Wolverhampton, never mind Vienna or Los Angeles.

It may be that Maria Tate could not give much individual attention to her ten children. One of the daughters suffered a cruel blow when very young: this was Marie, who was extremely beautiful and her father's favourite. One day she was playing at table, pushing her chair back with her knees, when one of her elder brothers was tempted to push it even further. The chair keeled over with her and she landed on her back, injuring her spine; she limped for the remainder of her short life, and had to wear a metal brace on her leg. This did not suppress her gay and vivacious personality, nor keep her from eloping, later, with a dark-eyed Tuscan immigrant named Odoli who had settled in London and was a waiter in the restaurant where Marie worked as cashier. Though frowned on by the family, their marriage went ahead; but Marie died when their first child, a daughter, Marguerita, was only nine months old.†

Jacob Tate put "gentleman" after his name; he had property and goods which though not of astronomical worth were substantial. After living some years at No. 12 Compton Road in West Wolverhampton, he bought a dwelling known as Dunstall House. This had been built in the picturesque grounds of Dunstall Hall, then the wildest and most uncultivated part of what was more and more becoming an urban area, only a mile from the centre of Wolverhampton. Dunstall House, of red brick in the style of a Victorian rectory, was very different from the formidable stone presence of the Hall, with its moat and Debussyan air of mystery, which until it was pulled down in 1912 remained Wolverhampton's last link with medievalism. On the far side of a belt of tall trees surrounding both houses lay meadows which looked over the town, still

---

* In Monte Carlo in 1907, Maggie Teyte shared the billing with Paderewski at her first paid professional concert appearance. See Chapter 4.

† It was this child, called Rita, left in effect an orphan in the Great War, whom Maggie Teyte was later to bring up. See Chapter 7.

giving a pleasant view crowned by a church on high to the south-east.[3] Long before, a treasured spring, Dunstall, had flowed there, deriving its name from the early British deity Dun, or Deon, who shared, Frazer tells us, a common origin with the Teutonic god of thunder and the oak, who lived in a sacred grove. It was a natural setting fit for Pan, for fauns, nymphs, and goddesses, and instilled in Maggie a feeling for magic and for solitude. After 1910 the gods were dispersed: the Hall became deserted and deteriorated rapidly. After it was demolished, the trees were cut down, the ground levelled, and the whole sacrosanct plot obliterated for ever under a mammoth factory constructed by Courtaulds for making rayon.

People born in Wolverhampton in the vigorous nineteenth century had the reputation of living a long time. The Member of Parliament at Margaret Tate's birth was the Right Hon. Charles Pelham Villiers; born in 1802, he was returned unopposed in 1895, having already sat in the Commons for sixty years.* But Wolverhampton's combined agricultural and industrial robustness declined during the tawdry first part of the twentieth century, so that by 1940, as one worthy unselfconsciously voiced it, Wolverhampton grew into the sort of place most people would hate to be found dead in: only one building stood out with any distinction from the general "dingy higgledy-piggledy"—so called by J. B. Priestley—and this was a brand-new dairy. Maggie's own 1943 outburst, "Good God, why Wolverhampton?", showed how little by then she relished the idea of returning there.

Nineteenth-century Wolverhampton was not without its solid layer of culture: to the Grand Theatre came touring companies with the popular operatic repertoire. Paderewski himself gave a concert there at the Agricultural Hall on 9 December 1892—special trains were laid on afterwards to take the audience home. This was only a few months after Maggie had made her four-year-old début in ice-cold water; but if the plunge was a prophetic preparatory gesture towards Mélisande, her precociousness did not as far as is known stretch to attendance at the Paderewski concert.

The older Tate sons formed themselves into a clan. When they left school they all studied engineering, and all—except for Jacob, the eldest—emigrated to Kenya, quick and keen to the advantages of being British at a time of rapid colonial growth. Here they skilfully built up a chain of

* Maggie herself recorded Gounod's "Ave Maria" in her eightieth year.

businesses and other interests, such as an art gallery in Nairobi called the
Tate Gallery, which lasted a long time. One of them, Jack, served in the
Boer War, later had a coffee farm among the Kikuyu, which he combined
with gold prospecting in the South African fields.*

The youngest son, Howard, a dark-haired bohemian, went to sea:
in the end he settled down and, as often with those who lead an ordinary
existence, departed any collective memory. Sidney, the next to the
youngest, also emigrated, not to Kenya but to South Africa. Years later,
back in England, he visited his older brother Bernard, by then retired and
living in Cheltenham. He rang the doorbell and Bernard answered it.
Sidney was amazed to find himself not even invited into the house. After
spending ten minutes on the pavement talking through a half-open door
to a brother he had not clapped eyes on for twenty years, he left again for
South Africa. Sidney never got over it: it was clear Bernard shared,
in even more marked degree, the traits of secretiveness and suspicion
which Maggie also bore.

Maggie in general held feelings of uncertainty, even hostility, towards
members of her own family and towards the idea of the family. Although
her younger brother Howard worked a short while for her when he
could not find a job, in the end they fought and he left. When she was
young, family life was, behind her parents' backs, something of a free-for-
all, and her elder brothers all disliked her. She quickly formed a highly
resistant, competitive stance towards men, and would always be daring
them to prove themselves. Her own prowess at golf, badminton, tennis,
and riding developed fast, and she loved life on the farm in which her
mother had a share. In fact, she loved nature in all its moods. But if being
heavily caught up in the male rough-and-tumble of her own family
helped to shape one side of her personality, it did not—as may seem
surprising—make her, at least when young, able to get on well with other
girls. Gertrude, her elder sister, once told her she was "stuck up",[4] and
she kept herself apart from her sisters and their friends, refusing to play
with them.

She appears to have treasured no childhood attachments at all: she
retained no pictures of brothers or sisters or parents, nor ever had any.
Neither did she have any pictures or mementos of herself as a child.
Intensely shy, she destroyed all that side, hiding away as much of herself

* As reported in the *Liverpool Echo*, 2 June 1976. He married a Liverpool businessman's daughter and they had six children.

as she could, and refusing when questioned to recall her family or to respond to approaches from them. Concealment was something she loved so much, with the sense of mystery it created, that not only did she hide her relations from the rest of the world, she kept her friends apart and pushed the world itself as far away from her as she could. Again, like Mélisande, she wanted to keep herself in the dark.

Her father must have been aware of her oddness. Though by turns shy and hostile, she had an excellent memory and applied herself to music from a very early age, so that by eight she knew fifteen songs by heart. All the Tate children could play an instrument of one kind or another, but most displayed a rowdy indifference to the need for practice. Maggie had only one brother who was musically gifted. James was a brilliant improviser on the piano. Light fanciful melodies would flow from his fingers, but he showed little application at first: good for a furlong but no stayer, his father used to say. But James would smile and not take much notice.

The old man was a little hated as well as feared by his large brood. It must be remembered Maggie was born when her father was nearly sixty, her younger brother when he was sixty-five: so he was more of a grand-father than a father, a stern Victorian grandfather. He had now been a Wolverhampton town councillor for some years, and was mindful of his own position in the town. The household, with its large preponderance of males over females, had strict rules, strict penalties for disobeying them. A worshipper of Cardinal Manning and a fervent adherent to the positive new wave of Catholicism which swept the land in the late nineteenth century, Jacob Tate sent Maggie to a convent in Wolverhampton where she learnt to read and write but little more, although the nuns were strict and piety was encouraged.

When Maggie was ten years old, her father had a strong and sudden ambition to pull up his roots and move to London. That he should at the advanced age of sixty-nine have taken this bold step, which meant that he had once again to suffer the throes of setting up a new business, is an example of the Tate waywardness which his daughter inherited. He bought a small hotel in the secluded and commanding position of Adelphi Terrace, south of the Strand, from which there was a magnificent view over the river and the Embankment, and a leafy, quiet garden below. His hotel was appropriately named (or was called already) the Caledonian, in deference to his Scottish forebears, and he hoped to fill it with prosperous and cultured foreign businessmen and tourists who much favoured such a quiet and yet central position.

Jacob Tate's early ambitions for himself had not been finally crushed, for that an old man should make such a spectacular move from the suburbs of Wolverhampton to the centre of the metropolis meant one thing: he wanted to belong, at least at the very end, to the "Society" to which he had always aspired, and from which for too long, as he slogged away in the Midlands, catering for the profitable tastes of the newly rich middle class, he had been excluded. So he sank all the money he had earned in his lifetime into the Caledonian Hotel and at once, by gratifying the dominant wishes of his heart, opened up a new prospect for his daughter.

Luckily, Maggie was young enough to take this new and exciting world in her stride. The hotel had an elegant salon in which there stood the grand piano they had transported from Wolverhampton. There she would practise when no one was about. She had started singing at St Joseph's Convent when she was six, but had as yet little notion of the scope of her talent. She never had much pleasure in her own voice, even when very young: it was never good enough for her. Her father, however, took her along to the Royal College of Music where Hubert Parry heard her sing. Parry decided she was too young to study singing, so she was entered for piano and theory, at which she concentrated, though she never worked hard.

In a top-floor flat in Adelphi Terrace across the road from the hotel lived the playwright George Bernard Shaw. She used to watch him, a spare gaunt figure with a springy stride, walking round and round the Terrace in his dressing gown. While guests at the hotel sometimes showed admiration for her singing, he did the reverse, one day sending a note over to Maggie's mother asking her to stop her daughter making such horrid noises.

The Tates' nurse, Holly, took the youngest children for walks in St James's Park and sometimes, in a horse-drawn bus, to Green Park. Some afternoons London, when caught in a certain mood by the sun or the mist, still looked as medieval as an Old-World city. Maggie loved this. The soldiers practising flag signals in St James's Park had as much charm as if they had been spotted on some foreign field; so also, when she walked in October in the Strand, was she dazzled by the vista of churches—the sun being perhaps overpowered by fog—backed by the roofs of the Law

Courts, with further off perhaps a striking and noble tower. She heard many young Londoners speak with contempt of the features of their native city and its growth of industrial eyesores, but to her fresh gaze it had all the vivid appeal of Rome or Florence.

One day an ugly row blew up in the household, which Maggie witnessed and which was significant for her development. Her brother James, whom no one thought very stable, had taken to frequenting the music halls with undesirable friends. He had even, at one of these smoke-filled palaces of sin and luxury, played and sung. Jacob Tate was beside himself with rage: that a son of his should be seen in such a place and, worse, go dressed in a brightly coloured, common and cheap waistcoat, was too much for his almost puritanical form of Catholicism. He summoned his son, and all at once that habitual smile vanished from James's face.

James argued along the lines of "You yourself have always given us music from the time we were small . . .", reminding him of the stories of Leschetizky Jacob had told them. This made his father gasp with horror. Sacrilege! How could Leschetizky be mentioned in the same breath as the common music hall? Yet James saw no difference, to him it was all music. "The great composers had a common touch, a streak of the vulgar. . . ." Jacob rebuked him once more: he had paid for James to go through St Wilfrid's College, no less, in Cheadle, Staffs. The rest of his sons had gone to Wolverhampton Grammar School. Could he afford to send Margaret to study anywhere privately? Margaret had shown promise. . . . James had now become silent. Margaret was only twelve years old. "Is this your gratitude?" the old man roared close to his ear.

James had now lost all urbanity. He had recently, together with the brightly coloured waistcoats which he resented his father calling cheap— for they were anything but that—acquired a monocle. At that very moment he let it drop from his eye. The effect was as if he had slammed the door in his father's face. "A monocle too," Jacob spluttered. "Why not a clown's nose or the cap and bells of a fool?"

Maggie, listening to their argument, shook with terror, for she had never before heard any of her brothers stand up to their father and answer him back.

"You're only against me," James said, returning to the attack, "because secretly you'd like to sing and dance and let yourself go in the way I do:

all this kotowing to snobbish musical taste is only part of your desire to please your customers in the hotel. Heavens, the disreputable lives led by some of the great musicians whose work you earnestly interpret as if the Apostles themselves had written it! Look, you may love Mozart but Beethoven blamed Mozart for writing music to licentious librettos. . . . There's something sacrilegious about all art, even the greatest, and there you are—with your deep religious devotion—behaving as if the glories of the great masters are as holy as the stations of the cross. . . ."

When the Tate children quarrelled the Irish side of their nature gained the upper hand. To make his argument even more extreme and unpalatable, James invoked the pitiful state of music in England, claiming there was little point in being a serious musician in such a philistine land. "The only place where music's at all vital is the music hall."

Jacob, now white with fury, looked ready to strike James. He sent Maggie to her room and she went, finding it all very confusing. Father encouraged them to love music. So they had. So why should James's love go so far beyond her father's tolerance?

The quarrel's outcome was that James left the hotel. He took to the halls; to Jacob the shame was unspeakable. But as a man, Maggie thought tartly, James would survive. And survive he did with a vengeance, becoming widely known, still sporting the monocle which had enraged his father so much, and picturesquely obliterated under a music hall pseudonym, the blunt throwaway epithet of "That!"—composer husband and accompanist of the ravishing Clarice Mayne, with whom he appeared in the first-ever Royal Command performance at the Palace Theatre, rattling out on the piano his own song, "I'm Longing for Someone to Love Me". Before Clarice he had been the husband of Lottie Collins, the blowsy Naughty Nineties act "Ta-ra-ra-boom-de-ay" which swept three continents, and at the end of which she regularly used to faint into the wings. A child of Lottie Collins, Jas. W.'s stepdaughter, was José, the "vibrant personality and remarkable voice", none other than the "Maid" in *The Maid of the Mountains*.

Jas. W. remained a strong anti-depressant all through life: once in Manchester, suffering himself from a bad cold, to cheer up a miserable fellow artiste, Clara Evelyn, he stuck a chamber pot on his head, and stuffed flowering sweet peas through the handle. She found it so funny she forgot her black mood—Victorian humour again! His and Clarice Mayne's most famous song was "A Broken Doll", and he also wrote

"Put on your Tat my Little Girlie", "Every Little While", and "I was a Good Girl till I Met You": songs whose titles alone evoke nostalgia and a naughty cheerfulness. Tate's additional number, "A Bachelor Gay" from *The Maid of the Mountains*, became a favourite with Maggie. She loved its Kiplingesque and masculine appeal:

> A bachelor gay am I
> Though I've suffered from Cupid's dart
> But never I vow will I say die
> In spite of an aching heart.

Jas. W. left only one child, Marie, from his marriage with Lottie Collins, and he died prematurely at forty-six, in 1922, having several shows and projects running at the same time and having caught, when travelling between theatres, a chill which later turned to pneumonia. Clarice Mayne lived to a great age, plying her exquisitely shapely long legs in pantomime, and marrying, in later life, Teddy Knox of the Crazy Gang.

But if, back in Wolverhampton in 1900, Jas. W.'s survival was never in doubt, what would happen, Maggie wondered, when it was her turn, if ever it became so? What would happen if her love of music impelled her towards a musical career? Would she be locked up, kept in a gilded cage like her aunt Rose Doughty who had, as everyone said, one of the greatest soprano voices ever heard in their part of the world? What if *she* had turned professional?

And that aunt's soul by some form of osmosis became absorbed by Maggie. The suppression of a gift in one generation in a family can, like rich produce turned back unharvested into the soil, feed the gifted in the following generation. It was that aunt Maggie saw, and in Rose's gentleness, her humility, her practical understanding—the very qualities that made her a good wife and mother—Maggie found a form of repression which she came to loathe while perhaps even benefiting from them. For in her aunt those qualities had dissipated a gift, they had made her like anybody else when she could have been like no one else, she could have been unique, she could have had the world at her feet in recognition of her talent.

Maggie vowed at a very early age, then, not to be like her aunt. If she had a gift she would be selfish with it, as her aunt's husband was in his

The Debussyan grounds of Dunstall Hall, Wolverhampton, where Maggie played as a child. (*Left*) Her beautiful crippled sister Marie. (*Below*) Clarice Mayne and "That!" (Maggie's brother Jas. W. Tate).

(*Above left*) Jean de Reszke's private theatre at 54 rue de la Faisanderie, Paris. (*Right*) Walter Johnstone Douglas, accompanist at the de Reszke school. (*Below*) De Reszke (standing, second from the right) with some of his pupils in 1910; Maggie Teyte is seated (in shirtwaist, third from the left) in the front row.

jealousy, as her father was in his sense of proper and moral behaviour, his snobbishness and his sense of what he wanted his children to do.

Maggie little knew that her father, too, had once had dreams of becoming a professional musician. He kept very quiet about the fact that Leschetizky had encouraged him to give a concert in Leipzig, which had been well attended and highly thought of. With what bitterness Jacob Tate had crushed this longing in his heart and turned his attention to the wine and spirits trade. Drink did not interest him in the slightest, as a consumer, but at least he went abroad to order his goods, at least he moved—if now only vicariously—in a world where he could indulge, as often as his stern nature permitted, his taste for concert-going, or could engage musicians for a hotel banquet.

As if the family violence over James were not enough, setting up conflicts of life versus art, of puritanism versus sensual pleasure, of—even worse—dilettantism versus the need for money, still more threatening clouds were gathering. The Caledonian Hotel was not doing well, and the Tates were having difficulty in remaining solvent. The younger children who were still at private schools were taken away from them, and sent to less expensive religious institutions; when Marie, crippled though she was, said she had found a job as a cashier in a restaurant, no one tried to dissuade her: these were bad times when daughters of gentlefolk had to descend to menial employment. One by one the older boys had emigrated. Only the eldest, Jacob, remained behind with his wife and family, living in the Caledonian Hotel and helping his father run it.

CHAPTER TWO

The Church of Corpus Christi
(1901–1903)

... and by her voice I knew she shed
Long-treasured tears.

JOHN KEATS

THE DOOR TO Jacob's room was open and the lights were burning.
She saw a doctor standing with folded arms at the bottom of the bed: in
the bed Jacob James Tate lay on his back, having died in the night. Feeling
the blood drain from her face, Maggie stood very still and, looking round
her, took it all in. Her mother sat on the chaise-longue, facing away from
her father. She recalled her as faraway and saying nothing; she had no
grief, only silence.

Maggie, now barely thirteen, was determined not to be put out of the
room this time. She would have a look. She came forward on tiptoe, she
remembered, pushing by the doctor to get a better view. For several
minutes she stood curiously still, weight on one foot, just watching—
reverently, reflectively staring at her dead father. Jacob Tate lay under a
knitted spread, in a long woollen gown, something she had all too rarely
seen him wear: once the Tate children said good night to their mother and
father, at quite an early hour, they saw no more of them. What they did
on their own none of the children had ever known: whether they kissed at
night, slept apart, quarrelled or were affectionate, no one had an inkling.

What struck Maggie vividly were her father's hands: they were veined
a pale reddish-purple, a lobster colour she had seen in a tank outside a
restaurant in the Strand where they kept live lobsters which swam around
for their customers' gastronomical pleasure. She had wanted passionately
to choose one and to taste it. The same reddish-purple veins were visible
in parts of his face, slightly discolouring, even disfiguring it. But his
defiant, finely etched features remained the same, his jaw stuck out in the
same self-denying and principled assertiveness, the nose carrying the
same thin, disapproving line.

She noticed other details . . . the ridge standing out on his brow, the drooping lids, the dry cracked lips. After a little while she remembered leaving the room. She was dazed at her sudden loss, but there were no tears.

The Tate family had barely seen in the new century when this tragedy overtook them. London had not been a success for Jacob Tate: in his will he gave instructions for his body to be returned to Wolverhampton, and laid alongside that of his first wife Hannah (somewhat slightingly to his second). London may have had the last flickerings of his life spirit, but he was not going to leave his flesh behind to rot there. He seems not to have cared much for the numerous children with which his second wife Maria, of whose sensuous nature Maggie liberally partook, had supplied him so rapidly—he himself had been an only child—for he left no money or property to Maria or to any of her offspring. The entire estate went to his eldest son, Jacob, Hannah's child: cash and effects to the value of £1,284, plus the highly dubious asset of the Caledonian Hotel, now fast piling up debts, and some other properties which yielded rent. Maria moved out of the hotel some time after her husband's death and settled eventually, until her own death twenty years later, on the other side of the river, in Putney. Life was not easy for her, though she received support from her children abroad.

Maggie was still attending piano classes at the Royal College. Her first opportunity as a singer came a year after Jacob Tate's death. With his resistance to a life on the boards, which he had been prepared to deny his offspring at any cost, gone once and for all, there was no one for her to quarrel with, as her elder brother Jas. W. had quarrelled with their father, over her choice of a career.

Her mother called her into the room to sing for the theatrical impresario George (later Sir George) Dance, and after she had done so, Dance suggested she should join one of his touring companies. When he inclined to ask her mother if she would give her agreement, Maria turned to Maggie and said, "You can make your own decision." Maggie hesitated. She felt quite desperately isolated, and with the isolation was mingled fright, as she had that very instant to make a decision on which her whole future would depend. "If you pay me what I want!" she answered.

Dance recoiled at this precocious demand and broke off negotiations. Of course she could have said, "I'll give you my answer tomorrow," and might, with more wisdom, have done so,[1] but either way there began here the obsession with money which lasted all her life. The removal of the security of her father as provider of it might well be one cause— or it may be merely that she became aware of an undying need for luxury. Whatever the explanation, a fantasy of wealth was born, and even in later life she would walk up and down a room, saying over and over out loud, "Money, money, money, I must have money."

But also in Maggie's treatment of Dance there was a strong element of her father's snobbery. She dreamed of Leschetizky and higher things: to tour the English provinces would have been to take a step backwards. Her demand, the first of its kind but by no means the last, was a presumption of greater possibilities for herself.

These came, indirectly, a year or so later. The Tates' local Catholic church, Corpus Christi, where Jacob had regularly taken his family to mass was in Maiden Lane, on the other side of the Strand from Adelphi Terrace. Built by Manning when he was still an Archbishop, it had not been long in service. It was a very tall, dark church, with a timbered roof and white-painted stone interior, and an impressive high altar carved out of Caen stone. Because so little light penetrated it, it had a solemn cavernous air, deepened by the generous candle offerings which blazed night and day.

It was here, at a charity concert one spring night in 1903, that the priest announced: "The next number is not on the programme. A very young person will sing Tosti's 'Goodbye' but I think that after hearing her no apologies will be needed. Miss Maggie Tate."

Maggie's slight figure moved from the back of the church—where, standing among the audience, she had heard the announcement with a shocked sense of unreality—to the sacristy. From there she came out in front of the altar as if a celebrant of the mass. And here she stopped, waiting for the opening bars of the accompaniment.

What the young man at the piano saw so enchanted him that he faltered over the first chords. Fortunately he knew the song backwards: an elegant, almost facile composition of *salon* sentiment, a mistress parting from her lover, turned in a simple yet effective manner, with a few striking high notes for the soprano to show her skill:

> Falling leaf and fading tree
> Lines of white on a sullen sea
> Shadows rising on you and me.

The voice began thinly and nervously, as if the singer were unable to supply her vocal cords with air; but then, quite unexpectedly, it began to pour out naturally, melodiously—so much so that the pianist could not believe his ears: the sound was swelling to a golden stream such that he straightaway found himself making comparisons with the greatest soprano voices of the age. But no, it was ridiculous. The girl looked hardly more than thirteen, though they had told him she was fifteen; she was barely five foot high, too, and had such an air of innocence, total untutored innocence, about her.

Still on and on gushed the lovely sound, and while his mind leapt with these extreme notions, he had no difficulty in keeping up the accompaniment, for he found he followed her instinctively. They passed the most tender *pianissimo* section:

> A voice from the far-a-way!
> "Listen and learn" it seems to say

and the church was hushed and reverential with listening; not a rustle disturbed the utter concentration of the crowd. Then she took a high note, exquisitely, and held it, while the passionate harmony from under his fingers seemed to expand with new radiance. How can a mere slip of a girl, he thought, have so much feeling to put into this trite song: where does it all come from?

But now they were at sea, chopping and twisting with a new sentiment:

> What are we waiting for? Oh! my heart!
> Kiss me straight in the brows!
> And part! Again! . . .
> Again . . . my heart . . . my heart.

Even though the words were banal, the pianist could see some of the audience almost murmuring in response. He himself felt almost moved to tears, but held back for he knew that to give way would be to ruin the song's ending.

And still she stood straight, unsophisticated, in a simple white dress, head held high, to all intents unaffected by what she was singing. How could she dramatize and understand such emotions, and how could she know how to break them up, and to phrase them so naïvely and yet so cunningly from a musical point of view?

They reached the end, an extravagant, powerful high note again, *fortissimo*: "Goodbye, for ever, goodbye? . . ." A final cataclysm of sound, the resolution; then silence. The girl suddenly looked very awkward, far away, vulnerable. She was almost crying.

The young man moved away from the piano and, taking Maggie by the hand, led her to the sacristy. Her hand was moist, clammy, limp like a child's. His mind was in a whirl. Part of him wanted to carry her off then and there, to make her his, to coach her, pay for her future, fashion her into a great singer—for such, he was sure, she would become with little difficulty. But another part of him was more cautious: Who was she? What was she like? What if she was stupid, what if, when you talked to her, she showed she was going to be a complete dud?

Maggie had now recovered a little from the ordeal. While she had been singing her mind had been a complete blank, but suddenly at the end of it she hardly knew where or who she was. She had felt very frightened and alone, and she missed her father dreadfully: why had he gone and died before she had a chance to know him properly? Then she saw all the people looking at her, and felt terribly, terribly naked. Then this kindly-looking young man had come and led her off. He must think her terribly simple-minded. She must pull herself together.

That is what she did, in the sacristy, becoming more collected; and then she in turn found the young man quite strange. For he was walking rapidly up and down and excitedly murmuring, "Quite extraordinary, quite extraordinary", over to himself, three or four times. She was at first sure it was not she that he meant, and wondered what else might have happened; but then she had to admit it was her singing that had brought him to this state, for the priest came over to her and said, "They are calling for you, you must make a bow," and only then did she become conscious of the rapturous applause, which had been continuing all this while. Her ears suddenly became unblocked, the sound rushed in almost deafeningly, and she moved out into the cavernous mouth of the church again, to sing an encore.

When he thought later about her, the young man, whose name was Walter Rubens, was sure he had made an unusual discovery. She was intelligent, he decided with relief, she would respond to teaching, and what was more, being fifteen instead of the thirteen she looked, she was ready to begin right away. There was no need to worry that the vocal cords might be damaged by exertion: they should be properly mature now, strong but also very supple.

Rubens was a stockbroker by profession, as was his father, so he was not given to making rash decisions. He lived in "Millionaire's Row", at No. 8A Kensington Palace Gardens. His Wykehamist brother Paul, a barrister and the lover of Phyllis Dare the famous Gaiety Girl, had already made a name for himself as a composer of light music.* Like Paul, Walter was a shrewd and gifted musician—an amateur, true, but he had the advantage of knowing and entertaining many of the most gifted singers and musicians in London. So he scrutinized his new find carefully, like a precious stone, turning it over to look at it from every angle, peering at it through every kind of magnifying glass and prism, considering all aspects of the influence it might exert. Being German by origin, Walter Rubens was thorough, and omitted no eventuality.

First he thought of her size. She was nearly full grown. She was small, though slightly taller than a friend of his, Olga Loewenthal (later known as Olga Lynn, or "Oggie"), who had a pretty voice but nothing quite as fine and unusual as this. This girl would never be a supremely commanding presence on the stage. If she became fat like most prima donnas, she would look dumpy and her smallness would be accentuated.

Nor was she built on the scale of a dramatic soprano. Her lungs, however well trained and well developed they might become, would never take in, hold, and expel air as might a more capacious bosom. But she looked as though she might have stamina, and when he talked to her he found she loved outdoor sports. He had also noticed, when accompanying her, her perfect teeth, her very small tongue and high palate—all these were in her favour.

Rubens assessed the girl's aspect, her appeal, quite coldly. At a distance she looked enchanting and winsome, almost, with an elf-like charm, but close to, her blue eyes were not pale and watery, or full of mystery, but rather sharp and level, almost cold. They were the eyes of a realist. The hair was reddish-auburn, thick and long, the figure thin, dainty, with an almost roguish quality. He wagered to himself that she would be a tease, in a year or two's time, for she had a somewhat wicked look, and a harsh naughty laugh. When she spoke it was still with a pronounced Midlands

---

* He wrote the score for Beerbohm Tree's famous *Twelfth Night* and later, with Howard Talbot and Jerome Kern, for the musical *High Jinks*.

twang which she tried to hide. That captivating boyishness would go far, he thought. But her greatest quality he singled out straight away: she was deeply mysterious; there was something unknown about her, something foreboding, even violent. And while she was sturdy in herself, when she stood in front of an audience what was most striking was that she looked so frail and lost. Everyone would want to protect her.

It was no great step from these thoughts to seeing her in various roles: she would be able to convey the sacrosanct quality of the virgin, the sexiness of the unawakened young girl, the bruised innocence of the *cocotte* who gives herself to many men, the trustfulness of the wife which invites male treachery. All these fantasies of her flashed quickly through his mind; it was hard for him to remain altogether disinterested, but in the end he did achieve it.

He could not help asking himself if the girl had that most important requirement for success, good luck. Good luck was a law unto itself, respected nothing, and rode above all else, supreme architect, archangel of success. He would ask her, he thought frivolously; and then, to prove his seriousness, he talked over with his father and mother, and with his brother Paul, the plan he was forming.

Walter Rubens became Maggie's patron. He introduced her to his parents, Victor and Jenny Rubens, and asked her to sing for them and for some of their friends, among them a noted patroness of the arts, Lady Ripon. The Rubenses took to Maggie at once, admiring her charm, her fastidiousness, and her devotion to work, all of which she was soon able to show them. The Tate family's circumstances were rapidly worsening, so when Mrs Rubens suggested that Maggie leave the Caledonian Hotel and go to live with the Rubenses in Millionaire's Row, Maria Tate consented whole-heartedly. From this time on Maggie's own family virtually ceased to exist for her: she had found another one to help her on the path of her career. So when Walter asked his now more or less adopted sister of fifteen whether she thought she had good luck, she said at first she did not know, but ventured a little later that only fate, or fortune—luck—could explain how he had come to play for her in the church that evening, and what had happened since.

Maggie took to the Rubens family like a duck to water. Stockbroking, at that time primarily the servicing of the wealth of the rich, had something in common with the hotel and drink business—the servicing more directly of the body—and Maggie did not find her foster family frivolous as many society people undoubtedly were, especially the Europeans who invaded London, with "their Sholte dinner jackets with the emerald facings, their Cartier watches, their Fabergé cigarette cases, their faint smell of Chypre and Corona cigars".[2]

The Rubenses, although Europeans, were not philistines. Rather, the family was cosmopolitan. Jenny Rubens, whom Maggie called "Mama", was sculpted in the grand style, dignified and serene. Like many society people she was repelled by politics, indifferent to national feeling.

True, it was right in the middle of what someone had defiantly nick-named "the Bad Old Days", but how could any days be bad, as so many pointed out, when cigarettes were 11d for 20, and champagne 5s a bottle? Although there were families living in poverty and privation, and imbalances of wealth as marked as the trade unionists claimed, there was also individual enterprise—or, as the Rubenses and their friends preferred to call it, fun.

To this deeply civilized society, then, Maggie became attached. Once accepted, she was part of it; she had to fight hard to maintain her position at all costs and keep on winning. She had no land, no inherited wealth, only a talent to manipulate. So she was quickly forced to develop a sharpness of mind—she had already a certain reckless and gambling spirit. Also amid the foreign diplomats, the to-ings and fro-ings of singers and their admirers, the desire to travel suddenly took hold of her. She acquired a passionate thirst for distant places, and, almost as quick and intense as an hallucination, she saw distant scenes of glamour and splendour—herself at their centre, a universally admired prima donna. Such fantasies of course she dismissed the moment after they occurred, but what remained of them had little connection with her native land.

Maggie's other patron, and a great friend of the Rubenses, was Gladys Herbert, Countess de Grey—better known then, as now, as the Marchioness of Ripon—who belonged to a breed now extinct. She galvan-ized Covent Garden into new life while before it had been "languishing in incredible tawdriness", though even so it was hardly yet a Covent Garden for lovers of pure music—though they did undoubtedly exist— but rather, a costly showcase for the mutual self-regard of the wealthy. A socialite don, E. F. Benson, who knew Lady Ripon well enough to share her box, avowed that she "could not, without aching weariness, have sat out a symphony of Beethoven unless she had been a personal friend of the composer, or the conductor".[3] Her superior feelings about

the English musical scene, slavishly followed by the rest of "Society",
were taken up with total conviction by Maggie, so much so that, when
she had been fully equipped as a singer by Lady Ripon's adored Jean de
Reszke, she hardly tarried more than a month or two of the year in
England for more than twelve years.

Lady Ripon and her kind had no sympathy for English composers and
English singers. They were bumpkin-like figures who wrote and performed oratorios in draughty cathedral towns. Sadly Maggie, who could
easily have become a magnificent oratorio singer, drank up this prejudice:
such snobbery early poisoned her judgement. Of course opera was the
only thing that mattered, my dear, and it had to be foreign. Little wonder
Maggie did her damnedest and succeeded in changing her personality,
artistry, and indeed nationality, into that of a Frenchwoman. She would
have swallowed the German *Zeitgeist*: she had a mind to do it, except that
war put a stop to that.

But what fun the cosmopolitan English élite did have, and how the
rest of the world lived vicariously off their private suppers, their recep-
tions, down to the "orts and greasy relics" devoured by the popular press.
The joke *was* that Lady Ripon had a *frightfully* small room in Bruton
Street where she gave little supper parties: "Then Réjane recited 'La
Poupée' "—so Lady Ripon's friend Benson recounts with such a perfect
sense of mingled magnificence and frivolity—

and after a few trifles of that kind, all rather uncomfortably bestowed,
Lady de Grey, purely for a joke, said to Edouard de Reszke, "Won't
you sing something?" He, instead of answering her according to her
folly and saying he hadn't brought his music, said, "But certainly I will,
though I have never sung in so small a room. I will sing you 'Le Veau
d'or' from *Faust*." He had a prodigious volume of voice when he chose
to open it out, and now he sang "Le Veau d'or" as loudly as he possibly
could, and the windows rattled, and the crystal festoons of the chande-
liers quivered. He sang it with extravagant operatic gestures, parodying
himself, with an eye all the time on the Duke of Cambridge, but he
never disturbed the light trance. And then Jean de Reszke, fired by this
noble exhibition, and slightly jealous, said, "But I want to sing too.
I will show you how to sing the 'Preislied.' So he found two footstools
and placed them in the middle of the room, and insecurely perched on
them proceeded also to parody himself. He sang it as he always sang it,

but with some absurd exaggeration of gesture and caricature of the way he took his high notes. Never was anything quite so ludicrous, and before he had finished his singing there was not, quite in the Victorian manner, a dry eye in the room except those of the Duke of Cambridge.[4]

What vivid pictures for a young singer's imagination! What prodigious cut-outs for a private pantheon!

CHAPTER THREE

Last Rays of Opera's Golden Age
(1904–1906)

Plato will tell us, that there was no such disease as a catarrh in Homer's time.

SIR THOMAS BROWNE, *Letter to a Friend*

A NOVICE ENTERING the strictest order could not have been more single-minded, more industrious, or more chaste than Maggie, when she first arrived in Paris, at the beginning of 1904. She had so impressed her patrons in England that they had collected a "purse" of £1,000 to send her to study for two years with Jean de Reszke in Paris (later she paid back the whole amount), and Maria Tate had agreed to let her go with Walter and Mrs Rubens to meet de Reszke and give him an audition.

Olga Lynn, Walter's friend, who had been at the school at 53, rue de la Faisanderie for some time—her father had read in the *Daily Telegraph* in 1902 that de Reszke was starting a school—was called in by de Reszke to hear Maggie sing for him. "She is only sixteen," de Reszke said to her, "and has apparently a really beautiful and phenomenal voice." Olga Lynn went along to hear her, writing later:

> I shall never forget the impression this child made on me. There she was, a simple girl with a huge auburn pigtail, singing as though she were a fully trained artist. She sang "Connais-tu le pays" from *Mignon*, by Ambroise Thomas, Tosti's "Goodbye", and a song by Paul Rubens. Those who were present at this audition could not refrain from shedding a tear. Her tone was round, true and noble, and of such beauty I could not believe she was real. Jean was much moved too, and from that day until the day of his death he never ceased talking of this wonderful pupil.[1]

Maggie joined de Reszke's opera class. Her devotion to singing became absolute. She followed his teaching, she absorbed his influence so fully—

and how much easier it is for a woman to imitate a man than vice versa, as she accurately noted[2]—that she quickly became his favourite pupil. In 1910 he wrote to her, after she had left Paris:

> My dear and charming Maggie, I cannot tell you how proud and happy I am at your success. All my friends write to me of your operatic roles and your recitals. In fact everything that you have done and are doing is appreciated as coming from a real artist and your example can serve as a model in method and style of singing. Do not tire yourself too much, but conserve your precious talent, because you will be an "éducatrice" to the present generation. Believe me, with the greatest affection,
>
> your master,
JEAN DE RESZKE[3]

De Reszke afforded an ideal example to copy. Midway through his own career he had systematically taken his baritone voice to pieces, destroying it to recommence, after a lengthy and taxing spell of vocal re-education, as a tenor. Born in Warsaw in 1850, he came from a music-loving, land-owning family* and as a boy had sung in church. Before his début in 1874 in Venice he had travelled everywhere with his master, Antonio Cotogni, the famous Roman baritone, and heard all the great singers of the epoch, including Francisco Graziani whose voice he recalled with special potency. A year after his début he sang the title role in *Don Giovanni* at Drury Lane, not altogether crowned with glory, and the following year he found himself plunged into inner doubt and confusion. He was singing Figaro in *Il Barbiere* in Paris, and very famously too, extending himself up to the B flat with extraordinary facility and command; so reverberant were the reports of his triumph that his father left Warsaw and travelled all the way to Paris to hear him. But after the performance Jan de Reszke was less than complimentary and told his son he was on the wrong track. He advised him to leave the stage and work at the tenor repertoire.

Here we get an insight into the courage of de Reszke's artistry, for in the midst of success as a baritone he turned once again to study, of a nature as severe and difficult as moving the *point d'appui* of his voice from

---

* His father, Jan de Reszke, a Polish aristocrat and a chevalier of the Order of Stanislaus, was also a hotel owner, like Maggie's father, and a gifted amateur violinist.

baritone to tenor. He must subsequently have worked his way through periods of great frustration, spending from 1876 onwards eight years travelling with his illustrious brother Edouard and his sister Josephine, hardly ever singing himself but coaching them and acquiring a passion for overcoming difficulties; indeed his whole method, if it can be called such—and he disliked the term—could be summed up as diagnosis of, and mastery over, technical difficulties. Beyond this zeal for technical, and thereafter interpretative, perfection, he was one of the most civilized spirits of the age. He was, wrote Felix Weingartner, in the highest meaning of the word, a "noble human being".[4]

After these austere years of self-imposed discipline—he worked for a whole year each on *Tristan*, *Siegfried*, and *Götterdämmerung*—he became, in the last dozen years of his operatic career, the world's leading tenor. It was not so much the notes he sang as the intonation and feeling informing them that audiences found so memorable. After his death in 1925, an admirer wrote to *The Times*:

> I have heard all the great operatic tenors since 1873. Three stand out pre-eminently in my mind, each so different from the others— Tamagno, Caruso, Jean de Reszke; Tamagno, a tremendous *tenore robusto*, who literally made you jump in your seat in *Otello*; Caruso, a golden tenor, who comes only once or twice in a century; Jean de Reszke, who did all the wonders that he did without a great natural voice by the illuminating magic of his genius, by his extraordinary magnetism, and by an artistic perfection dramatic and vocal, which subdued all things unto him.[5]

De Reszke was an extremely gifted linguist. English he spoke fairly well, though he never sang in it; this mattered little at Covent Garden, where Italian held sway. Of his German, Mancinelli the conductor said to him, "When other people sing German I don't like it, but when you do it, it sounds beautiful." His sung Italian was perfect in diction; he spoke it with equal fluency, and was especially possessive of its value. "Before every lesson," remembered Maggie Teyte, "every pupil who went on to the stage in the rue de la Faisanderie, whatever his nationality, had to pronounce the five vowels in the Italian, á é î ō ü."[6] But it was his French that was supreme, and this explains why he settled in France to teach when repeated attacks of bronchial catarrh, whose effect even he did not know how to circumvent, began not only to endanger his voice but seriously to threaten his general health.

In Paris he was made Artistic Director of the Opéra for a short while, but this was an unhappy appointment, and he is said to have remarked when he left, to his valet Louis Vachet, "Il y avait toujours la maîtresse de quelqu'un qui voulait se faire entendre." Then he was asked to sing the title role in Reyer's *Sigurd*, but another tenor refused to substitute for him if he should be ill, as long as his name was still listed in the company. So de Reszke refused, unable to tolerate working in an atmosphere of jealousy.

His French set a standard even for the usually chauvinistic French. The veteran music critic Camille Bellaigue wrote in the *Revue des deux mondes*, "The French language has never been pronounced and accented with such accuracy and force, or if need be with such charm and tenderness, as in the mouth of this foreigner." As a result when he did begin teaching, charging his students an astronomical 200 francs, or £8, per lesson for groups of four, he would send his pupils, 75 per cent of whom were American, back home at the end of their allotted time singing more perfect French than most French singers, even though their conversational abilities were still halting.

In 1901, de Reszke was made a Chevalier of the Légion d'honneur.* His retirement from opera to devote himself to teaching became permanent when his bronchial tubes were treated with iodine, its effect on them being so violent, not surprisingly, that they became dangerously inflamed. The pain of this treatment must have been dreadful. In 1905, having recovered, he was teaching full-time, having refused Heinrich Conried's much heralded offer, this time borne in person to the rue de la Faisanderie, to sing ten performances, spread over six weeks, at the Metropolitan in New York at $3,000 a performance. De Reszke's voice, as his accompanist W. Johnstone Douglas† attested, retained its original beauty and power until 1925, the last year of his life, when he was seventy-five years

---

* Maggie too was made a Chevalier, in 1955. Mary Garden was made an Officier, a rank to which Jean de Reszke was later upgraded. Had Maggie known of the differences of grade, no doubt she would have been furious—about Garden whom she never thought had much of a voice, but not about Jean.

† A saintly man (at least in old age, when the author met him), "J.D.", as he was known, was co-founder of the Webber Douglas School of Music. He was a member of the Queensberry family, a cousin of Lord Alfred Douglas, and later starred in Rutland Boughton's music drama, *The Immortal Hour*.

old: "The high Bs and Cs were then all right. The trouble was he had chronic catarrh, and was unable to sing more than a few phrases at a time without having to clear his throat, in other words to 'cracher'" (spit).[7] Most of the great singers of the day came to consult him at some time, and there were some strong assertions of the deleterious effects he could have on a voice; Melba affirmed bluntly that he "couldn't leave a voice alone."[8] Indeed, Melba sacked Olga Lynn at Covent Garden when she said she had studied with de Reszke.[9] Even more dramatically was he condemned by Enricheta Crichton, by repute a wonderful Isolde, though now virtually forgotten: "Jean de Reszke was sent for over a quarter of a century the cream of Europe and America and turned out nothing but skimmed milk—with *one* exception: Maggie Teyte."*

Maggie, who already had a taste for strictness, found this taste much developed and encouraged by her new life in France. Although morals were more lax than in England, there was a discipline even in licence which made France a more exciting, less lazy environment in which to develop a gift. France was a poorer country than England and though bribery and injustice were rife—there was an accepted tariff paid to secure a singing role at the Opéra-Comique—the corruption was open, even to some extent engaging in its openness.

Maggie's first sight of Paris was that of a child entering fairyland. She was now leaving her pottery birth town well behind. On the train, accompanied by her formidable guardian Mrs Victor Rubens, and by Walter, the sixteen-year-old girl felt very superior while still on the English side of the Channel, seeing ordinary mortals thronging to catch their local trains; and once on the other side she was prey to a new and unusual kind of exhilaration when the light dilated, the view assuming a wider dimension and sense of space, as the train plunged deeper into the French countryside. Not very much later, there it was: they entered by thrusting a noisy and echoing subterranean way through a ravine lined with windowed sides. High up on the right she spotted the hill of

---

* Rupert Bruce Lockhart, who reported this comment to the author, considered de Reszke a charlatan as far as vocal technique was concerned, shoving pencils down his throat and balancing books on his diaphragm; he said that Nora Valenti, the character singer, called him "l'assassino di voce". Many considered Mathilde Marchesi a far greater teacher. But Bruce Lockhart conceded that de Reszke was a first-rate operatic coach.

Montmartre and the unfinished church of Sacré-Coeur, partly hidden under rotting scaffolding, still awaiting the final touches. The traffic on their drive from the Gare du Nord to the hotel was much more fiendishly grating on the nerves—at least on Mama's nerves, for Maggie hardly knew she had them at that age—than that of London, though there was less of it: but even with a little, there always seemed much more going on. The vitality which came off the streets was vibrant and infectious. And she was amazed to see the extraordinary number of *maisons d'accouchements* advertised in large gilt signs—this in a city where the population was stationary, if not actually declining.

Within a day or two of their arrival Mama took her to the Opéra; and there she witnessed a sight largely unchanged in fifty years: a vast honey-combed interior, people reduced to ant-like proportions racing hither and thither, pushing their way past and arguing with the harpy-faced *ouvreuses* who fought and grasped for every sou. They attended the 1100th or 1200th performance of Gounod's *Faust*, noticing at once the rapt attention it received, just as if it had been a première, and the coordinated power of the choruses, the detail and concentration of the ensemble. She was staggered at some of the life-like portrayals of emotion by the principals, for this was the great age of naturalistic theatrical effect, as well as at their looks: women singers in Paris were of an almost indescribable loveliness compared with those of an earlier or later age.

Next day, still as a sightseer accompanied by Mama, she toured the colourful streets. They drove down the Champs-Elysées, still a dignified residential avenue where every afternoon a stream of elegant open carriages and fiacres with tinkling bells swept down towards the Rond-Point. They crossed the river to view the Luxembourg Gardens, spying the nursemaids in large white or blue aprons, the coachmen's huge hats, the toy balloons of the children, the subdued groups of students, decked out in large neckties and black hats, discussing anarchy or revolution. She viewed the brown trees and yellow chairs, the light-dappled leaves planted as if in a picture, and found herself susceptible to the gentlest of afternoon breezes.

Nevertheless there is good reason to suppose she remained extremely cool, though not indifferent to this wonderful new world opening up before her eyes. Curiosity in her always overrode excitement. Her sensitivity did not operate in this way. She would have noted it all with an appraising eye. She would have been amused at the young women, carelessly chic, some powdered, all talkative, sitting about in pairs with inviting looks on their faces. "It is not to be denied," she wrote later in a glossy London magazine, "that in many ways the Frenchwoman leaves her English sister far behind. It has been suggested, for one thing, that the Frenchwoman is remarkably witty, but I do not think that wit is an especial characteristic of the French nation. Wit is individual, not national, though one cannot deny that the Russians and Poles, en masse, have more brilliance, more wit, than any of the other peoples of Europe."

Further, from observation, she wrote:

But the French girl is vivacious and bright; her face is full of ever-changing expression, whereas the face of an Englishwoman is remarkable for its absolute lack of expression. The Frenchwoman has two secrets of success: one is that she can dress well, and the other is that she can flirt well.

I think it was Max O'Rell who said that a Frenchwoman was "dressed", an Englishwoman "clothed", a German woman "covered", and an American woman "arrayed".

But the second secret of the successful Frenchwoman is, perhaps, of even greater assistance. The Frenchwoman can flirt more easily and more delightfully than any other woman in the world. I do not say she can make love better. I am not prepared to say anything about that. But in the narrow borderline that lies between passion and indifference, the Frenchwoman reigns supreme.

She has a delicacy, an exquisite tact, that will guide a flirtation over ice of the thinnest. She has a way of looking, a smile, a droop of the eyelash, a glance, that are irresistible.[10]

Still, time to indulge in such curiosity was all too short. Her real life in Paris was not in the streets, the *salons*, or the chic dress shops, it was confined for the first two years and three months to the little auditorium seating a hundred people which de Reszke had built on to the house where he lived and where he gave his classes. In the auditorium a criss-cross wooden staircase had been constructed to lead over the orchestra pit on to the stage: there was a box either side, while on to the stage forty people could be crammed, at least for a group photograph.

Mama and Walter departed and Maggie joined Olga Lynn and Jane Wertheim, a Polish girl who was also at the school, at No. 40 avenue

Victor Hugo, in a pension run by a Scottish lady, Miss Julia Smith. Eight or ten girls lived there, and Miss Smith used to lecture them from time to time, pleasantly, in her Scots-French accent, telling them how to behave. Behind her back they mimicked her. Jane Wertheim, who was wealthier than the others, put a communal sitting room with an Erard grand at their disposal; Maggie used to practise diligently there. Artur Rubinstein, another Pole and a former student of Leschetizky, also practised the piano there frequently.[11]

Maggie was at the school every day. She was given lessons by the master three or four times a week, and otherwise she attended the opera classes, which were taken by Reynaldo Hahn, by Amherst ("Squib") Webber, or, later on, by Johnstone Douglas or another of de Reszke's assistants, Maurice Noufflard. When she was not attending a class she would often remain at the side in the theatre, watching and listening; from this she learnt just as much.

Some pupils at the school became almost part of the family, although the de Reszkes did have a son. Madame de Reszke, a dazzling beauty whose portrait by Flameng hung in the hall of 53, rue de la Faisanderie, and herself a fine singer, would also coach.* Some students even played golf, or went on holiday with the de Reszkes; J.D. found himself becoming a regular partner: "Jean was a golfer and when he heard that I was keen on the game it was arranged that twice a week I was to be his partner in a round at St Cloud. This led to my being used as an accompanist with an occasional lesson thrown in."[12]

Thrilled as she was with all this, Maggie appeared, on the surface, to take much of the novelty for granted. She became attached to the school straight away: she wanted and needed so much to belong. Her Wolverhampton background had been so strait-laced that its influence must by now have seemed non-existent, hence "refused" by her; she was still very guarded, very repressed, unawakened. If she left no account of the grand, often bizarre spectacle de Reszke presented on occasion it is probably because it was not in any way alien to her wishes or fancies.

The world of the grand nineteenth-century *seigneur* was at de Reszke's

---

* One day Maggie heard Mme de Reszke singing Paladilhe's "Psyché" in the little theatre and said to herself, "Ah-ha, I'm going to do that." Marie de Reszke had met Jean when she was unhappily married, and they had an illegitimate child together called Pratz. When Marie's husband died, they married. Pratz died in the First World War and de Reszke was heartbroken.

fingertips. The pupils would assemble in the hall in the morning and nervously wait for the master to appear before the class. The hall had a winding staircase with a wrought-iron and brass balustrade. First was heard Mme de Reszke shouting loud injunctions to the valet de chambre not to forget Monsieur's *châle noir* and to put it round him in case of a *courant d'air*. Then the procession would appear, led by the valet de chambre carrying the parrot, Coco's, cage, followed by the master, now a portly and bald middle-aged man, no longer the Tristan of yesteryear. Coco would be sitting on his shoulders, and after him followed his own Polish valet with the dachshund, Tchou, on one arm, and with the other trying to balance the black shawl on Jean's shoulders, while he resisted in voluble Polish.

Then he would notice his pupils, switching tongues at once. "Ah! Bonjour, mes enfants. Comment allez-vous?" He would say each one's name, often in pet or diminutive forms. Then he would come forward and kiss them all. His smell was clean and beautiful: a combination of soap and a very expensive hair tonic. Then they would enter the auditorium. Coco was more often than not put on his cage, not in it. Some of the students were terrified of this parrot and he would stroll or flap about, happily taking nips at their ankles. The accompanist would sit at the piano, the valet would kiss the master's hand and withdraw. "Maintenant, chantons," de Reszke would say, and they would begin.

The first ten minutes were generally spent on exercises, such as diaphragm exercises, jerking the stomach muscles up and down, and other means to try and get the voices into "place". Then they moved on to vocal exercises, of which de Reszke had fourteen; every day they did six or seven of these. There was one for scales, long-sustained phrases for breath control, taken from well-known passages in opera; there was one for *pianissimo*, the famous aria from *Don Carlos* in which Elizabeth recalls past happiness (Act V), which they sang moving it upwards in semitones, as high as they could go; there was one for staccato, one for *pianissimo* and head voice. Then they practised from Vaccaj's *Metodo Pratico*, de Reszke allowing them to imitate the quality of tone he was putting into his own voice. Then they would tackle various extracts, arias, and recitatives from operas.

For the first little while Maggie found the strain of trying to keep up so great that her brain felt like bursting. She longed to be back in Miss Smith's pension in the avenue Victor Hugo where the only sound was that of the bleating goats who drew the little milk carts. At the end of half an hour de Reszke would get up, saying, "Bravo! tu as très bien chanté," and Maggie would stagger exhausted from the room, full of grave doubts as to the truth of his words, but overwhelmed with admiration and devotion towards the master himself: he could do everything so easily, while for her it was so difficult.

But she made progress, even a little too quickly. At one time de Reszke, in his excitement to show off his phenomenal pupil, may have pushed her too hard. She had been there only six months when Conried, in Paris in person to try to persuade de Reszke to appear at the Metropolitan, was invited along to hear her sing. She had learned the 27 pages of the Queen's air from Meyerbeer's *Les Huguenots*:

> I sang the quiet opening passages without mishap, and then I had my first attack of nerves and broke down. There was a dreadful silence. . . . "Mais, voyons, ma petite—continuez!" As I started again, I heard him say to Conried, "You understand, she has only been with me for six months." Hot with shame, I finished the aria, all twenty-seven pages of it, with my throat choked with tears. . . . [When they had gone] I retired behind the upright piano on the stage, and cried for two hours without ceasing. . . .* I have never cried about my work since.[13]

Some of the voices that came to de Reszke had fallen into very bad habits, and he was not at all pleased with the production mechanism, so he would do what he called "*dérober*" (undress) the voice and build it up again on a more secure foundation. The pupils so treated often did not know at first whether they were standing on their heads or heels, and, after a few lessons, panic and flight would set in among the less patient and intelligent ones. De Reszke was not an easy task-master, and to break the voice of bad habits he would say contrary things, for which time and perseverance were needed to spot the connections and see the larger design of what he was doing. The wiser ones would hang on and benefit.

Maggie was a natural learner and from the start fell in easily with what he did, so that after a short while she had no problems at all. She may not have been able, at that age, to reason out what he told her through her own experience. But she obeyed him absolutely, and retained and

* She was later found by the elderly accompanist, Mlle Mange-Petit, who tried to restore her damaged self-esteem.

understood exactly what he directed her to do, because he was so good at communicating with her.

His great skill was in managing to find and then establish a proper connection between the voice and the breath support. A singer might have wonderful breath capacity and control but unless the voice was joined to it—as it were sitting on it—it was very little use. De Reszke showed Maggie that if one sang, as women often did, with a high larynx and was in addition physically tense, it became almost impossible to get the voice down on to the support.

Next he showed how to get the body behind the voice and how through this the voice could acquire a deep velvety quality, never be hard, and would also acquire personality. Here Maggie was able to lay down the basis for her singing personality, that curiously physical and distinctive character in her voice. Then he demonstrated how important the "grimace" or smile was for women's high notes. Maggie called this the raising of the soft palate. "There's a thin skin on the roof of the mouth, like a diaphragm. When it's flat, the voice is flat. Surprise lifts it. I had a high palate which made it easier."[14] The high notes of men were different, more a mysterious process of "covering" the note, difficult to explain without demonstration, impossible to describe in words.

He taught her the scales, the most primitive form of singing which, as Darwin observed in *The Expression of the Emotions in Men and Animals*, is even to be found in apes: "one of the Gibbons produces an exact octave of music sounds, ascending and descending the scale by half-tones." De Reszke's scales were somewhat more sophisticated, however. "When I first went to de Reszke," Maggie herself modestly asserted, "I'm damned if I could sing scales at all; it took me quite a time to master them." This is hardly to be wondered at: they started on E flat and/or C. They would go up in semitones, mounting on the ordinary scale of eight notes. Then there would be two notes added in the second scale; then four added on the third variation; and so on. The result was that de Reszke's pupils did eighteen scales and exercises, instead of the usual five or six. "And when you started on an exercise, you went through to the end. You couldn't stop for breath, or go out." One exercise for breath control de Reszke was able to do six times without stopping. Maggie could only ever manage it three and a half times.* He said himself of his

---

* See Appendix B for the full text of de Reszke's exercises. Lilli Lehmann had an even more difficult scale of two octaves, which she called the Great Scale.[15]

way of training: "Au commencement, les petits galops, puis le grand entraînement, et après ça les courses classiques, les Derbys." As J.D. summarized it:

> He knew that in the theatre one wanted all kinds of resource and colour in the voice, but primarily power, "Au théâtre il *faut* gueuler mais il *faut* savoir gueuler" (In the theatre you have to shout, but you have to know how to shout). He had an uncanny power of building up a voice out of little or nothing and under his hand ordinary voices were transformed into something rich and strange. But his power was never obtained by forcing or by the sacrifice of beauty or tone; it was said of him by Reynaldo Hahn: "Il est le seul ténor qui ait du charme dans la force." He also taught by exaggeration—"il faut avoir trop pour en avoir assez"—and in each point of his teaching insisted upon the supreme importance of that particular point. Not for many lessons did things become relative to each other; they were always absolute. In this way his teaching seemed to contradict itself at times, as the stresses on one side of technique seemed to be too heavy, but to those who had patience and faith the kaleidoscope settled down to a clear picture.[16]

Maggie always stressed how pedantic de Reszke was: "If you want to sing a difficult aria, learn one more difficult." The main value of this was that it developed endurance: strength of muscle and of breathing. By such means she learnt to sing Marguerite's "Anges purs" from the last act of Gounod's *Faust*, which rises by a semitone at each repetition. Even Melba, she reported, who sang this trio beautifully, had to rest the next day as she had not been trained quite so rigorously. But for de Reszke's pupils it was easy, they had a special exercise for Gounod's "little tricks", as Maggie called them. He also stretched her voice: she had a struggle to learn coloratura, but in time she was able to formulate those perfect high notes which she seemed to pluck from the air, though as far as can be judged she never developed a trill.

He also emphasized a feature much overlooked: he insisted above all that the singer sing in tune—the first rule of vocal intonation. "There was a famous coloratura, a wonderful singer, sang in Chicago, in London at the Albert Hall where I heard her later. But she always sang a little bit flat. The tragedy was ... no one told her. So when she came to make records, it was too late: she lost all her career."[17] This was Amelita Galli-Curci: Maggie overdramatized her plight, for she made many successful records, but it was true she sang out of tune some of the time. Even so, singers are taught by feeling not by ear; they have only their own sensations of sound issuing from their throats to go by, to judge the quality of what they are doing. For as Maggie rightly pointed out, "When we talk or sing, we become deaf."* So for a good singer a cultivation of the awareness of those sensations was essential.

Three of the pupils at de Reszke's during Maggie's time were, to her youthful eye, "over forty", though here again she was not strictly accurate. One was Lina Cavalieri, a noted beauty with a good figure, thick black hair, and lustrous dark eyes. Maggie described her own feelings as "wide-eyed at her fabulous beauty". Cavalieri made her début at Covent Garden in *Tosca*, and later went to Florence where she was killed in an air raid in the Second World War. Then there was Louise Edvina (The Hon. Mrs Edwardes) from Montreal, whose reputation was already established and secure—a pity, from Maggie's point of view, because Edvina later sang at Covent Garden many of the roles Maggie could have sung much better, and did.† According to Maggie she had a "good voice but a terrible tremolo". The third "older woman" was Minnie Saltzman-Stevens,‡ a dramatic soprano, "a shabby blowsy woman"[18] who was a member of the choir at the American Church in Paris, "without any culture or knowledge of operatic vocal art". These were special cases: Cavalieri had to be given a new voice; the other two had vocal faults which de Reszke corrected methodically and patiently. "I never saw him ruffled," said Maggie of her beloved Jean. Later at Covent Garden, when de Reszke was with them, she and Olga Lynn saw

* This was the reason she liked to sing in some big halls, like the Festival Hall, London, for she claimed that "when you stop, the sound goes on, and in that second you can hear yourself."

† Mélisande and Louise, for example. Edvina was a great barrier to Maggie's career for she was the mistress of the administrator of Covent Garden, H. V. Higgins. She was very wealthy and wore real pearls when she sang *Tosca*. One night in the scene where Tosca rushes over to Cavaradossi after his first torture, and flings herself on him, her pearls caught on the man's button and the string broke, scattering the pearls all over the stage. "Oh my gawd, my pearls!" exclaimed Mme Edvina in her North American accent. The curtain was hurriedly lowered, the stage cordoned off, while the stage staff went down on hands and knees and hunted for them.

‡ She sang at Bayreuth for Hans Richter.

Saltzman-Stevens, a "slender beautiful woman floating gracefully across the stage as Sieglinde". "Est-ce possible que c'est ma pauvre Saltzman-Stevens!" exclaimed de Reszke. He could not believe such a transformation had taken place.

De Reszke entertained royally. The King of Portugal, whose wife was the daughter of Louis-Philippe, came to 53, rue de la Faisanderie; so did the Duke of Connaught, the Grand Duke Vladimir of Russia, the Duc de Morny; younger students such as Maggie and Olga were assigned Dukes to dance with. Other distinguished visitors were Bernhardt, Réjane, and Sardou. One of de Reszke's two famous imitations—the other was drawing a cork out of a bottle, the final "pop" reducing the company to hysterics—was of Victorien Sardou at the dinner table. "Sardou never stopped talking. He scarcely ever drew breath while his food grew cold. When he raised an arm to drink he would splutter into the glass, lifting up the other hand to ward off any possible interruption."[19] He also loved to impersonate stars of the music hall: Vesta Tilley singing "Jolly good luck to the girl that loves a sailor" was a favourite.

The climax of de Reszke's entertaining undoubtedly came, for both Maggie and Olga Lynn, when Adelina Patti sang Rosina in an act of Rossini's *Il Barbiere*, in a private performance at de Reszke's theatre. Patti was in her sixty-fifth year, and this was her last appearance on any stage, though she went on singing until much later. Edouard de Reszke sang Don Basilio, and the students sang in the chorus. It is not on record whether Maggie was a guest or a participant, but she was certainly there.[20] So was old Madame Gounod, who sat in the small stage box with Reynaldo Hahn, "her pretty face surrounded by a large black bonnet, which was carefully arranged with a stiff organdie frill".[21] When it was over, Maggie remembered, Jean and Patti fell on one another's neck and wept. "Caro Giovanni, caro Giovanni! . . ."

The pupils also gave their own concerts, their little exclusive matinées to show off their talents before de Reszke's chosen guests, among whom could usually be found the most celebrated artists of the Opéra and Opéra-Comique. Even critics were invited. "Last but not least," wrote M. Pelca of one of these occasions, "the triumph was for Miss Maggie Tate who sang to perfection the duet from *La Bohème* with the tenor Mr Bertram Binyon. And in spite of her extreme youth—for Miss Tate is not quite seventeen years of age—she gave an admirable performance of that difficult aria, 'Depuis le jour', from *Louise*."

But a singer's life had to be balanced. There were holidays too. Madame and Jean once took the three girls from the avenue Victor Hugo to Deauville where they were given their own villa and cook. They went to the beach every day and met the de Reszkes. In heavy black stockings and thick bathing dresses they dipped themselves in the sea while the master and his beautiful wife watched from the shore and waved to them, Madame under her lace parasol, and Monsieur ready to offer them a glass of Dubonnet when they emerged from the waves. This image of de Reszke the man is possibly only capped by that of the plump retired tenor struggling to keep his weight down a little, though not too much, on the golf course. "His portly figure could often be distinguished on some high point, taking a swing at the ball with infinite care."[22]

CHAPTER FOUR

A Setting of Limits
(1906–1907)

But there is a limit to everything, and when someone gushed, "Madame Lehmann, you and Nordica are the greatest Isoldes I ever saw", Madame Lehmann didn't even smile.

IRA GLACKENS, *Yankee Diva*

WHILE DE RESZKE underwent a lengthy period of self-questioning and vocal analysis, only hitting upon a solution for his own voice after years of painstaking effort, Maggie had no such difficulties. When she first went to audition for him he had forecast that in two years she would be ready to make her début, and in two years and three months she did make it. Possibly the fundamental quality for early success as a singer is a discipline instilled so ruthlessly and without self-questioning that not for many years—or, as in Maggie's case, hardly ever—does a shadow of doubt cross the artist's mind. There was no need to question de Reszke's method, as it came so naturally to her and suited her temperament. The necessity of being methodical, of cultivating an even disposition, of learning not to be vain, brusque, or destructively temperamental, was all part of a professional personality which over and above their technical and interpretative training de Reszke gave his pupils; these qualities appear to have been central to his own artistic code, in turn enforced by his aristocratic sense of honour: in him the two were inextricably bound up. And like Pallas Athene born from Zeus's head fully armed, with wisdom and judgement matured, Maggie emerged from de Reszke's school precociously capable of technical and interpretative miracles.

Her own powers of observation contributed enormously. Surrounded by, and privileged to watch, all these gifted and experienced people who were part of de Reszke's entourage, she picked up a lot of tricks which helped the formal training no end. Physical fitness was absolutely essential. You had to be able to do without drugs. You must not be of a nervous disposition—though you might be very nervous before a performance—but you had to cultivate habits of mind which made you relax. "The voices of the golden age were not superior, but they had a better technique," said Maggie of the singers she knew and heard at the time; for it was true also that singers, and people in general, lived then under so much less strain: "they sat at home and did needlepoint". Just as medicine was based on old-fashioned natural cures, some of which were hopelessly misguided but others of which were, and remain, superior to the new, high technology drugs, so the cultivation of sensible habits of body and mind was a great preserver of vocal power. Maggie learnt such habits at this period, and maintained them throughout her life: for example, never to talk on the day she was to sing (she later extended this to the 48 hours before an appearance); never to go out to a restaurant the night before, because she would have to raise her voice to be heard, and, like as not, the atmosphere would be smoky and harmful to the vocal cords. "Keep away from cigar smoke," she advised; and never, curiously enough, go swimming: "sea bathing is the worst thing you can do, it relaxes you, makes you sing flat."[1]

Even the opera houses respected the traditions of voice preservation in their contractual arrangements. Melba and Tetrazzini never sang two nights running; sometimes, Maggie pointed out, they sang only once a week. And, she was to recall, of the meticulous contractual arrangements in France, "we had a clause in the contracts about periods".[2] Maggie always contrasted the quiet and solitary ease of concert performance with the rough-and-tumble of the opera house. There was the dust and the dirt, the waiting about, the clash of personalities, and even, sometimes, actual physical danger to take into account: "One day I saw a ballerina in the wings practising, picking her leg up, and thrusting it out like a donkey. Some tenor came walking by, not looking where he was going, and, my dear, she knocked the man down!" These hazards needed a philosophical approach, especially the waiting about, for it was absolutely essential to be in the opera house at least one hour before singing, and for a very good reason: the vocal cords had to take on the temperature of the house; just as orchestral instruments had to be tuned to the right pitch in accordance with the local conditions.

These tips, and many more, Maggie assimilated from de Reszke. Above all he put emphasis, in operatic training, upon the natural effect. With his parrot in attendance (who would intervene sometimes, when the lesson went badly, with a peculiar cry like a tenor in distress) he would embellish his explanations with similes drawn from nature: "Get your support on the note preceding the high note, and just carry the resonance of the high note further up by drawing back the uvula as far as possible, and when on the note itself, expand the ribs to support it, *like the pinions of a bird*."[3] The age of de Reszke we tend now to consider formal and heavy, by contrast with our own relaxation and informality; but this is largely a myth, as can be seen from strident, unrelaxed, over-assertive performances of *Pelléas* heard in recent years.* "But why in such a hurry, take your time," de Reszke told his pupils; "don't say it as though you were a schoolboy saying a piece as quick as you can. Sing as though you were improvising it; it gives you authority over the stage, over the orchestra, over the audience; you compel them to wait for you, to pay attention to you." The claims he made for naturalism in operatic effect have hardly been improved on. The key to such mastery and confidence was of course understanding, and deep sympathy for the reality of the situation portrayed in the opera: the artist must know more about the music, the character, the story, than anyone else. In other words the only real confidence is that based on hard work, on deep and painstaking study. De Reszke made *Faust* glowingly beautiful, and Werther and Charlotte "real people with real sorrows"; Meyerbeer was revealed "as something more than a synonym for insincere vulgarity".[4]

Towards the end of 1905 Reynaldo Hahn came to the de Reszke school to choose a Zerlina and a Cherubino for a series of concerts he was devising as a Mozart Festival to be held at the Nouveau-Théâtre in the rue Blanche in March 1906. Whole acts from *Don Giovanni*, *Le Nozze di Figaro*, and *Cosi fan tutte* were to be performed, together with arias, trios, and excerpts from chamber and orchestral works: altogether an exquisitely balanced and well-thought-out choice.

Maggie writes that de Reszke arranged with Hahn that she should sing the parts, but Olga Lynn claims de Reszke told her that *she* was chosen, presumably by Hahn, but that as Maggie was already making a success in public she needed to be encouraged in every way, and de Reszke insisted she be allowed this opportunity.[5] This sounds as if Maggie was already the school's shop-window pupil, but Maggie herself was adamant that this

* Such as that conducted by Boulez at Covent Garden in 1969.

was her first public appearance since she sang in Maiden Lane, where Walter Rubens heard her. Olga Lynn is probably the less reliable of the two, since she mistakenly names the venue of the concerts as the Salle Gaveau.

Maggie was not paid for this engagement, and rightly, though frostily, observes that it cannot properly rank as her professional début, though it is generally taken to be such. It was a fittingly grand occasion in any case. The stars, who were paid and who drew the public, were Lilli Lehmann, then nearly sixty, de Reszke's brother Edouard, and Mario Ancona. Maggie's code of behaviour, deeply inculcated at the school, insisted on perfect silence before a performance; this was rudely contradicted when she heard Lilli Lehmann, about to sing the Countess in *Figaro*, overpowering her niece and pupil Hedwig Helbig, who was singing Susanna, with vehement abuse and advice expressed in blistering German which Maggie did not understand. "I stood on the other side of the room, waiting for the Wagnerian storm to abate."

However, as she rapidly observed, remaining uncowed by Lehmann's behaviour—remember Maggie was not yet quite eighteen at the time, making her sharp, almost cynical perception the more astonishing—"the angry old aunt of a woman disappeared in what seemed to me a devilish grin, which stretched her mouth from ear to ear. As she moved forward into the applause, I thought to myself, 'So that's what you have to do, is it?' In my stupid ignorance, I thought it false and overdone, not knowing that the day would come when 'Ridi, pagliaccio!' would also be my password."[6] It did not ever really become her "password"; it merely became part of her professional mythology of being tough and going through with it, whatever she felt—although her technical appreciation of the need for a broad smile, an extreme grimace, to "fill a stage", was exact. But she was never very good at forcing smiles when she did not feel them or was not in the right mood.

Reynaldo Hahn, who conducted as well as arranged this festival, was a composer who had Mozart much on his mind.* Born in Caracas, Venezuela, he was only three when his family moved to Paris, where he became something of a child prodigy, dandled on his father's knee at the

---

* Of Dutch Jewish and German blood, Hahn took out French nationality in order to fight in the First World War, after which his enthusiasm for Mozart did much to re-establish his popularity in Paris. He later composed the incidental music for Sacha Guitry's *Mozart*.

grand piano, playing Offenbach in the *salon* of the celebrated Princesse Mathilde—

> Du do premier au final do
> Glissent les doigts de Reynaldo.[7]

—and regretting it was not something more serious. Like Mozart he composed brilliantly when very young and his most famous song, "Si mes vers avaient des ailes", a setting of Victor Hugo's poem, was written before he was fifteen.

But unlike Mozart, Hahn was by no means a pure and concentrated genius. Destined to fulfil a central social role in a glittering and diverse world in which he was as much attracted to literature as to music, and too gregarious to follow to the exclusion of all else the lonely path of the egocentric creator, he became one of those versatile figures such as Satie, Cocteau, or more recently Boris Vian, of which France—or should we say Paris—has made a speciality. The path of versatility, into which Hahn's rich and mixed blood led him, was full of perils yet offered great recompense in the form of almost universal adoration from society. Pushing him inexorably along this path was a strong narcissistic element in his character.

Maggie adored Reynaldo. His enthusiasm for everything was contagious, and his magnetic personality swept exciting projects along to triumphant conclusions. He was very good-looking, with brilliantly expressive velvety eyes—the velvet quality in men's eyes of which feminine observers at the time were much enamoured—fine brown hair, and very dashing pencil-stub moustaches. He was also on the tall side: Maggie liked tall men. Women, especially ambitious ones, often allow themselves easily to adore a man from whom there is no sexual threat: so she, at the age of eighteen, found herself fascinated by this polymath Parisian who was so wise and witty about everything under the sun. He turned other women's heads easily too, in particular that of the ravishing Liane de Pougy, who spilled out to him all her sexual confidences—she was often being pursued by as many as a dozen men at a time—and towards whom he remained chaste. "You are the only man to whom I would like to give myself," she wrote to him, "and who will not take me. . . . I no longer want to ask you to come to me: that will happen if it's going to happen. . . . No, we will not, my Reynaldo, pick the fruit of love. . . ."[8]

The fruit remained ungathered, overshadowed by an affair which, music apart, secured for Reynaldo Hahn a place among the immortals: his affair with Marcel Proust. Proust wrote to him generally in less passionate and more infantile terms than Mme de Pougy, familiarity in this case breeding diminutives; among the endearments he employed were "Poney", "Binibuls", "Bibul", and "Bichnibuls". But Proust was equally struck by that special capacity Hahn had for projecting his songs at the piano: anyone who saw him sit down and play and sing one of his own songs never forgot the experience. Maggie never forgot it, or his wonderful qualities as an accompanist;* she sang with him in 1946, not long before he died, at the British Embassy in Paris, for Sir Alfred and Lady Diana Duff Cooper.[9] "When he sits down at the piano," Proust confided in his *Chroniques*,

a cigarette dangling from his lips, the company falls silent, gathers round, and listens. Every note is either a word or a cry. The head is tilted back slightly, and from the melancholy mouth—a little disdain-fully—comes the saddest and warmest sound that ever was. The name of this instrument of genius is Reynaldo Hahn, and he wrings hearts, fills eyes with tears, bending, in silent and solemn undulation, one after the other. Never since Schumann has music, in its power of depicting pain, tenderness, and nature's soothing influence, borne features of so human a truth, or so absolute a beauty.[10]

Maggie added to Proust's description, specifically: Hahn had a light baritone voice, and a power of drawing very long breath (even with a cigarette in his mouth!). The manner or style was very suave. "No one could sing them better," she said, referring to his songs and discounting her own contribution, and she was struck by his beautiful rubato, a capacity for which, in the matter of the tempo, she called "stealing from Peter to pay Paul". His speeding up, his *accelerando*, and slowing down, *rallentando*, in the poem introduced a "very charming undulation in the whole concept of the song".[11] That she should, while never, as far as we can guess, having seen the Proust passage, light on exactly the same word, "undulation", to describe the effect—and from a distance of sixty years— only goes to show how strong an impact Hahn's special quality of inter-

* But when she heard him accompany Mme de Reszke in some of his *Vingt Mélodies*, he was "so overcome with admiration he collapsed in a heap on the floor".

preting his own work carried with it. It perfectly exemplified de Reszke's dictum, "Sing as though you were improvising it."*

Maggie never mentioned Hahn's homosexuality, though she did comment—sometimes scathingly, sometimes admiringly—on the sexual habits of many others, and on homosexuality in general; she had overcome prudery in such matters at an early age.† Homosexuality has been written of as a taboo subject at this time: the biographer and critic Gavoty portrays Tchaikovsky as dying from having "carried around in him an oppressive secret", while Saint-Saëns went to "hide in North Africa and the Canaries a vice to which he never made the tiniest allusion"[12] (possibly he never had it), but there is evidence to suggest that while certain codes were upheld in public, what people did and talked about in private was a very different matter. Maggie reported her friends discussing their homosexuality in front of her with complete frankness.

Hahn was one of the three men Maggie most admired during her Paris years, the others being de Reszke and Debussy; so possibly, like Liane de Pougy, she preferred to keep up the pretence that Hahn was, or might have been, as interested in women sexually as he was socially. At any rate, she accepted the general opinion that he was famous for his love affairs. She may genuinely not have known, for he was fifteen years her senior. After Proust's death, Hahn's love life remained promiscuous but shadowy, apart from one long-standing relationship with Guy Ferrant. "One thing is certain, Reynaldo's sentimental life was sombre. On occasions it led to the threshold of despair."[13] Maggie's own long friendship with him was touching, and unexpected encounters later on showed she had never lost her respect for and fear of one of her earliest masters.

His influence on her was as much literary as musical. Like de Reszke, like Debussy, Hahn stressed the value of the word, and the meaning of the word: he was at great pains to show that the two components of lyric creation, musical and verbal, came from an equivalent source: "No

* Maggie's best recording of "Si mes vers avaient des ailes", which has this quality, was made by Decca in 1937, with George Reeves as accompanist. The later, more celebrated recording with Gerald Moore, though of excellent quality, does not have the same interpretative excitement.

† Maggie was initiated early on into the manners and habits of the Parisian *grand monde* by her first husband, Eugène Plumon, whom she married in 1910. A lawyer of the Paris Court of Appeal, Plumon moved in the most sophisticated and liberal sections of society; their circle included the charming and gifted homosexual Jean-Jacques Ollivier, who was a friend of Isadora Duncan.

musical pleasure could exist without rhythm," he made his eloquent plea, "without cadence, without an interior source, without that mysterious and infallible dynamic which works all the movements of nature, from the gravitational pull of the planets to the circulation of the blood." Had the sense of this been expressed more analytically and fastidiously, it might have been Debussy himself writing—though Hahn detested Debussy both as a man and as a musician. To a child of nature such as Maggie, no view of music could have been more thrilling or more just, and later she paid tribute to Hahn, saying his songs were much underrated: they remained a "treasure-house"; everything he had written could be sung, she said, because of the unerring choice of poem, and because of the unity between poet and composer.[14]

That de Reszke's pet little pupil, this "pink and white rosebud", should receive her first public challenge in Mozart, under Hahn, could not have been more auspicious. Learning Mozart was one of the first disciplines de Reszke set his students and finding her *tessitura* or vocal range was crucial to Maggie during those formative years, as it had been earlier to de Reszke. The traditional Italian practice of cementing a range out of two different methods of voice production—the chest voice, the *voix de poitrine*, and the head voice, the high soft palate—were rejected by de Reszke, as their effect was to weaken the chest or cords at their limits; and so he had to find what Maggie called a "medium" to bridge these "breaks" without harming the chest or cords. This he found by putting the sound in these transitional passages through the nose. Maggie gradually settled down into the difficult *tessitura* of the lyric soprano (her voice, much to her disappointment, never had the weight for the full dramatic roles of *Carmen* and *Tosca*) by linking the three placings for the voice—the natural or speaking voice (or baritone, in a man), the chest voice, and the head voice—by "blending" them through the nasal passages.

Mozart demanded precision, delicacy, and vocal agility: he based all his soprano arias on two octaves and two notes, and if the range of the artist was not great enough for this, then it had to be stretched. On the principle that it was good to learn the most difficult things first, de Reszke had made Maggie study Susanna and Cherubino in *Le Nozze di Figaro*, Zerlina in *Don Giovanni*, and Pamina and the Queen of the Night in *The Magic Flute*. Susanna in *Figaro* goes from bottom A to top C, the Queen of the Night from D to top F.

Although Maggie was still too young to appreciate the finer points of the Mozart tradition, Reynaldo Hahn's enthusiasm for Mozart and his fervent interpretation at these concerts impressed themselves on her, and she acquitted herself admirably. He also taught her recitative, giving her a perfect balance between the artificiality of musical convention and a naturalness of expression. *Le Matin*'s reviewer spoke of a "Mlle Tate, whose soprano voice, wonderfully pure, expressive, and tender, brought a charming grace to the songs of Cherubino and Zerlina". An un-identified spectator, writing in her diary on Friday, 30 March 1906, compared her voice to that of Emma Eames. "She wore a short white frock, and white ribbons on her long braid. . . . Lehmann evidently felt that her days were over and . . . made the effort of her life to sing."[15]

Her operatic début came in the year following the Mozart concerts at the Théâtre-Nouveau. It was a modest beginning, so modest indeed that she omits it from her autobiography. Even so, it was impressive enough, and the company was not all that much less distinguished than Edouard de Reszke and Lilli Lehmann. The place was Monte Carlo, the date 7 February 1907, and her part that of Tyrcis in Offenbach's *Myriame et Daphne*, a new version of Act One of the operetta *Les Bergers* (1865), arranged by André Bloch, who was said to have "conducted to perfection".[16] Although the score of this short opera, paired with the première of Massenet's two-act *Thérèse*, has been dubbed a "musical jewel of exquisite freshness", and the artists, among whom were Hector Dufranne, Edmond Clément, and Yvonne Dubel, were applauded "voluminously",[17] Maggie forgot it entirely, remembering the more prestigious and hair-raising "début" in *Don Giovanni*, when she sang Zerlina to Maurice Renaud's Don.

She had been deeply excited by the prospect of Monte Carlo as a change from Paris. With Mama as chaperone, she left Paris on the *train de grand luxe* at 6 p.m. one evening in January 1907. The noise was ceaseless throughout the night, and Mama took a sedative to help her sleep; at 9.56 sharp the following morning they arrived at Menton, where they changed to a carriage which clattered along the tram rails to Monte Carlo itself. Here the white-painted villas were oddly at variance with Maggie's preconception of the place: because of the autocratic rule of Prince Albert she somehow expected spaciousness, and was disappointed to find it all very pretty and chic.

As Maggie was a minor and needed a special permit to visit the gaming rooms in the Casino, she and Mama decided to apply for one. So they addressed themselves to M. Raoul Gunsbourg, a short, fat, compact figure of a man, very ugly, who was always, she later heard, boasting in a roundabout way of his sexual exploits—saying, for instance, when a fine-looking lady passed him on the promenade, "She supped with me, very late, last night."

The Casino was a florid heavy building, and the foul air of the rooms, caused by the oil lamps which provided lighting, made Maggie fear for her voice. Oil had been restored as lighting because once a robbery had been attempted which began with the cutting of the electricity supply, thereby plunging the gaming halls into darkness and confusion. But the spectacle of all those large sums of money changing hands made her forget about the foul air: here was the Eldorado of the élite and she stood wide-eyed with astonishment. The Casino employed 1,000 people, 200 croupiers at any one time.

Maggie was entranced by a sound, a strange intimate music which has since passed away from such establishments: the actual chink of gold. It was like the little chattering background noise in the parakeet house at the Zoo, this chinking and susurration of hundreds and thousands of golden coins, passing from hand to hand over the undercurrent of voices.

Along with Mozart and Offenbach, during this busy month of February Maggie also sang three performances in the first revival for thirty years of *Le Timbre d'argent* by Saint-Saëns: Reynaldo Hahn had commented that "Camille Saint-Saëns is one of the greatest composers of all time and of any country", and Saint-Saëns was at the revival, attending a ceremonial dinner afterwards in his honour. Marguérite Carré, newly the wife of the director of the Opéra-Comique, was also in the company; it was she who thirteen months later was to be instrumental in securing for Maggie the part of Mélisande at the Opéra-Comique.

On 1 February, as a fanfare to these operatic roles, Maggie gave her first professional concert—that is, the first for which she was paid—at the Casino de Monte Carlo. The other artist, which whom she enjoyed equal billing, was "Mr J. J. Paderewski". With Paderewski, Maggie was taking the place of Aïno Ackté, a compliment M. Gunsbourg was at great pains to underline to her. Paderewski appreciated the value of having his instrument at the right temperature for the house, in accordance with the doctrine of the great Jean de Reszke: Maggie and Mama found him pacing the stage of the Opera House, a "huge empty cave of blackness", with both his hands stuck deeply into a muff. This was, Mama explained to Maggie, to warm up his hands.

In *Don Giovanni*, the Masetto was the stage manager, and there was no dress rehearsal for her first performance, a Sunday matinée at 2.30. Maggie was not well enough versed in the ways of the Monte Carlo Opera House to know that singers arrived only in time for the performance and then promptly left. Debussy had captured the spirit of the place in his *Monsieur Croche*: "The delightful adventurers who adorn that resort are not very particular, and the charming cosmopolitan young ladies only regard music as an unobtrusive and useful accompaniment to their smiles." The stage manager showed Maggie the moves; he was already half dressed for his part and she did her best to memorize his instructions. When the performance started Maurice Renaud, as the Don, pulled her about like an ice-block. Fortunately she knew the music backwards, though this was the first time she had sung the part of Zerlina all the way through. Otherwise she went through it, she said later, "as if doped". The movements Renaud made with his eyes were meant to impel her into some sort of action, but even these could not prevail on her except in the duet, "La ci darem la mano".

At the time of this baptism, another more sinister side of operatic life was also introduced: the casting couch. On this she refused adamantly to lie down, to the detriment of her future. Gunsbourg had summoned her one morning at 10 a.m., after Mama had left her to fend for herself. Closing and then locking the door of his office, he threw her down on a sofa, and, as laid down in the code of conduct for directors of the Monte Carlo Opera House, with himself ever the sole bearer of this office (one could almost hear Debussy's mocking tones), prepared himself to receive the traditional submission of a young and ambitious soprano to the will of *il grande primo uomo* (he did, on occasions, sing leading roles). But the traditional response was lacking in Maggie, who at once betrayed her stern Midland Catholicism by screaming in French at the top of her voice: "Unlock that door, unlock that door!"

Her punishment for this transgression was that she was left off the guest list of the banquet given every season by the Prince of Monaco for leading members of the opera company. No doubt even at this tender age her bluntness created a strong impression, and no doubt she could have extricated herself with more subtlety and circumspection—except that, as

Heraclitus observes, a man's, or woman's, character is her fate. Maggie showed no great talent or inclination for diplomacy, and possessing a good voice was only half, if that, of the battle of gaining a foothold in an opera house; the other half was to be a Metternich of diplomacy and cunning. Utterly deceived, she thought in her innocence that to have talent and ability was enough.

After Monte Carlo it was with relief she returned to Paris where de Reszke continued to coach her, and Albert Carré gave her a contract at the Opéra-Comique, where she sang first the small part of Glycère in *Circé*, by the brothers Hillemacher. A photograph in *The Tatler* showed an enchanting, kittenish-eyed maiden in a flimsy classical robe, with bare arms, gracefully clasping her hands together, but Maggie complained of her appalling clumsiness during the performance, when she even fell up, not down, a flight of stairs and the audience roared with laughter. *Circé*, Teyte★ apart, was not a success and was withdrawn, though Maggie remained a member of the company; her contract gave her 800 francs (worth £544 in 1978) a month for the first year, 1,000 francs a month for the second, and 1,200 for the third year. After *Circé* she sang a mezzo role, Mallika in Delibes's *Lakmé*, then tried to learn Poucette in Massenet's *Manon* (but did not sing it), and the Second Boy in *The Magic Flute*, which she later sang with Edmond Clément as Tamino and Lucien Fugère as Papageno. She also sang in Camille Erlanger's *Aphrodite*, based on Pierre Louÿs's book; a tiny role, but she sang it proudly, Pierre Lalo noted, providing him the only relief among "so many heavy hours". Then she was set to work to study the title role of Ambroise Thomas's *Mignon*, but did not sing it. Thus passed her first year.

Ill-suited to self-advancement by the methods of the *cocotte*, Maggie could not ascend the ladder by the other prescribed method: the use of money in the right places. The regular tariff for singers who wanted to make a start at the Opéra-Comique was exorbitant: 30,000 francs to sing *Carmen*. It was reputed that Calvé paid exactly that to make her début. For the title role of *Lakmé* it cost a mere 10,000 francs, while it was said that

★ Maggie by this time had changed the spelling of her name to Teyte to standardize its pronunciation: "In Paris," she said (in 1934), "they addressed me as Marjie Tot, so to keep the pronunciation correct I began to spell it Tête. De Reszke put in the 'y'— he feared the obvious temptation to attach 'swelled' to Tête."

Reynaldo Hahn had paid 20,000 to have his opera *L'Ile de rêve* performed in 1898.[18] Lacking that sort of money, Maggie had to wait her turn to rise by the equally traditional methods of patience, honesty, and good luck.

Graft and sexual favours apart, the Opéra-Comique was a strict place to work. The administration was very punctilious and precise about rehearsal times, with heavy fines stipulated in the contract for arriving late for rehearsal or failing to put on a costume or hat as instructed. Maggie found a dramatic contrast later in the casualness and *laissez-faire* of the Beecham opera company—compensated for by the galvanizing effect of Beecham's personality.

The authorities had wisely banned the use of gas for lighting Paris theatres and opera houses: it now had to be electricity. There was even a decree against cigarettes or matches in the dressing rooms, though in effect this came down to a fireman doing the rounds once a month preceded by the theatre or opera-house official who told everyone the *pompiers* were on their way, and to hide their cigarettes and matches.

On many nights, there was little for Maggie to do but sit in the wings and watch. Here, appearing in only one act of *Lakmé*, she could witness all the furtive activity, hidden from the audience, of an opera house at work. She watched the conductor, only recently banished from the stage itself, and now sojourning in the pit among the orchestra.* She watched the répétiteur, his head half screened by his wooden hood, untiringly following the score and holding the performance together with his clear low voice, as if he had some sixth sense of when something was about to go wrong. She watched the chorus master in the wings attempting to inspire and order the sheep-like droves of men and women, the principals pacing impatiently, clearing their throats, the fire- and foot-men keeping an eye on the curtain ropes, and then, above in the flying gallery, the agile, shirt-sleeved scene-shifters weaving their torsos amidst the pulleys and winches. What a complicated and specialized world it was: one slip on the part of any person and the performace could grind to a halt. And yet

* Felix Mottl, the first conductor Maggie had ever worked with—when still at de Reszke's—used to conduct Mozart from a seat at a piano next to the stage, directing singers with his baton and himself playing the recitative accompaniments, while leaving the orchestra largely to fend for itself. But now the conductor was firmly placed at the front of the pit, and Maggie could well have been turning over in her mind a *faux-pas* she had made at rehearsal in Monte Carlo, when she publicly contradicted the conductor over a question of tempo. The latter had been furious: "Not in front of the orchestra," he had told her—a good lesson she never forgot.

everything seemed to work so smoothly, so harmoniously, so inevitably: each one knew his place, and how he fitted into the scheme.

But what of the style of performance at the Opéra-Comique? It was an intimate house, seating 1,500, and in many ways the style of acting and performance was more popular and natural than today; at any rate it was not our same cliché of naturalism: the nervy pseudo-realism of working-class behaviour. Singers were, for example, very still, making themselves heard with great deliberateness. They would endeavour to suit the action to the word, the word to the action: they would, as Lucien Fugère pointed out, be judged on their ability to tell the story.[19] Various forms of naturalism flourished at the time, from an extreme Zola-esque crudity to the delicate performances of Antoine's Théâtre-Libre, and the enchanting performances of Chekhov, and it was these daring innovatory practices in the straight theatre on which Debussy drew heavily for *Pelléas*.* Indeed all the evidence shows that Debussy, who sought a simple portrayal of the mighty impulses of humanity, had very much his own way in the Opéra-Comique. Even more extreme forms of naturalism also flourished, as in the highly obscene and salacious Théâtre Naturaliste, with its simulated copulations: its leader was sent to prison for committing acts against public decency. The Opéra-Comique was not at all averse to more watered-down sex appeal: when they performed the Louÿs-Erlanger *Aphrodite* with Mary Garden as Chrysis, Carré spent hours experimenting with lights trying to make them pierce Garden's veil and show her nakedness beneath. Alas, to no avail, the lighting was not so strong in those days.[20]

It was a deeply hierarchical venture into which Maggie was launching. The prima donna, or *uomo*, was still at the apex of the opera-house power structure: the director of the opera house was a powerful figure, to a young person such as herself, but it was the star to whom he was beholden. Maggie understood little of what was going on at that time, she did as she was told and sang as she could, for her ego as a performer was as yet unformed, uninflated. For all her precocious musical intelligence she was ingenuous, and it was impossible for a girl of nineteen who had hardly any legal rights, let alone the bargaining cards of reputation or experience in her hand, to stand up to the reigning prima donnas—Melba, Tetrazzini, Garden, Edvina, Destinn, Marguérite Carré—each intent on making sure her position was secure *vis-à-vis* the others. "The more successful they

* See Chapter 5.

are, the more jealous they are. . . . Whereas they ought to be grateful to the world for their success," was how she put her feeling about them later on. The last thing any of them was prepared to do was to admit a new rival, and Maggie had to rely on the frailer and more upsettable craft of artistic respect, rather than the battering rams of politicians or machinations worthy of the *demi-monde*. It was first to de Reszke and later to Debussy that she owed her opportunities.

Experimentally, as a young woman whose pattern of life as it evolved became more like that of a woman of our own day than of her own, Maggie had during this first season at the Opéra-Comique her first short love affair—a quick dip in the sea, bracing and, extraordinarily enough, with a consequence whose proof can still be seen and heard today. She did not tell anyone of this affair for more than sixty years, until she received a letter from Romania disclosing to her that No. 5 of the *Sept Chansons de Clément Marot* of Georges Enesco, subtitled, "Présent de Couleur Blanc (Estrenes)"[21] had been dedicated to her in 1907–8. "I didn't tell anyone of this," she said, "because I wouldn't want them to say, 'Oh Teyte, she was a real little prostitute, she would go to bed with anybody.'"[22]

To the young woman of nineteen, Enesco presented an irresistible image of the successful musician: unusually romantic-looking, with hair agitated on the slightest provocation by quivers of passion, powerful intense eyes, and an extremely mobile and sensual mouth. His virtuosity on the violin was legendary, and he was to become world-famous as composer, conductor, and teacher of the young Yehudi Menuhin. Enesco was also an incomparably precise and clear-eyed observer of his contemporaries: like Maggie, an outsider from an even more distant land who was privileged and fortunate enough to be elected or "reborn" a Parisian, he had the gift of perception.

"Roger-Ducasse is ferocious and tender," he begins a wry account of the death of Gabriel Fauré:

Ferocious with those who love him, tender with those he likes. To tell the truth, he cultivated friendships but if he miscalculated he became terrible. . . . I believe Ravel deceived him a little—not musically for sure, but on the plane of human affections. . . . I remember an old story. . . . When Gabriel Fauré died, Ducasse and Ravel found themselves together by their old teacher's deathbed. Ravel seemed frozen to the marrow, he shook under his great overcoat of yellow ratteen:

"You know," he murmured in Ducasse's ear, "I've been ill."

" . . ."

"Very ill indeed!"

" . . ."

"You hear me?"

"Yes, I hear you," Roger-Ducasse said in a hollow voice. "You've been ill—but that one there . . . that one there, he's dead!"

He had a keen sense of irony, did Enesco, and loved to tell of Fauré's sense of inferiority to Debussy. Poor Fauré, such a charmer of the ladies with his prematurely white hair, though a bad loser at cards. He became in many ways better appreciated and understood in England than in France; he was even dealt a cruel blow by his favourite pupil, who was Ravel, practising a little deception on him: "It was in 1902. Ravel arrives at the Conservatoire carrying under his arm a carefully wrapped-up packet, which he tries to disguise from Fauré's eyes. Intrigued, Fauré orders him to open the packet: inside is the newly published score of *Pelléas*. Fauré doesn't bat an eyelid—he never got angry—but he says very softly, 'Ravel, you've hurt me. . . .'"[23]

Maggie knew both Fauré and Ravel. Fauré, "the perfect charming gentleman with white hair," she met at the Princesse de Polignac's *salon* one tea-time, where she sang "Soir" for him. She encountered Ravel at the house of the music publishers, Durand, and it was this same day that she met Puccini—she was at the piano singing *Butterfly*—and both said something nice about her singing. But she never bothered much about compliments: "They all say something even if they don't mean it."[24] So familiar was she with the great names of the epoch, taking them unselfconsciously for granted, that she later sang duets in concerts both with Enrico Caruso (the first act duet from *La Bohème*) and Charles Gilibert ("La ci darem" from *Don Giovanni*) without recalling either occasion afterwards, in conversation or in print.★ She had no gossip-column awareness of historic moments, devoting herself thoroughly to the work in hand.

★ She sang also, with Gilibert and John McCormack, at a musicale given for Queen Alexandra: "I can still see Her Majesty", McCormack wrote, "sitting on a settee near the piano listening with rapt attention. . . . Maggie had a great success. She sings French songs, to my mind, better than any French singer I ever heard, with the possible exception of Edmond Clément."[25]

CHAPTER FIVE

Partners in Pelléas

Mélisande: Je suis plus près de toi dans l'obscurité.
MAURICE MAETERLINCK

THE THIRD REPUBLIC, which brought stable rule to France from 1875 to 1914, a longer period than any since the Revolution, and saw the foundation of a deeply proud and richly productive culture, was established by a mere amendment to a law, passed by just one vote. Maggie Teyte, though she little knew it, was destined to become the lifelong beneficiary of the Republic's glory and stability, nearer "to being an expression of France of the broad acres and the vineyards" than were other reapers of "embattled glories" like Henry IV, Louis XIV, and Napoleon.[1] Danger to the Third Republic came not from the radical forces of the Left, who had passed their heyday, but from the Right, and Paris was a breeding ground for clubs devoted to the spread of Taine's hatred for democracy. The countryside, split up into millions of farms of less than two-and-a-half acres, showed that fragmented ownership, while producing little food, kept the peasantry conservative; workers in state industries—French railways, even then, were nationalized—were forbidden to join unions. In industrial production, France still lagged behind England and Germany, producing a seventh of England's coal, and less than a third of Germany's steel. Above all the Third Republic was the age of the small workshop, where a million businesses had less than five employees.[2]

The first and finest result of all this was that France held the dazzling position of being the luxury workshop of the world. All articles of decoration, sexual and sartorial allurement, could be individually crafted; every taste could be characterized, considered in isolation, and provided for. In this way, it was a golden age for individual virtuosity, and it was during the Third Republic that the French cult of the *métier* was established, a cult similar in many ways to the German cult of the superman: in music, Wagner incorporates the latter, while Debussy lives up to the former.

Not only music but the other arts reached the height of self-expression and suggestive power, nurtured in this atmosphere of freedom. There was a vision common to the Impressionists, common to the Symbolist poets, common to the naturalistic and poetic innovators in the theatre, which although deeply tinged with decadence and aestheticism, had a fundamental clarity and vitality about it. It was also an age when the discoveries of science had not yet been overwhelmed by their technological implications, or their applicability to mass destruction—the two going very much together, the former causing cultural deterioration only at a somewhat slower pace than the latter. Remarkable new discoveries retained a certain purity and directness of application beneficial to all, even to the human imagination.

In music the Third Republic also quickly captured the imagination with its variety and quality, although Paris had long been one of the world's greatest opera centres. The strength and influence at the Republic's beginning of such established composers as César Franck, Charles Gounod, and the partly Wagner-orientated Emmanuel Chabrier, was added to successively by Jules Massenet, by Ambroise Thomas and Camille Saint-Saëns, by the posthumous success of Georges Bizet, and then by the widely different but individual talents of, among many others, Vincent d'Indy, Gabriel Fauré, Maurice Ravel, Erik Satie, and Paul Dukas. Perhaps this new French repertoire could not challenge Wagner in self-confidence and formal grandeur, but, like that of the thousands upon thousands of self-employed French craftsmen and women, its beauties were of a rarer and more individual hue, shot through with peculiar and exquisite transparencies, composed of the fabric of dreams yet also not lacking in classical distinction; above all, fastidiously and professionally wrought. Claude Debussy was the musical personality who stood head and shoulders above the rest, and while in some respects his genius transcended his age, his and Maeterlinck's opera *Pelléas et Mélisande* is a lasting monument to an individual creative approach and power which died in 1914. It was in the deepest sense both an experimental, and a traditional, work of art. It became not only the work which established Maggie Teyte's reputation as an operatic artist, but the key to her development as a singer.

Even though music flourished, it was rather less than well paid, and there were not, possibly, more than three or four composers in France able to earn as much as a reasonably competent middle-class dentist. Into this category Debussy did not arrive until relatively late in life, and even then he complained that "Caruso would ask as much for his accompanist as I am getting." This was all the more poignant in relation to his early death, for cancer had possibly taken hold of him as early as 1907, the year he first met Maggie Teyte. With his hypnotic black eyes, black hair and beard, he had been dubbed "the Prince of Darkness" by fellow students at the Conservatoire, and a vampire-like power of sucking souls from young women was attributed to him. His early affairs became legendary and ended usually in disaster, some nearly in death. These and his later reckless and self-destructive acts, such as trying to seduce his stepdaughter,[3] could be explained by a lack of practical sense and an irresponsibility stemming from his being unable to earn a living and yet refusing to change his profession. As he once wrote to a friend, "I only face responsibility when it is forced upon me, and then it is insurmountable."

By way of compensation, his daemon impelled him to write an opera which would be unique—not one which would engender a series of operas measurable against Wagner's achievement, but a single work of manifold and truly innovatory qualities whose effects could not be repeated, even by himself. As a result, in an at least partly self-destructive manner, he spent on *Pelléas* the time and energy another composer with his powers would have expended on half a dozen major works. He spent twelve years trying to remove from *Pelléas* everything of a derivative nature that might have crept in. His intention was uniqueness, in the way a rare and perfect stone is unique, or the foliage of a tree which, while conforming to species and type, yet has a unique and individual growth, true only to itself. This was almost the complete reverse of popular art, whose ideal is the lowest common denominator, the apotheosis of species and type, the repetition of a model thrashed out in committee: the former is true to nature, the latter a purely social view of art.

Even Debussy's notion that the music should be one with, instead of dominating, the text—so the initial effect of the work should not be the same as with conventional opera—was for a composer uniquely self-effacing. He would have been immensely flattered had he known that when Arnold Bennett saw the original production of *Pelléas et Mélisande* at the Opéra-Comique in October 1903, he wrote in his journal, "This thing made a profound impression on me *as a play* (author's italics). I thought that the music neither helped nor spoilt the piece;* it did not offend me and at times it seemed rather good: it was 'always' in the key! But the play! I thought nothing could be more simple and more profound in its presentation of the essential quality of 'life'. The whole performance was a triumph."† For this must have been a remarkable echo of Debussy's own feelings when he first saw Maeterlinck's play, ten years before at its première on 17 May 1893, at a single matinée performance at the Bouffes-Parisiens. The audience on that occasion had largely departed by the end, intolerant of the apparent lack of action, impatient of the structure and missing the conventional qualities of wit and passion. But the contribution Debussy made to Maeterlinck's work was, in the first instance, as much one of critical perception as of musical creation. He saw exactly what it needed and what he himself could provide.

What exactly was the nature of the work which fired Debussy's imagination? In *Pelléas et Mélisande* Maeterlinck had been re-telling the story of *Tristan und Isolde* in his own way; their mysterious and melancholy names sometimes connected with the Arthurian legend, their actions sometimes with Irish legend, and their romance took place in a world divided from the normal everyday world by a kind of gauze veil ("Allemonde" equals "All-world"). Maeterlinck left the least possible scope for words and actions, and the gaps and pauses formed as important a level of speech as the very simply written words themselves, while the faceless, motiveless characters' capacity to withstand their irreversible fate is not orchestrated by any depth of emotion, but left in a very linear form. It is, if anything, nature which provides the movement: the dark, the light, the wind, trees, the water—all these are living characters. Even inanimate objects: mirror, key, lamp, tower, stairs, have sometimes as much dramatic impetus as the characters themselves. Conflict and crisis are useless; so are pathos and tragedy in terms of character. In other words, Maeterlinck's is a deeply contemplative drama.‡ "On occasions I had

* The first reception of *Pelléas et Mélisande* was in some ways similar to that of Samuel Beckett's *Waiting for Godot*. The latter had to wait for its hidden wit to bring it to acclaim, *Pelléas* for its hidden music.

† Bennett went to see *Pelléas* again, on 4 December 1903, when he wrote: "This time I thought Debussy's music very good. Sometimes really powerful"—i.e. he separated the effect of the music from the drama. But his first response had been as Debussy intended: he concentrated entirely on the representational aspect.

‡ The elements of nature are living characters in Beckett's plays and, like Maeterlinck's, his drama is deeply contemplative.

thought that an old man sitting in his chair, merely waiting in the lamp-light," he wrote in *The Wealth of the Humble*, "was in actual fact living far more deeply, humanely, and widely than the lover who strangles his mistress, the captain who scores a victory, or the husband who avenges his honour."

In sum, and without any humour to enliven it, *Pelléas et Mélisande* is not a very exciting story, though it does have this unusual power of suggestion, of what might be made of it. And the force or moral behind it is extremely powerful, namely that it is up to us to convert destiny to wisdom: which, of course, is what Pelléas and Mélisande fail lamentably to do in their love for each other. In this way the pessimism of *Pelléas et Mélisande* is perhaps ultimately the pessimism of a happy man, or of a man who has adopted certain terms in dealing with the universe and who practises philosophical, as opposed to passionate, art. Suitably enough, the Flemish name Maeterlinck means "the measurer".* But Maeterlinck, a fine and utterly original poetic innovator in the theatre, lacked the intellectual rigour to make *Pelléas et Mélisande* as great a play as it could have been. His observation, in its most colourful expression, remained too earthy and direct to be used in *Pelléas:* today his *Life of the Bee,* his *Life of the Ant,* and *The Intelligence of Flowers* seem more authentic and lasting works of literary and philosophical skill. Portraying man's absurd predicaments in the first half of his life, in the second half he rejected absurdity: his successors, some of the French playwrights of the 1950s and '60s, retain the absurd obstinacy, which he described so aptly, of the ant falling off a pebble a hundred times.

And here perhaps comes the most amazing act of direct artistic identification that history can show. Whereas for Maeterlinck the figures he created—Golaud, Pelléas, Mélisande—remained almost tapestry-like in their stillness, moved in moments of too ominous, even arch significance but with very pre-Raphaelite overtones, so that one can almost touch the drapes—suddenly, in this mysteriously unreal back-ground, Debussy saw himself, his own passions and complexities, his own failures, and, above all, his tentativeness.

He not only saw himself, but he saw also how to express himself:

---

* Flanders was in many ways the Ireland of the Continent, with its large estates, its folklore of ghosts and witches, and its numerous quirkish peasantry; Maeterlinck, coming from the smaller country, like Beckett adopted French as a written language, although it was also the language he spoke at home.

seeing *Pelléas* that first time, in 1893, triggered off in him the possibility of placing and unifying all those tenuous, diffuse, and yet psychologically true and profound qualities which made up his genius, at the same time as mirroring, quite literally, the natural world. The real dramatic existence of the wind, the light, the fall of Mélisande's hair, the rustling of leaves, the darkness of water, the subterranean depths of Arkel's palace, the mysteriousness of the grotto, must have played no small part in determining the choice he made, when he recovered from the performance and emerged from the Bouffes-Parisiens to find himself, with the poet Stéphane Mallarmé, among the few deeply interested spectators.

But what if Maeterlinck had refused him, rejected this staggering act of recognition he had made in wanting, not so much to base a dramatic opera on *Pelléas et Mélisande* as, more accurately, to set *Pelléas et Mélisande* to music?* Fortunately Debussy's friend, the Symbolist poet Henri de Régnier, knew Maeterlinck, and from him was able to secure a letter, dated 8 August 1893, giving Debussy permission to turn the play into a music drama, making whatever changes he thought were needed. This letter was to have its importance later when Debussy and Maeterlinck quarrelled, for it stipulated that Debussy was to have the final say in casting the production.

Maeterlinck was completely indifferent to anything musical,[5] but his mistress Georgette Leblanc—although she was known as Madame Maeterlinck they were never married, for she had not obtained a divorce from her first husband, a Spanish Roman Catholic—was a fiery prima donna. However, she was not yet on the scene; Maeterlinck did not meet her until 1895. Meanwhile Debussy travelled to Belgium to meet Maeterlinck, taking with him Pierre Louÿs, his best friend.

The playwright and composer could not have presented a greater

---

* *Drame lyrique* is the term Debussy used. Teyte always maintained it was the French who, because he was Flemish, belittled Maeterlinck's contribution to their great musician's *chef d'œuvre*. The attitude was quickly adopted: most reviews refer to "Debussy's *Pelléas et Mélisande*" though there is possibly no more "music" in it than there was in an ancient Greek performance of Aeschylus—considering "music", that is, as a specially formalized way of delivering the sounds of words, phrased as natural speech: i.e. recitative as Debussy used it. Some of the early performers of *Pelléas* were not great voices but they were outstanding actors. Debussy hated specialization. See *Monsieur Croche* (1921), his collection of powerful critical articles. When Teyte retired she toyed with the idea of acting in Greek tragedy.[4]

contrast. Maeterlinck was stocky, strong-featured, placid, with very pale blue eyes—a happy writer, another reason he is out of fashion today. ("The memories of happy hours are the only ones which I allow to live," he wrote in his last book, *Blue Bubbles*.) He was indifferent to failure or success, and his neighbours regarded him as an ineffectual day-dreamer which was just as he wished it, since no one expected anything of him and so he cultivated his hobbies, translated Emerson's essays, and kept fit.* Georgette Leblanc, herself no mean word-spinner,† described, at their first meeting, his "measured walk, neither slow nor fast—the walk of a person whose path is always smooth, and who has once for all calculated his objective and his strength."‡ By contrast, she found in Debussy "a painful sensitivity, a lingering suffering".[6]

When later Debussy played his first version of *Pelléas* to Leblanc and Maeterlinck, the experience was a torment to the playwright—not on account of Debussy's music in particular, but merely because it was musical and, as such, inimical to his soul. Leblanc, however, loved Debussy's score, and insisted on becoming the first Mélisande. Debussy took her through the part, but was in no way convinced that this former Carmen of the Opéra-Comique was suitable; yet her very definite impression was that she had been promised Mélisande in the first production, and she conveyed this news to Maurice.

Poor Maeterlinck! His Flemish peace had already been shattered by this ambitious lady whom Maggie insists had complex and varied sexual tastes of a lesbian variety. They had installed themselves in the vast monastery of Saint-Wandrille, near Rouen, and had a small Parisian base in the rue Raynouard in the XVIème. Gone, it seemed, at least for the present, was the happy tranquil fellow viewed with apparent distaste and incomprehension by Debussy's decadent friend, Pierre Louÿs, when he went with Debussy to see him. In his place was an immensely more productive

* By boxing in particular. At the age of fifty-eight, Patrick Mahony reports, he used to spar with Carpentier, the French heavyweight.

† From her several encounters with Debussy, Leblanc produced this remarkable description showing the extent to which he had been able to make the music of *Pelléas* autobiographical: "By small details of colours, manner, gesture, one guessed much of his hidden personality. His toneless skin was as white as wax, his fine crinkly hair misted the massive outline of his formidable skull. Beneath the bulging brow his sheltered glance shone dimly."

‡ *Pelléas et Mélisande* has so many of its author's qualities which Debussy lacked: straightforwardness, clear design, strong and bold characterization.

writer who, however, never departed from his philosophical ideas, or descended into the arena of realism or the attractive fashionable forms of despair in which Louÿs himself wrote, as in *Aphrodite*, the life of the Greek prostitute Chrysis.

Debussy, in the meantime, had his perfect libretto. He tightened it up and whittled down the characters, removing some of Maeterlinck's over-ponderous symbolic furniture such as the cumbrous doors opened at the drama's beginning, the washerwomen of the palace, and certain non-speaking parts. He made a play of epic trappings into an intimate chamber piece, strengthening it along French classical lines so that his version has a Racinian starkness about its scenic structure, though the language could not be more different from Racine's. As for the music, Debussy wanted to show a revolt against the aesthetic of both music drama and lyric opera: his objection to the latter was that a lyrical melody, or fixed melodic line, was too definite to express the "innumerable shades of emotion of a personage in a drama". In Wagnerian music drama, he maintained, spectators were invited to experience two distinct emotions, that of the music and that of the drama, whereas he held that the two should be merged into one, just as Arnold Bennett had experienced the end result in *Pelléas*. He thought the symphonic treatment incidental to music drama an attempt to render simultaneously the sentiment uttered and the internal reflections which govern the action: two distinct processes he held to be mutually harmful. And he intensely disliked the use of leitmotifs "which made the characters, so to speak, present their visiting cards every time they arrived upon the scene."[7]

In practice what Debussy did was scrupulously to avoid calling attention to the music instead of to the drama: but this is rarely achieved nowadays in performance.* In the score itself, there is only one formal melody,

---

* Pierre Boulez, in an introductory essay to the 1969 recording of the Covent Garden production, appears to understand the collaboration, but his interpretation raises a frenzied, psychologically intense barrier of music between the drama and the spectator. "They pay homage to the music, but they throw away the drama," Teyte said in an interview in the *Guardian* (22 August 1966). "Even with the music they are not sure of themselves. They think of Debussy as grey-blue. But he's not. All his colours are very distinct, but they're seen as though far away, as though through a gauze. He wants the music to act as a gauze between Maeterlinck and ourselves. Not a gauze exactly, it's . . . what's the word? Cloudy, *verdâtre*, smeared, *ternis* . . .". And later, "When Mélisande sings 'Ne me touchez pas', she has to move about. You have to feel this constant nervosity. She has a kind of shimmering quality. At Glyndebourne (1962) and at Glasgow (1964)

which Mélisande sings at the opening of the third act—a straight-forward setting of a "song" from the original text; the only symphonic intrusions are the interludes which were added later to "cover" the scene changes; there is one leitmotif which is associated with Mélisande, and which returns in the fifth act unchanged because, as Debussy justified it, "in reality, Mélisande is always unchanged in herself and dies without anyone—or perhaps only Arkel—ever having understood her."

In place of the traditional methods Debussy rejected, though perhaps did not entirely escape, he introduced the meticulous practice—copied, it has been claimed, from Mussorgsky—of studying with the utmost care "the phonetic quality of every syllable of the text, its prose accentuation, and its incidence in the natural rise and fall of the voice in speech", and out of the result of this study he fashioned his vocal line. Nowhere was Maeterlinck's language altered to suit musical requirements. Everywhere Debussy tried to make speech and music indissolubly one: "the attention is never diverted from the words to the tune, because the words *are* the tune."[8]

In commenting musically upon the melodic line Debussy avoided means by which interest would have been diverted to musical processes such as development. His method was purely selective. "It is put together you might say, rather like a film—thousands of little separate pieces put together with infinite skill, with genius," was how Teyte described it, a description hard to improve on. "When Pelléas and Mélisande, for instance, return to the cave in their vain search for the lost ring, we hear in the music first the sweeping of the water, then the moonlight, then the cry of Mélisande when she sees the old beggars sitting side by side against the rock. And these little pieces have to be put together. . . ."[9] From these and other statements Teyte made, she showed clearly that she grasped at a profound level Debussy's intentions in *Pelléas*, and his peculiar striving for uniqueness of effect, and to embody an otherwise indefinable experience. For his aspirations came to accord deeply with her own range of interpretive power, and through her mastery of Debussy's

---

she didn't move. And then the line which is the crux of the drama, when Arkel says to Pelléas, 'Pourras-tu choisir entre le père et l'ami?' It's because of his admonishment that Pelléas remains in the castle and hence the drama. You know what he did with this? He mumbled it as he went off into the wings."

difficulty, lay the effortless ease she was able later to bring to the whole field of French song.

Debussy had his perfect libretto, but his relationship with its author quickly became embittered to such a degree that on 7 April 1902 before the first performance, Maeterlinck was to write to *Le Figaro* accusing Carré, the manager of the Opéra-Comique, of trickery, complaining of the absurd and arbitrary cuts, and hoping for the "resounding failure of a play which is no longer mine." According to Georgette Leblanc, Carré had told her while she was singing *Carmen* that she must submit to his desires: "Even in the most State-run theatres there are . . . more or less capable sultans who too often exercise those rights which they have arrogated to themselves."[10] It became a question of either "giving in or getting out", so she resigned. "I was warned. Another woman was ready to take my place. This woman was Mary Garden."

The Scots-born American, Mary Garden, was never one to be chary with her favours, and she quickly established herself in Leblanc's place. But Leblanc bitterly resented the fact that Debussy, having shown a liking for her during the four or five rehearsals they had had together of *Pelléas*, either at his home or at Maeterlinck's apartment, failed to insist on her being the first Mélisande. Paul Dukas, she claimed, had insisted in spite of Carré's opposition that she take the title part in his opera based on Maeterlinck's *Ariane et Barbe-bleue*, performed in 1907.* Dukas got his way by threatening to withdraw the opera. But Debussy remained faint-hearted about Leblanc, no doubt afraid her overpowering personality would swamp Mélisande.

Maeterlinck was less phlegmatic. Quick to rise to any insult, in spite of his cultivation of equanimity—he would never sleep without a revolver, a Corsican knife, and a loaded shot-gun by his bed—he jumped out of the ground-floor window of his rue Raynouard flat, and was around to the rue Cardinet in no time at all, where he threatened to beat Debussy over the head with his walking cane. Debussy at once collapsed in an armchair,

---

* In *Ariane et Barbe-bleue*, whose action precedes that of *Pelléas*, though it was written later, the wives of Bluebeard, one of whom is Mélisande, are set free, and each in turn is asked by Ariane if they will come away with her, and each in turn says no. Knowing the lesbian Leblanc slept with each of Maeterlinck's mistresses, Maggie richly when she heard the opera appreciated the irony of life intermingled with art.[11]

saying he could do nothing to change the decision as it was the Opéra-
Comique's, not his, while his wife brought him smelling salts to revive
him. Maeterlinck then left in disgust saying all musicians were mad.*

Mary Garden, the winner, saw this incident very differently. Debussy
faced Maeterlinck very firmly, she said, called together a jury of musicians,
and had Georgette Leblanc sing an act of *Pelléas* for them. They
were unanimously against her.[13] Although this was the end of any
Debussy–Maeterlinck contact—they had never really been friends—the
Maeterlincks did later on attend a performance, in 1920, of *Pelléas*,
given by the Chicago Company at the Lexington Theatre, and Maeterlinck, who became much caught up with spiritualism, wanted to draw a
picture of Mary Garden's ectoplasm.

A woman not to be defeated, Leblanc, in 1907, renewed her campaign
to sing Mélisande, after her success in *Ariane et Barbe-bleue*, even going to
the length of organizing a petition to send to Albert Carré, for which a
thousand signatures were collected. "To Monsieur Albert Carré, Director
of the Opéra-Comique," ran the appeal: "We the undersigned patrons
of your theatre, grateful for the pleasure which we owe you, beg of you
to receive favourably our sincere desires, inspired by the beautiful performance of *Ariane*, to see Madame Georgette Leblanc in a revival of the
role left vacant by Mademoiselle Garden in *Pelléas*—a work that is
precious to us for many reasons." The delicate euphemism with which
she ended her appeal was hardly in character.

By this time, although Garden had gone abroad, a new rival both to
her and Leblanc had appeared in the rue Favart: Marguérite Giraud,
Carré's new favourite, whom he had married in 1902. Having displaced
Garden, she marched into the star's dressing room ordering everything to
be thrown out—curtains, furnishings, and any other evidence of the
previous incumbent.[14] And because the new prima donna was not yet
ready to sing Mélisande, Maggie Teyte was given her great opportunity,
not only to step into the breach as Mélisande but to sing the role no less
than nineteen times in the 1907–8 and 1908–9 seasons, her success in the
part possibly surpassing even that of her famous predecessor. Before this
opportunity came, however, and while the rivalries of the three older

* Edward Lockspeiser describes how Maeterlinck very nearly used the revolver:
he challenged Debussy to a duel and one morning, practising for this, shot dead his own
black cat.[12] Debussy's own movements were cat-like and he collected china cats, so the
symbolism of the action may have given satisfaction to Maeterlinck.

singers were violently reverberating in the corridors surrounding the Salle Favart (named, like the rue Favart, after Charles-Simon Favart, one of the Opéra-Comique's early guiding lights—unlike Maeterlinck one of the very few librettists perpetuated in a French memorial),[15] Teyte had to undergo the most strenuous preparation with the composer.

CHAPTER SIX

Stars in Opposition
(1907–1910)

Or if the women you portray
Represent a wish of your fanciful senses . . .
STÉPHANE MALLARMÉ,
"L'Après-midi d'un faune"

IN A "FAMOUS European opera house" which possessed the usual very narrow passage under the stage from one side to the other, two leading sopranos met one day; both waited for the other to give way, till finally one of them said: "Let me pass, don't you know who I am? I am Madame T——, the wife of the director." Whereupon the other replied: "Oh don't be silly, I was Madame T—— long before you."

When Maggie composed this vignette, as she called it, she discreetly omitted the names of the two rivals because she wanted to show a general principle of operatic life in those times but not the particular or personal source, and thereby find herself accused of bitchiness. But she had told the story* before writing it down, and the two prima donnas may be identified as Marguérite Carré and Mary Garden. A celebrated *Punch* cartoon of 1908 depicted Melba and Tetrazzini, gloriously ruffled up with pecking pride, blaring at each other through a pair of old gramophone horns; the animosity of Mary Garden and Marguérite Carré was beamed more directly and specifically on to the bald head of Albert Carré, the fifty-five-year-old director of the Opéra-Comique who looked like a senior bank manager—and the role of Mélisande was the prize.

Mary Garden herself saw the rupture of her relations with the Opéra-Comique in an entirely different light. It was by no means Marguérite Carré who had displaced her—how could her pride countenance such a thing even if it were true?—it had been Carré's jealousy of her great love Messager which had made him beside himself with anger. For one day

* To Richard Bebb.

Carré had proposed marriage, during the time of her affair with Messager (who was himself married to Hope Temple the Irish composer),* and Garden had turned him down. Like a good administrator, he had then made his offer in writing. No, she replied in writing, underlining her avowal of love for Messager not once but twice. Carré summoned her, leapt in the air brandishing her letter, pulled her contract from his desk, and tore it up, shouting "You're through!"[1]

Maggie kept apart from these rivalries: she was inexperienced at political scheming, and had no inclination for it anyway. She had no taste for the commanding position a great prima donna could wield in the political, social, and financial world. She had made no friends at the Opéra-Comique: "Never make a friend in the opera house until you have made your name," was her dictum;† and because she made no friends she made no enemies, for although she had plenty of *savoir-faire* her pride refused to allow her to mix in jealousies of that kind. She had none of the flamboyance or theatricality of Mary Garden, and she still had to gain self-confidence. Unlike Garden, who was accused of being slipshod and inadequate in musical training, Maggie, for all her extreme youth, was painstaking and exact in study. She needed the most deliberate preparation if she was going to succeed in the way her talents and power of application deserved.

When the publisher and impresario William Boosey met Garden, he noticed her desire to "assume more liberal proportions . . . Evidently she shared the opinion of the witty Frenchman who stated that there were three sexes: 'L'homme, la femme, et la femme maigre!'"[2] She was praised by him not so much for the quality of her voice as for the artistry of her singing, and Maggie, when she saw her, found her an excellent actress, whose method was so convincing as to hypnotize the audience. But she commented on a very "peculiar" quality in her style of singing, and judged her manner of pronouncing French very bad and the accent itself absolutely atrocious.‡ Yet she knew Garden to be a very clever woman and was convinced she did it all on purpose, playing subtly on the

* Garden's affair with Messager did not last long. One day he threw all his royalties at her, and thereafter she found him repulsive.

† See "Loose Leaves", Appendix A.

‡ As Maggie described them, Mélisande's opening words became in Garden's mouth "*Ne me too-shay paugh*," leading her to exclaim, "It was dreadful. Just like an Oxford don."[3]

snob appeal of her English intonation, by which she was converting her native deficiency into a positive virtue, even making it a distinguishing feature, appealing to the large *colonie d'outre-mer* in the audience.

Maggie was still partly a student while waiting in the wings at the Opéra-Comique. She had seen *Pelléas*, and in 1907 she went to see Georgette Leblanc in *Ariane et Barbe-bleue*. Then, in September 1907, she had been sent along to study the role of Mélisande with Debussy— originally at de Reszke's behest—and it was this fact which indirectly saved her career at the Opéra-Comique.

Towards the end of the 1907–8 season, ending a first year in the opera house which had been hardly more than desultory, Maggie had been summoned to Albert Carré's office and told she had no future at the Opéra-Comique, and ought to seek employment elsewhere. She was afraid that what had happened to her with Gunsbourg was being repeated: some weeks earlier, with a little more finesse than Gunsbourg—it was after all the rue Favart, and not Monte Carlo—Carré had made a gentle pass at her in the corridor, and just as tactfully she had disengaged herself. Her position was precarious and vulnerable: she had no guardian or relation in Paris to protect her, and no agent to stand up for her interests; would she be forced to embark on a supplementary career as a *cocotte* to support her singing? Or would she have to marry, or become someone's permanent mistress in order to fend off approaches from men like Carré?

Fortunately, before she could make a decision, Carré withdrew the notice he had served on her. He had been pushed to do so by Marguerite when she heard that Garden wanted to return to the Comique for the 1908–9 season. Mme Carré had decided she herself had not the time to learn Mélisande before the summer break, and the unknown Maggie Teyte would have to sing the role.

Forty years later, Maggie remembered her first meeting with the composer of *Pelléas*, when

at the age of eighteen,* very small and slight, I found myself on Debussy's doorstep with the score of *Pelléas* under my arm. He was living then in the house off the avenue du Bois de Boulogne which backed on to the Ceinture, the railway that runs all round Paris. It

* In fact she was nineteen.

must have been a noisy situation for a composer and indeed one of Debussy's critics said, "Oh, now I understand why his music is such a beastly noise."

Well, I rang the bell and was shown into the *salon*. My chief remembrance of it was a collection of china cats, some twelve or fifteen, of all shapes, sizes and colours. I had plenty of time to look at them— I learnt later, there wasn't a live cat in the house—because Debussy kept me waiting fifteen minutes before he came in.

He walked straight across the room to a little upright piano and sat down. Not once did he even as much as glance at me—but I had a good look at him. He seemed tall but thick and heavy and he slouched rather than walked. He had a black beard and a square head covered with black hair. It struck me he had almost an Oriental look. I was told that he was born in Marseilles.* All this I took in as he sat at the piano without even moving. There seemed to be hours of silence. At last he turned round. "Vous êtes Mlle Teyte?" "Oui Monsieur." Silence. "Vous êtes Mlle Maggie Teyte?" "Oui Monsieur." Silence. "Mais êtes-vous Mlle Maggie Teyte de l'Opéra-Comique?" "Oui Monsieur." He didn't believe it. "Une autre anglaise—mon Dieu." Mary Garden had been the first Mélisande—now another—because we were both Scotswomen. Ah well. And so Mlle Teyte—*anglaise*, really *écossaise*, became an instrument in his hand. Strange to relate he never even shook hands with me. He said to me, "I will have Mélisande as I want her." I was only too ready to agree.

As a teacher he was pedantic—that's the only word. Really pedantic. He sat one day at the piano. He never played without first getting into the mood. This took two or three minutes. I sat and waited. He raised his arms and was just ready to play when he saw a little bit of white cotton on the floor. He stopped and picked it up. He rolled it up into a ball and looked everywhere for a place to put it. Then again he concentrated. Dead silence for another five minutes. His whole body went still.

He never wasted any words. In fact in nine months he said hardly as many words to me. You may wonder what happened if he wanted to correct me. Well, he didn't—except in small details now and then. Once at a rehearsal of *Pelléas* when the conductor pulled me up he said: "Laissez faire Mlle Teyte." "Leave her alone." That may sound as if it was a remarkable tribute to me—but it was really a tribute to Mozart.

* Not true. Debussy was born in St-Germain-en-Laye, just outside Paris.

You see, to sing Mozart in the true style you must be, so to speak, pedantic. You must observe exact note values. This was ingrained in me. Perhaps Debussy had not heard his music sung like this before.

It is not easy to describe the impact of Debussy's character on me. He was such a many-sided character. Can I just give you some impressions as they come into my mind? He was volcanic: a volcano that smouldered. There was a core of anger and bitterness in him—I often think he was rather like Golaud in *Pelléas* and yet he wasn't. He was—it's all in his music—a very sensual man. No one seemed to like him. Jean Périer, who played Pelléas to my Mélisande, went white with anger if you mentioned the name of Debussy. Another thing I remember was that, like Delius, he seemed to care for no music but his own. He thought Wagner and Mozart just a waste of paper. Altogether my impression of him was of a man obsessed. But he showed another more pleasant side of his nature when he was with his little daughter Chouchou, as he called her. He mentioned me in a letter he wrote to Chouchou from Russia. He said he heard a singer that night with a voice nearly as beautiful as Mlle Teyte, and that was indeed a lovely compliment.[4]

Not to weaken the force of Debussy's compliment—indeed it strengthens it—but it was not a singer to which Debussy compared Maggie, but a bird. He had been residing at a house in Moscow, where he found two charming bulldogs with eyes like frogs whom Chouchou would love; also this bird which sang "almost as well as Mlle Teyte."[5]

Maggie had heard Debussy was very partial to sex, but although there were numerous reports that she became his mistress, he made no move towards her.* Had he done so, she might well have acquiesced. There is no doubt she found him fascinating, responding, unlike many others, to his unconventional (at that time), bohemian, "switched-off" quality. But he permeated her personality infinitely more deeply because they had no liaison. Those she numbered among her conquests, such as Enesco and later Sir Thomas Beecham, as well as her husbands, Plumon and Cottingham, were ultimately forgotten as lovers—which leads to the suspicion

---

* In 1940 she told Myra Hess, who was accompanying her in some Debussy songs at the National Gallery, "Women were afraid to sleep alone within a six-mile radius of Debussy." She said this to dispel the over-pretty and sugary view Myra Hess had of Debussy's music at this time.

that ultimately she may not have respected very deeply anyone she went to bed with, though they became feathers in her cap.* Those artists who remained sexually impervious to her had the more lasting influence.

The fact that Debussy's enigmatic, sombre, and morose personality sometimes spilled over into definite and even incestuous evil only made the fascination deeper. His evil designs extended to his own stepdaughter and subsequent heir—like Mme Debussy, formerly Mme Bardac, the girl was blonde and pretty, "like an Easter-lily"—whom he tried to seduce. It was an action hardly suggesting self-confidence. Another sinister feature was his walk: his steps were catlike, and he made no noise.

Maggie, who at one time in late middle age had a passion for orchids, for cultivating, collecting, and trying to make them grow on her roof—a a difficult proposition in view of their dependence as seedlings on a fibrous fungus which helps them absorb water and nourishment—found that Debussy conjured up an image of orchids.† His music carried for her the same evil yet fascinating, orchidesque overtones: predatory, guarding of its silences; beautiful, cold, with almost a decadent quality, as if not really wanting to get to grips with fear, love, jealousy, but preferring to peer at them through rose-coloured spectacles. Often it was as if the music pursued its own sensations, yet within this very decadence, the real quality of Debussy emerged. This was his obsession with truth: "Vérité, vérité, vérité"—all through *Pelléas* rang this obsession. Mélisande doesn't tell Golaud the truth about the ring, because she cannot tell Golaud the truth. Golaud puts Yniold up to the window to try and find the truth of Pelléas's and Mélisande's amorous behaviour together; then comes the truth about her child. But then, what is truth?

Maggie rehearsed with Debussy every afternoon for two hours, sometimes three. Debussy was an exceptional pianist, dating from the time his brutal father tried to make him a Paderewski, and drove him relentlessly on; he now played only his own music, for which he set his own standard, and never played very loudly. He marked the score of *Pelléas* for Maggie with a red crayon where he wanted an accent on a word, and he made her think of the text as a super-recitative: Mélisande

---

* Beecham of course was not forgotten as a man and a musician, though not very significant as a lover.

† This may have been related to her feelings about his deep sexuality, for the fascination of many varieties of orchid is that they resemble the male testicles, and the word orchid comes from the Greek for "testicle".

has no *bel canto* except for the song from the tower, while both Pelléas and Golaud do.

Debussy apart, when it was clear that she was to sing the role, Maggie learnt the French pronunciation of the text from the Régisseur-Général of the Opéra-Comique, who made sure she always placed the French at the very front of her mouth. She was very pliable and always did what she was told; fortunately her teachers knew exactly what was the desired effect: if not, she would have been terrible, she ruefully remarked. The tongue-twisting phrases were mastered with perfect diction, still retaining the beauty of the singing tone.

The other singers also helped her considerably. Jean Périer, although disliking Debussy, was a magical Pelléas, so much so that performances were cancelled if he was unable to sing:* he taught her much. Maggie recognized him as a true baritone Martin.† Hector Dufranne, the Golaud, told her about Mélisande's rape, how Maeterlinck beat his horses and bred bulldogs: the Mélisandesque silences belonged to him as much as to Debussy. To complete her schooling in what had become in five years a *Pelléas* tradition, the ravishing Mme Carré supplied her with trade secrets: "Mary did this," she would take her aside and point out; "Mary held her flowers like this." She was determined Garden should not return.

Maggie's patrons also rallied round: the spring before she opened, while she was still learning the role, Victor and Mama Rubens took her to Pontresina for a holiday; here she would set off with her score of *Pelléas*, her faithful student friend Olga Lynn in tow, find a quiet spot by a stream and go over the part again and again while Olga fed her cues.

It was a happy time. Happy hours have no history and there were no dark shadows to store in the memory. When the first night came, after months of arduous study, hardly anything went wrong, so there was little

---

* Garden held the role of Mélisande from 1902 through to the season of 1906/7 with *no* understudy: it was an age of individualism indeed, for if Garden was ill, Carré cancelled the performance. If Dufranne was ill, it was sometimes cancelled; and, again, always if Périer was unable to sing. Périer was not in *Pelléas*'s second season, 1902/3; his replacement was Lucien Rigaux, an inexperienced singer whom Garden took instead of Carré's choice, Jeanne Raunay, a woman who was to play *en travesti*. Debussy was said not to have objected, remembering a woman played Pelléas in the stage production.[6]

† Baritone of exceptional range, after Jean Blaise Martin (1768–1837).

to remember. Maggie, unduly modest, ascribed all her success to the efforts of her mentors. But it was her own memory and understanding of the role which held all the disparate elements in place, and the way she understood it was thorough and exemplary: sufficient to last a lifetime, as indeed it did.

To her the role was as follows: Because Mélisande is one of the wives of Bluebeard whose cruelty and rape caused her to fly from his castle, she is mentally bewildered and confused, as any child would be. She is very young indeed, as Golaud exclaims: "Vous avez l'air très jeune," and as a result left with a distaste, a terror of men which finds recurrent expression in the phrase, "Ne me touchez pas." If Golaud will not obey she threatens to drown herself. The crown that has fallen into the forest pool is the symbol of her ravaged virginity, and she cries out with horror, "Je n'en veux plus," when Golaud tries to retrieve it. From her loss of memory as a result of shock—vented in the Belgian-French idiom, the Flemish understatement of "Je ne suis pas heureuse"—her sense of personal misery, of foreboding, all stems. It was this phrase, literally translated, which made English audiences laugh when Mrs Patrick Campbell performed the stage part in London opposite John Martin-Harvey as Pelléas. It does not mean "I am not happy", but more nearly, "I don't like it," or "There's something I can't quite define"—in other words something almost psychic. Although she has only a dim recollection of being raped, and no mention is made of it, she exists in some kind of permanent premonition of being raped again. This is the key to her mystery.

Up to the Fourth Act this mist over her mind remains but in the scene of Golaud's dreadful jealousy, where he throws her about and pulls her by the hair, she suddenly comes to: it is like someone receiving electric shock treatment. Suddenly she comes alive, and in the fountain scene she goes spontaneously to meet Pelléas, and they kiss for the first and last time. She says to him, "I've torn my dress, I had to . . ." and he replies, "You are so strange, what's the matter—come to me here in the dark, otherwise they'll see us." And then it is that she boldly exclaims for the first time, "Je *veux* qu'on me voit"—"I want them to see me." Pelléas sees her at once in an entirely new light, and has the courage to declare his love. Then tragedy strikes, she sees her lover killed before her eyes and thrown into the well, and she subsides back into numbness, she goes back into the shadows, into loss of memory, confusion, and bewilderment, as on her deathbed after the miscarriage she sings:

Je ne comprend pas ni plus tout ce que je dis, voyez-vous.
Je ne sais pas ce que je dis. Je ne sais pas ce que je sais.
Je ne dis plus ce que je veux. Je ne sais pas.*

Arkel speaks her epitaph: "C'était un pauvre petit être mystérieux comme tout le monde"—and so she dies wrapped in mystery as she began: this is the essence of the Maeterlinck–Debussy portrait as seen through Maggie's eyes.[7]

The lack of physical contact between Pelléas and Mélisande must be electric with suspense, sexually charged; if Pelléas touches Mélisande before the right moment, the effect is ruined. It is by such economy, such restraint, that *Pelléas et Mélisande* gains its dramatic power. So here is the reason Debussy never wanted to touch Maggie: if she for him was a perfect Mélisande, he would flatter her, strengthen her image of herself as such, reinforce it by awe rather than by direct action, which can always be a disastrous let-down. For all his strong sexual feeling, art was far more important: he chose perfection of the work rather than the life. He chose the "heavenly mansion raging in the dark", as W. B. Yeats's vision of it was, and saw in Maggie a ruthlessly dedicated tenant. It was Mélisande he was in love with.

Maggie's début as the second Mélisande at the Opéra-Comique was to have been at the first of two performances, on 11 and 13 June 1908, but the 11 June performance was cancelled owing to the illness of Jean Périer. Maggie was to have appeared in the role in Prague on 2 May 1908, but this performance also was cancelled, so her first performance in Paris on 13 June, was "cold", without any preview or try-out. But when it came to the opening tableau, with the silent pool by which Mélisande is discovered, Maggie found herself not at all nervous. After her private coaching with Debussy she had rehearsed for two months with the rest of the cast, and then for one month with full orchestra—nine months in all. "My God, how we worked," she said. "But only with work can you get everything sliding in as it should. You see there are no duets, no double-singing. It's all so beautifully dovetailed and should show like a conversation. Yes, it's a damn difficult opera."[8]

Unlike Mary Garden, who claims she completely forgot who she was in the part, Maggie did not believe for one minute that she was Mélisande:

* I no longer understand all I am saying, you see. / I don't know what I am saying. I don't know what I know. / I no longer say what I want. I don't know.

she had far too much else to think about; at any rate her willing sense of identification lagged, at this stage, behind the huge mass of technical detail. There were the words to think of, Maeterlinck's contribution (Garden claimed she never bothered about the words); there was her impeccable singing technique to maintain, the Mozartian precision culled from de Reszke, adapted by Debussy; there was Albert Carré to observe, and his quite meticulous attention as director to life-like acting detail; and also, but by no means least, down in front there was that thickset, powerful man with a long dense beard and luxuriant moustaches—looking more like a forester than an orchestral conductor, François Ruhlmann.* And yet, for all these disparate demands on will and intelligence, Maggie for all the audience *was* Mélisande.

The production was very dark and misty in effect, with trees everywhere, the overriding impression one of sombreness. In Jusseaume's settings you could see the shadows of great poplars reflected in the deep and sleeping waters of the lake. The forest had "arbres touffus", the horizons of the sea a variety of changing tones. All the characters were strongly drawn. Dufranne as Golaud had great power, he used his voice "like Klingsor", and as for Pelléas, played by the melancholic and tender Périer, when he came on at the beginning of Act Four and delivered the words "C'est le dernier soir", it always sent a shiver up Maggie's spine: they, and the majestic Félix Vieuille as Arkel, all performed with such virility and "blood".

Pelléas was the fashionable thing to go and see at the time: it was the great musical masterpiece of the Third Republic, the summit of French creative achievement, established among warring critical factions, surrounded by the still potent mythology of Debussy's struggle for recognition, Maeterlinck's fury over the casting, the scandals created by Debussy's debts and marriages, and his now general eminence as a most acid commentator on the works of others. But the composer never went to see *Pelléas* unless forced to: "the atmosphere of a theatre makes me ill," he wrote to his publisher.[9] He preferred rehearsals, where he could still influence the outcome.

All Maggie's friends from 40, avenue Victor Hugo went along to share in her greatest moment of triumph. Devotees and patrons came from over the Channel: Lady Ripon, wearing a "dog-collar of diamonds", was

* It was Ruhlmann, who was strict on tempo, to whom Debussy had said at rehearsal, "Laissez faire Mlle Teyte."

there; Paul Rubens shared a box with his brother Walter and the latter's recently acquired wife, Olive; Mr and Mrs Victor Rubens had also travelled to Paris; all were excited and deeply gratified to share in the glory of their wonderful young protégée, and watch the audience proclaim its enjoyment of her touching simplicity in singing and personality.* The reviews gave Maggie a more rapturous welcome than has probably ever been accorded in Paris to a British artist singing a French opera in French, even though she was following hard on the heels of an American of Scots birth. Maggie's predecessor Garden never forgave her for it, even told her she was "imprudente" to follow her.

Debussy seems to have been well satisfied: on 18 June 1908 he wrote to his publisher Jacques Durand, "You have read that Miss Maggie Teyte has not had too much to suffer from her illustrious predecessor," while in 1909 he wrote, about Rose Féart the first Mélisande at Covent Garden: "She is unspeakably ugly, lacks poetry, and I continue to wish that dear Miss Teyte were with us again."†

Maggie sang *Pelléas* nineteen times in the 1907–8 and 1908–9 seasons, and it was dropped from the 1909–10 season possibly because she did not want to do it again; she began also to make concert appearances in Paris, Berlin, and London, some of them with Debussy and some in others of his works, such as *La Damoiselle élue* and *Le Martyre de Saint-Sébastien*. Two of these concerts supplied Maggie with illustrations of the cocoon-like, impenetrable nature of Debussy and how he broke out of it in volcanic eruptions. On the first occasion she was appearing with the Sechiari

* Maggie liked to play down the importance of such occasions: when asked in a BBC interview on 29 October 1959 how she interpreted the role of Mélisande, she replied, "Very thin and very young . . . like a parrot"—which, under pressure from her inquisitors she qualified, with a shriek of laughter, to "like a bird of paradise". In a broadcast of a concert from Lewisohn Stadium in New York in 1948, the applause was so great and went on such a long time, that to bring it to an end Maggie said, "Thank you! That's enough!"

† At another time he commented to the singer Jane Bathori on Maggie's "very accurate idea" of Mélisande's character, though on a third occasion, in a typical and violent fluctuation of mood, he complained that she had as much emotion as a prison door, and was a "more than distant princess". His feelings about Périer, too, had their ups and downs: "People find Périer more and more admirable," he wrote to Durand in June 1908. "This is undoubtedly due to the fact that he no longer sings my music at all."[10]

Présidents d'Honneur : MM. Camille SAINT-SAËNS et Gabriel FAURÉ

Directeur : Charles DOMERGUE

SÉANCE SUPPLÉMENTAIRE

donnée le **Vendredi 21 Janvier 1910**, de 3 heures 1/2 à 6 heures

AVEC LE CONCOURS DE

MISS MAGGIE TEYTE

MM. CLAUDE DEBUSSY, HAROLD BAUER

LE QUATUOR FIRMIN TOUCHE (MM. Firmin Touche, Dorson, Vieux, Marneff)

LES CHŒURS DES CONCERTS COLONNE

et M. E. R. SCHMITZ

PROGRAMME

1. **Trio** (A l'Archiduc). . . . .   Ludwig van Beethoven
     a) Allegro moderato.
     b) Scherzo allegro.
     c) Andante cantabile — Allegro moderato.

   MM. HAROLD BAUER, FIRMIN TOUCHE et MARNEFF.

2. *a)* **Ariettes oubliées**, nᵒˢ I, II, III. . . . .   }
   b) **Green**. . . . . }   Claude Debussy

   Miss MAGGIE TEYTE,
   accompagnée par M. E. R. SCHMITZ.

3. *a)* **Fantaisie Chromatique**. . . . . . .   J. S. Bach
   b) **Suite** pour piano (*Prélude, Aria, Finale*). .   César Franck

   M. HAROLD BAUER.

4. **Quatuor** pour archets . . . . Claude Debussy
     a) Animé et très décidé.
     b) Assez vif et bien rythmé.
     c) Andantino doucement expressif.
     d) Final.

   LE QUATUOR FIRMIN TOUCHE.

5. **Trois Chansons** de Charles d'Orléans, à 4 voix
   mixtes sans accompagnement . . . . . Claude Debussy
     a) **Dieu ! qu'il la fait bon regarder.**
     b) **Quant j'ai ouy le tabourin.**
     c) **Yver, vous n'estes qu'un villain.**

   Miss MAGGIE TEYTE
   et les CHŒURS DES CONCERTS COLONNE
   sous la direction de l'AUTEUR.

PIANO PLEYEL

VENDREDI 4 FEVRIER, de 4 h. à 6 h. de l'après-midi, Salle de la Société Française de Photographie,
51, rue de Clichy, 5ᵉ SÉANCE DE L'ABONNEMENT.

Quartet, which was playing the String Quartet to open the concert, while Maggie and Debussy were in the Green Room; Debussy was pacing agitatedly up and down, breathing very heavily, "smoke coming out of his nostrils like a bull". The piece was finished, the applause ended, and suddenly Sechiari came in, saying to Debussy: "Eh bien, maître, comment c'était?" Debussy who up to now had not said a word suddenly went mad, hissing at him, "Vous avez joué comme des cochons !" He then went out and accompanied Maggie in the *Ariettes oubliées* absolutely without comment.

Then there was the Schmitz incident. Robert Schmitz, the celebrated promoter and accompanist who had arranged a series of concerts at the Salle Gaveau, was playing for Maggie at a rehearsal and made a mistake. Debussy was provoked to such rage that she thought he was going to knock the other man off the piano stool. Instead Schmitz got out of the way and Debussy sat down and played the opening bars of the same *Ariettes*, so nearly stifling with rage that he could hardly play a note. All the blood drained from his face, he went completely white and then reddened with the sheer effort of self-control.

How could his music be more expressive of this behaviour? The emotion is constantly about to explode, overburdened with inner tension, about to carry everything before it like a dam breaking. Then some inhibitory factor rears up, sometimes with majestic force: this was the essence of Debussy's disconcertingly modern quality, the arresting of natural emotional impulses and their interplay with the refined, the artificial, as well as the encroaching technology. This new kind of alienation was typified in the noise of the Ceinture outside the windows of his house by the Bois; in his neglected bohemian days, when he dressed "somewhat like a Spanish pirate", he had lived right over another railway, near the Gare St Lazare in the rue de Londres. Here he had worked on setting these *Ariettes oubliées* Maggie now sang, their delicate evocations oddly at variance with the shunting of rolling stock and the whistles of departure:

> C'est l'extase langoureuse,
> C'est la fatigue amoureuse,
> C'est tous les frissons des bois . . .

CHAPTER SEVEN

English, and a Tiny Thing
(1909–1919)

The Victorian cook lived like a Leviathan in the lower depths, formidable, silent, obscure, inscrutable; the Georgian cook is a creature of fresh air. . . . Do you ask for more solemn instances? All human relations have shifted—those between masters and servants, husbands and wives, parents and children. And when human relations change there is at the same time a change in religion, conduct, politics and literature. Let us agree to place one of these changes about the year 1910.

VIRGINIA WOOLF, *Mr Bennett and Mrs Brown*

DE RESZKE, DEBUSSY; de Reszke Debussy . . . the names of diminutive Maggie's two great father figures have a similar sound, not unlike that emitted by the steam of one of those luxurious trans-European expresses whose speed made the life of these early commuting musicians so remunerative. Alongside their noble sibilants the name de Plumon strikes a lighter note: a father figure indeed, but a transitory and more frivolous one, dropped quite early on the track, lost, it may be literally, alongside a sleeper.

From 1910 to 1921, the year of her second marriage, Maggie lived a life of uninterrupted hard work and success. Everything else was subservient to this blaze of activity: the fact that she divorced a husband, had numerous affairs, fell in love and even at times contemplated more marriages, was quite irrelevant to the trails of glory her voice spread across three continents—though the three were narrowed down to one in 1914 when at the outbreak of war, and though still a French citizen by marriage, she remained in America, leaving her first spouse, Eugène de Plumon, behind in Europe.

This marriage remains a mystery, shrouded in Gothic gloom, dark corners illuminated with a stab of sunlight but lapsing even more quickly into obscurity. Various Parisian *arrondissement* records yield nothing of

Plumon, the *mairies* of the fashionable quarters retain no trace of his background; there are only certificates or entries in law registers to the effect that he completed his "stage" as an *avocat* in 1910. A brief candle reveals that he and Maggie were married in London, at the Kensington Registry Office, on 16 October 1909, and that Olga Lynn was a witness.★ But after this, not even a death certificate; though it is said that this by then venerable old gentleman lived to a ripe age, at least into his mid-eighties. Sentimentally given to pondering over his own past, he even telephoned Maggie in the 1950s, some forty or so years after their marriage was over, and asked her if she would see him. But she would not. "My dear," she said, "think what he would look like now!"

What Plumon looked like in 1909 we do not know either. But we do know he was possessed of immense charm and courtesy of manner, and that he was some years Maggie's senior, a fact which seems to have been evident to a marked degree. He was once escorting her down Unter den Linden in Berlin, when she was singing at the Imperial Opera, when a passing and flirtatious German officer took him to be her father and ignored him pointedly while making eyes at Maggie. Eugène stopped and tore a strip off the Junker in fluent German—an accomplishment he had acquired while studying law at Heidelberg University—and the young man disappeared. It was true Eugène's companions had called him a cradle-snatcher, but this was only in fun, and after all his friends were French not German: what passed as *badinage* from a friend became, in a foe, mortal insult. Forty-eight hours after the incident Eugène burst excitedly into their Berlin hotel suite. "Pack at once, we're leaving!" The Junker had sent his seconds round to the lobby, and Eugène decided post-haste that discretion was the better part of valour, even though he was no stranger to duels.

Indeed at another time, when they visited Heidelberg, he took Maggie to see a duel between two students who had quarrelled the night before. To be a witness to such an exclusively male rite a woman had to be smuggled in and remain hidden, and Maggie, standing on tiptoe, watched the sinister contest, or as much of it as she could stomach after first blood had been drawn, through a grille in an iron door. She remembered the two rivals in love, attended by their seconds and a doctor,

★ Maggie states in her autobiography that the marriage took place in 1910, but she got it wrong; she makes many such elisions for the sake of chronological convenience.

dexterously flicking their wrists, their arms being stiffened with bandages. Blood did not dim her perception of technicalities.

If Eugène did not have to use his sword to defend his marital rights over Maggie, his own wrist was highly dexterous in wielding a pen and compounding fees, and he was useful in other ways, some flippant, some serious. As a trained *avocat* of the Paris Cour de Cassation or Court of Appeal, he knew how to plead a cause, and became extremely skilful at promoting his youthful protégée in her career. He gave musicales where she sang: at one such, on 19 August 1910 in the White Salon of the Savoy Hotel in London, Mrs C. Edwardes (Mme Edvina) helped, with a selection from *Faust*; the guests included Lord Westbury and Andreas Dippel, the impresario of the Chicago Opera Company, the latter accompanied by Kochmann, the conductor Campanini, and an un-identified Mr Marx. At another, lower-keyed event, Eugène even stood in for Maggie when she had a cold: not by singing, of course, this was clearly not his forte, but with some inimitable conjuring. At an evening in aid of the Forest Row Cricket Club he turned the waistcoat of a member of the audience inside out without once removing his coat: so effective was this that the unfortunate victim was as much congratulated for his courage in passing through the ordeal as was the aggressor for his sleight-of-hand. The age was a genteel one, at least on the surface. Later in the same evening Plumon gave a display of coin- and card-manipulation which left the audience gasping.

Maggie was in good hands, though not destined for long to be loyal to them or to find them to her taste. Yet she never appeared to lose admiration for Plumon's roguish qualities, supported as they were with charm. And he signed all the cheques, a business which irked her. She loved money, but she was a romantic; she was no businesswoman. After a while, their relationship cannot have seemed very romantic: she became attracted by fellow artists, creatures nearer herself in temperament and emotional needs. Another side of her, a remoteness and idealism, needed satisfying. She was as yet too young to think of secure accounts and companionship in old age.

But she and Eugène laughed a great deal, and not always at what was considered correct for a demure young lady. Maggie's taste for crude jokes, an anomaly in one whose appearance was so dainty and whose appeal so lyrical, dates from her association with Eugène and his friends. Jean-Jacques Ollivier, the homosexual *littérateur*, told graphic anecdotes of nights spent dining—and more—with Austrian officers, for both sexes at the time symbols of the stud male. At one such dinner Ollivier found himself paired with Isadora Duncan while much to his annoyance a dishy young Austrian had been snapped up before his eyes by Siegfried Wagner. To his horror he was expected to take Isadora to bed, and, worse, she insisted he undress her. "I found myself in bed with Isadora and didn't know what to do." With another Austrian officer he was luckier, except that "Il m'a mis un instrument si grand qu'il m'a fait souffrir"—images not designed to provoke mirth in an English girl of tender years, yet Maggie was definitely amused.[1]

The Maggie–Plumon pattern is so often repeated with ambitious young women of independent talent: a need for protection while a career is being built up, then, with the realization that protection is no longer necessary and freedom desirable, an urge to discard. We can only say this urge came over Maggie sometime after 1913 and before 1915, and that when she and Eugène separated he was well provided for. Whether it was good for her in the long run to cease to be "la Dame Plumon", as she was styled in the divorce document, and revert to plain Miss Teyte may be questioned; possibly it was a sign of an immaturity which dogged her to her very grave, an impatience and lack of long-term trust which made her ever ready to change, an inability to settle down for any length of time which left her ill-equipped to hold the position of leading soprano in one of the world's great opera houses. For her talents—except that her voice was a little on the small side for some of the great dramatic roles—equipped her for such a position, and her musical intelligence and social skill more than made up for a somewhat limited range of repertoire.

But somewhere in her was an obstinacy, more of the creative artist than of the performer. She always had her own idea of what she wanted to do, always wanted to be in control. You could envisage her singing Mimi or Mélisande five times, but hardly fifty, and never five hundred: the effort of repetition was too taxing on her sense of individuality. There were elements in her which made her slide so perfectly, almost as though prepared by heredity for it, into the end of that Golden Age of French music; her spirit typified in both its profane and its pure elements the twilight of romanticism. She was part of the *langueur*, of that "*extase langoureuse*" which so perfectly expressed the conscious and unconscious yearnings of the *avant-guerre* years; part both of the august pride and the hidden unseemly titillation which were elements of the same ethos, and which we see joined together in the statues of famous Frenchmen who, as reward for their disinterested travail, were always depicted with naked or near-naked nymphs on their knee or curled up admiringly at their feet.

Maggie's obstinacy possibly covered two further deficiencies. Educationally she had grave shortcomings—apart from music, she had received no formal education at all, or little to speak of. Poems, librettos she knew backwards, but with history or politics, the novel or fashionable corrective reading, she had no acquaintance. All her life her thinking remained untutored and instinctive, and she could only appreciate others' points of view if they were close to her own. Equally, because she had been uprooted early from family life and remained deeply distrustful of it, she was utterly backward in conventional womanly matters. All her life she was admired, publicly and in private, for her capacity to take part in manly competitive activities: at Edwardian house-parties she would challenge the young bloods to after-dinner billiards, or play tennis and badminton; her golfing exploits became legendary. Her immaturity in these things may have helped her career by maintaining her level of aggression at a high point: she was free-lancing at a very peculiar time, and the career she pursued was not a normal one, as it would be considered today. Obstinacy, outspokenness, individuality—only these qualities could have helped her survive and sustain a career through two World Wars, two marriages, a depression, and finally inflation, though they were not calculated to make her very nice or understanding.

But why, one might ask, did she ever marry at all? This was a function of the inspired self-interest that goes by the name of realism; though the effect, in truth, came limpingly behind the cause. Eugène was the first man to come along who seemed to have some of the assets required. She could have embraced the calling of a *cocotte*, as she had thought of doing in 1907, and earned far greater sums than she ever did in opera.* Or she could have been stand-offish and old-maidish, a line of conduct calculated in such a calling to close all doors at once. So she married. She married quickly.

Under the laws of France, at the time when she launched herself upon

---

* This was a tradition well established in France since the time of Cardinal Mazarin, who took as his mistress the illustrious Leonora Baroni, thereby inaugurating the "long and frenzied tradition of operatic 'stardom'."[2]

matrimony, all the money she earned, according to the contract she rashly put her name to, and the nationality she took on, belonged to her husband. So even more easily than he would have done in the Paris courts, and far more amusingly for him, Eugène became a prosperous man. This turn in fortune began when, in the Viennese hotel Sacher's, she signed with Andreas Dippel of the Chicago Opera Company. Her host at a concert had already given her a bouquet fastened with a brooch of real diamonds. In one week at the Alhambra Theatre, London, she reportedly earned $2,250, her fee for a London concert was a minimum of 50 guineas, her pay per performance in Chicago $400.[3] Who would not with alacrity abandon advocacy for the promotion of prima donnas?

Though it worked later with other prima donnas more prepared to settle down, Maggie was too young for such a mature arrangement. After some years of receiving a fixed allowance, or pocket money, for her art, she began to rebel. It occurred to her that there were plenty of men who, given the resources, could fulfil the task of host, publicity manager, accountant, and concert promoter without her having to be permanently tied to them. There were even women so gifted.

So overworked was she, so taxing the life her childish innocence had led her into, that by 1912 her weight was down to about six stone (84 pounds), well below her usual 100 pounds which American journalists found so incredible a weight for a prima donna to carry about. There was only one way for her to break the hold Plumon had over her career: she would be unfaithful to him. His pride as a Frenchman would not tolerate that for long, and he would leave her and return to France. Separation, and the contention she could make before a French court, would then lead to divorce. So she was unfaithful to him, she left him behind in France, and he obtained a divorce in the Paris courts. It was to take her until 1920 to regain her British nationality.

Sexuality is often the subject matter of art today, but there is little expression of it through art: greed and hostility are more often the driving motives behind the urge to self-expression. For Maggie in 1912 the power of sexuality was that of a trapped energy, it gave force and motion to what on the surface were more innocent threads of romance. Today one might see her as an active lesbian, or an active bisexual, or a voracious man-eater, and all the less interesting she would be for it; in her day the camouflage of sexual behaviour gave intrigue, in all its glints, colours, and deceptive chiaroscuro, a breathtaking complexity. She had a "romance", it might be deemed, with a leading baritone; she "fell in love" with a young composer; she was "courted" by a world-famous violinist—today all these might mean one thing and one thing only: that she went to bed with these men one after another in quick succession. But for Maggie and for others at the time there was such a delicate variety of nuance that we do not really know what happened, only that it did. For there was one code of behaviour, in public, before the world, another in private, and the newspapers had not yet been licensed to rip away the veils.

Eugène and his playmates gave her sexual freedom, but her marriage to him had one permanent and tragic effect. Like a child, under his mentorship, she submitted to the destruction of her own reproductive capacity. Convincing her that, for the uninterrupted pursuit of her career, a small and safe operation was necessary, Plumon arranged for her to be sterilized by the most efficient means then available. When she thought with horror this might mean removal of the ovaries, which was fashionable particularly in America at the time, she was assured that there was a much better, if costlier, method, that of double tying the Fallopian tubes. Maggie had never wanted to have children and could never imagine that she would; even so, it was claimed if the tubes were not completely severed but only ligatured inside, the procedure was reversible. At any rate she agreed and the operation was performed in a Passy clinic; and so, far in advance of the rest of her sex, she had freedom from the constraint of a possible pregnancy. Perhaps even at that early age she had a glimmering of the power this freedom could give her over the opposite sex. Yet it led, some fifteen years later, to the tragic situation in which she could not give the man she deeply loved the only thing he really wanted, a child. This would only serve to harden her in the course of loneliness and the placing of her career before all else.

But hardly a cloud formed over her work until war came along, and then it was the same war cloud over everyone. She had signed with Andreas Dippel to sing in Chicago in the 1911–12 season; but in 1910, after Paris, it was London that first experienced the full impact of her charm, when she appeared, first in Thomas Beecham's season at His Majesty's Theatre, and then later in the year at Covent Garden. In the autumn of 1909, a series of concerts at the Aeolian Hall had already gained her a large and interested public,* but from 25 May to 12 July 1910, Thomas Beecham conducted her to "a succession of operatic triumphs", primarily in Mozart.

Her London début, however, was not in Mozart, but in the part of Melka, in Missa's *Muguette*. Missa was one of Massenet's pupils, but his work is now largely forgotten. Maggie was called in to sing Melka at the last minute, but made a very distinct success of it; all agreed it was the cleverest piece of work of the evening, though by no means the biggest role. She also sang Antonia in *Les Contes d'Hoffmann*, which she was to sing again frequently in the winter season; but her chief impact was in the role of Blonde in *Die Entführung aus dem Serail*, and Cherubino in *Le Nozze di Figaro*, promoting the maid and the page respectively into the chief plaudit-winners of the evening.† Both operas were conducted by Beecham, and both sung in English, with the additional interest in *Figaro* of spoken dialogue substituted for the *secco* recitative. Maggie's musical phrasing was judged by all and sundry to be deliciously refined, though *The Times* rapped her over the knuckles for forgetting, since she had been in Paris, how to pronounce English.‡

Working with Beecham after the Opéra-Comique could not have presented a more nearly opposite extreme to the mind of a young singer. In Paris singers had been fined for late attendance at rehearsals, and for those days comparative efficiency reigned in the day-to-day running of the company, whereas in Beecham's province all was the reverse, at least while the maestro himself was not around. The pianist in attendance was Tommy Chapman,

> the funniest man I ever met in my life, and the biggest man I ever saw, the biggest *boned* man I ever saw. He had a coat, the "original" of

* With them, in fact, she became something of an Edwardian celebrity, singing, as it were, a requiem for the age. One day at the Rubenses in Kensington Palace Gardens the housemaid came in to tell them King Edward VII had died. Maggie was due to perform that night at the Aeolian Hall, with Olga Lynn: Lynn was to sing the German songs, she the French. The concert was postponed until after the royal funeral, and when it did at last take place, the singers—both tiny, Olga Lynn several inches shorter than Maggie—wore black chiffon, each "with a little lace collar." The audience was a sea of black.4

† Though all the singing was praised, particularly the fine bass Robert Radford was commended for his Osmin in *Die Entführung*.

‡ She was announced to sing in G. H. Clutsam's *A Summer Night* on 16 July but withdrew because of illness. She was also announced for a matinée of *Hänsel und Gretel* but seems not to have appeared.

Schaunard from *La Bohème*—on 1 October, when the Calvary Fair began, he would put it on, never removing it for the whole winter. Chapman sat at the piano, the score of *Bohème* sticking out from one pocket, and *Figaro* sticking out from the other, and fell asleep. Eleven o'clock came: no Beecham. They did a little bit of rehearsal: some dialogue, say (no longer recitative), and someone gave the word, and up Tommy Chapman's hands would jump on to the piano, those huge hands like tables, suddenly transformed into butterflies because he was such a wonderful Mozart player, never missing a note. Anyway, twelve o'clock came and went, and then at half-past Tommy [Beecham] would stroll in, and suddenly like electricity the whole place sat up.[5]

But Beecham chanced his arm, Maggie thought, by under-rehearsing and when, fifty-seven years later, an interviewer asked her directly, "How was Beecham at rehearsals?" she replied quick as a flash, with the absolute certainty of truth, "He never was at rehearsals."

Even so, she never found anyone as exciting to work with, and everything went smoothly in the His Majesty's season. There were peccadilloes, of course; one night the Act Two sextet of *Figaro* was all over the place, to which Beecham's twinkling assessment ran, "Now there, wasn't that marvellous—we all finished together!" Maggie was entirely thrilled; though she did not believe in reincarnation, there was no doubt that for her Beecham *was* Mozart. He was naughty, like Mozart; he smiled, dancing his eyes here and there, full of wit and dancing merriment, fully aware of every *double-entendre*. In his very reticence about his deepest feelings—for he was a very "North of England character, like Arnold Bennett", as Sacheverell Sitwell said—Beecham had much in common with Maggie.*

Beecham's struggle against English snobbery in music made little headway in that pre-war decade, and his 1910 season lost a huge amount of his father's, Sir Joseph's, money. "We are not interested in our fellow countrymen," Beecham said, "only in the picturesque foreigner with an unknown background." In the early 1920s when he went bankrupt, his counsel in Chancery claimed he had spent all his money disinterestedly

---

* "Massenet's *Manon* is worth the whole of the St Matthew Passion," he once said, just as Maggie once said to her grandnephew John, a Bach lover, "You can go to bed with your Mr Bach." Unknown to either at this time, she and Beecham were to become more closely associated both in 1914 and in the 1930s.

on music; "And what good does that do anybody?" asked the judge. The élite often had no contact with the music it patronized, enjoying it almost as its ancestors had enjoyed cock-fighting or, perhaps more aptly, cock-crowing competitions. The dizzying "white" voice, the *rossignol* trills, the twenty-second-held notes meant far more to this audience than the truth of the drama or well-discriminated feeling in the music.* Yet almost in spite of this—for Mozart is one of the very few composers whom it is impossible to sacrifice somewhere along the line to vulgarity— Beecham managed to re-establish the Mozart style in England, just as Richard Strauss had done in Munich, Reynaldo Hahn in Paris, and Mahler in Vienna. "Clearly Mozart has a future," began a review of *Figaro* in the *Daily Telegraph*.

Universal praise of a new English singer was continued into the Beecham winter season at Covent Garden, when between 5 October and 31 December Maggie sang well over twenty performances in five operas, including Marguérite in *Faust* and Nuri in the first-ever English production of Eugène d'Albert's *Tiefland*. The season was to have opened with *Tiefland* on 1 October, but a wave of "indisposition" swept over the principals, and that opera, along with various alternatives, was postponed —a sign, possibly, of Beecham's disregard for contingency plans. *Tiefland* finally opened on 5 October. As a footnote on props used in that day, John Coates, playing a Spanish shepherd, carried a large dagger or *navaja* which had actually belonged to a notorious Valencian brigand, and which had been used to kill at least two men: what a *frisson* this sent around the house!

Maggie was presented to Queen Alexandra after one performance, but as Her Majesty was somewhat deaf she could not make out Maggie's reply to her question, as to how many years she had been singing. Sooner than waste time, with roguish forthrightness Maggie stuck out five fingers, which the Queen duly comprehended. "Irrepressible" is how one onlooker described Maggie's action, somewhat taken aback at this public exposure of the Queen's disability.

---

* When, after singing Desdemona, her greatest role, the audience clamoured for an encore, Melba had a piano pushed out on the stage by grubby stagehands; she then sat down, still in Desdemona's nightdress, plonked out a few chords, and sang "Home, Sweet Home". The story, probably apocryphal, was also told of Patti; but in any case the most romantic adherents to the myths of the Golden Age might have found the reality decidedly mundane.

Marguérite in *Faust*, which opened on 1 November, is a demanding role which shows up well the power of a young singer's voice, and Maggie used the opportunity to the very best effect; her Marguérite also had the advantage of looking like a Goethe heroine. She may have thought that judging by the reception she need have no fear as to her future activity at Covent Garden. However, this turned out not to be the case. For it was for one performance only, on 19 December 1910, that she sang Mélisande; Golaud was sung by Jean Bourbon, Pelléas by Georges Petit, and the conductor was Percy Pitt. She put herself heart and soul into this single opportunity to show her brilliance, but the powers that be, or rather the formidable support that existed for Mme Edvina in that role at Covent Garden, made sure she did not sing it there again for twenty years, and then only twice,* while Edvina, by all accounts an inferior singer in the part, sang it eleven times. What conclusion can be drawn, except that the organization preferred second best?

The same charge cannot be levelled at the critics, who without exception were ecstatic in their praise: "She is Mélisande, and all other singers have only pretended to be," wrote one; another, that "she has . . . never had an equal in the part, . . . nor ever will."† Honesty and unpopularity went together: Maggie never paid a claque and was not at all popular with the Soho Sicilians at Covent Garden; this may have been another cause of her failure to whip up support. But what a tragic example this was of a great artist working below her capacity, not being fully stretched. Over a span of forty-six years of singing opera she sang Mélisande little more than thirty times, and more than half of these were at the Opéra-Comique, within a year or so of her début. One has to conclude that in general English appreciation was very much against the level of truth and reality she was capable of depicting.

Although English to the core Maggie felt in later life that she had not

* In 1930; see Chapter 9.

† Victor Gollancz was another admirer: "It was not till December that year (1910), after the grand season was over, that I was to hear as Mélisande a singer and actress of the kind that, once heard in a role, comes to mean it for ever after in the listener's consciousness, Maggie Teyte: who I cannot help thinking, to judge from rumour, must have greatly surpassed her more famous predecessor, Mary Garden. Her adorable *mignonesse*, a quality of mingled freshness and gravity in her smooth gentle singing . . . and the child-like ingenuousness of her acting, if acting it must be called, moved me to an affection for her such as I have felt for few other singers."[6]

been fully appreciated in her homeland. Had she been born into the *nouveau-riche* plutocracy like Thomas Beecham, she might have forged, against the tide, a strong eccentric personality able publicly to flout the philistinism. But she had none of Beecham's money to back her up, and therefore none of his licence to fail on a grand scale—the only kind of failure likely, in this case, to lead to ultimate success. She could not afford to put a foot wrong: what could she do but go abroad, where her background had the same kind of romantic exotic appeal as that of an Italian or German had in her own country?

Viewed from a distance, her few months in London in 1910 make it appear as if she was impatient to break entirely from her English background. How inaccurate a reading that was to turn out to be: it was elsewhere that she was unable to put down roots, elsewhere that she showed continued impatience to move on.

But her departure for America did sever certain ties. It marked the end of her relationship with Walter Rubens. While, some years earlier, Walter had been in love with Maggie, hoping against hope she would marry him, she had insisted from the start his devotion to her be disinterested and that she would accept it only on these terms, it being clear that he and his family were her patrons, her family in art. His mother she treated as her own mother ("the kindest person in the world," she declared—even so she never had a photo or keepsake of her). As for Walter, he had no real luck in his own life, the discovery of Teyte apart. When he was thirty he had married Olive Elizabeth Chalk-Hood, the daughter of a squire. Younger than he, she had been a concert artist, and quickly, with her charm and good looks, came to combine singing with the role of hostess. The idyllic life this pair led was to be cut short by the Great War, in which Walter saw service as a captain in the Essex Regiment. He was at Gallipoli and barely survived the horrific ordeal, from which he never fully recovered; he became, literally, the shell of a man.

The shell had a semblance of motion, though, by virtue of Olive's notorious love affair. Like a hermit crab, a lover slid into hers and Walter's marriage—Lionel Lord Sackville, father of Vita Sackville-West the novelist. Lord Sackville, bewitched by Olive Rubens's tall, dark, and slim looks and her flirtatious and seductive manner—even though she was nearing forty—insisted she remain almost constantly at his home, Knole, where he installed her in an apartment. Walter tagged along, he and Olive still living outwardly as man and wife.

The shell remained intact until Walter's death in 1922. Lord Sackville and Olive lived together until Sackville's own death some years later, maintaining sexual relations to the very end. Vita Sackville-West ascribed her mother's flight from Knole and the break-up of her parents' marriage to Olive, for whom she invented the name "Rebecca". "He had by then got rid of his stringy, wispy Lady Constance, and from now dates his friendship with another woman, Rebecca, who with her husband spent a lot of time at Knole."[7] Olive was godmother to one of Vita's children by Harold Nicolson; a lover of golf, healthy and strong, she was nicknamed "Bom" by those children because she was a sort of "booming contralto".[8] After Sackville's death, Olive married again, this time Foch's ex-Quartermaster, General Nation, holder of the Croix de Guerre and a Commander of the Légion d'honneur. This brave fellow couldn't resist World War Two either; he sailed off to France with the British Expeditionary Force as a war correspondent, and then became a zone commander in the Home Guard, dying in 1946. Olive was awarded a Grace and Favour House at Hampton Court and passed away in 1973. She was Maggie's last contact with her patron's family, and they saw each other till her death.

Maggie's years in America were cheerful, oblivious of self, breezy, and suited to her adventurous temperament. She moved about frequently, as one opera historian observed, flitting brilliantly from place to place like a hummingbird, never staying very long.[9] The Americans were enchanted with her: "A little dear, just as cute and sweet as she can be," wrote one critic.[10] Another remarked that her voice was as big as she was small, "a mite of a soprano about twenty with a voice four times as large as she is." Almost in the same breath it was pointed out that Mme Tetrazzini was the size of "three or four Maggie Teytes"; yet "Little Maggie Teyte...received almost as great an ovation for her Cherubino ... as Tetrazzini had for Lucia."[11] Her nicknames became "Tiny Teyte", the "Petit Proteus" or the "Pocket Prima Donna". American critics were quick to perceive the distinct personality coupled with the beautiful singing. "Unique among all singers," Walter Anthony called her. "She has this quality of genius—there isn't anyone else quite like her."[12] As for her background, they said she was Irish, Scots, English, and, according to one reporter—about as remote from the truth as it was possible to get—she had a pronounced Cockney twang.

Outspokenly, accurately, even wantonly, they compared her with Mary Garden. "Whereas Maggie Teyte seems a younger Mélisande because she is small and slight," Henry Lahee wrote, with all the bitching innuendo of green-room gossip and yet withal a fairly shrewd objectivity, "with a voice that is unquestionably more pleasing, being a dramatic soprano of surprising warmth and carrying power considering her physical limitation, Miss Garden's way of dressing is, to most people, more successful. Miss Teyte's interpretation is simpler, but because it is less dramatic has neither the grace nor the mystic allure of Miss Garden's."[13] At any rate Maggie was not going to get a chance to show her colours as Mélisande, so the critics, disappointingly, would not have the chance to judge for themselves. One wonders indeed if Lahee had himself seen Maggie as Mélisande. Mary Garden had more or less a monopoly on the role in the States, a monopoly broken several times by Leblanc, who was no real rival to either.*

Maggie was certainly not in the same publicity stakes as Garden. Both were in the Chicago-Philadelphia Opera Company in 1911, and when Garden arrived at her suite at the Blackstone Hotel, Chicago,

> as usual she brought with her trunk upon trunk of gowns and during the interview she modelled some of these for reporters. The first one was made of thousands of little steel discs put together in overlapping rows like the scales of a fish. She looked something like a mermaid with it on. "But I can't wear it long," Mary said. "You see it is just like chain mail and it weighs twelve pounds . . . I think it is a becoming gown for crowned heads, because it's bullet proof." "What would you do if it ripped?" one of the reporters inquired. "Could you pin it up?" "Hardly. Instead of dressmaker, I'll have to find a blacksmith!" Then Mary came out in a black dress all of fringe. "All of my gowns are clinging," she said. "I don't wear corsets, you know."[14]

She behaved with the customary flamboyance the press loved.

* Leblanc did not sing the role but "chanted" it, relying otherwise on her "originality": she was now allowed to do it—as a sop to Maeterlinck's great influence and reputation—even while she herself voiced a preference for Fauré's incidental music over Debussy's score.

Little Teyte had no such captivating powers. There was to be no throwing of kisses to win her public, no camping it up for the press corps. She was far more prepared to turn her back on them than open up her front. She would win through, if ever she was going to win through, on the quality of her technique. After all, as she so often thought and often said, who gave a damn about Melba's personality? It was the voice which mattered. When Teyte made headlines, Quaintance Eaton wrote, it was usually on behalf of righteousness; a stage manager was bullying a female member of the chorus in Philadelphia and she "threatened to have him horsewhipped" (actually, she said, she remonstrated forcibly). Another time she skilfully ensnared the leader of the Philadelphia claque, a sinister *bonhomme* by the name of Nathan Arlack who demanded $500 to ensure she would not be hissed, into repeating his demand so it could be heard by opera-house officials and press men in an adjoining room. The press burst in, the villain was unmasked.

Her American début was as Cherubino with the Chicago-Philadelphia Opera Company on 4 November 1911, at the Philadelphia Metropolitan Opera House. Otherwise the cast was Gustave Huberdeau, who sang Figaro; Alice Zeppilli as Susanna, Carolina White as the Countess, Louise Bérat as Marcellina, and Mario Sammarco as the Count. Campanini conducted. "The elements were a little racially diverse for a well-blended performance."[15] On 25 November in Chicago, opposite Mary Garden as Prince Charming, she sang the role of Cinderella at the American première of Massenet's *Cendrillon*. This was so successful she repeated it the next season, with Helen Stanley in the travesty role. Maggie wore her size $3\frac{1}{2}$ glass slippers—hardly a journalist missed picking this up—and looked utterly unearthly at the ball: there is to this day in the Art Institute in Chicago, on the fifth-floor landing, a painting of her in her spectacular jewel-studded and brocaded gown. According to the *Chicago Tribune* the scenic display was the most "attractive" and "pretentious" ever shown in Chicago, but the lighting left much to be desired: they never learnt the trick of handling it during the transformation scene.[16]

Andreas Dippel's Chicago-Philadelphia Company also produced, in Maggie's first season, Jean Nouguès's five-act opera *Quo Vadis*, in which she sang Lygia: this was based on the Sienkiewicz novel and was already showing its cinematographic potential, for several miles of painted scenery were needed. As was tartly pointed out, the conflagration scene would scarcely have warmed anyone's hands; however, on a reciprocal arrange-

Cover of the programme for the
Monte Carlo concert in 1907 at
which Teyte made her professional
début. (*Left*) Reynaldo Hahn, in a
drawing by Jean Cocteau.

Creators of *Pelléas et Mélisande*: (*left*) the playwright Maurice Maeterlinck and (*below*) the composer Claude Debussy, in a photograph by Pierre Louÿs.

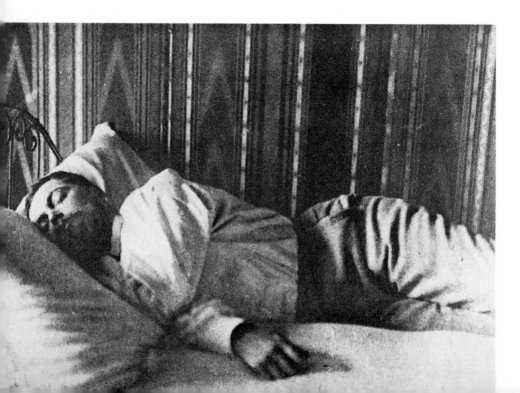

Teyte as Mélisande in the 1908 production of *Pelléas et Mélisande*, with (*below*) her Pelléas, Jean Périer, in a cartoon by Luc, and (*right*) décors by Jusseaume for the Paris production: a forest (*top*), Act I, sc. i, and a fountain in the park (*bottom*), Act II, sc. i.

Posters for productions of the Chicago-Philadelphia Opera Company,
with which Maggie Teyte sang, 1911–14.

Stars of the Chicago-Philadelphia Company arriving in New York, November 1911: Teyte with Mario Sammarco and Gustave Huberdeau (left), Hector Dufranne (extreme right), and others. (*Right*) As Marguérite in the Company's production of Gounod's *Faust*.

Teyte in four of the operatic roles
she sang in America in 1911–18:
(*above*) the title role in *Cendrillon*
by Massenet; (*right*) Antonia in
Offenbach's *Les Contes d'Hoffmann*;
(*facing page*, *left*) Cherubino in
Mozart's *Le Nozze di Figaro*;
(*right*) the title role in *Mignon* by
Ambroise Thomas.

(*Above left*) Teyte as Mimi in Puccini's *La Bohème*; (*right*) in costume for
a recital of old French songs; (*below*) with Charles Wakefield Cadman
(right) and Indian Princess Redfeather in California, 1915.

ment the Chicago company had with the Met,* *Quo Vadis* was given one performance in New York, as was *Cendrillon*.

In May 1912, amidst a hectic European itinerary, Maggie appeared twice nightly in variety at the Alhambra Theatre, London; she wanted to test de Reszke's technique to the very limit. "Vissi d'arte" from *Tosca* was her first "number", followed by Herman Bemberg's "Chant de Bacchante", the latter suiting her style better than the passion-laden aria. (She was said at the time to be going to Paris "to study an opera by Bemberg specially written for her", but no other mention of this work exists.) Her encore, after nearly a dozen curtain calls, was "The Minstrel Boy". She filled and silenced the immense house: "how this can be managed in a tobacco-laden hall, ask the high gods."[17]

In the 1912–13 Chicago season, her second with the company, Maggie also sang the lead, Dot Peerybingle, in the big novelty, Goldmark's *The Cricket on the Hearth*, based on the Charles Dickens story. The *Tribune* predicted it would achieve a permanent place in the repertoire. Maggie sang it with Hector Dufranne, her Golaud from the Opéra-Comique, and George Hamlin, "wearing one of the most extraordinary sets of whiskers that ever diversified the human countenance." Sung in English, *The Cricket* was given at least four times, and once the following year.†

Maggie also added Mimi and Mignon to her repertoire in this season, which was otherwise notable for the appearance of Tita Ruffo as Rigoletto, an event which put even Tetrazzini in the shade. The *Tribune* said of Maggie's Mimi that it was "by far the finest interpretation of the part that Chicago opera lovers have witnessed in recent years," *Musical America* that she "gave a truly touching and absolutely convincing portrayal" and that she sang "with plenitude and sweet quality of tone, modulated at all times to the appropriate emotional aspects, and directed invariably by exquisite taste and deep sense of artistic proportions." Even Gatti-Casazza left his office at the Met to attend her portrayal of Mimi, and later of Butterfly—a procedure quite unheard of for him.[18] In both cities there was equal enthusiasm for her Mignon. Her salary per performance was raised

* This Chicago company had come into being after the Met had paid Oscar Hammerstein \$1,200,000 not to produce opera in New York for ten years. Hammerstein came to London and built his opera house in Kingsway. The acoustics were considered poor. At the opening, King Edward VII had to mount a large flight of steps, at the top of which stood Hammerstein in the full regalia of a New York impresario.

† In *Opera in Chicago* (1966) Ronald Davis states, inaccurately, that it was given only one performance.

from $300 to $400; not inconsiderable but far short of the $2,000 Tetrazzini and now Tita Ruffo were said to command. Maggie gave a concert with Ruffo in New York at the Hippodrome, and was recalled when she sang the aria from *Louise*.

Tetrazzini was one of the two great stars—Garden was the other—of these Chicago seasons, but she fell out with her brother-in-law, the conductor Campanini, during a tour in 1912. They had a preliminary row in which she told him she was the box-office attraction and he only the conductor. Hurt, he bided his time until one night in Los Angeles his opportunity arrived. She was singing Gilda's "Caro nome" in *Rigoletto* and in the cadenza she lost place and pitch, ending on a very high note but not quite the right one. Instead of tactfully concealing her mistake, Campanini, sensing a devastating revenge in the offing, invoked a jubilant chord that screamed the distance of her departure from true pitch . . . Tetrazzini never sang in Chicago again until after Campanini's death, and he was not to die for a good many years: in her autobiography she made no mention of Chicago, or of Campanini, except that he had married her sister.[19]

Maggie admired Tetrazzini and found her marvellous in *Traviata*—she had been at the star's celebrated first performance at Covent Garden—but had a strong preference for Melba's voice, rhapsodizing over the top E which Melba held while bowing six times, lifting up her train, and then withdrawing—still holding the note ("They used those tricks"). She used them too, but not for many years, not till she was over sixty and then almost deliberately to invoke echoes of the Golden epoch. Melba's laconic comment, Maggie reported, on Tetrazzini's vocal shortcomings was to "ask her to sing me a slow scale."[20]

Maggie was constantly amused by the disparity between her own tiny appearance and the impact her voice made. In 1912 she was in a café on Seventh Avenue in New York: it had a little balcony with tables around it, and sitting at a table were a man and a woman, the woman facing in her direction. "It looks like Maggie Teyte," she heard the woman say, and hearing her name she naturally turned round to see who had said it, thereby giving a fuller view. "But it isn't!" said the woman furiously, to her partner.[21]

After touring England and the Riviera in the summer of 1913, Maggie's second season was extended into a third, 1913-14. But this was the last, as Andreas Dippel resigned, and Campanini took his place.* The first two seasons of Dippel's administration had been very successful, but the third showed a net loss of $250,000: true, this was mostly accounted for by contracts with singers for a 1914-15 season which was now not going to take place, and which the company had no intention of honouring. In the bankruptcy petitions there were ten pages of claims from singers, among them Garden (at $1,600 a performance), Teyte (at $400 a performance), John McCormack (ten weeks at $1,200 a week), Saltzman-Stevens ($250 a performance); the company's defence was based on the "in case of war" clause in the contract. Of course there was no war yet, so far as the United States was concerned, but it supplied a fine point for lawyers to argue over.

Maggie was undeterred at the sudden drying up of her Chicago-Philadelphia career, and went straight on to the National Grand Opera company in Boston, where she made her début in *La Bohème*. Her first Rodolfo was Léon Lafitte, her second Giovanni Martinelli, held by many to be Caruso's successor. According to Quaintance Eaton,[23] at this time Martinelli was forcing his voice to the point of abuse. Later, when Max Rabinoff took over the company from Henry Russell (the latter had had his credibility shattered by presenting Wagner in France on the very eve of the First World War), Maggie sang *Bohème* with Luca Botta. This was one of the Boston Opera's most successful productions, and she repeated it in 1916, after Rabinoff too had run into trouble.†

There were several memorable tours after Maggie's engagement at

* Dippel's resignation was a mystery, the only real cause of criticism being the appalling lighting; if, it was said, during the first few years of the Chicago Opera, there was ever a time when a change of lighting was made on cue, "neither memory nor record reveals the fact."[22]

† Other parts Maggie sang in Boston were Nedda in Leoncavallo's *I Pagliacci* with the great Zenatello—it impressed the distinguished critic Philip Hale as the best since Mme Basta-Tavary; one performance of Desdemona on tour, possibly opposite Zenatello: she learned it in a week and claimed no great result. She sang a solitary performance of Gilda in *Rigoletto*, though she also sang Gilda with the Davis Opera Company in Pittsburgh—she seemed to hold no great affection for this part. She sang Gretel in Humperdinck's *Hänsel und Gretel*; she was later an excellent Hänsel at Covent Garden. In January 1917 she sang in *Faust*. Amram Scheinfeld of Milwaukee wrote of this Marguérite as "one of appealing beauty and wistfulness. She sang it in a voice of peculiar beauty . . . invested it with a simplicity, a gentleness and truth, wholly devoid of apparent stagecraft."

Boston, the first being Henry Russell's fifth season at the Théâtre des Champs-Elysées in Paris, a venture backed by the Baron Frédéric d'Erlanger, the millionaire composer, by Lady Ripon, and Otto Kahn. They leased the theatre for five years, a singularly ill-fated move to make in 1914; but they began brilliantly, with a rich Italian repertoire staggeringly well cast and performed, so that even Messager at the Opéra had to juggle his schedule to face up to this competition. Melba sang Desdemona in *Otello*, while in *Un Ballo in Maschera* the principals included Emmy Destinn, Ancona, Martinelli, and "little Maggie Teyte", who sang Oscar. *Un Ballo* was taken to Parma, to celebrate Verdi's centenary. Maggie also sang with Destinn in *Don Giovanni*, and in the first Paris production of Wolf-Ferrari's *Il Segreto di Susanna*—the frivolous story of the young Countess who has a guilty secret: she smokes cigarettes on the quiet—she sang Countess Gil. Her exploits on the Chantilly golf course were also much commended: she played there with Francis Ouimet, the American Open Champion.*

Their work done, the company then returned to the States on the *Cincinnati*,[25] though Maggie had stopped off to tour England with the Czech violinist and composer Jan Kubelik. She also sang in a memorable concert at the Albert Hall: quite apart from ungrounded suspicions that her voice might have been found "short" in such a huge auditorium, she, Fritz Kreisler, and Wilhelm Backhaus, then billed as "Willy", proved an irresistible attraction, and her "beautifully produced voice penetrated the vast spaces of the hall like rays of sunlight". The *Daily Mail* called her "by far the prettiest and one of the most accomplished of our singers," wishing her selection of English and American songs had not been so trivial.

But she did not come to England only for this concert: there was a more interesting catch bobbing up and down, if only she knew how to pull it in. In 1914 Melba's reign at Covent Garden was beginning to draw to a close. Her Mimi that year both opened and closed the Grand Opera season; at her last performance there had been seven kings and queens in the audience. It was possible, though, that an English singer such as Teyte might detach from her one or two roles, like Mimi, in which she had more than proved herself abroad. The English press were campaigning very hard on Maggie's behalf, and she had been engaged for the

---

* Quaintance Eaton places her exploits with Ouimet in Paris, while Maggie claims modestly she managed somehow to beat Ouimet in America.[24]

first time in the Grand Opera season of 1914 to sing in her two favourite Mozart operas, *Don Giovanni* and *Figaro*. "The fact that such an exceptionally attractive artist as Miss Teyte has not appeared more often at Covent Garden has frequently been the subject of comment, and her admirers will hope that she will be seen and heard here more often in future," wrote the *Westminster Gazette* in June 1914, on the occasion of Mme Edvina's participation in a revival of *Pelléas*. Though its comment appeared on the same day as the review of *Pelléas*, it was not quite so frank as the *Globe*, which said that while it appreciated Mme Edvina—others, like the *Observer*, did not even go so far as that—it hoped Maggie might yet be seen in London in a part in which she triumphed in Paris. The *Globe's* writer was quite oblivious to the review the paper's then critic had written of the London performance in December 1910, which had deemed the performance of *Pelléas* the greatest ever seen at Covent Garden.[26] So quickly did the glory of Maggie's one London appearance fade!

Even so there seemed more hope for her at Covent Garden in 1914 than there had been in 1910.* But although extremely well-attended, much better than some of the half-empty Wagner houses in the same season, the productions of *Figaro* left much to be desired. Only Scotti (the Count) and Teyte showed a semblance of the Grand Manner, said the *Telegraph*. The rest of the company—including Rosa Raisa, "not suited to it", Alice Zeppilli a "weak Susanna", Jean Aquistopace "too heavy a Figaro", and the conductor, a "slow and lifeless" Ettore Panizza—were written off by most critics.[27] Only Maggie won unanimously good reviews, *The Times* calling her "wholly delicious", the *Pall Mall Gazette* "the most truly Mozartian figure". Her "Non sò più" one would not have had one whit otherwise, said the *Mail*; her "Voi che sapete" was perfect.

From the stage Maggie was able to observe the end of an era. The war she now, from what she had seen in Paris, believed imminent, and it was going to sweep away this whole society and its absolute insistence on

---

* A further augury—if a rumour then current was based on truth, as seems likely—was that she had now begun a spasmodic liaison with Thomas Beecham which was to last until the late 1930s. Beecham at that time was conducting his historic Russian season, with Chaliapin, only a block or two away at Drury Lane. It was a great pity, Maggie was reported as saying, "that Beecham visits me reeking of Elsa Stralia" (the Australian-born soprano who made her début that season at Covent Garden).

patrician virtues and foibles: whether the most beautiful woman in the house was Lady Drogheda or Lady Curzon or some pretty interloper with a foreign name, would no longer be important, neither would the splendour of Edwardian peacockry. Gone soon would be the lovingly lingered-over menus of audience attire: on the first night of *Figaro*, for example, there was listed Lady Harewood in oyster grey charmeuse, Lord Portsmouth in heliotrope, Lady Kimberley in black jetted net and a black ostrich feather. Ah Lord Portsmouth, where, a few months later, would be your suit of heliotrope; and where, Lady Kimberley, your black ostrich feather?

Employing Teyte, all agreed, was a wise move, even though the production of *Figaro* suffered by being relegated to the very end of the season (the company included Caruso, Melba, Martinelli, Dufranne, Huberdeau, et al.). But our dainty rogue in porcelain also sang in *Don Giovanni* and was no less applauded: fortunately the rest of the cast, Emmy Destinn, Maggie's apparent rival Stralia, Scotti (a superbly sung Don) and John McCormack (a lifelessly acted Don Ottavio), didn't this time manage to isolate Maggie in her excellence. It was certain she could look forward to more roles at Covent Garden, and according to the *Daily Mail*, which published an article about her entitled "A Great English Singer",[28] she had been engaged to sing opera at the Gewandhaus in Leipzig with Nikisch, one of the greatest conductors of the day. She had already sung Butterfly in Berlin, noted the *Mail*, an honour unprecedented for an English soprano.* Who knows but that she was about to begin increasing her repertoire with German roles hitherto unknown to her? But, as her life showed so often, and not that she enjoyed it the less, she had not been born at quite the right moment. The cruel intervention of war put an end to German ambitions, which she was not really to revive until after the Second World War, when she decided to tackle Schoenberg and for this reason went for a time to live in Vienna.† At any rate, concluded the *Mail* article, when will London have a chance to

---

* But no records of this remain, just as no facts are known of a tour made of pre-Revolutionary Russia—apart from a Tsarist passport dated 1909 and that she visited Kiev and Warsaw.

† The reason Beecham was not wholly successful with Wagner, she once said, was that he had come to it too late in life. The same might have been said of her as Eva in *Die Meistersinger*, a role Edouard de Reszke had suggested to her (as well as Norina in *Don Pasquale*, which she never sang but which would have suited her).

hear Miss Teyte's Mimi, "a part in which she has achieved such immense success elsewhere"?

But did Teyte really fit the foreign prima donna tradition of Covent Garden? Was she at all compatible with the good plodding, earnest English tradition of outstanding voices such as Walter Widdop, of singers who could not act and did not in any way behave like opera stars, content to let the conductor, the new ascendant power in the opera house, increase his hold over what had hitherto been the territory of the prima donna and *primo uomo*. It is hardly surprising that when war was declared she joined the international circuit of opera stars, untypical of her yet temperamentally related to the prima donna world of her formative years, instead of staying behind in the highly reduced circumstances of the London musical world. At this time the American cities responded far more to Teyte's quality of Paris-based refinement: curiously enough the perhaps brasher and more outwardly vulgar Americans hungered after the Third Republic refinement more than did the staid English, who in their opera house worshipped though they would not quite own up to it, the broad, even the vulgar.

One thing at least is sure: both English and Americans served French art song and the Opéra-Comique tradition more devotedly than ever the French did.

In 1914 Teyte saw Debussy for what was to be the last time. She had made a startlingly vivid realization of his musical ideas,* and now, in an interview for the American *Opera Magazine*, not to be outdone in journalistic efficiency, had even taken her own photograph of him. "'You mean that your style of music is not sufficiently appreciated?' I gasped. 'Not at all,' he answered, smiling. 'It *is* appreciated among the *cognoscenti*. And about the rest of the world I care little. You will find in ten years

---

* Though he accompanied other singers, and made a record with Garden singing Mélisande, Debussy rarely appeared as a conductor (and was by no means considered a great one). Maggie claimed the distinction not only of having been coached by him in Mélisande and in his songs, and of having frequently been accompanied by him in recitals before the First World War, but also of having him conduct for her, as he did on 21 January 1910 when she sang the solo part in his *Trois Chansons de Charles d'Orléans* with the choir of the Concerts Colonne. The last concerts Maggie sang with Debussy accompanying her were on 25 March 1911, with Jean Périer, and on 5 March 1912, when she sang *Le Promenoir des deux amants* and the *Fêtes galantes*.

everyone will be singing and playing my music. The general intelligence of the public will have caught up with me by that time'." The interview proceeded in this vein, containing on the way the most rounding condemnation of Wagner Debussy ever voiced: "'a great literary and dramatic genius . . . but no musician. . . . On the whole Verdi was a more original composer.'"*

Scarcely two years after voicing these thoughts, Debussy was operated on for cancer of the rectum; the operation had, for those days, a short-term success, and he was able to linger on until 25 March 1918, unproductive and in great pain, dying amid the sound of the long-range German shells falling on Paris. The funeral procession passed nothing but military trucks in the wide boulevard, the shopkeepers stood in their doorways looking puzzled: "Il paraît que c'était un musicien," they said. Thus was laid to rest one of the most diversely gifted and monumental figures of the glorious Third Republic.

In 1914, also, Maggie and Eugène separated. After practising as a lawyer in Paris for only a few years, Plumon had given up his legal career for Maggie. In the opera world a woman singer is either ruthless herself, or has someone to be ruthless on her behalf. In the short term Eugène had been very successful in managing Maggie. He concocted newspaper stories. He arranged meetings. He entertained lavishly on her behalf. He took care of his breadwinner with the most sophisticated tenderness. He took her part with some of the critics—very few—who were not as kind as they could, or should, have been, over her choice of songs, writing them letters—polite, disarming, and intelligent letters—so that in their next notices the critics tempered judgement with a certain wary respect, and even a desire to please. Up to a point Maggie had been a perfect object to own and manage, combining with the attributes of the girl-mistress those of the sexual connoisseur in which he had so carefully schooled her.

But patterns of personality are strong, though they may take time to emerge. Maggie craved independence. She wanted to manage herself. She felt she had never really experienced love.

So they began to row. Eugène disapproved of a certain "*manque de raffinement*" in a pair of shoes she chose, and he would grow slightly hysterical, betraying hundreds of years of conditioning in French preciousness. What business was it of his, her taste in shoes? she thought;

* The whole of this remarkable interview is reproduced as Appendix C.

they were comfortable, practical. She wasn't on a stage all the time, as he would have liked her to be.

In a little while she sensed that, intellectually, she had the upper hand. True, he loved music, but only as an embellishment, a decoration on life, he had no searching critical quality such as she sensed in herself. Other singers were *"pas mal"*, "too sharp", a "little heavy", or just "lacking charm". Ah yes, that charm, that was everything at the time, wasn't it, she thought. But there must be such a thing as musical intelligence. . . . She noticed that when he was with her musical friends such as Reynaldo Hahn, or the Rubenses, he vanished behind a smoke-screen of utterly empty persiflage. She soon found herself dismissing him, as they did, as a lightweight.

"Why did you lie about ——?" she asked one night after they had been out to supper. "Oh, I didn't want to hurt him, poor fellow," he replied. "He is a nice enough chap." "You should have told him what you thought. He respects having the truth told him," she said. "Oh, *ma chère* Maggie, you are uncouth. You must flatter people's ideas of themselves, else you will lose yourself a lot of friends." "I have no friends," she countered. "A young soprano is alone in this world but for her immediate supporters. I have the Rubens family." What else could he answer but "You have me", which prompted, "What good are you? You never tell the truth." So he had to make a stronger case for himself. "I protect you from the worst in yourself. A certain tendency towards vulgarity. It is very English." This made her furious. "So you want me to lie? Lie, lie, lie!" To which his answer betrayed a smug French cynicism: "It is the very fabric of which the world of the performer is constructed."

But for her . . . she could not do anything if she lied, that was death to her performance, as de Reszke had taught her. They were talking about two different kinds of lie, of course, but it is not uncommon for two people who are quarrelling to confuse the meaning of words. Now she looked at him coldly. Her eyes became dismissive and piercing when they lost their Cherubinesque sparkle. He saw hatred there and felt very uncomfortable. "Get out," she said. "Leave me on my own." "No, please, look, you don't understand . . . In no way did I mean to cast a reflection on the truthful quality of your art." "Get out," she repeated. "You disgust me. You are a coward. That's why you wanted no children," she went on, recalling with a shudder the operation he had persuaded her to undergo for her career—and his own uninterrupted pleasure. He threw up his hands in a lightweight gesture. "You don't understand, my darling child." But she did. "I'm fed up with having you on top of me. In the morning there you are, jealously guarding your little vedette. You take me out to lunch, you meet me from the opera house, you are suffocating me." "But you need me," he retaliated plaintively. "Where would you be otherwise? You were a waif; you had no address to speak of. Monsieur Carré had his eye on you. Others did too." She had a reply for this too: "It would have been better if I had let them all have their way. It would have made me more tough!"

As a final resort Eugène's Jansenist legal streak came into play. He would appeal to her love of perfection. "You are too good for them. You belong to . . ." But she was too quick for him. "To no one but myself." "Exactly," said Plumon. He had been going to say to her art. "You are a vulnerable person at heart. You need marriage, a husband. . . ." "A child?" she hit back. "Your career is your child." The conjurer played his final card: "Our child."

So it went on. Only each time it got worse. Until finally the various combinations of "I hate you", "I never wanted you in the first place", "I can't see what you ever saw in me, if that's what you think of me now", were countered by the wrong set of "But you don't mean it", "It's merely temperament. You're taking it out on me because of the tension of performance . . .", and so on, and she said bluntly, "It's no good, I'm leaving for America alone. I cannot have a career, by myself, and have you too."*

In such a manner the child-wife, though hardly this by now except that her emotional life remained strangely undeveloped all through, left the guardian and protector who possibly now—third or fourth in succession from her dead father—had gone furthest in sharing her life. While Eugène had at first been to her all kindness and protection, he was in the end all wool and *eau de sucre*. He had not challenged her to grow up, only sought to arrest her at a convenient stage as a productive investment on which he would secure, and indeed did secure, his future—from fees she earned and which he kept.

Maggie and Plumon were divorced in November 1915, the divorce and costs awarded against Maggie, with the following judgement: "For some time the marriage was happy, but then the independent character of

---

* Prima donnas often seemed to lead parodies of one another's lives. Compare Olive Fremsted's preaching of celibacy: "Marriage is not for serious artists."[29]

Madame Plumon became stronger from day to day ("le caractère indépendent de la dame Plumon s'affirma de jour en jour davantage").[30] On arriving in America Maggie wrote Plumon that she wanted no more to do with him, and wrote again six months later to him, "Let me tell you once and for all I've finished with married life." This was the last he heard from her.

From the time of Maggie's adoption by the Rubens family she had severed all connection with her own. There was one exception to this: Marguerita Ninetta Odoli-Tate, the child of her crippled sister Marie, whose guardian Maggie became during the Great War. After Marie had died from puerperal fever, nine months after the child's birth, her husband, the Tuscan Odoli from Cameri, had looked after the child with help from the loyal Tate nurse, Holly. Odoli, who worked day and night as a waiter and spoke little English, had his troubles: he had erysipelas, and fell from the first-floor window of his flat, badly cutting himself. When the War began he returned to Italy to join his Alpine regiment, and was never heard of again, though later his daughter was apportioned some family land, the right to which was waived by Maggie. The nurse, Holly, responsible for the child, took to drinking with a man called Walter, leaving her charge outside pubs. Maggie, who had been contacted by Father Lawton, a Catholic priest from St George's School, Southwark, where the child went, sent instructions from abroad that she was to attend a convent in Croydon. There the child felt even more deeply deprived of any parents of her own.

Maggie bitterly resented her guardianship, as an interference with her own life and career. Far from considering the child a compensation for having none of her own, she treated Marguerita (who was known at the convent as Maggie Odoli but whom she insisted be known as "Rita", so as not in any way to clash with her own name), in cavalier, half-competitive fashion, always paying generously for schools, shopping expeditions to Harrods and other treats, experimenting on her when she first came to give lessons, but never visiting her at the schools she sent her to, or providing consistent and responsible attention. Rita never felt she belonged to Maggie Teyte at all, although as a child she hungered to belong somewhere and to someone.

When Rita was summoned to visit her guardian, after the First World

War was over and Maggie had returned to England as she thought for good, a grey-haired and stately looking maid, Mitchell, opened the door at her Cadogan Mansions flat. Rita was overawed, and when she was shown into the drawing room to meet Maggie, she took an instant dislike to a pair of snorting Pekingese dogs on silken cushions. "What's the matter, haven't you got a tongue?" were Maggie's first words to her niece. "This must be the effect the convent is having on you!" She then removed her from the convent and enrolled her at a healthy seaside school, the Girdlers, at Herne Bay in Kent, bewildering and smothering her with gifts of clothing. For the three years before that, Maggie had not written her a word and the nuns had been privately rubbing their hands over thoughts of a new novitiate. All through her early years the child was subjected to these violent alternations of mood on the part of her guardian: yet that Maggie loved Rita in her fashion there is no doubt.

Maggie's own mother Maria had an enviable death. Being very elderly and tired, and with a sense of life's completion aided no doubt by the eight lusty children she had borne and raised, in 1916 she informed everyone that her end was near, retired to bed, and shortly afterwards passed away without pain or apparent illness. Maggie took this for an assertion of will-power on her mother's part, which she herself attempted to copy without success, sixty years later; it may well have been something more passive, the recognition and acceptance of a different kind of will. But apart from this one attempt at emulation, Maggie seems to have had little feeling for her mother; and Rita became in the end the sole family tie that lasted.

Back in the States in 1915, Maggie subjected herself for the next four years to a hectic round of concerts, recitals, opera performances, and extensive travel. She toured with a famous company formed by Max Rabinoff, performing opera and ballet. They did two operas, *Madama Butterfly* and *La Bohème*, the first with Tamaki Miura—whose interest Maggie found to lie in her complete lack of sex in the Western sense, for she had the unawakened coquettish quality of a little girl—and the *Bohème* with Maggie as Mimi. After each opera performance there would be a ballet-divertissement in which Pavlova appeared, and which always ended with the "Dying Swan" from Saint-Saëns's *Le Carnival des animaux*.

Maggie was captivated by the beauty of the dancer's legs, which she saw as being like the stem of a flower; but Pavlova herself was quite ugly, "which you don't hear anyone say when they reminisce!" And she was a very bad-tempered so-and-so. But how she could dance! Watching her as often as she could, Maggie never stopped marvelling at the way her feet floated, appearing never to touch the floor: there was not a moment when there was not a space between toe and stage. Another undying impression was of Pavlova's sadness: on the train she would pass through from her drawing room to the dining car, "a tragic, almost wraith-like figure drifting past, with just a pause for a greeting, spoken in French but in so subdued a voice as to be barely audible—then she would be gone."[31]

The old cob swan passed that way later too, in Teyte's time; almost, yet not quite, dying. On his last trip to America, when he was "about ninety-six", as Maggie related with huge relish, Saint-Saëns descended one day on the director of the Chicago Opera, causing a terrible how-do-ye-do. "Je veux une femme," he panted; "a woman . . . tout de suite." Everyone rushed about in a panic, until a suitable—and willing—candidate was found. But when they took her up to his room they found him lying on his back flat out on his sofa, a sad look on his face. "C'est trop tard," he said, "trop tard."

Now a single woman herself, Maggie leaned more in these years towards the profane side of her nature. After the divorce she never again called herself Madame Plumon. She appears to have formed, fairly soon after leaving Eugène, a serious attachment with a highly sensitive and intelligent young composer pianist, and there is no doubt she had other affairs. While not being exactly promiscuous, she decisively followed her inclinations, even if they often turned out to be short-lived. And when the affair was over her attitude was "Never let anything get you down— I give myself two weeks." Or, "I had an affair. It broke up. I moaned. And cried. And then"—here there would be that decisive choppy and catarrhal sound she made with her throat, reinforced by the descent of a hand on some hard wooden surface—"*chonk*!! On to the next thing." She showed wisdom in setting aside a short period in which to wallow in grief: she knew, even early on, the value of such a thing as emotional health.

The serious "romance" was with Charles Wakefield Cadman, who was seven years her senior, born in 1881. His special interest was in American

Indian music, on which he lectured after visiting the Omaha Indian reservation. It was shrewd of Maggie to spot his talent, for after their liaison he became the first American composer ever to have an opera done at the Met in two consecutive years: *Shanewis* (*The Robin Woman*), first produced on 23 March 1918.*

As early as the summer of 1912 Maggie had given two successful recitals in London at which only American songs were presented, and she continued her tremendous service to American music by including in her repertoire a liberal offering of the best-constructed examples, to encourage the native school of composition. In this way she was transferring to America the experience she had gained in Paris of the fertile interchange between artists of the first rank and composers, just as she brought to her operatic impersonations a simplicity and directness, a technical relaxation which overwhelmingly proclaimed the virtues of de Reszke's training.

Along with Cadman's songs she sang works by John Alden Carpenter, C. Whitney Coombs, Rudolf Friml, Sidney Homer, Marshall Kernochan, Charles Martin Loeffler, Ethelbert Nevin, James H. Rogers, and many others. She went with Cadman on his tours, and was present at a concert given by the Indian mezzo, Princess Tsinina, or Redfeather. Another person who was there,† ten years old at the time, has supplied this eyewitness account:

The time: Tuesday March 9, 1915.

The place: Backstage at the Loring Opera House, Riverside, California.

The occasion: Concert given by Charles Wakefield Cadman, composer, pianist and lecturer in America Indian music, and Princess Tsinina or Redfeather, soprano, presented by the Tuesday Musical Club of Riverside through the auspices of L. E. Behymer, Los Angeles impresario.

My mother, Mrs B. K. Marvin, President of T.M.C. at that time, promised to introduce me to Princess Tsinina.

* The libretto was by Nellie Eberhart, who had kindled Cadman's interest in indigenous folk music. Mrs Eberhart also wrote the words for his set of *Four American Indian Songs*, which Maggie sang at concerts. One of these, "The Land of the Sky-Blue Water", had been made popular by Lillian Nordica.

† Elma R. Marvin, who wrote this in 1977.

Imagine meeting a real live Indian Princess!

In honour of the occasion I picked a bunch of violets from our garden and just before the concert Mother took me backstage where I gave Princess Redfeather my small offering.

It was then that I met Maggie Teyte. She and Mr Behymer had accompanied the artists to Riverside for the concert. I fell in love with Miss Teyte because she was so beautiful and gracious.

While she was in California Maggie herself gave concerts, the following Sunday afternoon, and again a week later, which the *San Francisco Chronicle* reviewed. But she was not to settle down in California as Cadman did soon after this; he later turned his hand to a different kind of indigenous music, with works such as his *Hollywood Suite* (part of it dedicated to Charlie Chaplin), and was one of the founders of the Hollywood Bowl. He had poor health, a tendency to tuberculosis for which the Californian air did wonders, and this may well have been why their romance failed to blossom into marriage. So the hummingbird, whose nationality (at least in press notices) became markedly more English the longer she tarried in America, and less French, Irish, or any of its other components (not that her passion for America ever then, or ever afterwards, seemed to diminish), remained still in the mood to flit from place to place, resting only a little while on each bough, though Cadman's was an especially congenial one.

The American was out of the picture by February 1916, when Maggie became engaged—briefly and unconvincingly—to a British war hero, Lieutenant Seymour Robertson. This whole episode smacks of a shrillness Maggie usually managed to keep out of the headlines and revealed only in private. In London briefly after the battle of Ypres, she noticed in the casualty lists the name of a Second Lieutenant Robertson whom she had known in her youth. She had to wait to see him while he had his left arm amputated. When they met she declared at once, "I want you to marry me." The Lieutenant protested that he was a "broken and shattered wreck", but she had her way and they became engaged. In this vagrant variation of love-sickness she seems to have taken French *symboliste* inspiration too far. At any rate a few weeks later the announcement was forgotten and Maggie was back in America.[32]

Mexico was another area of the New World which briefly claimed her attention. Engaged to sing in Mexico City in 1916, she found herself travelling in the company of the great Spanish basso Andrea de Segurola. He dressed very suavely, crossing often to London to order his suits in Savile Row, and considered himself, in Maggie's phrase, "the bee's knees". When they entrained at New York he had two great trunks crammed with his wardrobe.

The journey took four days. When they reached Mexico Maggie, gaping in horror out of the carriage window, saw numerous dead bodies hanging in a matter-of-fact way from telegraph poles along the track: two or three years before there had been the Revolution, and they were still mopping up. It was a Monday when they arrived in Mexico City. When de Segurola went along to the luggage compartment to fetch his trunks, what did he find but that everything had been stolen. "And, my dear, do you know what they left him? A grey topper. That was all!" De Segurola was beside himself with fury, "but it served him right!"

Another de Segurola adventure unfolded one night when the singer met a beautiful woman and went to bed with her. The next morning he was lying back surveying everything with calm satisfaction when he noticed a boa constrictor sliding out from under the bed. "My God, with what speed he left her," said Maggie, "stark naked, clutching his clothes as he ran. And do you know what it was? He had forgotten he had gone to bed with a snake charmer!"

Artistically, Mexico City was a great disappointment, for an obvious but easily overlooked reason. At 6,000 feet Maggie found she simply could not breathe, and after ten days there she abandoned any attempt to sing and went back to New York. The thin air had defeated her, but the boisterous audiences in the few operas she had sung, she relished hugely.

In the last two years of Maggie Teyte's first American career—she was to have a second, based mainly in New York but separated from the first by twenty-five years—she gathered still more operatic honours. Ruth Miller, the fine American coloratura, tells of an incident in Pittsburgh. Maggie was to have sung Gilda in *Rigoletto*, but stood down for Miller when the latter expressed a desire to try to impress the conductor of the Ravinia Opera Company, with which she wanted a contract. About four in the afternoon Maggie called the manager to say she was "indisposed", and suggested that Ruth Miller take her place. So Miller got her chance, won her contract, and this led to her singing later with Maggie in New York. The story of one prima donna standing down for another is unique, declared Miller. "I know of no other singer to be so generous."[33]

For the Davis Opera Company, as well as Gilda Maggie sang Giulietta and Antonia in Offenbach's *Tales of Hoffmann*. With the Henshawe Company, which toured the Middle West, she sang Fiora in Montemezzi's *L'Amore dei tre re*, with Moranzoni conducting, while for the Society of American Singers, at the Park Theatre in New York, she sang Mignon. In the latter role she opened the season, on 23 September 1918, before an audience of habitués of the Met, managers and devoted patrons of music, and men and women themselves eminent as artists. Grenville Vernon in the New York *Tribune* wrote that Teyte's portrait was a veritable masterpiece; rarely had the operatic stage witnessed such an exquisite blend of acting and singing as was provided by this "little Englishwoman". Geraldine Farrar was in a box, noted the *New York Times*, following the action of her prototype Maggie Teyte with undisguised and rapt attention. That *Mignon* had been written by a composer born in Metz, now in German hands, and that its heroine, darling of France, was (although originally from Goethe) the brain child of an artist of the "lost provinces," gave the production an added fillip. An enthusiastic gallery sent down the first thunders of applause. Sylvester Rawling, in the *Evening World*, noticed a particular Teyte trait, when faced with overwhelming adulation: "the floral tributes", he wrote, "were not obtrusive, save for Miss Teyte's reluctance to notice them."

Equal honour was accorded Maggie in the concert field, leading her to quip that her concert manager assured her there was no future for her in opera, her operatic impresario to claim that she could make no further progress in concert work: "Wouldn't it be terrible if they were both right!"[34]

Covering the many concerts she gave between 1911 and 1919, the American critics left a record of her singing which can hardly be improved on, either as a description of her particular voice, or as an account of any singer's voice at a particular time. For this was a golden age of vocal appreciation, with writers such as W. J. Henderson, Philip Hale, Richard Aldrich, H. E. Krehbiel, and Henry Taylor Parker all vying with one another to sustain the mellifluous and ecstatic stream of valuations, all remarkable for their loving grasp of vocal technicalities. It is little wonder that the great singers all congregated in the States at this time—money apart, that is, which was not quite everything to them, for in addition there was such a wealth and quality of critical appreciation.

How, at her best, Maggie responded to being in America was best summed up by the *Ohio State Journal*: "With a voice like a thrush, eyes as roguish as a March wind, and a smile like a breath of spring, this diminutive prima donna sings as if singing were the best fun in the world, and there is a freshness and spontaneity about the way she does it which makes her most captivating." Less rustic and down-to-earth, Henry Taylor Parker still spoke of this child of nature who was Maggie Teyte in distinctly open-air imagery; her *symboliste* quality, before all else, was the appeal he was able to render in exquisitely turned prose: "A distinctly French voice," he called it, ". . . a very bright voice which has been polished into a kind of dry clearness. . . . It falls on the ear much as the light of a very clear, dry, cool, still autumn day falls on the eye. There are glints in Miss Teyte's tones; they are transparent, prismatic, catching many reflections from the music and the mood of the songs. . . . It is a voice for connoisseurs."

Impossible it might seem to improve on such a description, yet in a notice which appeared on 17 November 1911 of her first New York concert, the great *New York Times* critic, Richard Aldrich, had made a remarkably specific assessment of her art:

Her voice is an almost startlingly powerful one to come from a person of her diminutive stature . . . she showed in her singing yesterday a talent and temperament of no mean order. In its best tones, which are heard in her *mezzo voce*, her voice has real beauty, though it has no great range of color and expressiveness. It is not a luscious voice. It has often a reediness; its prevailing colour is pale. When it is used with greatest power it is apt to take on a hard, even acidulous quality. . . . She is a singer of exceeding intelligence, of fine taste and musical feeling, of a commanding temperament that produces results sometimes unlooked for. In phrasing and in finish of style her best is of remarkable excellence. . . . She has the power of entering deeply into the spirit of what she sings and finding characteristic expression for it, and in her most successful attempts the results were exceedingly interesting and had individual beauty. Such were the two poetical songs by Duparc, "L'Invitation au voyage" and "Extase" and Hué's "J'ai pleuré en rêve", presented with a seizing intensity. . . . Equally appropriate to their character was her singing of songs by Debussy, "C'est l'extase langoureuse" from Verlaine's *Ariettes oubliées*, the "Fantoches" from *Les Fêtes galantes*, and "La Chevelure". Her enunciation in the songs in her native tongue was not quite so good as in the French ones.[35]

Like the London *Times* the year before, it was now the turn of the *New York Times* to rap her over the knuckles for forgetting her English.

CHAPTER EIGHT

The Nightingale of Maidenhead Thicket
(1919–1930)

For everything that's lovely is
But a brief, dreamy, kind, delight.
W. B. YEATS

BED-RIDDEN, VOICE CRACKED with age and slurred with arterial deterioration, only a year or two from the end, Maggie remembered the nightingale she had heard fifty years before: "The last time I heard the nightingale was at Woolley Grange, outside of Maidenhead, the other side of Maidenhead . . . Woolley Grange. And the night—it was a most beautiful moonlight night—and I heard the nightingale in my grounds. The silence, its supreme silence . . . and that's the only way we can hear a nightingale. . . . Have you ever heard a nightingale? Oh, it's the most marvellous thing in the world . . . and there was a brilliant moon and it was—'borne to me'—let's quote the poet . . . it was—un-moody . . ."[1]

The memory blurs finally, the recollection is too taxing. The poignancy is unexpected too, and seemingly never otherwise shown in talking of the period she spent at Maidenhead. She lived there from 1921 to 1936, till the death of her second husband, though by 1936 she was no longer living with him, and he had remarried.

The nightingale is a shy, retiring bird, dowdy and short of length, an unglamorous version of the robin redbreast. The cock sings, the hen does not—a sexual contrast Maggie noted with irony when talking of the greater power and ease of the tenor voice as compared with the soprano—but the voice lasts only a short time each season. It has a brief climax of beauty, manifested not only in the night but in the daytime, and then diminishes to a croak, even before summer is ended.

The thicket to which Maggie retired soon after she returned from the United States, after almost fifteen years of uninterrupted work as a prima donna, could not have been a more favoured and congenial country seat. It lay on the western edge of Maidenhead, in Berkshire, on the Bath Road which intersects the town at the thirtieth milestone from Hyde Park Corner. The Thames Valley air must have recommended itself at once to her gentler senses, even though many times during the following fifteen years she was to demonstrate a capacity like that of Lady Macbeth for screwing her courage to the sticking place—though stopping short of murder, in deed if not in thought.

Littlewick Green, the nearby village, had existed since Roman times, although subsequently like the rest of England, it became a place of barbarian decline, the inhabited areas overgrown with woods and plagued with wolves—the name Woolley is derived from the Anglo-Saxon *Wulfa Leage*, meaning "Wolves' Glade".[2] The open wood to the north was at the beginning of the eighteenth century called "No man's land", having but a few hovels scattered about it. The character of the neighbourhood must have been deeply attractive to Maggie: not only had woods been part of the landscape of her early childhood, consciously and unconsciously assimilated in the picturesque, tree-covered part of Wolverhampton where she had lived—the name of Lady Wulfruna of Dunstall was also intimately linked with the presence of wolves and woods—but also she had lived imaginatively for so long in the sylvan recesses of Arkel's estate, its sombre majesty and brooding unplumbed mysteries, that it is not surprising that the first chance she had had to inhabit in reality something near to it in beauty and force, should have been seized upon vividly and eagerly. She needed something as different as possible from the ceaseless exposure night after night from coast to coast in America, from the fêted transatlantic trips home prior to World War One, from the equally demanding though extremely luxurious tours of the French and Monégasque Riviera.

So at the end of the First World War she had sent a cable to Lionel Powell, her London manager: "Must come home. Please find me something to do."[3] There had been restrictions on travel from the States during the war, and ever since the *Lusitania* had been sunk—Maggie had had a passage booked on it, but arrived late for its sailing—she had been cautious of sea travel, except under the most favourable conditions. Powell had replied: "Messager is having his opera *Monsieur Beaucaire* presented. Would you like to be in it?" She wrote at once to say yes, she would.

After the taxing roles she had sung in America, creating the part of

Lady Mary Carlisle, which she did on 19 April 1919 at the Princes Theatre in London, must have seemed a prelude to the calmer and more peaceful life she was to enjoy over the next years. She spoke of this period as her "retirement", by which she meant she sang little and felt no pressure to earn money. Messager, who had conducted the world première as well as some of the performances she gave of *Pelléas et Mélisande* at the Opéra-Comique, was an old friend.* Maggie was also on excellent terms with his wife Hope Temple, whose songs she sang in recitals. Messager's operettas were popular: *La Béarnaise, Véronique, Mirette, Les P'tites Michu,* and *Monsieur Beaucaire†* all at one time or another enjoyed successful runs on the London stage. They were clever, pleasing, gay and full of touches of musicianly refinement: the recipe for success in a now-vanished canon of taste. They conveyed an atmosphere of relaxed charm, with spirited duets and sparklingly innocuous intrigues, "avowedly light but undeniably pretty." Maggie was delighted with the stage production of *Monsieur Beaucaire*, and Messager's score, its inimitable orchestration—"he does the most delicious things with a simple flute, or a clarinet backed by a light pizzicato on the strings, or a simple arpeggio on the harp"⁵—and she loved the song "Philomel" which Messager wrote specially for her, after seeing the preview in Birmingham, in the twenty-four hours before the opening. This, as often with last-minute additions, became the great success of the show, although it hardly cut deeper than the surface of its subject matter:

> Philomel, Philomel, waken as of old,
> Sing a violet into the dell,
> With every note of gold,
> Till the rose's cup uncloses,
> Under the summer rain,
> All the earth is joy and mirth,
> The gods are come again;

* Messager came to the dress rehearsal of *Monsieur Beaucaire* and the pre-London try-out in Birmingham. Some years before he had been artistic director of Covent Garden, a post he held for several seasons with, as Debussy said approvingly, "the perfect and unerring taste which everyone expects of him."⁴ He had also been general director of the Opéra-Comique and joint director of the Paris Opéra.

† Rudolf Valentino later starred in a Hollywood verson of *Monsieur Beaucaire*, derived, like the opera, from the famous stage play by Lewis Waller; but the first film of it, made in London with Maggie Teyte, probably silent extracts, was never released.

—no hint here of the grim and bloodthirsty tale of Pereus's lust for his wife's younger sister; of his forcing her to lie with him; of the older sister, tongueless, wandering around in circles; of other even more gruesome occult griefs leading to the nightingale's melancholy song. The story of *Monsieur Beaucaire*, a romantic tale of high society, had nothing to do with a nightingale either, but in "Philomel" the mixture of a gay Scottish folk-song element with an occasional dark and melancholic shade, to bring out the natural mezzo colours of the voice, showed how well Messager knew his Maggie Teyte.* More prophetically, the librettist—who was not Messager's usual librettist, Albert Carré, but Adrian Ross—may not, in the few hours available to him, have managed to find any original images: but he did capture an element of significance with two lines of the second verse:

> And the nightingale in the dusky dale,
> Gave word that the gods were coming.[6]

The "gods", as far as Maggie was concerned, were a pair of Canadian–American millionaires, Walter Horace Cottingham and his son Walter Sherwin, or "Sher" as he was known for short. Father and son had crossed the Atlantic a few years before and settled in Maidenhead, from where they assumed ownership and then ran the long-established paint firm of Lewis Berger & Sons, whose founder, 130 years before, had invented Prussian Blue. W. H. Cottingham, born in Omemee, Ontario, in 1866, had risen the hard way, reputedly by peddling paint in Montreal, then by manufacturing it on a $25 formula, and for some years before settling in England had been a power in the world's largest paint organization, the Sherwin-Williams Company, based in Cleveland, Ohio.[7] The offspring of impoverished Protestant Irish merchant stock, he showed many of the admirable traits, and some of the less admirable ones, of the self-made transatlantic pace-setter. Dark-haired, powerfully built, with a square determined jaw, punctilious and efficient, he had been talked into taking over the London business by Bergers' North American manager, James W. Garson, and when he arrived, in or after 1905, he set to work with commendable energy, augmenting the range of paint products,

* "One hardly knew if it was those dainty trickeries or the charm of Miss Teyte's singing," said *The Times* about "Philomel".

launching into the manufacture of chemical insecticides, and establishing, with great rapidity, large factories in Sydney, Australia, in Durban, South Africa, in Wellington, New Zealand, and later on, in 1925, a Paris branch of the business. Curiously enough Bergers bought a house in rue de la Faisanderie only doors away from No. 53 where de Reszke had had his school.

Business was Cottingham's sole interest in life, and he was a multinational visionary. "Cover the earth" was his cry—he dreamed of his company as a self-contained unit, producing its raw materials, owning smelters and oil mills. He believed in a diversified line and in sales campaigns—"Get out and hustle," he told his workers. One of his favourite sayings—he was a man of codes and mottoes—was "A dead fish can float with the stream, but it takes a live one to swim against it." A devoted reader of the biographies of great men, he wrote a booklet called *Business Success*, where these verses appear:

> A little more persistence, courage, vim,
> Success will dawn o'er fortune's cloudy rim.
> Then take this honey for the bitterest cup,
> There is no failure save in giving up.[8]

Before W. H. Cottingham bid for Woolley Hall and Grange, and the surrounding estate, on 18 September 1912, partly by private treaty and partly at an auction, it had been owned by George Dunne, a Catholic of kindly manner and gentle temper who had died in his forties of pneumonia. Dunne had lived all his life as a recluse.* It was rumoured that his withdrawal from the world, which was total—he refused a high post in the British Museum and this can hardly be described as being in the public eye—was the result of his brother's elopement with his fiancée, though which brother it was—one was a Monsignor stationed in Fulham who conducted the requiem mass on George's death—was never established.[9] George Dunne was one of "England's most learned men", as the Maidenhead *Advertiser* wrote on his death (their obituary notice copied almost word for word from that in *The Times*), his collections of rare bindings, of monastic books of the thirteenth century, and of rare clocks—he had more than eighty, all of which he could mend himself

* Dunne broke his seclusion once a year, when he would take his horse and trap, drive to Henley, and there pay his rates.

(they were later sold at Christie's)—all being unique. He also kept at Woolley Hall a telescope which weighed a ton; it was one of the finest in the world, and took some of the largest and most highly detailed photographs of celestial bodies then in circulation. Whether these were adequate compensation for the loss of terrestrial bodies to contemplate is not known, but poor George Dunne's astronomical and antiquarian concerns did not bring him long life and happiness. He fortified his desire for solitary scholarly pursuits by planting trees, on which he is credited with spending, between 1887 and 1912, some £70,000 (though this is more likely to have been £7,000).[10]

One of the 4,051 millionaires who in 1912 owned 87 per cent of America's wealth (top of the league were John D. Rockefeller, with $600 million, Andrew Carnegie with $300 million, and W. W. Astor with $200 million), W. H. Cottingham, a widower, was worth an estimated £4 million, or $20 million, so the upkeep of such an estate cannot have taxed his resources unduly. The year he moved into Woolley Hall with his fifteen-year-old son—his wife had died and was buried in Lakeview Cemetery, Cleveland, and his other three children remained in the New World—Maggie had just given her first song recital at Carnegie Hall in New York.

Oddly enough, Cottingham did not, as might be expected, open the estate to let in the fresh air of the outside world; his first action was to build gates everywhere: main gates, side gates, iron fences, boundary gates. He converted Dunne's observatory into a summer house, dug a deep lily pond, and added a magnificent balustraded and paved terrace.[11] He also, once he was a little more settled and the First War out of the way, took a second wife, on 12 March 1919, a Mrs Jacqueline Miller, formerly Devereux. She has been described variously as handsome, attractive, beautiful—with auburn hair, a tall figure, and excellent taste in clothes. So Walter Horace had made a good catch, if an unconventional one, for she was twenty-six, French, and only a few years older than his son Sherwin, while he himself was fifty-two. Jacqueline had a strong practical sense; an ante-nuptial agreement with Walter insured her of a settlement after his death. Being Canadian, Walter liked travelling to France, and besides Jacqueline Devereux, he acquired an interest in Citroën cars, which strengthened the connection.

Sherwin Cottingham was still living part of the time in Cleveland when he and Maggie met, in 1919. He was very tall, six foot two, with dark wavy hair and a boyish, engaging smile. He was athletic and competitive, a quality Maggie admired in men. He played golf, as she did. He liked expensive fast cars, as she also did. He was rich, and she loved money, and above all what it could buy cheaply at that time—service. He was also faithful, not being a womanizer, but he had a gauche, instant generosity— if he saw an attractive woman at a table in Fouquet's he might send over a basket of flowers without ulterior motive—and this warmth of heart Maggie found appealing. He was, for Maggie who was now in her early thirties, a highly desirable prize to be won and enjoyed. Because he possessed a certain North American flamboyance, and spent his money without reserve, he attracted a good deal of attention wherever he went. He was aware of his attractiveness and of his high degree of eligibility, and his father kept him under scrutiny, vetting his would-be wives and checking his business arrangements. "He was so beautiful," Maggie said, "I was surprised he ever looked at me."[12]

Though Maggie was beautiful too, she was some years older. She knew how to use her charm, how to be roguish and provocative; how to appeal perfectly to a very well-defined, sporting type of masculinity. And she knew how to keep her distance, as he did. Had he fallen for her instantly and displayed lapdog devotion, she would have spurned him quickly and without mercy. She held such men, who were legion at that time, in utter contempt, and felt absolutely no pity. That was a kind of weak love whose nature she understood only too well. It existed for her solely to be trampled on, though it gave her no pleasure to do so.

On many counts Maggie and Sherwin were an ideal match. She possessed independence and prestige of the kind that conferred a certain aristocracy on her partner. She was a very much sought-after member of society by now. She was witty and tough in a way few women at that time permitted themselves to be, but her success, especially the American side of it, gave her licence to say as she pleased and do as she pleased, and she took advantage of it. It was true that she was a divorced woman, but the Cottinghams were a liberal-minded family and ignored local gossip. Walter, after all, had married a woman twenty-six years younger than he, and people had gossiped then.

Maggie and Sherwin both led very active professional lives. Sherwin had been given a post in Berger paints, and helped his father run his other interests, in Oceda mops, and in Cubitts the builders. There was no reason why he should not build himself a career as his father had: he had plenty of time to do so. He had already distinguished himself in the war, as an officer in charge of a balloon in an artillery Forward Observation Post.

And he and Maggie had genuine feeling for one another. They were in love. Maggie, who always claimed she believed in fate, had consulted for the second time in her life a famous clairvoyante, Evangeline Adams, who read her horoscope. Miss Adams, whose reputation had been enhanced by a celebrated trial, at the end of which the judge concluded that she "had raised astrology to the dignity of an exact science",[13] had been visited by many opera singers, among them Caruso. Fortune-telling flourishes in any age of intellectual and sexual emancipation, and Maggie had been to see her in 1917, at her famous studio in Carnegie Hall. Miss Adams had told her, rather banally, that she was going to marry a tall, dark, handsome young man. Maggie was so deeply superstitious—her life had been taken out of her hands and directed by others from such an early age—that no doubt her will, when she saw the opportunity, assisted her to make the prediction come true.[14]

The opportunity came on her voyage back to England to play in *Monsieur Beaucaire*. Sherwin Cottingham was travelling on the same boat. If he had not already spotted her and sent over a basket of flowers, she would have been decisive enough to forge the introduction herself. They had plenty to talk about because Sherwin went frequently to the theatre, when he was in London, and often invited the principals back to Woolley Grange for the weekend. Beatrice Lillie (later Lady Peel), Gladys Gunn and Fay Compton were among his friends, and he may have known Maggie's brother, Jas. W.; he certainly had entertained Jas.'s step-daughter, José Collins. He and Maggie met soon after, in London, at a party, and as they grew to know each other better, he told her his age, twenty-eight, and she told him hers—thirty-two. Four years was not an insignificant gap, if they were thinking of marriage, which he un-doubtedly was. But red-headed, petite as she was, she looked as young if not younger than he; the pace of life was already beginning to tell around his eyes.

Love between them grew over the succeeding months, but not intimacy or knowledge. Maggie now had a house over the road from Harrods, Knightsbridge Cottage, tucked away entirely surrounded by a garden, and she saw Sherwin on his trips to town, to Hackney where the Berger paint works had been since the eighteenth century. She was a frequent visitor to Woolley Hall, where she became friendly with Walter, and with Jacqueline. They found her charming, worldly, and highly intelligent, and Walter respected her shrewd sense of business and loved to hear her sing. Sherwin was not enamoured of the human voice to a marked degree; he was more interested in flying, driving fast, playing golf, and, more ominously, in drink. By nature he was a dolphin: he loved simply to play.

A curious feature of that age was that servants often knew their masters and mistresses better, and vice versa, than masters and mistresses knew each other; a chauffeur was often a better confidant for a man, a cook or maid-in-waiting for a lady, than a wife for a husband. If Maggie had talked to Sherwin's footman, Fred Cummings, or the butler, Henry Scribbins, or the chauffeur, who went by the unlikely name of Roland Beresford Wheeler and was known as Bert, she might have been fore-warned of the problems she was shouldering in marrying Sherwin. For he was weak on two fundamental counts: in health and in character. These for a while remained hidden under his outgoing charm and generosity, his bravery and good humour, and his considerable prowess, endearing him to his country neighbours, at outdoor sports.*

It was his heroic qualities in the 1914–18 war which led to his weakness in health. Artillery observation balloons in northern France were sitting targets for German aircraft and guns, and the crews often had to para-chute to safety: "Quick out of the basket" was their motto. Sherwin's balloon had been no exception; while all his crew were killed, he had escaped with a back injury and some damage to his kidneys.† He was often in pain and continually on drugs, heavy doses of pain-killers which he supplemented liberally from his cocktail cabinet. But he was not deterred from flying by this crippling experience—rather the reverse: he seems to have been stimulated to embrace greater danger. He bought a weird and exciting outfit known as the Personal Flying Service, based at No. 92 Piccadilly, which flew out photographers and reporters to cover major disasters and other world events, for the delectation of the readers of the *Daily Graphic* and other Fleet Street papers. Herds of stampeding elephants and earthquakes were their speciality, and they employed such

---

* He was captain of the Temple Golf Course near Maidenhead for three or more out of the eleven years he played there.

† Lillian Nordica's husband, curiously enough, was also a balloon pilot.[15] One day he went up in his balloon, and never came down again.

dare-devil pilots as Nobbie Clarke (who went down with malaria in Marseilles on one trip) and Captain Starling, who flew an eccentric collection of machines. One, a Sikorski amphibian, was towed across the Atlantic behind the old *Mauretania*; on arrival they had to pull it out of the dock at Southampton where it had sunk. There was also a Junker, and a more conventional three-seater Henley fitted with a glass floor to give a good view of stampeding elephants.

In flying, as in much else, it was a carefree, highly individualistic age, in which people did not seem too much to mind dying. You could "stand still in the air", and air crashes were just beginning to become part of the national consciousness.* Air France had three crashes in one week, and one of the most spectacular crashes of the time was that of the airship R101 diving into a hillside near Beauvais. But a passenger in the 1920s did not suffer quite the utter helplessness of the jet airline age: Sherwin is reported on one Air France flight home to have disagreed so violently with the pilot on the course they were taking, that the two had to be restrained physically from coming to blows.

A balloon basket casualty on the one hand, Sherwin had also suffered emotional wounds which went much deeper and became, as time went on, harder to assuage. His mother had died when he was young, and his father had not been able to give him the care and attention he needed and deserved. The elder Cottingham travelled widely and frequently, and though he had an enviable ability to pick loyal and efficient servants who looked after the boy, he was not the kind of man to spot what was missing in his own son's development. He was too busy expanding the Sherwin-Williams and Cottingham paint empire, and when not doing that, improving and maintaining the Woolley estates. Added to this, he had a pretty and vivacious young wife, only a few years older than his son.

Sherwin had a younger brother, William, who is said to have died in 1932 by accident or by suicide (so it was rumoured in Maidenhead) in a garage in the States, and two sisters. War wounds apart, there was a discontented and melancholy streak in the Cottingham family, heightened possibly and pushed to extremity by the family's wealth,[16] and certainly more in evidence to the outside world as a direct result of that wealth. For Sherwin the possibilities of satisfying any desire he might have were

* R. B. Wheeler, Sherwin's chauffeur, was taught to fly while in the service. He had many narrow scrapes with Sherwin.

endless, but he lacked the motive or drive that might have stretched him beyond the point where he was bored or unhappy. It is people such as he who fall deeply and impulsively in love, and this is what he did when he met Maggie.

So much so, that he completely misled her about his own age. She promised him such a great deal—a firmness, an emotional stability, a strength of character he sorely lacked—that he grew terrified of losing her. He told her he was twenty-eight, when he was really twenty-four.

She for her part was no less deceitful. She kept from him the full facts of the operation performed in Paris when she was married to Eugène which made it impossible for her to bear children. In any case she had only a hazy notion of what had been done, and had been assured the operation was reversible. So she remained silent about it.*

Maggie and Sherwin were married on 12 March 1921. By then *Monsieur Beaucaire* had come to an end, cut short by a strike of backstage workers. It had played to packed houses for six months, and Maggie had been signed up more or less straight away to appear in another light opera, this time Viennese. Another pretty and not too taxing role was ideal to combine with the last stages of hers and Sherwin's engagement, and for William Boosey, one of the managers who presented *The Little Dutch Girl* and who went across to Vienna to make arrangements with the composer, Emmerich Kalman, Teyte was exactly right for the *hollandaise* Princess Julia.[17] The piece opened in December 1920† and, like *Monsieur Beaucaire*, ran for six months before the Lyric Theatre was shut down in the miners' strike of 1921.

There was no honeymoon, "No Honeymoon for Me", ran the head-lines, "Prima Donna Too Wedded to Her Work".[18] The Lyric Theatre management were not informed of the marriage until the night before—the wedding took place on a Saturday morning—and Maggie played the Saturday matinée, receiving an enthusiastic reception from the matinée

* Other traces of Plumon she could and did erase, such as her French nationality. She did this on 4 June 1920, when her name appeared in the *Gazette* in a list of 310 aliens "Naturalized British".

† "Miss Maggie Teyte's voice is heard to such great advantage that one could not help regretting at times that it had not been possible to keep the production on the level of comic opera. But then, presumably, we would not have had such fun" (*The Times*, 2 December 1920).

audience and bouquets and baskets of flowers from Cicely Debenham, Lauri de Frece, Jack Hulbert, and Martin Iredale, the other leading singers in the cast. "I will go straight on with the work I love," she told a reporter, but even so the management let her off the evening performance.

The ceremony took place at the Buckingham Palace Road Registry Office, in the District of St George's, Hanover Square, on a sunny day when the papers carried photographs of springtime in St James's Park. Maggie and Sherwin had planned to marry quietly, but the plan went astray and they found themselves facing a battery of cameras and the smiles and greetings and pressure of scores of people who wanted to see "The Little Dutch Girl" marry. They had to wait in the prosaic office for twenty minutes, and when their party was called in the bride, it was reported, had reached a state of extreme nervousness. She laughed hard, and then looked almost grim. She shuffled her feet and toyed with her white kid gloves. The bridegroom was quite self-possessed. "Miss Teyte made a charming picture all the same. She was dressed in a walking costume of silver grey voile, with dainty cloak trimmed with satin of the same shade. Her hat was *en suite*, with tiny forget-me-nots."[19] The witnesses were Sherwin's father and John Burlison, husband of a sister of Walter Rubens; Olive Rubens was also there—Walter was too ill to attend—a Mr Josephs, and Maggie's faithful dresser Mitchell.

As they prepared to leave the Registry Maggie gazed in horror through the glass of the door. "Oh, what a lot of people. I cannot face them," she cried. "It's no good trying to hide yourself now," answered her more philosophical husband.[20] So the newly made Mrs Cottingham pulled the fur collar of her cloak round her face and ran like a frightened hare to the waiting car, which was large and blue, according to another reporter, who described Maggie as a "tiny, golden-haired woman".[21] A third noted that Mr Cottingham "has a slight American accent".[22]

As well as being confused by the throng, Maggie had seen something else which displeased her. Marriage ceremonies pass for most people in a haze of anxiety, euphoria, or intoxication of one kind or another. But Maggie, who retained her sharp eye and her judgement even in that moment, turned to Sherwin as soon as they were alone and asked him: "Why did you give your age on the marriage documents as twenty-four? You told me you were twenty-eight." "It's true," he replied. "I'm very sorry. I lied to you, for I feared you would never marry me if I told you how old I was."[23]

It was too late, but Maggie found herself bitterly and at once regretting she had married him. Outspoken she may have been, but she respected truth, and there was a crucial difference between a woman of thirty-two marrying a man of twenty-eight, and a woman of thirty-two marrying a man just turned twenty-four. She would be thirty-three in only a few weeks' time—nearly ten years his senior. Sherwin had been quite right: had she known his true age she would not have countenanced marrying him. And the reality of her situation was brought home even more sharply when she considered that her father-in-law was married to a woman also younger than herself.

Walter gave Sherwin and Maggie the dower house, or Grange, a few hundred yards from the Hall where he lived, as a wedding present. It was a whitewashed farmhouse with dark wood panelling in the main rooms and on the staircase, on the same pattern as that in the Hall itself. The Grange had escaped the excesses of many of Walter's additions to the Hall: the stained-glass windows of dubious taste, depicting subjects like Christopher Columbus on the high seas, making for the New World; the elaborate ceiling mouldings of roses; the liberal display of the Cottingham armorial crest—a bearded goat's head, or camel's head, above the letter C, and beneath it the motto *"Mens cujusque is est quisque"* ("As the mind of each, so is the man"), pressed out in white plaster. Like his own mottoes, Walter seems to have taken this last seriously.*

To her niece and charge, Rita, who now had a home to go to during the holidays from her school in Kent—otherwise she still shared a small flat in Bloomsbury with her old nurse Holly—life at Woolley Grange was absolutely marvellous. "Maggie was very happy," Rita says, "Sherwin was rich, handsome, they had this lovely house, they had three cars, a cook, maids, gardeners, everything that money could buy. Maggie was a very good driver, and with me in her own car, a Morris, we would pick up Sherwin from Maidenhead station. They were both good golfers,

---

* The crest and motto seem to have been borrowed from that of the 4th Earl of Cottenham, "a camel's head in erased or, bridled and gorged with a ducal coronet," with the same motto enlarged as

> He that has light within his own clear heart,
> May sit i' th' centre and enjoy bright day,
> But he that hides a dark soul and foul thoughts,
> Benighted walks under the mid-day sun—
> Himself is his own dungeon.[24]

and used to play a great deal at Sunningdale golf course. It was always open house at the Grange and many people came in for cocktails at noon and again at 6 p.m. and a great deal of drinking would go on. I learnt to play badminton there,* and also clock golf on the lawn. We always dressed for dinner. Maggie did quite a lot of sewing during the evening. She played the piano. I never heard her sing except if we went for a drive in the car and then she would do exercises for her voice. Sometimes Sherwin would take Maggie and me out for lunch, and would always buy me something such as peaches or an enormous box of chocolates. I was really spoilt, but I loved it. I hoped things would never change."

But even here the class barriers came down, causing their own separations, harsh for a thirteen-year-old girl: "The first blow came when Nana (Holly) was with me. Maggie said I must understand that I would not see so much of Nana, as she would be eating with the other servants, and living with them. I was very unhappy with this, as I had always lived with her."

Like her niece, Maggie enjoyed the luxury without any scruples, and without any guilt. She wore her superiority easily, gave her commands without fuss, hired and fired with her customary acuity, and spoke her mind, as ever, bluntly. One day she had to call in on a local firm called International in connection with a car, and found that one of their workers, a young man still in his teens, had fainted. Something about the boy took her fancy, and she sent her butler off to fetch some brandy to bring him round. When he recovered his senses, the young man was extremely surprised to find himself looking up at a well-dressed lady, who was plying him with brandy. When she offered him the chance of joining the Cottingham household, he was very much attracted. A private chauffeur's life could be an extremely good one, especially if you loved cars, and the very best cars, as he did.

"When would you like me to start, madam?" he asked. She fixed him with her shrewd blue eyes, one brow raised and half furrowed. The eyes were so bright and clear they seemed to be twinkling, bubbling over with amusement. "On Monday," she said. But that was impossible: "I'm afraid I shall have to give them a week's notice here," he told her.

* Again ahead of her time, Maggie was "one of the few prima donnas who keeps slim by exercise," wrote the *Liverpool Echo*. "At the house parties she gives she takes part in several genuinely energetic games of badminton. Miss Teyte's court has artificial lighting and a spectators' gallery just like a squash court."

"If you don't start on Monday, you won't get the job," she said, and strode off with her butler.

The would-be chauffeur stuck to his original promise and refused to come till he had served out his notice with the other firm. Finally, though, Maggie did take him on. In her eyes he had proved himself, and for her, loyalty was the first quality required in a servant. "Good," she said to him the first morning he drove her out in her two-seater Daimler. "If you don't let International down, you won't let me down." But she was impatient of his driving. "You're not going fast enough," she told him, and when he speeded up she said, "Now you're going too fast. Slow down!" He did as he was told, reserving his judgement of this curious and diminutive lady who was so imperious.

Their first visit to London by car almost saw the end of his employment at the Cottinghams'. She made him drop her off first at Harrods where she did some shopping. "Here's a pound for lunch and tea," she said. Then he took her to Savoy Hill, where she did a broadcast. The session here must have gone badly because on the way back to Maidenhead she was in a foul mood, and picked on his driving, telling him he was too near other cars, to keep away from them, when to overtake, when not to overtake. Near the end of the journey, he could not take any more of this. He turned round to her—she was sitting beside him—and said, "If you feel that way about me driving you, madam, I think you had better drive yourself."

She stiffened. "Don't you be insolent to me," she snapped, drawing her mink around and over her knees. "I'll speak to Mr Cottingham about you." It was then that Wheeler noticed her extraordinarily tiny feet, size 3 they must have been, strapped into a pair of high heels. "Pull up alongside the road!" was her next peremptory command.

He braked, and took the car straight away in to the side. "Get out," she said. He opened the solid Daimler door and stepped down on to the road. She hopped across into the driver's seat, and the Daimler shot off at full speed.

He started to walk the ten miles to the Grange, hoping he might pick up a lift from someone. But after a while what did he see but Maggie's Daimler come careering back, gravel and dust flying—she always drove very fast—and shuddering to a halt beside him. She wound down the window and, still thin-lipped and grim, said, "Get in!" to him. Then she drove him back to Maidenhead.

Next day she had forgotten the incident. He was not fired, and when she saw him she said, "Good morning, Wheeler, you've been a long time." He mumbled something, and thought he had better be sure what was happening. "Shall I drive, or do you want to drive, madam?" She exploded: "What do I employ a chauffeur for, if I don't want him to drive?"

Dogs were enjoyed, as well as servants. Maggie changed the pair of snorting Pekingese that had so intimidated her niece in London for bigger dogs, more of the golden retrievers owned by the stepmother-in-law younger than herself. She would exercise these dogs in the grounds, among the fifty or more varieties of trees which Dunne had planted, and which were now beginning to make an impressive spread of foliage. In all this hearty outdoor activity, the Teyte voice took a long rest, and recovered its pristine quality. She knew how to look after her greatest asset, and it was not by cosseting the vocal cords, by wrapping them in heavy protective clothing, that they were going to serve her as long as they did.

For two years she sang virtually nowhere. There were various explanations for this, such as that she had failed to secure a permanent position in one of the world's leading opera houses because she came at the tail end of the so-called Golden Age, and all the places were filled. But she hadn't the temperament, in any case, to thrive in a permanent position. She was too much of an adventuress, and quickly became impatient and would be seeking something new. Once she had done something well, she hated repeating herself. After all the record was there, in the notices, and she always scooped the notices; indeed it is hard to find one, except very early on, in which more space is not devoted to her than to anyone else. She had a strong sense of historical importance. She wanted to move on. She loved the restless, energetic pace of American life, and the great financial reward; but even there she had had no desire to settle.

But at Woolley Grange she refused almost all engagements. She loved Sherwin so much, she never wanted to sing again, she told her niece. When she and Sherwin visited the United States on holiday she had a lot of contracts offered her, but she turned them all down. In England she said "No" more subtly: she priced herself out of the market. She had given a recital on 4 December 1919; she gave a recital on 29 May 1924* but hardly anything between, except for a few appearances at Covent Garden, mostly as Butterfly. The Queen attended a special matinée of *Madama Butterfly* at the Chelsea Palace Theatre. Maggie sang so well the Queen sent for her. "Butterfly, in her make-up and kimono, looked like a Japanese doll against the tall lady in soft grey furs, but the 'doll' blushed through her paint as the tall lady rose and congratulated her on her performance." Maggie charged 50 guineas a recital, then a considerable fee in England, where a tenet of artistic life has been, and still is, that quality may be expected without the recompense being generous. In her case her rare appearances were almost an assurance of quality.† In one such rare prestigious engagement she toured Britain in 1926 with the French violin virtuoso, Zino Francescatti.[25]

Maggie was always willing to sing for her old patron Olive Rubens: Walter's (and now Lord Sackville's) Olive, still a beautiful woman, still an *artiste manquée*, but even more a great social figure. "I never refuse the Rubenses," Maggie said. She sang for the Duke of Westminster on the occasion of his departure from Grosvenor House, when he sat with her at the artists' table; she sang Debussy's early work *La Damoiselle élue* at Sir Walter Gibbon's house in Carlton House Terrace, with Churchill and Lord Beatty in the front row, their evening shoes sticking through the

* Both recitals were at the Aeolian Hall. At the first she sang old French songs (Méhul, Grétry), contemporary French, and some English songs; her accompanist was Amherst Webber. "Miss Teyte's power of throwing herself into the emotional effort without losing her purity of style was wonderfully shown," wrote *The Times* on 5 December 1919.

The American poet Ezra Pound, at that time reviewing music for *The New Age*, wrote (18 December 1919): "Maggie Teyte has what is usually, and can without irony be, called a 'divine voice'—fluidity, charm, ease, and notably the quality of seeming to fit snug into all the corners and crevices of the hall; whereas most voices, even quite good ones, seem to fill only a sort of amorphous area ending a yard or so from the edges of the room and leave the auditor with a sense of strain, or strained attention."

At the second recital she sang Franck, Webber, Dobson, and groups of old and modern French, Italian, and English, "mostly new to us" (*The Times*, 29 May 1924).

In between, she did appear—for the week of 17 October 1921—in Variety, at Sir Oswald Stoll's Coliseum. Sir Oswald made it well worth her while for "the well-known Operatic and Musical Comedy Artiste" to appear twice daily, at 2.30 and 7.45. Will Fyffe was on the bill with her.

† A possible exception was a production of *Pelléas* in 1924, at His Majesty's Theatre, with Percy Pitt conducting. The performances were sung in English, and as a result not, it seems, Maggie Teyte's best.

gauze and tickling the lovely titled ladies in the chorus; she sang it again at Lady Aberconway's house in South Street, where one of the angels was Tallulah Bankhead, huskily rasping out Debussy. She sang it later, with Boyd Neel, at Londonderry House for the Greater London Fund for the Blind, and again, in a Prom. Maggie was always prepared to dabble in rich bohemia, and to oblige friends. She attended wealthy functions, like the Shakespeare Ball at the Albert Hall: Lady Diana Cooper remembers her there, in a black velvet suit, as one of the princes in the Tower (the other was Olga Lynn). Even in frivolity her fantasy sported with the role of the innocent victim in need of protection, the child-like Mélisande. On a sombre note, she later sang at Percy Pitt's funeral the "Ave Maria" from Verdi's *Otello*.

She was also invited to entertain at the very apex of society. Between 1919 and 1923, the Prince of Wales travelled more than 100,000 miles, round the world. After his Indian tour Lloyd George and his Cabinet entertained him; and to the dinner they invited Maggie Teyte and Leila Megane, a Welsh contralto who had also studied with de Reszke and sung at the Opéra-Comique. Tom Jones, Lloyd George's private secretary, arranged the programme, and when they discussed it with Ivor Newton, who was to be the accompanist, Lloyd George told Newton, "Go easy with the programme. Not too high-brow. No one here understands music much. I mean Bonar Law might be able to manage 'Drink to me only with thine eyes', but for the others . . ."—the others being Lord Curzon, Lord Birkenhead, Lord Milner, Lord Lee of Fareham, Lord Balfour, Sir Eric Geddes, and Churchill.

The Prince was the only true connoisseur. Drawing his chair right up close to the piano, in front of the other members of the audience—a daunting procedure—he savoured the voices, beaming his bright blue eye and winning smile on the performers, and made a strong impression of youthfulness compared with the rest of the assembly. He reminded Newton of Vesta Tilley. "When he thanked us, he said to Maggie Teyte, 'I carried one of your records with me all through the war. It was "The Land of Might-Have-Been".'"*

But while Ivor Newton felt, and lovingly recorded,[26] the aura of majesty, Maggie did not. She shrugged it off, as she did other kinds of

* The record is unknown. It is possible the Prince was referring to "The Homes They Leave Behind" (Walter Rubens) or "Your King and Country Want You" (Paul Rubens), issued by Columbia on both 10-inch and 12-inch discs.

flattery. After the evening was over Lloyd George gave the three performers signed photographs—not of the Prince, but of himself. Had they
been of the Prince, Maggie might have kept hers; Newton certainly
would. But Maggie gave hers away—to the daily, or the cook. Ivor
Newton later sent his to Jeremy Thorpe, who appreciated Liberals more
than he did.

Life in the romantic kingdom of Allemonde, otherwise known as
Woolley Grange, lasted as long as any life conducted according to the old
high ways of love could possibly have done. Sexually Maggie was able
to satisfy Sherwin. She was a strong sensualist and frankly enjoyed the
act of sex, and after her schooling as a child wife, or little more, in the
sophisticated milieu of her first husband and his friends, the composers of
the Third Republic, the *symboliste* poets, Sherwin for her had something
of the earnest, well-meaning *ingénu*. She was a devoted wife, however,
and when her husband's back ailment worsened and he was sent away to
Bournemouth, Maggie went with him and nursed him with great
devotion—an action quite inconceivable to anyone who knew her later
in life, when she made a point of never visiting anyone she knew in
hospital.

The illness required more drugs. More drugs resulted in more drinking,
and outbursts of a new addiction: a boundless generosity. Maggie noticed
as the years went by that Sherwin's friends were not really to her taste.
They were a hard-drinking parasitic crew and, to a man, they egged
Sherwin on. At first their flattery was sweet, but soon she could not
tolerate their fawning. She tried therefore to keep them away from the
house, and as a result Sherwin grew devious and resented her interference.
She locked away the drink, she was becoming so desperate. She pointed
out his friends' shortcomings to him, and he hated her for it. He felt he
had even less self-confidence than before, and was driven to drink more
and more. He knew that no one in Morning Lane, Hackney, minded
whether he went to work or not, even though he had once carried out an
impressive piece of negotiation in the States for Berger Paints—only his
father appreciated it, promising him anything he wanted. (Sherwin had
chosen as his reward a Mercedes with a supercharger and new Bosch
plugs, its exterior body work covered in choice leather.) So he began
reasingly to take himself off to play golf, dispensing largesse quite

literally sometimes by the wayside, and to caddies—those in particular employed on Lord Nuffield's golf course, who were physically handicapped.

The prodigious way he gave away money grew alarming: whereas Maggie would give her chauffeur Bert Wheeler one pound for his day's expenses, Sherwin would give him five. "Here's five pounds to go to the pictures," he would say. It was more than the man's whole wages for a week. If a woman was at work washing down the steps on a stairway he was climbing, he would apologize for disturbing her and press a couple of pounds into her hand.

Sherwin's desperate emotional need for company cut across the class system. On the road he would not let his servants go and dine by themselves, eating a sandwich while he ate his oysters: he insisted they join him, and ate oysters too. The servants worshipped him, considering him kindness itself. Once one of them said to him, "Don't forget I'm only a servant." Sherwin replied, "I don't want you to say that. You're a friend."

A paradox of the twentieth century is that strong and independent women often choose as their husbands weak men, as if to prove to themselves that the male sex as a whole is petty and tyrannical and that they are therefore right in asserting their own power over it. Maggie, being older than Sherwin, tried to mother him, and while he may have wanted this, or needed it at a much earlier time, sadly it was too late now. And having sacrificed all of herself for him and for love, or so she thought, she began after a little while to wonder what she had left that truly belonged to her. Sherwin owned just about everything in sight: the houses, the farms, the old Titan tractors, the Mercedes with its gigantic chrome exhausts, and even some of the planes that flew overhead, from which he used to spy, very good-humouredly, on his tenants and their workers in the fields. But there was one precious thing, more precious than anything else, which he did not own: her voice.

One day they had a row over some of his cronies. He had promised to be back at a certain hour, and had kept her waiting. She was furious, and told Sherwin that if it was not for him, his friends would be selling matches outside the Piccadilly Hotel. Because she did not like to feel owned, she had spoken her mind when nine out of ten wives would have kept quiet.

Sherwin was coming to the stage where he needed a less exacting partner, someone who would not be jealous when he eyed a pretty parlour maid, someone whose sense of time was as hazy as his and who would not be for ever watching him and trying to keep him off the bottle, away from his friends. Maggie was the kind of woman he could never have looked at and lied. She had to be told the truth. He began to need a woman who could pretend a little more easily—someone who loved him weaknesses and all.

Worst of all Maggie found herself beginning to pity him. Her only out was to find her way, gradually, imperceptibly, back to singing. Oddly enough she found an ally in this in Sherwin's father, with whom she began to be more in contact than with Sherwin. He it was who raised the ceiling in one of the downstairs rooms at the Hall, installing a grand piano for her there, so she could come over and practise.

And gradually, imperceptibly, singing began to become for Maggie something different from what it had previously been in her life. She was no longer the precocious, perfectly trained technical artist whose interpretation was partly instinctive, partly a near-faultless memory of what she had picked up from the composers and interpreters of her early years. Singing began to take on for her something approaching a power of self-expression. This is perhaps why she had retired, or withdrawn. This is what she had wanted to find.

One day she looked at Sherwin. "I pity you," she said harshly. "Oh yes," he replied, half slewed as usual by eleven o'clock. "I feel sorry for people who can't sing." She looked quizzically at him. "Why do you look at me like that?" he asked her vaguely. "You've become a different person," she told him. It was true. Now when he drank he was beginning to change into another being altogether. He would not dress properly in the morning, going round until noon in dressing gown and slippers. He began to believe the servants were whispering behind his back, and laughing. On one occasion Mrs Howlett, the wife of the gardener who laid out the herbaceous borders with such care that Suttons Seeds in 1930 proudly used a photograph of the Woolley grounds to advertise their Spring catalogue, was chatting with Mrs Everett, the senior lady on the staff, when Sherwin fixed them with his drink-glazed eye: "What are you talking about?" he asked them. They told him it was just about a friend. "Oh, never mind," he said. "I thought you were talking about me. I thought you were laughing at me."

Maggie found the people she had to entertain with Sherwin more and more of a trial. They were business people: Australians, Canadians, and Americans, connected with Berger paints and Walter's great fit of expansion, and she was expected to chat with their wives, with whom she had nothing in common.

She might have had more in common with them if she had had a family. This was the crucial failure. She consulted specialists in Harley Street. She had an exploratory operation in which the whole of her abdominal cavity was opened up, from which she carried for the rest of her life a scar similar to that left by a Caesarean section. Still she was unable to conceive: the operation she had had years before in Paris, on her Fallopian tubes, was clearly not reversible, as she had believed.

It may be that if she had had a child Maggie would not have made a good mother. As it was, she tended to blame Sherwin for being impotent, a charge she clung to even after the end of their relationship.

So it was that the two lies told at the moment they came together began to weigh more heavily, even though the first, Sherwin's lie about his age, was exposed straight away. Another event was soon to give Sherwin a different kind of freedom from any he had hitherto known. This was the death of his father.

Evangeline Adams had foretold in 1917 that the year 1928 would be a lucky year for Maggie, but it was a curiously distorted form of luck, prefiguring the end of the marriage. For this was the year her father-in-law contracted infantile paralysis. He did not die for two more years, but it was his death, as Maggie said, that "caused the end of my married life".[27]

Walter Cottingham's great wealth hardly made his decline easier for him. At one time it was thought the creeping paralysis would necessitate the amputation of his fingers. In order still to be able to travel he paid over £1,000 to have the chassis of his car lengthened, to stop it vibrating. "With all my money," he told Mr Smith, the tenant of Feens Farm, "I can't buy health,"[28] and so in the end he was confined to an upstairs suite in the Hall, with two male nurses looking after him full time. He would call Maggie on the telephone: "Will you come and sing for me?" And off she would go, hurrying along the path between the trees and over the lawn separating the smaller mansion from the large. For this last of a series of father figures she had had since her own father died, she would sing the Hahn, the Debussy, which he genuinely loved. She sang Reynaldo Hahn's songs with little voice, like Reynaldo, accompanying herself on the piano. At other times she would push Walter around the grounds in a wheelchair, through the bluebell wood, across one of the "rides" he had fashioned which ran, straight as a die, to the top of a hill where he had built a small triumphal arch. When he was a fit man he had walked up there and back every day before being driven to town. She would wheel him down the lavender walk from the rose garden to the tea house, once the observatory from which the solitary Geo Dunne had scanned the planets. Cottingham Senior loved the mixed wall-flowers planted by Mr Howlett all round the terrace under the windows; in the evening the scent of stock would float in through the open windows.

And now she was singing more and more for herself, and practising more and more. She had started to become busy again, and she could be heard singing all over the estate. The servants would hover in the corridors outside. The high notes drove Sherwin mad, as years earlier in Adelphi Terrace they had driven the very differently addicted George Bernard Shaw, whose own father had been an alcoholic. When Sherwin's hangover was worse than usual the sound would make him flee the Grange. He was beginning more and more to go off by himself anyway. Maggie began to suspect that he had another woman, and she threw herself increasingly into her work—above all into broadcasting for the BBC, which blossomed at the end of the Twenties. "I have to work hard to live, and you have to work hard to live," she told her chauffeur.

It was at this time that Maggie began the deepest and closest friendship of her life, with a young woman called Grace Vernon—known to her friends as Gay, after the heroine of Scott's *Rob Roy*—who lived near by in Maidenhead. Gay, who was Jewish, had been given away by her parents, through an arranged marriage, to a man very much older than herself, the playwright and impresario Harry Vernon, who wrote *Mr Wu*, a successful West End play. An innocent young thing, she almost died on her wedding night—so shocking was her first encounter with sex—and from that night she hated Harry Vernon. They had a son, Bobby, whom she hardly ever mentioned, though he was around the place.*

* A very nervous person, Gay was not good at imparting confidence to others. One day she was very upset because her son was sitting a music exam, and he became so frightened he walked out of the exam. It was said subsequently that he went to bad, and died.

Gay was Maggie's opposite in may ways. She was thin, gentle, very feminine, quite an easy person to dominate, and deeply unhappy. She began coming over to see Maggie in the afternoon, with horror stories of her marriage, and Maggie responded with the tales of her own misery. They would cry together, and they had the most perfect means of lessening their misery: music. For Gay, a composer of musical-comedy numbers, was an excellent pianist and accompanist, as well as singing teacher, and she would play for Maggie. It was a stroke of great good fortune, for this was exactly what Maggie needed at this moment: another pair of ears, which were in a way an extension of her own, someone to act as a critical mirror who was at the same time very much in awe of her.

Maggie was beginning to put her training into a personal mould. As she matured as a woman her power of interpreting Debussy grew instead of diminishing—a tribute to the human experience of pain, of emotion and sensation he was able to distil in his work, and to which, where it concerned her, she held the key. And not only Debussy, others too: so Maggie came to the unusual situation of finding her singing, not only a discipline at which she worked to gain perfection of interpretation and technique, but a romantic form in a more personal sense, a form into which she managed to pour, in distilled shape, her own emotions, disciplining and purging them—and exalting them. This is why she remained such a balanced and fit person, and why she kept her voice and her vigour so long: she began to find release, poise, and beauty in what she sang. This is why, as she had said to Sherwin, "I feel sorry for people who can't sing."

Debussy cried much, a capacity of which he was inordinately proud. And Maggie, at this time, cried a great deal over the songs she sang. She would sing a song, with Gay accompanying. Then she would cry at the emotion she had awakened: cry so much that she did not want to cry any more. Then she would sing the song again. And this was the point at which she would be able to make her audience cry. So well now did she master this ability to convey an emotional experience, something of which she had never been capable before, that twenty to twenty-five years later this emotional quality was still uppermost in her singing. For the first time, therefore, Maggie found an identity in her singing: this was the real she. And she began at once to understand and explain, and to find her way around the songs and scores she had been singing for years.

This hardly lessened the blow when Sherwin at last admitted that there was another woman, a divorcée whom he had met in 1929 in Paris, where he often went on business; she was slim, very seductive, with a Russian accent. Slightly younger than he, having been born in Kiev in 1899 of Russian Jewish parents, Vera Sklarevskara had fled the Bolshevik Revolution at its height, and married a Captain Owen, said to be a British officer, at Constantinople in 1920. A friend of Francis Lorang, the absconding chairman of the Blue Bird Petrol Company who was later arrested in a Paris cabaret, she was reported in the press to be a familiar figure in many well-known resorts, where she attracted attention by playing for high stakes in the baccarat rooms, and by the expensive jewels she wore.

Maggie fell into an unspeakable rage. Plates flew fast across the spacious dining room at the Grange, shattering on the walls, and the servants all thought they were going to be given the sack. Sherwin, no doubt, like the gentleman he was, remained very detached, to some extent gratified that he was at last the centre of attention.

During these troubled years Maggie's niece, Rita, began attending the Royal College of Music, at which she gained a place with the help of some expert tuition. "Maggie announced to me that I was to leave the Girdlers and get ready to go to the Royal College," she remembers. "As Nana and I did not have a piano, I was to come to her at Maidenhead and she would coach me. She taught me the French and the interpretation of the Valse song, from Gounod's *Romeo and Juliet*. Such was her tuition that I got into the College. I learned a great deal from my teacher who was Johnstone Douglas.*

"Money was now coming from Bergers in the form of a cheque for £12 per week made out in my name, which was very generous of Sherwin. Maggie never came near the College to see me or any of the performances that I gave. Suddenly some of the other students and I heard of an audition for *Just a Kiss* being held at the Shaftesbury Theatre, so as a lark we decided to go. I sang a ballad and they asked if I could dance the Charleston. I said yes, which was not true as I had never even seen it done. I felt ashamed of lying, but even so they asked me to sign a contract, giving me two solo lines to sing, at £7 a week. I went back to college and told J.D. He was furious, and took me to Sir Hugh Allen the principal who told me that as I had signed the contract, I would have

* See Chapter 5.

to leave the College." Having started her off, Maggie was not taking enough notice of her niece.

Rita was now a highly attractive young woman, with jet black hair like that of her Italian father and soft brown eyes, but whose other features, if not quite as hard, bore a strong resemblance to Maggie's. During this time Rita had met Cavan O'Connor, also a student at the Royal College on a scholarship. Cavan, a gifted tenor of romantic appearance, tall and powerful, with the legendary Irish dark hair and blue eyes, had been born into a poor Nottingham family, and had served in France in the Royal Artillery. At other times he had worked down a mine, in an iron foundry, a barber's shop, and as a street busker.

"I had been seeing a great deal of Cavan," Rita recalls, "so we decided to tell Maggie that we wanted to become engaged. As I had been living since June 1926 with Nana in Redcliffe Gardens, Maggie came to meet him. Cavan will never forget that meeting. After all, Maggie did not associate herself with many people who were unknown. Or were not rich. She gave him an imperious look and said, 'What have you got to offer my niece?' He replied, 'Nothing now, but I hope to earn money with my voice and perhaps go into business.' But she bet me £10 that in two years I would change my mind.

"Cavan came with me once to meet Sherwin. We were invited to spend the day at Ascot. It was very lavish. Champagne flowed like water, and there was caviar."

Rita found, on her now less frequent visits to Woolley, that the atmosphere had changed. She heard gossip about Sherwin; she heard arguments, and jealous rows. She thought they were over some servant who had caught Sherwin's fancy. She married Cavan during the break-up of Maggie's own marriage, so Maggie's reaction was not marked by great generosity of spirit. "Cavan and I got married in 1929, after an engagement of three years. Maggie gave me away. She was not at all pleased. She said to me, 'You have made your bed, now lie on it.' Then she actually gave us a bed to lie on. As well as a table, and an old sideboard, all from Woolley Grange. My allowance from Lewis Bergers was stopped. Cavan and I started life together with very little, and it was a good thing. We were living in Notting Hill, where some years later our eldest son was born, and Maggie consented to be his godmother."

Then, in 1930, Walter Cottingham died, who had represented stability and continuity at Woolley Hall. "One evening, returning to my

music-room, I found there a bird, fluttering to escape. Two days later
my father-in-law died," Maggie wrote.[29] He died of pneumonia: after
remaining indoors for a long time he had gone outside, in March, and
caught a chill. He left instructions that his body was to be embalmed,
transported by sea back to Cleveland, and laid to rest in the family vault
alongside that of his first wife Gertrude. Sherwin, with his brother
William, saw to it that these instructions were carried out and left
Southampton with his father's body on the S.S. *Majestic*. Walter's wife,
Jacqueline, departed as well, visiting in Gloucestershire and then going on
to the United States, where she disappeared, at least from the view of the
occupants of Woolley Hall—no doubt to enjoy the fruits of the ante-
nuptial settlement.*

Walter's will dated 1922 and ratified in June 1930, was marked by the
same fairness and meticulous regard for detail as he had shown in his life.
In it he dispensed numerous legacies to his children, his other relations,
and his friends, and did not forget the servants of Woolley Hall. The
bulk of his fortune was in shares, of which in England his interest in
Lewis Bergers was the most substantial. But he left over £400,000 in
cash, as well as Woolley Hall, the surrounding farms, and the Grange,
to Sherwin.

When Walter died Maggie was in the second of her three years of hell.
For a time she moved over to the Hall, where she put to good use the
grand piano that Walter had installed for her; one of the parlour maids,
Mrs Coleman, often heard her practising. The first of her broadcasts of
which we have a record was in 1927. In 1928 she sang in two light operas
on the radio, Cuvillier's *The Lilac Domino* on 30 January, and another by
Emmerich Kalman, *The Gypsy Princess*, on 28 March. Also in 1928, she
sang in an English production of *Pelléas*, on 29 October on the Daventry
Experimental Service. In 1930 she gave several recitals over the air,
Sunday Symphony concerts with Sir Henry Wood and Percy Pitt, and
took part in another Messager operetta, *La Basoche*, as well as in a further
production of *Pelléas*, this time promoted to the London Regional Service.
She also sang *Pelléas* at Covent Garden, and *Madama Butterfly*. At least,
then, while being in hell in her personal life, she was fortunate to have a
wonderful range and variety of outlets for the emotional turmoil within,
caused by Sherwin's infidelity.

Once back from Canada, his father safely deposited in the family tomb,

* She died in 1973.

Sherwin picked up the threads of his new love, and again took up with his old friend the bottle. "I suppose you'll be seeing *her* again this weekend," Maggie screamed at him one night over dinner. He viewed her philosophically, as he had the reporters at their wedding now nearly ten years before. But he was by now heartily tired of her prima donna fits of temperament, which he had never seen or suspected before they were married. The last time he had been to hear her sing at Covent Garden, and had gone backstage she had had the most frightful row with everyone, her dresser—still the faithful Mitchell—the stage manager, the other singers, bawled them out with no femininity or charm.

Yes, he must have thought, the charm is wearing thin. And she is nearly forty-three years old. He might well have reflected, in his moods of maudlin suspicion, on her relationship with Gay Vernon: were they conspiring behind his back; did Maggie now care more for her than for him? If we had something to share, a child, it might be different. But we have not. It seems reasonable, he may have said to himself, that I should have a little peace and happiness on this earth, and, with all my money, an heir, a son, someone to leave all this to, before it's too late . . .

So Maggie Teyte and Sherwin Cottingham went their separate ways, though until his death five years later, the ways were not very far apart. She went back to living in the Grange, a few hundred yards away from the Hall which now became his. She was very bitter at having to move out, and one evening she came through a back entrance into the Hall, went into Sherwin's bedroom suite on the first floor, locked the door behind her, and argued with him for two hours, shouting at him finally, before she left, terrible warnings of what would happen to him if he left her and lived with the other woman: "She'll kill you, she'll kill you!"*

They were not divorced until the following year, in May 1931. There was an arranged co-respondent, part of the deal Maggie had made with Sherwin, who wanted no scandal. The lady accused by Maggie of committing adultery with Sherwin, and well paid for it, was called Gladys Mary Levy. Maggie was the petitioner, and while Sherwin denied the charges, he did not contest the petition, a convenient formula by which no one lied in court, and no feelings were hurt. Maggie's counsel stated before the judge, Lord Merrivale, that "at the end of 1928 she had

---

* This the parlour maid, who was in the next room, remembers hearing through the walls.

to complain of her husband's neglect and of his being away a great deal. He took a flat for himself in London. A letter signed 'Dolores' in March 1930 aroused Mrs Cottingham's suspicions, and she asked her husband about it, and he made admission."[30] Sherwin was said to have committed adultery with "Dolores" in Earls Terrace, Kensington.

Maggie was granted a decree *nisi* with costs. After the divorce Maggie went into the garden at Maidenhead, and "howled like a dog". The "Decree Absolute for Dissolution of Marriage" was issued six months later, on 7 December 1931; there having been no sufficient cause shown in the period between why the divorce should not proceed. Just four days after this, on 11 December, Sherwin, who gave his address as 38 St Johns Wood Road, St Marylebone, his age as thirty-five, married Vera Owen, aged twenty-seven, who gave her address as Woolley Hall, Littlewick, Berkshire. The marriage took place in the Registry Office at St Marylebone. Sherwin arrived back at Woolley as tight as a drum. Gladys Mary Levy was not heard of again.

Maggie was to hear the nightingale again, in the fine nights of May and June, for a further five years, because under the generous divorce settlement she wrung from Sherwin, she was allowed to remain living at Woolley Grange. He also made her a yearly allowance of what amounted, finally, to £2,000, tax paid, to continue for the rest of her life. Maggie's astuteness made her able to foresee vast changes in the income-tax laws, and to exact such a provision was an act of prescience. The allowance was secured in Lewis Berger shares. Sherwin complained in a light-hearted telegram to her that she had taken the rolls but left him the butter.[31] A little later, when she was having lunch with Ivor Newton at the Savoy, she told him, "I shall never have to worry about money for the rest of my life."

It was true: whether it was good for her singing was another matter. Maggie had no sense of money. She always spent it like water, but from now on at least she had advisers who told her when she had to stop. That early period of being without money had scarred her to the extent that she never wanted to feel deprived of it again. It may be that Sherwin was an easy touch, for her as for his boozing companions, but she had married in good faith into his family, and she must have seen the very best of him, certainly in terms of his appearance. The transformation of a slim

Maggie Teyte in the title role of Emmerich Kalman's *The Little Dutch Girl*, in which she was singing in London in 1920 at the time of her second marriage.

Woolley Hall, the estate of the Cottinghams near Maidenhead, Berkshire. (*Far left*) Sherwin Cottingham, Maggie Teyte's second husband, and (*left*) his father, the multi-millionaire Walter C. Cottingham. (*Below*) Maggie exercising her dogs in the grounds at Woolley.

The Grange at Woolley, where Maggie lived from 1921 to 1936. (*Left*) Sherwin Cottingham in the late 1920s. (*Below left*) Sherwin Cottingham with Vera Owen at their marriage in 1931, and (*right*) Vera with their daughter Patricia, born in 1934.

(*Right*) Programme of the 1930 Covent Garden production of *Pelléas*, in which Teyte made one of her rare appearances in England as Mélisande. (*Above*) Maggie Teyte in the 1930s, at the time of her liaison with (*below*) Sir Thomas Beecham.

ROYAL OPERA
: : COVENT GARDEN : :
Lessees: Covent Garden Opera Syndicate, Ltd.

THIS EVENING'S PERFORMANCE

Tuesday, June 17th, 1930, at 7.45

DEBUSSY'S OPERA

PELLÉAS ET MÉLISANDE

In French

Arkel	. .	FERNANDO AUTORI
Geneviève	. .	JEANNE MONTFORT
Pelléas	. .	ROGER BOURDIN
Golaud	. .	JOHN BROWNLEE
Yniold	. .	EVELYN HANSON
Le Médecin	. .	RICHARD WATSON
Mélisande	. .	MAGGIE TEYTE
Conductor	.	GIORGIO POLACCO

Teyte in two of her singing roles of the 1930s: as Puccini's Madama Butterfly, and (*right*) as Hänsel, in Humperdinck's *Hänsel und Gretel*, thumbing her nose at the world.

Rita Odoli-Tate, Maggie's niece and ward, (*right*) with the Tate family nurse, and (*above*) in the 1920s, before her marriage to the singer Cavan O'Connor.

Cavan O'Connor, in a 1963 drawing by his son John. (*Left*) Maggie's friend Grace Vernon with the O'Connors' eldest son, Maggie's godson Michael.

Maggie Teyte in New York in the 1930s with Joe Brogan, owner of the Gramophone Shop, who started her on her successful career as a recording artist. (*Below*) "Mélisande's tower": the apartment building in New York where she lived after the war.

young man into a middle-aged debauchee took no more than ten years.

With no Maggie to point an accusing finger at him, Sherwin pursued his derelict journey, possibly a little more speedily than he might have done with her, to the grave. He must have wanted to arrive there quickly, and may even have resented her slowing him down, for soon after he and Vera were married they had the Catholic chapel which George Dunne had built in the house, but which was now deconsecrated, turned into a cocktail bar.*

So Vera took Maggie's place alongside the new owner of the Hall. Vera moved her family, not only into the Hall but into Littlewick Cemetery, for after Sherwin's own death and burial, she made strenuous efforts to reserve space for four further graves: her own and that of her nephew, her sister Countess de la Marche, and her sister's son.† For her it must have been odd, moving into an English country house thousands of miles away from her home, with a Canadian-born dipsomaniac English gentleman, knowing his first wife was only a few hundred paces away behind some trees. What Vera and Sherwin had in common was love, the very same love Maggie and Sherwin had had in common.

In a little while he virtually retired from business, refusing any longer to take a salary as vice-chairman of Bergers, which had never in any case been much more than a nominal title, and stayed at home at Woolley. One day the gardener, Mr Howlett, was outside the drawing room, where Sherwin was sitting. "Come in," Sherwin said. Howlett told him that Madam would be furious as she hated dirt in the house. "Damn Mrs Cottingham," he said. When Howlett went over to him, he was surprised and shocked to see tears streaming down his cheeks. "Here, take this," Sherwin said. And from his wrist he unstrapped his gold watch. "I can't take that, sir," Howlett said. Sherwin insisted. So Howlett took it, and

* Maggie was most emphatic that this did not happen during her time at Woolley Hall, so much so that when the *Daily Telegraph* reported in error on 23 March 1963 that Dame Margaret Cottingham had "bought the Hall in 1912, and the chapel was turned into a cocktail bar", she wrote to the paper (28 March) that "converting the chapel into, or use as, a cocktail bar was never for the moment contemplated by her, and it had not been so converted when her association with the Hall ended in 1930."

† There is a fascinating exchange of letters of 1936–9 between the Reverend R. S. Wormald and Vera Cottingham's legal representatives, swopping land for grave spaces, with the church showing a certain intransigence about allocating what was required. Mrs Cottingham's nephew Lonia de Prascovsky is buried at Littlewick.

when Vera came back later on he gave her the watch. She told him, "If Mr Cottingham offers you anything else, don't take it. If everyone took everything Mr Cottingham wanted to give away, I should have to close Woolley Hall."

These gestures of a man ending his life by bidding for love and attention were copied almost exactly in their incontinent *largesse* by Maggie when she was approaching the end of her own life, adumbrating how strong a love she had had for him. Where there is love, the urge towards imitation is strong. Sherwin's attraction for her went very deep and was altogether lasting, heightened and intensified by the fact that he was sick and weak. Heightened at least in imagination, though impossible to face in reality, and to live with for any length of time. The myth of the rich man, war-wounded, charming and in many ways perfect, but weak in character, unable to leave the bottle alone and with a capacity for romance, was one of the most potent of that age, and had proved irresistible.

While Maggie lingered on at Woolley Grange, Gay Vernon moved into a flat in the Grange, in the stable block. Harry Vernon, who was always promising he was going to make a million but whose hand stuck in his pocket as he reached to pay for the next round of drinks, had gone to America to try and make his play *Mr Wu* into a film. That was the last that was heard of him, and no regrets were felt by Gay. Maggie's sense of humour being irrepressible, the pair of them would sometimes, when they thought Sherwin and Vera were out, go over to the Hall and have a peep round to see what was going on. One day they were almost caught by Vera.

Sherwin and Vera entertained a lot, but the xenophobic servants, at least, disliked the influx of foreigners all speaking French and Russian, and they said Sherwin would often become disgusted, get up and walk out. What did overjoy Sherwin was the advent of his and Vera's daughter Patricia, born in Paris on 12 June 1934.[32] Sherwin was so delighted with her, he nursed her on his knee. Maggie was furious over this, and did not till her own death have a good word to say about Vera or about the child.

On 22 January 1936, aged only thirty-nine, Sherwin Cottingham died of a cerebral haemorrhage. None of the cures had worked on him, and the pair of male nurses he had had looking after him for some years had not been much help either. One of them, an Irishman, was alleged by other servants to have let him drink as much as he wanted. In the obituary notice published a week later the *Maidenhead Advertiser* wrote:

The heir to the beautiful house Mr Walter Sherwin Cottingham kept up the traditions and even went beyond those of his late father's largesse. He made himself beloved by the large staff of servants who almost "worshipped him", to use the words expressed by one of them. He never had a cross or angry word with one of them. They naturally are long-service employees; neither they nor their master liked to part with each other. He was ever ready to help anyone in distress, being most generous to those in genuine need. He was fond of entertaining the children and was largely responsible for the village maypole celebrations that Littlewick Green has been noted for in recent years. At the last Christmas party he gave recently he himself impersonated Father Christmas and went round the Hall bestowing presents on everyone. Some of the little folk found a crackling new £1 Treasury note placed in their hands as a make-weight with the present.

The beautiful garden and shrubberies with all varieties of conifers, the classically designed pergolas with their arcades of festooned rambling roses, and the layout of the expansive lawns and flower gardens bear a deep and attractive charm in the many and varied pictures they present. Here was work for six gardeners who were kept continually busy in looking after the surroundings. Mr Cottingham's death will be keenly felt by those who have benefited by employment besides the local tradespeople. A great deal of money has been spent by him in improvements to the estate since he became its squire.

The third and last of the three great squires of Woolley* had passed away, a tragedy for the estate. The funeral was splendid and old-fashioned, like the interment of Tolstoy or a Czarist prince. A hand-propelled bier carrying Sherwin's coffin, a massive panelled coffin in dark oak which in contrast "enhanced the beauty of the floral emblems which surmounted it", including those from the widow and "Mother", his Russian mother-in-law, was wheeled by Vera and members of the Cottingham and Sklarevskara family past the lodge, through the massive iron gates installed by Walter Horace, and down the Bath Road to Littlewick church. The mourners followed on foot. The service in the church was held under the great east window put up in 1893 by the mother of a man who discovered

* There are no more squires. The hall is now the headquarters of the Southern Electricity Board, and a large number of the mature trees were felled to meet a shortage of wood poles. The trees now carry supply lines in Reading District.

the way to remove phosphorus from pig-iron.* The window itself depicted St Joseph in his rich cloak, with the ox and ass behind him: "The ox knoweth his owner and the ass his master's crib", and indeed the congregation might have been an echoing tribute to this, for the aisles and pews were overflowing with representatives from Sherwin-Williams and Lewis Bergers all over the world, with staff from Woolley Hall,† with his North American relations. There were massed choirs—from St Mark's, St Luke's, and St Mary's Maidenhead, backing up the local one— singing Russian *contakions* and English hymns.

Maggie was there, unnoticed: she had never been known to miss a good show and she went out of respect and love for other members of the Cottingham family who were to remain life-long friends and admirers.‡ She used her histrionic skill not to be noticed, to slip in and out of the ceremony. What she saw was amazing: vivid demonstrations of quite un-British grief from Vera and her family. Vera, leaping into position beside the open grave, and sobbing away, tried to touch the coffin as it was lowered into the ground. At one moment Maggie thought she was going to jump into the grave itself, like Laertes, overcome at Ophelia's death,

> Hold off the earth awhile,
> Till I have caught her once more in mine arms.

and try to throw open the coffin, to hold Sherwin once more in her arms. But it was then that her mother and her sister took her firmly by the elbow, and pulled her back from the edge of the gaping earth.[33] Ah yes, Maggie mused, before she escaped from the broken cortège and dispersing mourners, one thing was sure, everyone loved Sher. And now he was dead she could love him again, he could belong to her, he could remain her Pelléas, the only man in her life she had loved and was to go on

* Sidney Gilchrist Thomas.

† Among them the butler Henry Scribbins and the footman Frederick Cummings, who, in a typical Sherwin gesture, had been witnesses to his will.

‡ One of them, Kenneth Allen, managed in part her triumphant career in America after the Second World War. Some of them visited her forty years later as she lay dying in a Holland Park nursing home; Sherwin's sister left her a legacy when she died. A younger member of the family, named Walter Sherwin Cottingham after his uncle and grandfather, called his own daughter, born in 1962, "Tey"—after Teyte—and Maggie gave her her own engagement ring from Sherwin.

loving. As for Vera, her opinion was that "she was a gold-digger, but good luck to her."[34]

The grave was lined with evergreen boughs on which was "powdered a profusion of red carnations and daffodils". The wreaths and other floral tributes made a galaxy of splendid colour, and on the gargantuan grave-stone, erected—in contrast to the rest of the graves in the vicinity—not facing east, was etched a maiden kneeling, her hands clasped in grief over her head. The epitaph ran:

> Long ago with love's arms I bound thee,
> Now the everlasting arms surround thee,
> Through death's darkness I look and see,
> And clasp thee to me.

Vera could have reflected that it was not all that long ago, indeed barely four years, that she had bound him with love's arms.

The tribute Maggie left behind on her wreath was more succinct and to the point, showing that she had tried at any rate to confront Sherwin with the reality of his situation, or at least did not want it then, on his death, to go unrecorded. Her words were:

> To a troubled mind that has found peace at last.
> MAGGIE*

A chambermaid later found this note, crumpled up and torn, in a pocket of Vera Cottingham's coat as she was putting it away for her in a wardrobe.[35] She had removed it from the wreath.

Vera's own tribute had been "To my beloved husband, with a love that will never die." She later married Thomas Lilley of Lilley & Skinner, and, after his death, Roger Hue-Williams, a stockbroker, coming to be numbered among the richest women in England. When in her seventies Maggie visited Sherwin's grave, with her niece Rita, they found it neglected, overgrown with cow parsley and dandelions. Such was the end of a man whose wealth served to maintain, if not his own life, those of his servants, his exquisite garden, and, for the rest of her long days, Maggie Teyte. Summer's guest had departed.

* The wording is exactly that reported in the *Maidenhead Advertiser*, where it strikes an odd note, strongly discordant with the rest of the report.

PART TWO

NIGHT

Alone in a sky dark and gloomy,
Roamed Night, the silent thieving prowler,
Around his head a sliver of gold,
Moon and stars attached to his belt,
Ever seeking for a silver river
To mingle with the gold upon his head.

One night he roamed far in the sky
Attracted by Earth's wondrous light,
Valleys deep with silver streams
Mighty oceans, bluish-green;
"This indeed is a jewel rare,
It must be mine, it shall be mine."

To earth, supreme, haughty, and proud,
Riding high in her misty shroud,
Night begged, pleaded and even insisted—
"For just one of your silver streams,
I'll give you back your moon and stars"—
But with scorn and disdain, she turned away.

His heart full of venomous hate,
Night flung his wrath high in the sky—
"Bring forth your steel-wingéd weapons,
Go fetch me that sphere who denies my right";
His shafts of fire, so deadly swift,
Struck deep in mountainside, and silver stream.

They placed a star upon his knee,
As yet unnamed, as yet unclaimed,
His eyes still seeking a silver river
Knowing now he would never find,
Bowing his head he uttered a prayer:
"Give me oh God, if God there be,
One tear, one bitter tear, to shed."

MARGARET TATE, 1974*

* She signed this poem, written when she was eighty-five, with the early form of her
name.

CHAPTER NINE

Breaking the Ice with Red-hot Irons
(1930–1940)

Hard fate! to have been once possessed
As victor, of a heart
Achieved with labour, and unrest,
And then forced to depart.
THOMAS CAREW

PELLÉAS WAS DEAD, not by a sudden jealous blow but from war, infidelity, and drink, hardly less dramatic causes. But Mélisande was not pregnant, or if she was, it was now with art, with stored-up voice and unimpaired vitality. She itched to return to a career such as she had in 1910.

But it was not 1910. There was no great operatic circuit. There was cold comfort to be had from Covent Garden; because of her disinclination to pursue her career heartily in the Twenties, her performances there had been very scattered, and often only due to the cancellation or illness of some other singer. She had sung in the British National Opera Company in their 1922 winter season: one performance as Mimi in *Bohème* (Melba sang the other, to help the impoverished BNOC). That season opened with *Hänsel und Gretel*, Maggie taking the part of Hänsel; the performance on 6 January 1923 was broadcast over Station 2LO of the BBC*—the first opera ever transmitted from a theatre in Europe.[1] Later, she sang again, in the summer: a few performances of *Madama Butterfly* and, in the most frequently performed and most popular work of the season, the Princess in Holst's *The Perfect Fool*, a new opera, the rarer for being British.†

Maggie's snobbish and basically profane nature deprived her of one of

---

* Kenneth Wright recalled listening to the broadcast in Manchester, by the first land-line relay, as "the most exciting moment of radio pioneering".

† Holst was delighted with the clearness of Teyte's words, and her pure and effortless singing. According to Imogen Holst, she lifted the opera "out of ordinary comedy into a mood that was like my father's music at its most serious".

the most rewarding paths her career could have followed when she wanted to return, especially now that she had passed the age when her appeal as an *ingénue* passed unquestioned—that of oratorio. She tried it once. "One of my outstanding memories of the 1924 Norwich Festival", wrote Sir Henry Wood, "is Maggie Teyte's interpretation of the soprano part in *Elijah*."

> When I first approached her about it she was doubtful about taking it on. "I'm an opera singer," she told me. "I don't think I want to sing oratorio. But if you teach me the part I will see what I can do." Her performance was a triumph and proved my contention that oratorio is a *sacred drama*. Her rendering of the widow's part was a lesson in interpretation. I wish every oratorio singer could have heard her performance. What a lesson, too, for the contralto, whose duplicate parts of the Angel and Queen are so often sung with the same stodgy delivery; what a chance there is for varying colour of tone, and expression—that of the Angel so very beautiful and full of feeling, and that of the Queen—a virago, calling forth all the drama that Maggie Teyte knew so well how to portray. I shall never forget the pleading tone of her voice when she asked the man of God to help her: "My son is sick. Help my son! There is no breath left in him."[2]

Such was Sir Henry's astute verdict, but she knew better and pooh-poohed the idea of further such displays. The influence of Lady Ripon had left its mark.

Now, in 1930, when she wanted to make an operatic comeback during the break-up of her marriage, there was a general impatience with old-fashioned opera. Galli-Curci ridiculed it, calling it "pompous" and "obsolete". One of the absurdities she pointed to was lying Mimi on a couch to breathe her last, "singing exquisite passages with perfect clearness as she passes away."[3] The public was indifferent to opera and there was a shortage of good singers at a national level. In January 1929 it was proposed to pull down the Covent Garden Opera House and in 1930 it was up for sale. Even so a season was mounted, acknowledged to be the most brilliant since 1914 (a season in which Maggie had also sung).

Meanwhile word had gone round that Maggie was keen to appear again, and in June 1930, at short notice, she sang Butterfly when the Irish soprano, Margherita Sheridan, became ill. She sang in English, while the rest of the cast—Dennis Noble was Sharpless—sang in Italian. The opera was being broadcast, so listeners who had heard the first act with Sheridan singing in Italian, were subsequently treated to the last two with chauvinistic Teyte in English; even so Teyte's Butterfly eclipsed that of Sheridan.⁴ She gave more performances of the opera in 1931, and in the 1933–4 season at Sadler's Wells, all with Tudor Davies as Pinkerton.

Her *coup* on the rebound from Sherwin, however, was not a new boy-friend or lover, but an engagement at Covent Garden for two perform-ances of *Pelléas*: only two, mind, but priceless, and sufficient once again for her, in typical Teyte fashion, completely to scoop the notices. The season was in two parts, a German and an Italian, and *Pelléas* came in the Italian part, giving rise to such comments as: "In its way . . . the most completely satisfactory of the Italian performances of this season—it was sung in French", from the *Telegraph* (18 June 1930), which went on that Maggie's performance remained on "as high a level as those which occurred when Miss Teyte represented Mélisande in the years before the war—the most effective and attractive Mélisande I can recall at Covent Garden." The blithe reviewer did not seem to know she had only ever sung it there once before. "Time has left her the ingenuous, forlorn little princess of Maeterlinck's and Debussy's dream," pronounced the *Evening News*, while the *Yorkshire Post* proclaimed quite openly its patriotic pride: "It was generally admitted in the foyer that we had seen no finer and more finished example of the prima donna's art than this English singer gave this evening."

Despite the rain of compliments on her and Golaud (John Brownlee) as an attractive pair (not quite how the story matched them, but never mind, Roger Bourdin as Pelléas was patted on the back as an after-thought), Maggie, at forty-two, felt a good deal more womanly than she looked—and indeed she now looked rather less fragile. But the reviews gratified her ego, gave her an illusion of temporary revenge on Sherwin and Vera, and she hoped, rather cynically, that it would not be like the last time she had sung the part—and not been asked back. Perhaps the management, or possibly other artists with a vested interest in keeping her out, recoiled from her very ability so nearly to produce perfection. It was not the first time the realization had come over her that maybe she was a little too good, and that only the connoisseur, the truly perceptive, could really appreciate her.

When she came to re-study the part for these two performances it was not as though she was rusty, for she had sung Mélisande at His Majesty's in 1924, broadcast it in 1928,* and in Giorgio Polacco, the Venetian-born conductor brought up in St Petersburg, and then conducting in Chicago, she had the conductor of her dreams, who combined restraint, judgement, and power. "So beautifully did he draw out the colour from the orchestra that it seemed as though the score had become an illuminated manuscript in sound," she wrote of him.⁵ In a maturity compounded of her personal shock and defeats, her aspirations, her loves, and her sheer technical acuity, she was able in 1930 to piece together the most delicate and beautiful study of the part she had ever given or ever was able to give. Inside she felt absolutely at one with the shadowy personality Debussy builds up by little imperceptible touches, flicks of sound, and with, beneath it all, the clenched violence she herself had seen the composer show on several occasions: a violence always under the surface, always about to erupt—and sometimes erupting. And how the negations of which Mélisande is made up answered her deepest convictions: she could show them what it meant to be unhappy, for now she knew.

The performance on 17 June 1930 was definitive—so much so that one commentator, Marion Bauer, wrote that Debussy himself had said "she does not act Mélisande; she is Mélisande": this may not have been strictly true, but it summed up how everyone felt. Debussy's stammering phantoms were back in force.

The other singers too, were excellent: true, Roger Bourdin was a bit dull to begin with, though he had a fine clear voice: but suddenly and quite unexpectedly, after his declaration of love, he began to become thrilling. In the final scene he was infused with greath warmth. And Brownlee's Golaud more than made up for Bourdin's erratic moments. Here, Maggie thought, in this Australian singer from the Paris Opéra, was something of the Hector Dufranne quality, and she felt powerfully challenged by his full-blooded jealousy and manliness. Fernando Autori's Arkel, too, had great reserves of emotional power.

But offstage the triumph was short-lived and, incredible as it may seem, Maggie was not invited back to Covent Garden till 1937, seven years later. And during those seven years she sang in few other operas.

Her failure here was on the human, more than on the artistic, level. Like Lady Ripon she remained somehow deeply a dilettante, not in musical terms, but in the sense of feeling able to pick and choose. She

* On Daventry Experimental 5 G.B. with Walter Hyde as Pelléas and Roy Henderson as Golaud. The opera was sung in English.

never perhaps tried hard enough to broaden her operatic appeal, content to stay in the somewhat rarefied world of the rich musical coterie: she was stand-offish, not a good mixer, and her social ideas were still those of the pre-war celebrity.*

Her withdrawal, her "retirement", had done her no good either. A year, maybe two, was one thing, but after the seven years of 1923–30, people imagined her dead, or permanently abroad. Life with Sherwin had spoiled her, as had life in the Rubens circle; that practical, gritty Midlands independence had still not fully asserted itself, though always remaining part of her.

Her next few years were full of soul-searching. The search began with that dog-like howl which had so shocked the household and inhabitants of Woolley Hall. Where had she gone wrong? Why had she, with Sherwin, the Pelléas of her life, committed the same kind of fault as with Eugène, the Golaud-like protector? Why had she not learnt to see where she began and ended as a person, not presuming on her attraction for him, and the charismatic effect of her career? Why could she not have seen his personality and needs—even his need to kill himself—for what they were, instead of giving him what she needed to give, to show herself she could give, the protection and mothering which he, naturally enough, hated?

Strong understanding of others was never a marked feature of Maggie's character: it may be that the Scots have no great sympathy for the hourly movements of the soul. But she was a great imitator. If she liked a person, her liking found expression in copying that person's mannerisms, adopting his expressions: she had done this with Sherwin, as with de Reszke, and Plumon; and she did it with roles as well. As she grew older, possibly the Scottish side came to be more dominant: it was, as in many people, the hardiest strain. But it had in it a great blindness, and a great impatience: it despised growth, slow change, understanding. It worshipped strength, smartness, aggressive charm. It was a very masculine set of values that Maggie, after parting from Sherwin, came to embrace as her own. The rumour went around that she went to bed with every baritone in the business. Was she going to turn out like her rival from the earliest days,

---

* Even so she had enough foresight to apply her energies to the new electronic substitute for that coterie, the newly emerging radio channels. She even invented, with the help of Pamphonic Ltd, an electrical device called Teytone which printed out on a paper strip the vibrations of the voice as received by the microphone, thus allowing a singer to see when his tone was overloading.

Mary Garden, a voracious man-eater always boasting of her conquests, but at heart frigid, with lesbian tendencies? Once, found with a young man in her bed at Woolley Grange, Maggie shocked her niece Rita when she declared, with melodramatic violence, "You may as well know!" Men had become male meat. And if these values had, in the short term, a bad effect on her life, they could in the long term have a bad effect on her singing.

And at times, because she was now solely the performing artist, constantly attentive to how she was going to sing, constantly under pressure from an inner directive to do the best she was able to do, and never closely involved with a man or woman she considered compatible, her sense of other people's states of mind and emotions began to suffer. She became egotistical. Hers was a life measured out in performances, hard study, and then more performances, for if opera made less calls on her, radio and concert work kept her fiendishly busy.

Between adolescence, when she had no time for such things, and middle age, she was subject to quite sudden, unavoidable depressions. In an instant the inner winch would come unfastened and down, down the bucket would plummet, till there was a faraway splash in the darkness so faint as to be hardly more than a tinkle. The depressions had to do with her lost father—that was the unnamed grief which underlay much of her personality, just as Bluebeard's rape underlay Mélisande's unhappiness— but they were not so much a diagnosable illness, even the serious ones, as dead pockets of the psyche into which she plopped. She would linger in one of these until almost without volition—for the mind, like the body, if left to itself in repose tends towards normality—a chance remark, an idea or image, would bring her back to herself. This was true in her earlier life; later on these dark moods became a well harbouring ill-begotten memories of her dealings with the male sex, a breeding ground for resentment. Unmitigated by any influence from a distant, coherent father, this stagnant breeding ground of treachery, jealousy, and regret in the end took the place of the earlier depressions. Her will no longer partook of these states: it observed from outside, gratified by relationships it could glimpse, which were only partially distorted, such as that with Gay Vernon, her companion in these distressed years, or with a temporary man. Her will could not quite tolerate the normal without a shudder. After a resumption in this period of her not very resounding affair with Sir Thomas Beecham, Maggie quite seriously and deliberately broke off relationships with the opposite sex, even though there is evidence she long remained prone to passion and sudden desire.

These were years of deep frustration. Her great thirst for operatic roles was never gratified.* Opera apart though, her career in some ways

Victoria Palace handbill, 1932

flourished. She sang at numerous Proms, often the opening or closing concert, and Sunday orchestral concerts with Sir Henry Wood. She gave impressive radio recitals with, among other artists, Cortot, Rudolph Dolmetsch, Tapia-Caballero, Cassadó, and Frank Laffitte. She sang

---

* Though there were no more Mélisandes for her to sing in England, a further English revival, this time with Lisa Perli (Dora Labbette, another of Beecham's friends), provoked an outburst that was heard as far away as Delhi: Kaikhosru Sorabji, the reclusive Sicilian-Indian composer, complaining of Perli's performance, went on rhetorically, "But where, in a season boasting the cream of all available singing talent, was that past mistress of the art of Debussy, Miss Maggie Teyte, a Mélisande of European fame?"[6]

numerous operettas on the radio, and appeared in the highly successful revival of the comic opera *Tantivy Towers*, by A. P. Herbert and T. F. Dunhill, at the Lyric Hammersmith with another former de Reszke pupil, Steuart Wilson, the tenor who later became head of BBC music. She also did a 30,000-mile tour of Australia with Tudor Davies, like her a terrific "study"—they sang duets, and visited Melba's house, at Lilydale, where Maggie heard a kookaburra, or laughing jackass.

But all this was not quite enough for one still possessed of her power and potential. She tried, abortively, to find work in America, but they had forgotten her there. An engagement she had been booked for in a new theatre in California failed to take place because of a lumbermen's strike, and so back to England limped the former leading soprano of the Opéra-Comique, Covent Garden, the Imperial Opera Berlin, and of Chicago, Philadelphia, and Boston. It was all deeply humiliating, now that she was approaching the age of fifty. She even quarrelled with Fritz Reiner in Philadelphia over the tempo in a Mozart aria, and he asked her, "What do you English know about Mozart, anyhow?"

Of Maggie's many projects at the end of the Thirties which failed to get off the ground, *Mozart*—the Sacha Guitry–Reynaldo Hahn collaboration—was possibly the most bizarre. Maggie had been engaged to sing in the Salle Gaveau in Paris, and only forty-eight people turned up to hear her. What disappointment she felt, and with what ghosts the hall was now redolent, ghosts of thirty years before when Debussy himself had conducted her there to a full house. She had chosen some numbers from her early repertoire and among them one of Reynaldo Hahn's songs from *Mozart*. As she started to sing it, what did she see, sitting several rows back from the front, not a ghost, but someone very much alive. A familiar tall figure, older now, greyer, still as suave as ever, draped languidly over several seats and surrounded by empty places on which his accoutrements were neatly laid out: Reynaldo.

Oh God, she thought to herself, faltered, and then her memory failed. She stopped the accompanist, asked him to start again, and tried to dismiss Reynaldo from her mind. But her memory failed again. She came to the front. "It's all your fault," she said to him. "You make me nervous." "Very well," said Reynaldo, picking up his hat and cane. "I go." "No," retorted Maggie. "Sit down—don't be silly. I'll start again. But you *do* make me nervous." "I am very honoured," he answered. The audience was now openly shrieking with laughter at the exchange. "But try again."

So she did, reading from the music, and the song was the great success of the evening.[7]

After that they revived their friendship. They lunched at the Ritz. Reynaldo, who was conducting Mozart at the Paris Opéra, tried to get her into the Company—as Susanna in *Figaro*—but this came to nothing. Then she had the bright idea of having his *Mozart* translated and done in English. She arranged for Reynaldo to see the impresario Charles Cochran. "Votre proposition me charme et je serais ravi que ce projet pût se réaliser" he wrote to her, but later when he had seen Cochran, it was a different story: "I would be most impressed if you succeed in convincing M. Cochran. . . . The way he acted with *me* was astounding!"* Maggie kept on with the project, and found a translator, Dennis Arundell, who was interested. But it progressed no further, being finally vetoed, she told some friends, by Sacha Guitry's wife, Yvonne Printemps.

Trite as it might seem, her nationality did not stand Maggie in good stead. In the *Daily Mirror* of New Year's Day 1937, Godfrey Winn took as his sermon, after visiting Covent Garden, the performance of *Hänsel und Gretel*. It proved, he wrote,

> infinitely better, my companion Mr James Smith told me, than the one he had seen at the Metropolitan Opera House in New York. In the London Philharmonic Orchestra we possess an orchestra which, when it goes on tour in Germany, packs out every concert hall in which it performs. In Miss Maggie Teyte we possess an English singer who, if she changed her name to Marguerita Teytarina, would be world-famous. In Sir Thomas Beecham we possess the greatest musical conductor of the world. Well, why don't we do something about it?

The two artists named in Mr Winn's article, and pictured side by side, did do something about it. They promptly renewed their pre-World War One attachment ("You may as well know," one can almost hear Maggie again telling her niece), Maggie enjoying for a time the eye-opening kudos of being Beecham's mistress. She wore it for some years as a consolatory feather in her cap, giving rise to certain fits of bravado. Once after World War Two, she was travelling by train from Paris to

---

* Maggie got her own back on Cochran, after a fashion. She caught him in a theatre foyer, and demanded how he *dared* put on Offenbach's *La Belle Hélène* without her. Apparently he cowered in a corner.

London with her accompanist, Anatole Fistoulari the conductor and George Weldon. Discussing Beecham's Old-World manner, one of them said, "I've never heard anyone call Beecham anything other than Sir Thomas."

Maggie said briskly: "I always call him Tommy." All three men turned to look at her. They were extremely impressed. "Anyway why shouldn't I?" she went on. "He was my lover for years." A silence fell. Their awe could hardly be reckoned. Finally one of them plucked up courage and asked, "Was he a good lover?"

"Wonderful. Wonderful," she replied abruptly. That was the end of the conversation.

But on the quality of his lovemaking, there is evidence to the contrary in other, more private remarks she made. Beecham's whole body when he was conducting reflected the music, it was a complete sensual act of love-making, his hands gently drawing music from the strings, his left hand turning over to denote some delicious shading or making a rapier-like thrust for dramatic strokes, the right hand shooting out to ripple up the brass section, to reach climax . . . . Yet in the interval, where he sometimes in the dressing room asserted his manhood in different fashion, with obligatory, Saint-Saëns-like regularity, it was disappointing: "Oh my dear, I cannot tell you how *disappointing* it was."★

Beecham's public personality was an elaborate artefact; even mistresses were built into the structure, along with his own family ("Not my best work," he reputedly said of his two sons) and his studied lateness and eccentricity. "When he came into a room he was so unsure of himself that he *had* to create an attitude, outside, arrange himself," Maggie said of him, adding, "Take a little time to put himself into the part, before we went in." Unfortunately for Maggie she did not manage to break down the elaborate defences whereby this gifted individual hid his sensitivity from the world; nor did she truly become part of his private life. She was probably too old for this.

But if Beecham was not to be a lasting sexual partner, as artistic director of the 1936 and 1937 seasons at Covent Garden, with Vladimir Rosing as director of productions, and Percy Heming as organizer, he did give Maggie's operatic career a welcome boost. Percy Heming had been a

★ So Maggie told a close friend, though it may be on this occasion she was surpassing her normal truthfulness. Perhaps she was thinking back to 1910 when she found Beecham the reincarnation of Mozart: "Naughty, full of wit and dancing eyes."[8]

friend of Maggie's since 1915. A descendant of John Heming, a member of Shakespeare's company and part editor of the First Folio, he knew every side of opera, and was full of good humour and amusing stories.

The triumphant Philharmonic tour of Germany mentioned by Godfrey Winn showed how music, and Beecham in particular, had been sucked into the maelstrom of international politics. "I should have liked so much to come to London to participate in the Coronation festivities, but cannot risk putting the English to the inconvenience my visit might entail," Hitler said to Beecham when he heard the Philharmonic's concert in Berlin, hoping to ingratiate himself with Edward VIII with whom he believed Beecham to be on friendly terms. "Not at all. There would be no inconvenience. In England we leave everybody to do as he likes," was Beecham's nonplussing reply, which onlookers say left Hitler looking bewildered. A faked photograph was published in the papers, purporting to show Beecham hobnobbing with the Führer in his box although he had never gone there. Later Beecham, who had gone to Bayreuth to engage Furtwängler for the Coronation season, managed to sidestep Hitler's summons to join him at the Festspielhaus, and afterwards refused further invitations.⁹ The following year he dashed over to Paris, gathering the Légion d'honneur while he was there. Maggie, who went travelling in Germany—with or without Beecham we cannot be sure—also met Hitler, but did not sing for him. They were introduced: "He was a horrible little man and he smelt."¹⁰

In this Coronation season into which Beecham put such effort, Maggie sang Euridice in Gluck's *Orphée*, in the presence of Queen Mary. Though it was generally considered by the critics that she alone achieved anything worthwhile in the production, Beecham's assistant, Berta Geissmar, thought *Orphée* superb, and that "press and public failed to appreciate its high artistic merit."¹¹

She sang Hänsel again, with Olive Dyer as Gretel, before finally "putting him to bed," and Butterfly again and again, sometimes with Heddle Nash as Pinkerton (also with Heddle Nash as des Grieux, she sang a radio performance of Massenet's *Manon* of which an incomplete recording remains).* Many now believed her to be the leading British exponent of Butterfly, the *Liverpool Post* writing (2 November 1938)

---

* The *Manon*, given at St George's Hall on 21 January 1938, inaugurated the BBC Music Productions Unit directed by Stanford Robinson. Dennis Arundell's English version was criticized as sometimes being stilted, as in "Will you name on her bestow?"

that she catches her fragility and childish faith, "pitching it for the most part in an emotional low key by which device she gains enormous emphasis for the high-lights."* She owed much to her careful examination of Tamaka Miura's performance in America, and its "complete lack of sex in the Western sense". "I was told that the lower parts of an Oriental's legs are likely to be shorter than ours," she observed grandly, as if incapable of making such assessments for herself, "which makes the constant small but always graceful movements on and off the knees easier for them to manage."[12]

She also, just before the war, made her début in Wagner as Eva in *Die Meistersinger*, which she sang in Edinburgh and Glasgow. Edouard de Reszke had suggested Eva to her, but she was a little late in taking up his suggestion, and though she sang it perfectly well, and was much applauded, she considered it a failure. But she never had much luck with the German repertoire: just as she had been going to sing in Leipzig when the Great War was unleashed, so now when World War Two was in the offing she came around at last to Wagner: bad timing.†

"There came a moment in my life," Maggie said, "when I had to decide between love and companionship, or music and solitude. I chose the solitude. The other could never have made up for that void of music."[13]

This choice came when she was just fifty, when she decided once and for all that her love for music made her less able to love, in the ordinary human sense, another human being. It coincided with her leaving the countryside, her beloved Woolley Grange, where she had lived for seventeen years, and which now, after Sherwin's death, was put up for sale. When she was packing, her housekeeper cook, Mrs Deacon, who was helping her, found a photograph of Sherwin. "Do you want me to throw it out?" asked Mrs Deacon. "I'll keep it," said Maggie, and put it in her bag. Henceforth she was to be an urban artist.

---

* She almost invariably sang Butterfly with Edith Clegg as Suzuki. While it is said Teyte's first act was good, her second act superb, especially in the letter duet with Sharpless, she had not in act three the poignancy of feeling in her farewell to the child shown by other singers—Elizabeth Rethberg and Miriam Licette, for example: perhaps a sign of how much personal feeling she projected into what she sang.

† She of course loved Wagner, and once promised to take her grandnephew to the *Ring* cycle at Covent Garden. But no production came along which she thought would do it justice, so she gave him the librettos instead, which he still has.

Towards the end of the Thirties her career was still in the doldrums, her private life hardly inspiring. But fate sent along its rescuer, a true *deus ex machina*, the machine being the gramophone. The 'god's' name was Brogan, and his intervention galvanized her work and laid the basis of future success. Of Scots–Irish blood, Joe Brogan had emigrated to the States from Scotland, and had spent his youth as a total "melomane". In or out of a job, in times of prosperity or depression, he would always be found at the opera. Later, after working for one of the established record companies, he started his own business, the Gramophone Shop in New York, which grew in time to near-legendary proportions, so that he could boast among his customers the Mikado and the Maharajah of Mysore, who relied on him to choose their collections. Maggie had met Brogan in 1915, when she was singing in a James Wolland Bagby "Morning Musicale" at the Waldorf Astoria.* Brogan himself had once tried to be a tenor, singing Alfredo in Verdi's *La Traviata* with an English touring company: if feeling jolly among friends, he would tackle "De' miei bollenti". It is possible that his joy at possessing Violetta sometimes, even though he was homosexual, extended to possessing Teyte, for he told her more than once that he wanted to marry her, which was something more than affectionate bravura. So total and romantic an opera-lover was Brogan that when he sold his business he retired to a town on Lake Lugano, from which he would have easy access to the world's great opera houses.

Around 1935 Brogan tried to interest the Victor Record Company in New York in the idea of recording an album of Maggie Teyte's Debussy repertoire. When they refused he approached Walter Legge of HMV. Legge, however, "raised an eyebrow" when Maggie's name was mentioned in connection with Debussy,[14] and later claimed that when she took over Mélisande from Garden, Debussy asked, "Why am I condemned to suffer English accents in *Pelléas*?"[15] So Brogan went over Legge's head, and talked to his boss, Fred Gaisberg. Gaisberg was delighted with the idea and suggested Cortot as accompanist. He cabled him: WOULD YOU LIKE ACCOMPANY MAGGIE TEYTE IN ALBUM OF DEBUSSY SONGS SHARING ROYALTIES DURING YOUR VISIT ENGLAND MARCH DO YOU AGREE STOP PLEASE WIRE REPLY REGARDS GAISBERG.

* Geraldine Farrar also took part in that concert, and together they sang the letter duet from *Figaro*—Chicago's Cherubino (Teyte) as Susanna opposite the Met's Cherubino (Farrar) as the Countess.

MAGGIE TEYTE

AND

CORTOT

DEBUSSY

Recital

Saturday Afternoon, November 6th

at 3

STEINWAY PIANOFORTE

Tickets (including Tax): Reserved, 12/-, 9/- and 6/-; Unreserved, 3/-

May be obtained at the Box Office, Wigmore Hall; usual Ticket Offices; and

IBBS & TILLETT, 124 Wigmore Street, W.1

Telephone: Welbeck 2325 (5 lines)
Telegrams: "Organol, Wesdo, London"

Ticket Office: Welbeck 8418
Hours: 10-5; Saturdays, 10-12

BAINES & SCARSBROOK LTD., PRINTERS, LONDON, N.W.5 1937)

For Programme P.T.O.

While waiting for Cortot's reply, Maggie bit her nails furiously. They tried to think of a substitute should Cortot say no. Joe suggested Artur Rubinstein, who used to come and practise at 40 avenue Victor Hugo when she had been a student. They had days of agony. Then WITH PLEASURE DEBUSSY TEYTE, wired back Cortot from the rue Budapest.

Their album of seven double-sided discs was so successful it sold over 1,000 copies in one year at the Gramophone Shop alone,* and led to numerous other recording contracts. The two artists gave an extremely successful concert in London, which was repeated in Paris. Cortot, one of the few international artists to accept an invitation from Furtwängler to play with the Berlin Philharmonic after Hitler came to power,[16] had pro-German sympathies as well as political ambitions, and later wrote articles in support of *Pétainiste* principles, and received a "Francisque", Pétain's emblem, a Gallic axe and a marshal's baton.

Brogan then had another recording idea, more ambitious even than the Teyte–Cortot album. Carried away by his absolute devotion to Maggie he threw himself into attempting to arrange no less than a complete recording of *Pelléas et Mélisande*. He hoped Reynaldo Hahn would conduct, though his reasoning may have been a little obscure—because of Hahn's well-known detestation of Debussy and of his music. "I know of no other man better suited to it," he wrote to Hahn after they had discussed the project over cocktails at the Ritz. "The other artists should be equally as great (as Teyte). It is a tremendous undertaking and must be of the highest artistic standard, something that can be handed down to posterity, and the most perfect example of Debussy. You mentioned a great Pelléas, someone who had no name, but to your mind was the perfect voice for the part. I would like Vanni Marcoux for the Golaud, if he has any voice left." But this letter, ominously, was dated April 1940. War—

> But hark! My pulse like a soft drum
> Beats my approach, tells thee I come

—was soon to put an end to Brogan's industrious striving on behalf of his long-cherished dream.

* When the Dutch-born American composer and opera director Richard Hageman heard the recordings, he wrote to Maggie, "You are one of the very few great artists alive, sad to relate." For Constant Lambert, Maggie's Debussy was a "revelation".

CHAPTER TEN

Cows & Concert Artists
(1940–1945)

You are quite right to prefer dogs—they are more entertaining than
concert artists and cows, more prepossessing than great prima donnas.
CLAUDE DEBUSSY, letter to Jacques Durand

WITH THE ONSET of war, Maggie seemed to accept a new fate, one
with which she had not up to then positively identified herself: she was
becoming primarily, indeed exclusively, a concert artist. Opera had been
her first love, and while she had been singing a predominantly French
repertoire in concerts for over thirty years, it was opera, along with the
high life, the personal dramas of love and marriage, even outdoor sports
such as golf, which had mattered most to her. Her concert work she
had often rather tossed off, just as she had earlier engagements at musical
soirées. Now, however, the conflict she had joked about in 1917 to an
American journalist, of her concert promoter versus her operatic impresario, was ended.*

But every decade had a different flavour in Maggie's life, as it did in the
times at large, and the flavour of the Forties was peculiarly suited to her
temperament, a temperament now in its sixth decade. The Thirties—the
age of what Hilaire Belloc called the "parvenoo", but also of volatile
political allegiance, of empty-headedness, and social and economic
depression—was not really her style at all. But the character of the
Forties suited her resilience and her individuality, and in her maturity as

---

* Even so she tried out new operatic works: on 27 May 1940, in the Parry Memorial
Theatre at the RCM, she sang Penelope in the first act of Inglis Gundry's *The Return of
Odysseus*, for which Boyd Neel conducted the LSO. Neel was staggered at her musician-
ship and capacity for hard work: she had memorized the whole thing in a very short time
while the other singers used scores.[1] Later in the Forties according to Jack Henderson who
lent her the score, she was thinking of performing in Britten's *Rape of Lucretia* in New
York.

an artist she knew exactly where she was and how to do the right thing
at the right moment. The reward for her painstaking professionalism and
artistic consistency was that French song again became popular in Great
Britain and America, and she was now its only outstanding Anglo-Saxon
interpreter. In the Thirties and Forties, nicely assessing that popularity
would return to her chosen composers, she had added considerably to her
repertoire. It now included not only Debussy, Ravel, Fauré, Dukas,
Chausson, Hahn and Duparc, but also the more recent figures of *Les Six:*
Honegger, Auric, Durey, Tailleferre, Poulenc, and Milhaud.

She had little idea of this, however, during the "phony war" when she
and Grace Vernon, who had continued to live in the flat at Woolley
Grange after Maggie's break-up with Sherwin, found another temporary
country retreat, though on a much less grand scale. The house in St
John's Wood in which, on Sherwin's death, she had taken a flat had been
requisitioned by the Air Ministry. London was overflowing with visitors,
refugees, and expanding ministries, and accommodation was scarce, so
for the time being Maggie moved her piano and other furniture into a
butler's cottage on a Berkshire estate near Yattenden. Both she and Grace
had cars, and petrol was as yet unrationed, so they could commute to the
city. But in Berkshire suddenly, the night after their move, these two
ex-wives in their fifties—Grace a few years younger than Maggie—
used to refined living and the constant attention of servants, found themselves on their own: "We were cold, we were hungry, we were tired—
we were near to tears. All we could do was to lie down in the beds, pull
over us anything we could grope for in the dark, and pray for daylight.
We had never felt more homeless, cast-out, and unhappy."[2]

Although Maggie was the smaller of the pair, physically she was very
tough and she did the lion's share of the hewing of wood and carrying of
coal. She dressed herself in an old siren suit, with a scarf over her head,
motoring goggles, and wielded a huge hammer: Cherubino and Hänsel
had at last attained full manhood. Butterfly had been extinguished once
and for all.

Such innocent, atavistic enjoyments were short-lived, for the war took a
serious turn with Dunkirk and the fall of France, and petrol rationing cut
short this final country visit. Maggie and Grace then moved into another
house in St John's Wood, No. 73 Hamilton Terrace, Grace taking the
top flat and Maggie the one underneath. Then, as she put it, "Tragedy and
comedy began to walk the streets hand in hand."[3] Beecham, who had

lived not far away, left England, first for Australia and then for the United States. Maggie had abandoned her native land in the First War, but not the Second; the reverse was true of Beecham.

Patriotic feeling ran high, and before Maggie could be persuaded that singing was the means by which she could best help the war effort, she decided she wanted to learn to drive an army truck. The pocket-sized prima donna was accepted by the Civil Defence Authority, and went on a special mechanic's course, rising every morning at seven after spending the night in a dug-out. Ah, Bohemia in excelsis! Bohemia, no longer in tiaras, but overalls!* 1940 vintage: it suited Maggie right down to the accelerator pedal, even though she had to stand to apply the brakes. But alas, they took away from her all too soon the glories of physical labour, making her give orders in a depot rather than take them, and to a rebel, a bohemian still at heart, this was the kiss of death. Then she found her throat affected by the dust and fumes of the depot.

Everyone thought she was mad, not the first time or the last, but it was a passing phase, serving perhaps to put her in a mood whereby, refreshed by contact with the actual and physical, she could begin, or again want to begin, to sing. It was, like many of her real-life gestures, deeply romantic, short-lived, but vitally executed, clearing body and mind of work-resistant toxins.

France fell on the day Charles Münch was to have conducted the first concert of a Festival of English and French Music at the Queen's Hall, under the patronage of the French Ambassador, and of Duff Cooper, erstwhile British Ambassador in Paris. Thomas Russell, manager of the London Philharmonic, had been in Paris to engage Francis Poulenc: "Suddenly Poulenc burst into the room, made the briefest apologies, explaining almost breathlessly that he and Pierre Bernac, who was waiting below in a car, were leaving at once to rejoin their regiment at Tours."⁴ Maggie was one of the "salvaged events"⁵; she gave a concert at the National Gallery on 21 June 1940, with the LPO under Constant Lambert, singing three of Berlioz's *Nuits d'été* and two songs by Duparc, "Phidylé" and "L'Invitation au voyage".

Then came the blitz. The hazards of the LPO have been graphically described by Russell, in an incident concerning his assistant: "Felix Aprahamian answered the telephone in my absence just as a couple of oil-bombs whizzed over the roof, sounding as though they were making

* To adapt E. F. Benson's phrases.

for the office. The person at the other end of the line heard an astonished 'My God' from Felix as the receiver was slammed down as if it were a red-hot coal."[6] Orchestral players and soloists threaded their way to work between bomb craters; streets were torn open, buildings roped off, as they might at any moment crash, and tops of houses smouldered with incendiaries. There were air raids for fifty-two consecutive nights. In November concerts were resumed. One night a woman phoned the Queen's Hall, asking for a ticket. They warned her of an air raid: "I'm not going to come unless there is," she replied.

In 1941 it eased up slightly. The LPO had just given a splendid performance in the Hall of *The Dream of Gerontius* and, feeling relaxed, the orchestral players decided to leave their instruments behind. Next morning the Queen's Hall was rubble. Twisted drum frames, bits and pieces of charred double basses, bent and blackened bassoons were all that remained. Only Sir Henry Wood's bust stood in one piece. An appeal was made over the wireless, and the results were overwhelming: a bus driver came all the way from Kent clasping a brown paper parcel under his arm. "It's a fiddle," he said. "I cannot bear to think that owing to the loss of an instrument, a player should be out of work."[7]

The LPO then took to the suburbs and the provinces. Felix Aprahamian, as Russell's assistant, planned for Maggie to sing Ravel's *Shéhérazade* with the LPO under Leslie Heward at the Albert Hall, Nottingham, in 1941. He had first heard her sing "that most beautiful of orchestral song cycles" at a BBC Symphony concert under Sir Henry Wood ten years before: "Once Maggie Teyte had charmed the magic casements opening on to Ravel's 'Asie', the spell was cast. It lasted long after the orchestral sigh that ends 'L'Indifférent'. Truth to tell it has lasted till this day."[8] He was distraught to find now that she was once again driving an army truck. Aprahamian persuaded her that singing Debussy was just as laudable a gesture of hostility to the Germans (never forgetting Debussy's feelings about German musicians), and that he would organize some Debussy.

As resistance to Hitler stiffened, so musical activity in London increased. There was Polish music, Russian music, Norwegian music, Greek music, all under the auspices of exiles who had fled Europe. The international milieu bore in certain respects, though material deprivation was only too evident, a curious resemblance to the Paris of the Third Republic. Everyone believed in freedom and the individual, in refinement—when they could get their hands on some—and it restored to the music of the Third

Republic its timeless appeal: in the face of terror, mass murder, bombing, and universal displacement, from this music was distilled a delicacy, a purity, an intimacy of mood, and an ennobling perception of nature. War can be a great purifier of the artistic tradition. Concerts of French music drew large and appreciative audiences.

A French broker, Tony Mayer, who had joined the Free French as a paymaster or financial expert, united with Aprahamian—the pair had used to play together as amateurs, Mayer the violin and Aprahamian the piano and organ—in organizing a first concert. And so began an illustrious series under the sponsorship of the French Committee of National Liberation, in which 104 concerts were given altogether. Maggie figured often in the early ones: "She made it a condition that I should rehearse with her once a week," wrote Aprahamian.

The thought that she considered me a fit rehearsal substitute for Gerald Moore was flattering enough. It was also rather terrifying. My weekly *trac* used to be taken care of by a Maggie Teyte cocktail ($\frac{1}{3}$ tumbler grapefuit, $\frac{2}{3}$ gin). I soon found out that my partner knew far more about the accompaniments than most singers. It was no rare thing to be stopped at the opening phrase of "Je tremble en voyant ton visage", the third song of *Le Promenoir des deux amants*, and be corrected with: "Now, Claude played it like this, but Artur (Artur's other name, I learned, was Rubinstein) played it like *this*."[9]

Together, on Thursday afternoons, they rehearsed not only Debussy songs, but others by Fauré, Duparc, Chausson, Ravel, Poulenc, Milhaud, and even Szymanowski. Maggie was shrewd and happy in her choice of accompanist, for with Aprahamian's boundless enthusiasm she was able to extend and deepen her repertoire, learning many new songs.

In 1943 Maggie was given, in recognition of her service to France, a gold Cross of Lorraine, the extempore Free French award, with an accompanying letter in General de Gaulle's handwriting. The cross was handed her by René Massigli, the French Ambassador, at a dinner at the Connaught.[10] The concerts of French music continued until well after the war was over: she sang at the fifteenth in the series, after France had been liberated, with Gerald Moore as her accompanist; the other soloist was Jacques Thibaud.

Less glamorous, but no less rewarding, was working for ENSA (Every

Night Something Awful, as one wag had it, originating a typical Forties joke). The Entertainments National Service Association was a pioneer in the expansion of music into the popular domain. Tours for ENSA were planned, under Basil Dean's direction, by Walter Legge, who had originally turned down the Teyte–Cortot recording—Maggie seems to have been a blind spot for him, which she never forgave. "A cruel, sarcastic, but clever man," she called him, telling an amusing story (possibly apocryphal) about his attempt one day to conduct in Birmingham, wearing a Russian blouse, "Like Moiseiwitsch. He took up his baton, broke it. Second time he took up the baton. PAM PAM . . . the orchestra walked off."[11] These opinions of Legge were much echoed by others, none of whom disputed his power and ability.*

Seven artists congregated for a first meeting at the Drury Lane Theatre to sort out their programme: Maggie, George Baker (baritone), Alfred Cave (violinist), Olga Hegedus (cellist), Josephine Curtis (contralto), Colin Horsley (pianist), and Josephine Lee (accompanist). "I sang during bombings and strafings, during hot weather and cold, sang the classics and some popular songs, even to a rendition of Porter's 'Begin the Beguine' in Spanish."[12] At the end of this particular tour, playing in small halls to audiences of all nationalities, English, American, Greek, French, Polish, Canadian, Indian, Maggie told her accompanist that it was a pity she had been born a woman, or she would have asked her to play for her at other concerts; but alas, it was the rule for a soprano to have a male accompanist at recitals.

Maggie's two men accompanists during this prolific period were Ivor Newton, and then, with greater frequency, Gerald Moore, who as a boy in North America had first heard her sing nearly thirty years before. During the blitz at one National Gallery concert, with Moore accompanying, she shattered the spell of a Fauré song: "Damn. Start again. I swallowed my eyelashes."[13] Though she cancelled one tour to her birth-town, Wolverhampton, in 1943, she did sing there, in fact twice, at the Wulfrun Hall: once in 1942, with Gerald Moore, and again in 1943. On the first occasion she wore a beautiful white dress with the Cross of Lorraine across her chest, and sang "La Chevelure", that painfully tender distillation of the hair scene from *Pelléas*, Emile Paladilhe's exquisite

---

* The *Sunday Times Magazine* (16 October 1977) quoted Legge as saying: "I ran the Philharmonic as a benevolent dictatorship. Democracy has no place in the arts . . . democracy is a euphemism for deterioration."

Under the auspices of the French Committee of National Liberation

A PROGRAMME OF FRENCH MUSIC

PLAYED BY THE

LONDON PHILHARMONIC ORCHESTRA

CONDUCTOR:

FISTOULARI

BERLIOZ : Ouverture de Benvenuto Cellini
DUPARC : " L'Invitation au Voyage " et " Phidylé "
DEBUSSY : Fantaisie pour piano et orchestre
DUKAS : Scherzo, L'Apprenti Sorcier

INTERVAL

RAVEL : Shéhérazade   FAURE : Pavane
CHABRIER : Rapsodie, España

MAGGIE TEYTE
(SOPRANO)

MARCEL GAZELLE
(PIANIST)

MONDAY,	DEC. 6, at 6.15	.	Town Hall, BIRMINGHAM
TUESDAY,	DEC. 7, at 6.30	.	Central Hall, COVENTRY
WEDNESDAY,	DEC. 8, at 6.30	.	Civic Hall, WOLVERHAMPTON
THURSDAY,	DEC. 9, at 6.30	.	Victoria Hall, HANLEY
FRIDAY,	DEC. 10, at 6.30	.	Town Hall, WALSALL
SATURDAY,	DEC. 11, at 2.45	.	De Montfort Hall, LEICESTER
SUNDAY,	DEC. 12, at 2.30	.	Adelphi Theatre, LONDON

MUSICAL CULTURE LIMITED   .   295, REGENT STREET, W.1

VAIL & Co. Ltd., E.C.1.

"Psyché" which sent shudders down the spine, Berlioz's "Absence", and songs by Quilter and Elgar.

All over England she went, with England's tireless music providers. During the 1942 concert season, said Sir Malcolm Sargent, he averaged more than one symphony concert a day. Payments were small and erratic. The artists received £5 apiece for the French music concerts. When the bombs got too bad in the National Gallery, Myra Hess's concerts retreated underground to the basement. Maggie sang there several times. She sang with the LPO conducted by Fistoulari in 1943, at Birmingham, Coventry, Wolverhampton, Walsall, Leicester, and finally in London, at the Adelphi Theatre. She sang at the Albert Hall with Sir Adrian Boult. The international Edwardian celebrity was at last returning to her roots. As the tide of war turned, and France was at last liberated, town and civic halls all over England echoed to the strains of Debussy and Ravel—some of them, as the *Oxford Times* (8 September 1944) noted when Maggie visited there, not at all designed to do justice to such music. Even so, in Oxford she "revealed herself as ever as the only singer in this country capable of a real sympathy to the French idiom". But she charmed with the favourites, too, doing in February 1944 two numbers each in three "Workers' Playtimes" for which she received the "special" fee of 150 guineas. It was rare for BBC artists to be paid more.

Maggie's gravest shortcoming at this time was that she stood too much on her own. She dominated Grace Vernon almost totally, and saw less of her niece Rita, who now had two small boys and was occupied with them. Maggie found the presence of the children irksome. At the war's commencement, when Rita and Cavan lived in Edgware during the blitz, she would drive there sometimes, to be away from the centre, but would never stay long at their house. Later Rita and Cavan moved to North Wales, where Cavan broadcast almost continuously through the war on the BBC—touring in between—and they saw Maggie when she came to sing in Bangor. She tried to stir up jealousy in Cavan: their marriage made her quarrelsome and provocative, possibly reminding her of her own failures. After the birth of Rita's second son, she sent her to Dr Helena Wright, the gynaecologist, saying, "Don't have any more." She told Rita that everything she really loved, she destroyed: bitter words.

Beecham had been the last of her ships passing in the night, though that affair went on longer than most. Now she seemed to be withdrawing apart. She was undergoing, and for a woman of her vanity the effect must never be underestimated, the fading of her youth. She became mysterious, liking to keep everyone guessing as to what her next move would be, and whom she was seeing. She would phone to say she would arrive somewhere, then at the last minute change her mind and cancel the arrangement. She would promise to give someone something, then forget all about it; even, after a period of time, give the same thing to someone else. She would study to keep her friends separate from one another. She had a secret life.

But the truth was that she was seeing nobody. She would go up to her room twenty-four hours before she was going to sing, do up her hair in a neat prim way, like a pre-adolescent schoolgirl, and spend the evening entirely on her own, doing her "tatting".

CHAPTER ELEVEN

Park Avenue to Mélisande's Tower
(1945–1950)

Th'assay so hard, so sharp the conquering . . .
CHAUCER

AFTER WORLD WAR Two the past life of Maggie Teyte became fable, the present fairy story. Early in 1945 she received a cable from America: HAVE CONTRACT OF THIRTEEN WEEKS FOR YOU WITH COLUMBIA BROADCASTING SYSTEM CAN YOU COME PLEASE REPLY IMMEDIATELY LOVE JOE BROGAN. The Cortot–Teyte recordings put out under Brogan's initial sponsorship had been increasing Maggie's reputation during the war years; no less had the additions of excellent recordings of Duparc, Chausson, Hahn, and Fauré, made with Gerald Moore. Now, on the other side of the Atlantic too, Maggie was considered the foremost living interpreter of modern French song.

A second cable arrived from Joe Brogan; then a third, pertaining to the long-cherished dream: RODZINSKI AND NEW YORK PHILHARMONIC WANT YOU FOR COMPLETE RECORDING OF PELLEAS FOR GODSAKE DONT FAIL ME LOVE JOE BROGAN. A fourth cable even revealed a battle going on between CBS and NBC as to which network would have the privilege of presenting Maggie, due to be "the first European artist to visit America since V-E day". But Maggie's main problem was how to arrive in the States: the excitement was such that she gave herself trismus, a mild form of lockjaw. She could not eat, and when she finally docked in New York in July, having obtained by the efforts of Ed Murrow—although CBS were no longer in the running—a passage on a banana boat from Glasgow called S.S. *Eros*, the first thing she did was to announce to her sponsors, NBC, that she was unfit to sing. Everyone was extremely nervous for a week or two wondering why they had made such a fuss. But then her jaw improved so that she was able to give her first Bell Telephone Hour concert, which was broadcast live.

It was her first appearance in America for twenty-five years, and some people went so far as to say it could not be she, that she had died and was being impersonated by her daughter. "I felt I was hearing the true vocal French for the first time in my life," wrote Wally Magill, the Telephone Hour executive. "It was a caressing sound—I'd never heard anything quite like it. In fact, when it decided to take Maggie Teyte for its Telephone Hour program, the Bell system, who were the sponsors, had no idea they were doing so much for the art of America."[1] Maggie made them pay for the privilege: she received $3,000 for each of the twelve programmes and sang only three or four songs on each, though the programmes were rebroadcast again and again.

Little surprise then that she booked a suite at the Waldorf-Astoria: a change indeed from the NAAFI canteens and barbed-wire perimeters of provincial England, where she had often performed in near-anonymity. Not only did she consider it her due, now, this luxury, but she basked as never before in the publicity given her. At the end of 1945 she gave two concerts in New York's Town Hall, on 31 October and 28 December, both of which were sold out within hours of the announcement. The audience at the first, wrote Robert Hague, received her tumultuously, with a welcome beside which "a Sinatra demonstration at the Paramount is a feeble thing indeed".[2]

But in what shape really was her voice? Many old admirers and fellow artists were conspicuous in the audience at Town Hall in October, among them a parterre of prima donnas—Grace Moore, Jeritza, Swarthout, Jennie Tourel—and all had but a single thought in mind: Could she still sing? The critics, too, were highly sceptical, some bored and blasé. Were they going to see yet another artist past her prime clinging on embarrassingly?

It turned out to be one of the greatest recitals of her career. She cracked a top A in one song, and in the awed silence that followed it, with a glance at the formidable ladies who confronted her in the front rows, said quite serenely, "Now we'll just do it over again!" A second time she hit the A fair and square, and then all hell was let loose by way of applause. Afterwards the critics did marvel. For most it was the return of an artist in the great tradition, the like of which they had not heard for years. "One harbours emotion to project it at the right moment," Maggie told a reporter.[3] "You can really tell that woman's lived," one young admirer blurted out to her friend.[4]

While twenty-five years before she had been known as the "baby prima donna", the "pocket diva", and by other such epithets, in this second American career she was bathed in descriptive hyperbole: not only was she the "toast of New York", "a living legend", a "doll-sized magician", or Virgil Thomson's "a miracle and a monument", but one dared to say "she seemed to climb right inside the microphone and make love to it"; another proclaimed that, armed with "exquisite artistry and machine-gun wit", she came as "an experiment and remained to conquer." "British good-will ambassador extraordinary" was another title and she earned this by travelling to Toronto, opening there Canada's ninth War Loan drive. She gave a recital in Washington at which President Truman was an enthusiastic member of the audience.

Her New York triumph was followed by a tour of Philadelphia, San Francisco, Los Angeles, Portland, and Seattle. With the San Francisco Symphony Orchestra, under the veteran French conductor Pierre Monteux, she sang seven out of the twelve scenes of *Pelléas*. Perry Askam sang Golaud, and Theodore Uppman Pelléas.* She had sung a substantial fragment of *Pelléas* in London early in 1945,† with Pierre Bernac and accompanied by Francis Poulenc, but Mélisande with Monteux was the first time she had broached the role in the States. Even so, nothing came of Brogan's hope of recording the whole opera, and he had to console himself in the end with mere snippets: Maggie doubling Pelléas and Mélisande, singing in addition the role of Geneviève, on a famous set of records made specially for his Gramophone Shop.

The prize plum of this comeback was yet to come. Maggie was now doing very well and engagements flowed in from her two New York managers, one Austin Wilder, who had a lot of trouble with his eyes, the other a nephew of her second husband Sherwin Cottingham, Kenneth Allen jun.—youthful, wealthy, and an excellent liaison officer for Maggie. Bookings correspondingly increased back in England. The BBC no

* Maggie arrived late for the first rehearsal at the San Francisco Opera House, and Monteux filled in for her in a "French monotone—his matchless (speckled grey) walrus moustache twitching, and his black eyes sparkling as he intoned, 'Ne me touchez pas. Ne me touchez pas, ou je me jette à l'eau . . .' When Golaud says, 'Vous avez l'air très jeune. Quel age avez-vous!' Monteux could not resist, and . . . he answered 'Seexty-tree'."⁵

† In this memorial concert for the critic Edwin Evans, who had died on 3 March 1945, given at the Fyvie Hall of the Polytechnic, Regent Street, they sang the two fountain scenes. Harriet Cohen also played a piano solo at this concert, and Arthur Bliss spoke.

longer balked at the special fee of sixty guineas she asked—not knowing
she was soon to ask for more—and she sang in a Fauré programme, then a
Variety Cavalcáde (with Tom Ronald); she sang Tchaikovsky, and Gluck;
in April 1946 she gave a recital at the Wigmore Hall. Edward Lockspeiser,
Debussy's outstanding biographer, judged in a report circulated privately
to colleagues in the BBC (17 April 1946) that:

> Maggie Teyte is now singing very well. She has improved a lot. Her
> trip to America seems to have done her good. Her voice is in good form.
> What is remarkable in her singing of French songs is the temperament
> she puts into them. She does not believe in making Debussy so tenuous
> that he fades into thin air; she underlines and brings out all the harmonic
> and vocal colour in his music—as Mary Garden seems to have done,
> judging from the records she made with Debussy. There was a time
> about a year or two ago, when Maggie Teyte's deliberately "robust"
> approach to French music became coarse and overemphatic. Her voice
> was less good than it is now, and nervousness may have obliged her to
> force her expression.

He was but echoing the enthusiastic young woman who gushed, "You
can really tell that woman's lived." And what good fortune, to be
actually improving in voice towards the age of sixty: yet this does appear
to have been true. Had Maggie seen this report she would no doubt have
been gratified but a degree chilled at the reference to Garden, whose voice
she never revered as she had those of Felia Litvinne, Melba, Caruso,
Chaliapin, and, more recently, of Flagstad.

Her New York base was still the Waldorf-Astoria. She could have
lived better, probably, more modestly, but the hotel was in the old
tradition too, the revived rays of the Golden Age, and she meant to draw
from them every last glimmer of heat and comfort. New York loves
people prepared to live out their own myths publicly, and this, now more
than ever, Maggie was prepared to do,* unleashing her wit, her irrepressible vivacity, her memories, punctuating her talk with, as Allene Talmey
of *Vogue* noted, "eyebrows she uses the way the French do their hands",
and laughing "a low crumpled laugh that is not at all soprano".

If the fame element that she bathed in was, ultimately, a little cold,

* For quite a while, she even paid a publicity agent $500 a month, which her friends
thought a waste of money.

and she had long since fed too much off the lonely marrow of herself, there was still the ever faithful Gay Vernon, far away from the pinnacles of New York glamour, back at camp in Hamilton Terrace. She could be relied on to serve, ever zealously, her mistress's commands. "Darling," Maggie writes to her, "I have not come across the manicure set I used to keep on my mantelpiece in the little room. I am a little nervous because inside are the two front crowns that Thompson* made for me in case I broke one." Gay dutifully airmailed them, and there follows the next request, wrapped up in an exciting social titbit:

The trip was very smooth owing to fog! I was at the purser's table— Mr Carme, who is still very charming—the others were Alfred Edwards, M.P., quite nice and a little smitten—Bobsie Godspeed, a friend from Chicago, Jack Buchanan also afloat. I mentioned *The Marquise*—and he said he was free next September—so who knows!†

I am in great need of an article by Newman‡ re conductors and composers, perhaps you remember the one I mean. Would you please get a copy, date, etc., and send it by airmail. Sorry to give you the trouble of having to go to their offices for it.[6]

It was all excitement. Her New York friends kept her busy and entertained her royally. A friend of Joe Brogan, Hayes Sturges, used to invite prima donnas to listen and compare his rare vocal recordings: this kind of gramophone salon flourished just after the Second War when there were not as yet so many records that the sport became bewildering. Among the singers he put on were Frieda Hempel, Edyth Walker, and Maggie. Maggie was a great favourite, as she had such witty and perceptive comments on singers she had known thirty years before: Garden, Delna, Vanni Marcoux, and Edouard de Reszke among them. (Of Destinn, with whom she had sung in Paris in 1910, she said she was the ugliest woman with the most beautiful voice she had ever heard.) Sturges's circle included

---

* Her dentist, Allan Thompson.

† *The Marquise* (almost certainly a musical adaptation of Noël Coward's play written for Marie Tempest) was something Maggie had the idea of putting on herself, but when Buchanan, she, and Gay Vernon—who knew Buchanan well, having played golf with him—met, Buchanan said, "Have you the slightest idea what you would be letting yourself in for? I tried it once, but never again—it's an awful headache." So the project fizzled out, but not Maggie's idea of putting on something herself.

‡ Ernest Newman, the critic Maggie "swore by".

the publisher Theodore Purdy, and through him she also met other publishers in London and in New York: Max Reinhardt, Roger and Moyra Lubbock, Hamish and Yvonne Hamilton. With Theodore Purdy and his wife, Maggie went to see a pre-war French film, *La Kermesse héroïque*, with Françoise Rosay and Louis Jouvet, as she wanted to refresh her accent; even so no one could quite claim her accent had the freshness it had when she bore the name Plumon, and was herself *citoyenne* of the *République française*.

One night she was invited by Hayes Sturges to share a box at Town Hall: "We'll go along, hear the 'divine' Mary give her *lecture—un événement assez drôle*." Surprisingly enough to Sturges, Maggie accepted; she could never resist something like this, especially if she could steal in unseen and unknown, play at being *en bohème ce soir*. The *lecteur* was Mary Garden, now long retired, no longer stout but thin and bony, in a tight red dress with too-brightly dyed hair. What money she had not lost on the Chicago Stock Exchange she had gambled away in Monte Carlo, and she was now living in retirement in Aberdeen. She delivered a huge rambling concoction of supposition, scandal, and promiscuous adventure.* She was introduced by Virgil Thomson and to those present she looked bemused, as if she had been drinking.

Great artist but what an immodest boaster she now seemed, and how she dug her nails into the musical *monstres sacrés* of the Third Republic. "Then there was Massenet . . . I'm afraid I never much cared for Massenet. I know how the French adore him and the French know how much I adore them. . . . But he would pour out to me the most sickeningly sentimental and gushing letters . . ."

She did not know Maggie was watching. If she had, most likely she would not have cared. They had sung Massenet's *Cendrillon* together in Chicago, New York, and Philadelphia—ah, well, only a mere thirty-five years before; what was that between Scots-blooded prima donnas? Maggie could never stand her, but she was amused, fascinated. But, ruthlessly, with her greater age and experience—and her complete sexual amorality —Garden had forestalled Maggie ever singing Mélisande in the States.

". . . Thanks to that body of mine I was the perfect boy," went on that

* William Miles, director of the Berkshire Playhouse, Stockbridge, Massachusetts, was also present on this occasion and talked to the author of it, 1977. Later, Louis Biancolli spent the better part of three months interviewing Garden, the basis for their amusing book.

prick-teaser divine. She hardly looked it now, Maggie thought: how unscrupulously she had used Massenet, his fawning admiration for her, and Carré too, and Messager, saying she loved them all. "I was in my dressing room, still in my Chérubin costume and wig, and at the door, on his knee, a bouquet of flowers in his right hand, was one of the greatest writers of France . . ."

Maggie began to get impatient and look restless. Her companions, seeing this, began to grow apprehensive even though Garden was mainly an object for pity. Now it was Debussy's turn: God forbid that she should claim Debussy had pursued her wildly and passionately, throwing himself on his knees and pouring out his soul to her. That was not Debussy's style, though it was very much Mary Garden's. But Debussy had loved Mélisande, no doubt about that: he was utterly infatuated with his own, or Maeterlinck's, heroine. Could he distinguish the character from the actress who played her?

Garden told the heartrending tale of how Debussy's first wife, the sweet and lovely Lily Texier, had come along ecstatically happy to a performance of *Pelléas* in Paris after Debussy's death. There was Mary in her Mélisande costume, in the dressing room after Act Three (two still to go), being slain by compliments from Prime Minister Aristide Briand, when Lily entered. (Was the Prime Minister really there? Still, we'll let that go: Prime Ministers make good fodder for punch lines from prima donnas.) Texier had bought two tickets for the performance, one for herself and one for Claude. "Claude is with me tonight," she said, radiant with joy.

Then appeared Madame Debussy *numéro deux*, Mme Bardac, in black, tottering on a cane, convulsed with sobs. All this in the dressing room, with the opera's climax still to come! "And who," the divine Mary asked Briand after they had gone, "do you suppose really loved Debussy for himself?"

What an actress she was! But then she presumed more than Maggie could take: it made her blood boil instantly. "Of course," Mary confided to the hushed house, "you know I really *am* Mélisande." "Oh, for God's sake!" Maggie turned to her companions. Something had snapped. She had to speak out.

If Maggie had had over the decades the smaller slice of the Mélisande cake, she at least had the last bite, for she made her New York début in the part in 1948, a few days before her sixtieth birthday. By all accounts the divine—"getting more divine by the minute"—Mary fled town, for previously, as *Newsweek* told the people, whenever Miss Teyte wanted to sing the role, "La Garden arrived fastest with the mostest." He who knows how to wait wins out in the end, as the proverb goes. The miracle was that Maggie still had the energy and stamina to take on this demanding role which taxed not so much robustness and lyrical virtuosity, as emotional subtlety and musical perception.

The Met had not wanted to chance Maggie as Mélisande, but to the courageous and enterprising Laslo Halasz it came as a challenge and so he engaged her for the New York City Opera Company and also for some Carnegie Hall concerts where she sang Mozart. So there she was, in Mélisande's golden tresses, almost forty years to the day after she made her Paris début in the part, ready to do it all again. There were several cases of nerves as to whether it would go down well. Jacques Jansen had first been engaged as Pelléas, but he could not arrive in time. Theodore Uppman, from Hollywood, who had sung Pelléas with her when Monteux conducted the concert version, went under at the very last moment, feeling inadequately prepared, and withdrew;* his place was taken by a young French Canadian called Fernand Martel, a former pupil of Maggie's.

Komisarzhevsky's set and staging presented a variety of platforms and other permanent structures which terrified Maggie to begin with. Virgil Thomson, writing in the *Herald-Tribune*, advised the audience to keep their eyes closed. Gone was the mystery and fear of the forest, the naturalistic shadows and eeriness of the damp foundations of the castle. The production was prophetic of director and designer taking over control of opera, in the next twenty years, with their narrow, brutalist imaginations.

---

* According to Uppman,[7] Maggie insisted on replacing Jansen, the Company's choice. Uppman arrived late for rehearsals, and by the first night felt less prepared than he wanted to be; his début was delayed until the third performance, thus giving rise to the impression relayed in *Newsweek* (5 April 1948) that he took fright. He was still, in any case, terribly nervous at the third performance. "The sets were treacherous—steep stairs to trip on— and everything darkly lit." But he acquitted himself well, the *Herald-Tribune* writing (22 April 1948) that his singing and acting as Pelléas had been "rarely matched in this city". He disliked his costume so much that Maggie had a new one designed for him, which she paid for herself. He wore it later at the Metropolitan, making his début there as Pelléas in 1953. Uppman created the title role in Benjamin Britten's *Billy Budd* in London in 1951, and during his stay Maggie asked him to sing *Pelléas* with her again in aid of Jean de Reszke's destitute niece in Poland; but this came to naught.

Objects dominated a set described variously in terms of local phenomena, such as the entrance to the Holland Tunnel, a cistern top down on grandfather's farm, and a wall of Sing-Sing. The lighting was dim too, to add to Maggie's problems in moving about the stage, so her acting appeared on the stiff side, and by the end she was totally spent with mastering obstacles. Even so, little touches thrilled Maurice Maeterlinck's biographer, Patrick Mahony, who found the way she threw the ring away a stroke of genius.

Vocally and musically the performance was a triumph. It was, for Virgil Thomson, "beautiful work", so much so that he went on to claim that French opera was the one repertory that made dramatic and musical sense. Teyte's influence was strong here: at one rehearsal she stopped the conductor and said, "Sorry, Maestro, you are losing the story. You have to give the full value to MAETERLINCK's *Pelléas et Mélisande*."[8]* As well as for Maggie, the plaudits rang out for Carlton Gauld's Golaud and Jean Morel's poetically authentic reading of the score. Even for Olin Downes, who had once chided her for overacting,† "Miss Teyte is not only authoritative mistress of every measure from the standpoint of musician-ship and style but she colours her tones with the text and accomplishes everything that dramatic interpretation suggests by means of vocal delivery."[10] Physically Maggie may not have had the resources she had when she performed the part forty years before, but technically and interpretively the miracle was that she had over it as great a hold as she had ever had. De Reszke's teaching was still alive and well.

The experience had its detractors. Leo Lerman, who adored Maggie, could not refrain from noting a certain "ghoulish pleasure" at seeing a Mélisande over sixty, especially with such a young Pelléas—Fernand Martel was only twenty-eight. Maggie's final arbiter, the box office, affirmed her popularity, however: the first performance was a sell-out, and its reception at the City Center was, so *Time* said, the noisiest ovation of the year. Four more performances were given in New York before the opera was taken on tour. But "Dammit all," Maggie said, "one can't go on forever." She felt now as she had felt over Cherubino, over Zerlina,

* Very rarely did Maggie dictate to a conductor, though it was on Debussy's instruc-tions that Ruhlmann, her first conductor of *Pelléas*, followed the *tempi* she herself had learnt from Debussy.

† Maggie's reply to this comment was, "He has no soul, no imagination. He is stone cold, like a piece of mutton fat."[9]

over Mimi, Butterfly, and Hänsel—the time had come to put Mélisande to bed.

While her triumphs in the U.S. had a certain poetic justice, in view of her neglect before World War Two, in Portland Place, W.1 a flurry of internal memos was set in motion by Maggie's demand for 100 guineas for a Debussy recital on the Third Programme. She felt now she was worth this price, but the BBC, after earnest deliberation among its A/DMs and A/Cs (Ent) and A/OMDs, decided to offer her but 80. Worse than this, another member of the BBC, sent to what was clearly a bad concert Maggie gave on a flying trip to London from New York— she was probably tired and in Edward Lockspeiser's words, "forcing her expression"—found a deterioration in her singing. "For many years now," submitted another mandarin sent along to hear her who, having found her errors in taste and style more noticeable than they had been, was asked to expand on his initial reaction, "matters of interpretive style have taken second place with her to vocal effect."[11] Here was a marked difference of view from Lockspeiser's comments made barely a year before.* But then on 1 September 1948 she gave a superb concert with Gerald Moore at the Freemasons Hall, Edinburgh; opinions were at once reversed and the BBC agreed to the 100 guineas, the Music Booking Manager arguing that "no other British singer of the present day had reached international status." A little while later Maggie decided, however, to forsake her homeland and become an American.

She felt unappreciated in England, as ever. When she tackled Sir Adrian Boult at the BBC over the Honegger–Claudel *Jeanne d'Arc au bûcher*, Boult replied that he would put the idea up to the HOM (Head of Music): that was the last she heard of it. "The whole business of music in England has gone to pieces," she said, "because they don't appreciate it any more. Musical appreciation and culture is far greater in America today. I remember when it used to be the other way around."[12]

She backed up her words with deeds. After her success as Mélisande she found a large studio twenty-four floors up, at No. 404 East 55th Street. She called it her Mélisande's Tower because it was dominated by the building's huge water tank. It had a large garden space, a gallery round the studio where she slept—with little privacy—and she was so taken with it she summoned, giving immense trouble to all her friends,

---

* The postwar BBC line was very much against voices of emotional and temperamental quality like Teyte's, preferring the "off-white", highly restrained effect.

her furniture from London. Her relations came on business: Cavan, Rita, and their youngest son. "Rita had a grand time," she wrote to Gay Vernon "in spite of having to watch Johnny every minute—but poor old Cavan couldn't get away fast enough,"[13] the latter possibly because Maggie had overspent herself, and had recourse to him for loans.

Her faithful Gay in London kept minding her material possessions, obeying her directives, and desperately serving all the schemes her fertile brain spun off in all directions. "You seem to be having a nice time in and out of bed!" she writes to Gay in February:

Do the doctors know the reason of the boils? I suppose really it's all because of certain things lacking in diet!! Well, darling, I hope you are better now, and on your "tootsie-wootsies".

First let us talk about the car—if it is not used, it is better to jack it up but not empty the engine, as it should be run now and again to keep it in running order—it is better for the tyres to have them off the ground—it would save a little money as well to have it jacked up.

Then she asks Gay to find her a book: "I want to prepare a television programme telling the funny side of opera—between numbers, and I am collecting these anecdotes . . ."

She reels off the trials of her furniture, of meeting up with her old friend Olga Lynn, now "stouter than ever", looking "even shorter "than before—when curtseying to the Queen she needed only to bow her head—and of the ever hectic life of Kenneth Allen, Sherwin's nephew, her New York agent, known as "Kenny". "My furniture is still going through the customs, but here's hoping that I shall be definitely installed sometime next week. I don't think Harrods were very good—many papers I should have had never came, and it delays everything—for instance a copy of the insurance certificate."[14]

Next month she is in more of a domestic mood, as she tells Gay about "Mélisande's Tower". "This place is really fascinating, and I consider myself very lucky to have found it—it is the first time that I have ever made something to my own liking—decoration etc.—grey walls, grey net curtains, scarlet curtains, which makes my black wrought-iron stand out—there are still a lot of little things to be done, a bit of paint here and there, windows to be readjusted to keep out dirt and draught—but I am very happy." Her next Telephone Hour broadcast, which came off that

June, went well, and Maggie found herself briefly drawn into the battle royal between radio and television, proclaiming that she was fighting for "tele", the new medium, but that money was scarce there.

In August she made her first venture as producer-actress, in spite of Jack Buchanan and others warning her off it, and in spite of her failure with Hahn's *Mozart*.★ This was with a concert version of Gounod's *Faust*, the poet Stephen Spender having prepared for her something between a libretto and a commentary, basing it more on Goethe and bypassing Barbier and Carré, Gounod's librettists.

I have the first two performances of *Faust* scheduled for Aug 4th and 5th at Stockbridge, which is close to Tanglewood, the big summer Festival here—it is my first venture as a producer-actress—I start with a group of six songs—and then the concert version of *Faust*—myself as narrator. Saw Stephen Spender about 10 days ago (Gee he's a handsome brute !)— he is revising it a little from the original manuscript I had—the Goethe metre is very interesting, like a man composing in 4/4 time, with bars here and there in 5/8 and 3/4. He is very clever—Stephen I mean.[16]

This enterprising *café-théâtre* or pocket version of *Faust*, purely Maggie's brainchild, could have belonged more to the Seventies than the Forties. After her mini-recital, mostly of Debussy, the stage darkened and Maggie, dressed in a pale blue dinner gown, marched to a lectern and began to narrate: "Behold Faust in his cell . . ." Then came the Gounod, sung by three men—representing Faust, Mephistopheles, Valentin—and a soprano as Marguérite, accompanied by two pianos. They wore dinner clothes and capes, and the stage business was effectively simple.

Her inspiration came from the war. "Hitler really started it all. I could just see him†—reaching out, twisting, destroying. He was the real Mephistopheles. I always thought he should be the centre of the opera— not that milksop Marguérite or that weakling Faust." According to Irving Kolodin the feat required "a strong will, the courage of a fool, and the conviction of a saint":[17] she had all three, and relished the whole

---

★ She had met Hahn again just after the war at the British Embassy in Paris, where Lady Diana Duff Cooper briefly revived old-style musical patronage, and Hahn played for Maggie. The Labour Government was in, and another time the entertainment consisted of Ernest Bevin leading the singing with "Daisy, Daisy, give me your answer do".[15]

† And she had met him, of course. See Chapter 9.

thing, auditioning seventy-five sopranos for Marguérite, finally picking a nineteen-year-old radio singer, Lillian Murphy. She really put the cast through their paces—she had been taught the opera by Jean de Reszke: "Not too much passion," he had said, "or you can't finish the *bel canto* properly"—and they stood up to it. "One cannot learn to be a good singer through flattery. I wouldn't let them wave their arms—no windmills for me!"

Confidence characterized the whole venture. Her old friend, Fritz Kreisler, said to her: "You have put the pearls on a string," and while most agreed they preferred the old pearls to the new string, namely Spender's, everyone felt it was a bang-up show.[18]

Maggie's own reaction was as cool as usual: she never had much time for praise, and once gave a dressing-down to a correspondent who had written extolling her recordings, asking him if he hadn't something better to do. "Heifetz was playing here last night," continued her American chronicle to Gay from Stockbridge, "which brought us a lot of critics first. Kolodin of the *Herald-Tribune* (not Virgil Thomson this time) apparently has given us a wonderful column, he has fallen for Spender—I wonder where Spender is?" In her, some might say, dilettante fashion, she did not pursue her *Faust* further, although demand was there to exploit it from coast to coast. She wanted to do something else, so she got down—Spender having disappeared—to doing her own narrations for *Romeo and Juliet* and *La Périchole*, to try out in Philadelphia. Time was short: she felt she now had only a year or two more of active work.

And money was in short supply. She had two flats to pay for, until giving up the London one, and Gay partly to support,* as well as her travelling across the States, and frequent crossings of the Atlantic—all these undertaken in the most expensive fashion. Some of her musical competitors in New York were resorting to dirty tricks: She claimed to have seen a circular letter sent out by a leading rival concert bureau, alleging to people who asked for her for dates that she would not prove satisfactory, and giving reasons.† A plan she contrived through her

---

* Gay Vernon taught under the aegis of the "Teyte-Vernon School of Singing", even staying at the Waldorf when Maggie lived there, giving lessons as Maggie's assistant for twenty-five dollars a time (she charged a pound in London).

† About this time *Colliers' Magazine* published an article purporting to disclose the nasty methods of these big combines, whereupon one of them promptly sued *Colliers'* for a million dollars.

solicitors to convince Vera Cottingham (now Mrs Lilley) to settle on her a lump sum of £50,000 instead of the annual income running now just under £2,000 a year—Maggie had during the war fought and won a High Court case to make the Cottingham estate pay the surtax on this sum—failed to impress Sherwin's widow. "I doubt if she will ever part (with the £50,000)," complained Maggie, giving up one hair-brained notion she had of settling in Jamaica. She was rapidly running out of stimuli as well as money, and at the beginning of 1950 she confides to Gay: "Darling, I have got to get away from here if only for two months— otherwise it looks as if I shall have to return for good."

The impatience which she showed in New York through her constant employment of at least two agents—a sign of uncertainty—had led to her dismissing Ibbs & Tillett as her London agents, then, after a short spell with Al Parker, returning to them. "Is there a good concert agent in London, or shall we be forced to return to Emmie [Tillett]," she asks Gay in January 1950, and then later, "I suppose we may as well have Emmie do the job, and see what she can do with the old man Boult." Olga Lynn offered her a flat in Chesham Place; nothing doing—"I prefer just a room in a hotel on our side of the Park. . . . Would you be an angel and find out if they have rooms at the Cumberland where I could cook little things—and the higher the better overlooking the Park." For the third and final time in her life, even though she had many more engagements to fulfil in the States, she was preparing a homecoming.

CHAPTER TWELVE

Girls Eternal
(1950–1952)

Then everything includes itself in will,
Will into power, power into appetite.
Troilus and Cressida

PRIMITIVE NATURE IS most often depicted as female, but in maturity it was the male aspects of Maggie's personality which became dominant—just as years earlier she had switched over from playing Gretel to Hänsel in Humperdinck's opera. To what extent life forced her to this, to what extent it was an inner need in which, as she aged, she found herself less inhibited—a sort of inner freedom of will if not of desire—is harder to measure. All one is saying, perhaps, is that she now did exactly what she wanted. As indeed she always had.

While she had never wanted to be a mother and would not we can be sure have made a good one, she could well have made a good father. She was imbued with a cavalier masculine spirit, best shown in a little poem she wrote:

> I travel the road to Nowhere,
> Down past the hillside green,
> Down past the watermill
> White clouds gather lazily
> As I travel a road to Nowhere.
>
> My memory returns to the watermill
> In dappled light and shade,
> Golden brown maid so fair so see
> A cottage and a flowering tree
> Light my road to Nowhere.

> I saw not the whiteness of her arm
> As she plucked the ripe fruit from above,
> Nor the delicate curve of breast and hip
> That might cradle a son of mine
> As I travel a road to Nowhere.
>
> Grey clouds billowing with ice and snow,
> When suddenly on my road I turned,
> For my heart cried aloud in joy and pain,
> Will she be there? Will she be there?
> Or does my road still lead Nowhere?

In these verses she assumes completely a male identity, while in her old-age ramblings she poured forth deep resentment at being a woman: "A man's life is more interesting than a woman's: if I came back, I'd come back as a man . . . and I'd have a hell of a time! I wouldn't be a woman again. I've had a very easy life but when you think of a woman's life, some of them, they're nothing but slaves, and *dirty* slaves at that."[1] But for her the liberated woman of the Seventies did not exist and confidence was equated with masculine prowess: asked after her New York success, which went on more or less until she was sixty-five, what was the secret of her lasting vigour, she responded: "I think it is largely a matter of personality: energy comes with experience and knowledge which leads to self-confidence, and that increases vitality."

Gay Vernon had much to do with this increased vitality; they released energy from each other, giggled, compared dates, even, who knows, sported and cavorted with one another—no one would have put it past either. Gay was the more feminine of the pair, and Maggie, while showing a protective spirit—"I walked home through Rockefeller Plaza last night, and stopped to watch them skating—thinking of you!—how is the arm?", at other times is cheekily pally: "How about it, kiddo the monko?" she asks about Gay's coming to New York. Another time she makes what seems an overt reference to Gay's sexual tastes, mentioning a garageman who "has a *very pretty daughter*"; she had let the girl know she was writing to Gay, she informs her friend later. Maggie herself was prey at times to a rampant, devil-may-care sexuality: "Hope you will be feeling much better by the time I arrive so we can have a little fun during my short stay. P.S. I am in a wild mood—the spring sap is rising, my doctor has got under my skin, and of course he doesn't care a hoot about grandmothers." Who and what the doctor was remains for ever a Mélisande-like secret, but the drive seemed hardly all to have been directed at Gay. And she too had men friends.

They found companionship in each other, and each had a rather wicked sense of humour and plenty of what they called "pep". Both were singing teachers now and both good pianists, Gay having improved greatly since the Twenties when Maggie first took her under her wing. She practised with Gay, and in time Gay was good enough to play for her at concerts, though Maggie would go over Gay's head to employ someone else if the concert was special. Gay never minded.

Gay was light-hearted, thin, taller than Maggie. She had been very pretty when younger, but with Maggie around she was content to remain in the shadow; though her wry sense of humour never deserted her, she allowed herself to be completely dominated. Maggie gave her confidence, and she found life with her exciting. Maggie's own looks had hardened: There was something embattled about her face now. She still had her girlish manner and crumpled laugh, but the soft, mysterious element had vanished. The bubbling wit, formidable and rapier-like, had banished the outward traces of mystery; an inner vulnerability remained, but it was no longer to be seen in her face.

When Maggie was at the full height of glory in New York in 1945, she was much in demand to give lessons to wealthy New Yorkers, and could charge them $50 a time. So she had Gay join her, "signing" her up for the summer. Many of Maggie's pupils were outraged by her bluntness. She would poke an overfed woman in the tummy: "You haven't got a girdle on. Go and put a girdle on and come and see me again." Some of them found Gay's kinder and more tactful approach more humane. She was the temporizer, the smoother-out of thorny encounters, the one who made faces behind Maggie's back telling the affronted person to take no notice. But she was not, like Maggie, a big person, and she was actually terrified of performance.

While Maggie was singing well she was impatient of teaching and often passed her pupils on to Gay, taking them back again if her mood changed or times got hard. One of their finds, back in London, was a little Cockney girl they nicknamed "the Countess". She was Maggie's and Gay's Eliza Doolittle, a fat little dumpling with stringy dark hair and a gopher face who tottered along on thin legs. Maggie heard her sing and impulsively decided that with Gay's help she would do for "the Countess" what the Rubens family had done for her: she would take her to live with them in Hamilton Terrace, they would teach her de Reszke's way of singing, and then they would dispatch her to Paris for the final polish. The girl had a good head voice and no temperament, which Maggie took as a virtue, for she saw in this a parallel with herself when young. But what she failed to see was that "the Countess's" lack of temperament was sheer dumb-headedness—a form of suet-pudding insensitivity— whereas with her it had been a mixture of inhibition and extreme sensitivity. When she sent her protégée to Paris, "the Countess" returned with her voice totally ragged and disintegrated. Maggie persevered a little longer, finding work for her in a touring company of *The Pirates of Penzance*, but when the girl announced that she was pregnant and then got married, that was the last straw. "You can't make a silk purse out of a sow's ear," thundered Maggie.

Another protégé of Gay's and Maggie's was a young French tenor, a swarthy Algerian type, slim in build, who professed himself crazy about Gay's numerous and very pretty girl friends. He too lived for a while in Hamilton Terrace, always alluding to his teacher and hostess as "Madame Teyte". "She always used to go for pale-voiced tenors," certified a friend. But the Frenchman's attachment to Maggie remained hazy, and no one was very complimentary about him, even Maggie, who called him a "bit of a *blagueur*" though they all went along, as they said, to hear him "bleating his way through *Les Illuminations*".

Elizabeth Schumann, the great Mozartian soprano who had fled Hitler, had been about to take a long lease on a cottage, No. 40 Hamilton Terrace, when she fell ill and died. Born in almost the same year as Schumann, Maggie bought the lease of No. 42 in 1952 and lived there for almost twenty years. She became very much the "local enchantress" and loved it there, writing vitriolic letters to the Council about its decision to replace the old lamp posts by concrete monsters with sodium boxes—she wanted them hung with flowers. She kept an open fire in her cottage, chopping up bits of wood for it, and she would get down on all fours to blow at it.

Maggie still had a few adventures left up her sleeve. One of these followed hard upon New York: she wanted to form an understanding of Schoenberg's twelve-tone method, and in particular the *Sprechgesang*, used in his cycle *Pierrot Lunaire*. So again leaving Grace behind in London to do the donkey work, she went in pursuit of the right "word colour", which she hoped to find with a certain Max Kundergrabbe, who lived in Vienna. On Wednesday, 2 November 1951, she wrote from the Pension Schneider, VI Lehargasse 3:

> Gay darling, I finally got here with ¾ of my luggage left in Zürich. God only knows when I shall get it—I was an awful fool not to take Swiss francs along with me, because the dear darling Swiss won't take anybody's money! It's a long story—I'll tell it you some other time. The rate for excess baggage is exorbitant—they wanted £17 from Zurich to Wien, and of course I didn't have it, so I am waiting to have it come Air Freight, which will cost me £8. So the allowance of £150 is dwindling fast. I sent a telegram to my bank asking them to pay immediately £10 in Swiss francs to Cooks in London for payment to the Zürich office. They must have received my telegram on Monday Morning the 19th. If you are passing—or perhaps Perman* could telephone—perhaps we could get the lowdown. Cooks here are doing their best, and Brass at the British Council has been most helpful. Must get this to the post. Have lots to tell you. Everything is very interesting. Je t'embrasse,
>
> MEG

She added as a postscript that her pension was the home of musicians "en route". Hans Hotter was there and Furtwängler was expected soon. She even saw "W.L." (Walter Legge) peep round the door at "Elisabeth S[chwartzkopf]'s" recital.† "She had a full house and a wonderful reception!", winding up, "Je t'embrasse encore, MEG."

She stayed four months, like a child with a toy, curious to take *Pierrot Lunaire* apart and see how it worked. She also had a lovely time at the Pension Schneider; although the British currency restrictions led to constant financial difficulties, her bohemian spirit leapt to embrace them:

> Dear Gay, Would you be an angel and do something for me? This rationed money doesn't go very far. I enclose you a cheque for £5. Would you take one pound at a time, say once a week, and post it to me,

* Her accountant.   † Legge and Schwartzkopf were married in 1953.

very flat between a thinnish paper. *Do not on any account put any name or address* in case it is picked up. Just off to lunch with Peter Habig, an old sweetheart of mine. Heard Fournier last night in an all-Bach programme (cello alone). You can imagine how wonderful he is, and was, for us to stay to the bitter end. I will send you a picture p.c. every time something comes through.

Herr Kundergrabbe, when she found him, recoiled from the purpose of her visit, and so in revenge, and to escape the English spoken in her pension, she went along to the Berlitz School to have some German lessons; she was soon put off there, though she went on with another tutor. The Schoenberg quest thus ground to a halt, but the fresh pastures she surveyed had a remarkably familiar contour: "Please excuse pencil but my 'fountain' has run out. I have been to hear *Salomé* this evening—I took a ticket thinking it would be Welitsch,* and was rather disappointed, when seated, to find that it was someone called Goltz.† The last time I saw *Salomé* at C.G. I thought how very old-fashioned it had become—but believe me, or am I telling you so to speak, tonight's performance has been an eye-opener—there is only one word, 'colossal'." The first *Salomé* she had seen had been Beecham's in 1910, when Herod's luxuriant moustache came unstuck: he held it up with two fingers but every time he needed both arms for emotional effect, "down came one side of the moustache again." Not all the mesmeric glances of Beecham could save the situation.[2]

"Now for the story—and a nice little joke on myself," she went on.

I saw in the paper that there was a performance of *Wozzeck* at some place called the Parkring Theatre. I got the people here to ring up for a ticket last Sunday—Full house, and I said to myself Ah! Ah! Alban Berg is a success in his home town—and the answer was "perhaps" you can get one at the Box Office! Sunday morning I go walking to find the Parkring Theatre—I plucked up courage and asked an Austrian (not Russian) policeman—he didn't know of such a place, but he directed me close by to a theatre ticket office, and there right enough was an announcement of *Wozzeck* taking place in the *Keller* [cellar] of the

* Ljuba Welitsch, the Bulgarian soprano, whose special starring role was Salomé.
† Christel Goltz, German soprano, one of the most prominent singers of the Vienna State Opera.

Café Parkring. You can imagine my secret reaction to the "*Keller*" part. Anyhow, merrily I go along to the *Wozzeck*. I walk through a dingy-looking café downstairs to the *Keller*—a moderate narrow room with peculiar drawings on the walls, I should say [painted] in a peculiar way—tables etc., one or two people only—at the next table to me was obviously an old actress—I spoke to her, everyone understands English or French—and learnt that she teaches *breathing*. I noticed that the name Berg did not appear on the programme, of course you know now what's coming—Yes, it was a play—whether it is the same plot I don't know, I have to find out—it was quite short and very interesting—I understood bits here and there—it was beautifully acted.* I found out that the *Keller* opened on the Saturday night, and a kind of co-operative company of actors and actresses who are out of work at the moment. So, thinking of Adèle,† I have not heard Berg's *Wozzeck* yet.

The Pension Schneider housed almost every singer or musician who came to Vienna—they were all artists there, and apparently the nice little Fräulein in the office had said to Maggie on her return from *Salomé*: "'But Mme Goltz will be coming in any moment now, if you want to speak to her'—which I did—and said amidst other things, 'When are you coming to London?' and she answered, 'In December—to sing *Wozzeck*'."

Wozzeck apart, Maggie was much taken by some songs of Berg's, the early *Sieben Lieder*, which she heard in Vienna, though somewhat rueful when she found out that Berg, under Schoenberg's influence, had later disowned them.

Meantime the ills that flesh is heir to took their toll. She did not want to bother Gay with more troubles, she wrote, but she had grown worried about her arm which she had mentioned several times and which did not get any worse but also no better. She thought she had strained it cranking her car on some cold London morning. Gay knew quite a lot about these things—so if it was a strain, should she rest it, but if it was rheumatism, should she use it? She didn't want to start "monkeying" about with doctors there, but didn't know how to find out. It was always the same amount of pain day in day out—sometimes a little worse in the morning,

---

* It was of course the play by Georg Büchner.

† Adèle Leigh, soprano who sang leading roles at Covent Garden and elsewhere, also a pupil of Maggie's.

and there were moments when she felt the muscle in her right thigh, which might be connected with the pressure she put on the right side for "cranking purposes". So she went on with scientific clarity, working out her body's problems in terms of weights and balances, ending by asking Gay to contact her doctor Janvrin on her behalf.

Even with an ailing arm she rooted about for bargains. Gloves were "wonderful" and "priced between Sch. 125–150 = £1/15/–. If you tell me what colour you want I will bring you a pair. Do you like the stitching on the outside?" Nylons were expensive—about 18/– a pair. Again there were errands for Gay to perform: a letter to forward from a man in Mainz who had sent her an album of Yvette Guilbert photographs, and once again, in her eternal passion for Bile Beans—the practical Wolverhampton girl who took good care of herself—"I'm sorry to be bothering you again, but I didn't bring enough Bile Beans with me—please be an angel and when you have time, would you post me two bottles (large)."

Through all this, German still makes small headway, as she got no chance to try out even her mistakes on anybody.

German is becoming more difficult every day—when I went for my German lesson yesterday, my teacher informed me that he has been living in South Africa for the last twenty years and couldn't stand the German language—never read it and never spoke anything but English with his English wife. He had heard my records and we talked music— a nice German lesson! The climate is quite good here—the winds are cold though, blowing straight from the Russian steppes. The only bad thing about Vienna—it would be Russian too! They look a surly lot too, when you do come across them.

In her musical studies the wheel returns full circle back to Schumann and Schubert.

So Maggie's Christmas in Vienna came and went, an "Alpenstock" Christmas: no snow but ice everywhere and trees covered with hoarfrost. The narrative to Gay quickened. The Pension Schneider was clearly becoming something of a reincarnation of that pension at No. 40 avenue Victor Hugo where she had spent her student days. "Somebody is singing top H's in the next room—probably Zerbinetta from *Ariadne auf Naxos* for next Thursday"—very sad, perhaps, but she rather wallowed in it, so was it really sad? There was red wine, white wine, and cherry brandy, though no gin (she told Gay to buy herself a bottle, sending her a cheque). There was rich food in plenty, and, unusual for her, she indulged herself: fried food, tournedos, potatoes, chocolate cake, cream. One could almost imagine the ghosts of indolence, of voluptuousness and luxury, filling her with images of a departed life. But even the ghosts had to be regulated: on 5 January she writes:

Thank you so much Gay darling for the Beans. It may interest you to know that the manager of this pension was at the Bristol Hotel old and new, as he says, from 1921 to 1926. [CENSORED PASSAGE]* I wondered if you knew him. He was talking about Kalman and his children, a boy and a girl who picked flowers and put them inside shoes and boots outside hotel doors and filled them full of water. He has a picture of Lehár in the office. I was wondering why the place was so well run. The Bristol is still going strong—the Yanks have made it their headquarters and the Imperial which is down to the left on the Ring [CENSORED PASSAGE]. It is so funny to see barriers shutting off the pavements there. I suppose they are afraid someone will throw something nasty at them!! They look a sorry lot!

With early spring, she made ready to return. She had learnt more words of German and no longer knew what to do with or where to put them. The Viennese skies became overcast, her eyes began to trouble her in the poor light and her arm now hurt again badly. A different season in her life was nigh, the season of mists and mellow fruitfulness—the memoirs season—and as if with divine foresight, her wartime friend Felix Aprahamian, now on the *Sunday Times*, sent her Mary Garden's book to review: let battle be joined in public between the two great Mélisandes of their day. Meg (she now refused to be known any longer as Maggie, so on her express orders we are forced sometimes to employ the crisp, blunt "Meg") sensed a fight, and she would never miss a fight if she could.

Would you please telephone Felix for me and tell him I have received Mary Garden's story and I am trying my best to review it—it's a bit difficult because it is 60 p.c. drivel—but perhaps "we" can (that is if you will help) do something about it—it lends itself to some very

* In Vienna in 1951, the Occupying Forces still censored mail.

nasty "cracks". I don't suppose you've read it yet. George* had read it in the States, I believe, and said how terrible it was. Tell Felix that if he can wait till the week of the 17th, I will then submit it to him.† Au revoir, sweetheart.

There was now a concert in the offing at home. "Is Gerald's fee still 15 guineas?" she inquired. "On the other hand Ivor has been very nice re Mermaid Theatre‡ and other things—what is his fee, by the way?" She had one new group for the programme of her concert, some songs by Joseph Marx, but found herself at a loss ("Stumpt") for the other parts. She could not bear repetition of all those old numbers, but supposed she had better please the public.

She had visited Joseph Marx in Vienna, a fine-looking man, she found him, over six feet tall and with a leonine head of white hair, and she was so grateful to make contact again with a living composer over his own music: "He freely revised his own expression marks on my copies of his song," like so many of the composers she had known, Fauré, Reynaldo Hahn, Gabriel Grovlez, Messager. "Debussy was the sole exception— he stuck to his own markings, and woe betide the singer who did not heed them!"[3] Alas when she came, pluckily, to perform all this new repertoire, Edward Lockspeiser, again sent to report for the BBC, wished she had stuck to her own repertoire. The age of specialization was at hand, the specialization so loathed by Debussy: "It reminds me of those old horses who, in bygone days, worked the roundabouts and died to the well-known strains of the 'Marche Lorraine'."[4]

While Maggie was in Vienna, Gay was having, in between errands she performed for "Meg" and her own teaching, second thoughts about a relationship on which for twenty-five years now, since she first went to stay in the flat above the stable at Woolley Grange, she had been largely dependent. She too was now sixty, and although well-preserved and healthy, did she want to pass into old age as a female companion, an appendage, to an increasingly ruthless and dominant prima donna? It was no good arguing with Maggie: she saw your point of view only in

---

* George Reeves.   † For the review, see Appendix D.

‡ Ivor Newton suggested Maggie to Sir Bernard Miles for Belinda in *Dido and Aeneas*. See below, p. 220.

so far as it accorded with her own, but ultimately—although she never questioned your right to do exactly as you wanted—being obedient was the only way to get along with her. Not only obedient, but with a certain tolerance towards tyranny: Maggie was a wilful and often contradictory mistress.

To their pupils, Maggie and Gay were often a good balance: Gay understood them and mixed with them, while Maggie made them afraid, brutally telling them the truth, so they would go back to Gay for warmth, for encouragement. One was the builder-up, the other the cutter-down. With Rita, too, Gay was often on closer terms than Maggie, taking an interest in Cavan and the children. In this way, Gay's and Maggie's was very much a union and, in the eyes of most people, they were inseparably joined.

Gay saw Maggie's intention only too clearly. But she had not, like Maggie, had two marriages, one of them to a man who might still have been her husband, had she not let a streak of selfishness make marriage impossible for her, curbing her sense of freedom, inhibiting her imperious will. Maggie had never asked herself how she could live with another person—the overriding question one carries from birth to death; it was always a matter of how other people were to live with her, to fashion their own lives around the demands her career, her ego, and her way of pleasure made on them. She sucked in everything around her, and those whose point of view she could not see, although her judgement was often shrewd, became in her mind weak, pusillanimous, or conceited. She would have nothing to do with them.

Grace Vernon, however, had been the victim of an arranged marriage: her Jewish parents had forced a husband on her acceptable to them. She had never chosen a man for herself. So when the opportunity came to her to break her fetters, she thought: Why not try again?

The man was not a dashing romantic hero many years her junior. Far from it: he was lugubrious and hardly ever spoke a word. A musician, true, a violinist; a wonderful player, but it was not, as someone snidely remarked, the kind of playing anyone much liked to hear. After all, there is, in musical execution as in morals, a kind of perfection which is unutterably tedious.

His name was Cave, Alfred Cave, suitable nomenclature for a man who would disappear noiselessly into himself, and from company, so that no one knew where he was. Those such as Miriam Licette who had travelled through North Africa with him in the Desert Rats concert parties might notice he had vanished again. "Where's Alfred?" someone would say. No one had seen him go, and no one grew very worried, very concerned. He was utterly mysterious, utterly negative. But women liked him, and sooner or later he would be spotted again, in a densely smoke-filled corner of the NAAFI, with a WAAF girl on his knee.

This was Alfred Cave, tall, dark-haired, big-boned. The mystery man. The rift in the lute. Maggie never for a moment took him seriously and, when Gay began seeing him, did not hold back from telling her what she thought of him, "the most boring man I have ever met in my life," she avowed. "He looks just like an orang-utan." And laughed her crumpled wicked laugh.

Nor did Gay seem to find him all that attractive. Once, at supper at Enid and Gerald Moore's with Maggie, she rounded on the poor anthropoid: "You have a face just like a chimpanzee." He may have ascended a rung on the evolutionary ladder from the orang-utan, but it was still enough to make anyone choke over his soup. Alfred stuck it out, as ever inscrutable, silent.

Maggie's tyranny stiffened Gay's resistance, and more and more she found herself liking Alfred; his very negativity was a quality she came to admire. So much so that one day she decided, when he asked her, to marry him.

"Treachery in the house! Murder! Betrayal," thundered Maggie. In a way it was, though who can blame Gay for wanting to be happy? She did pass a long and contented old age, living in Walberswick, Suffolk.* Even so, though a lesser artist and person than Maggie, she was in one notable way the better human being. Her love for Maggie never faltered and she admired her to the very end.

But Maggie never saw Gay again. Never forgot. Never forgave.

* She died in 1974.

CHAPTER THIRTEEN

Last Performances & Immortal Longings (1952–1960)

Haply you shall not see me more; or if,
A mangled shadow.
Antony and Cleopatra

ASTONISHINGLY ENOUGH, MAGGIE sang well in public until she was sixty-eight, and privately—in little snatches—till well over eighty,* but she would not allow the later voice to be heard. Her fiftieth anniversary as a singer and farewell concert was planned for 22 April 1956, at 3 p.m. in the Royal Festival Hall, where she was to be assisted by the English String Quartet (a perceptive critic much earlier noted how well her voice sounded with string assistance). Her last recitals in America took place in 1954, when George Reeves again accompanied her, to her intense satisfaction. Irving Kolodin found that though power was in short supply, and an occasional F or G marked the upper limits of range, yet she sought no effects but "virtuous" ones and the ultimate result was a remarkable precision, and complete expressiveness. She was "still trading with solid vocal currency rather than merely on the reputation that brought her a long salvo of applause when she entered."[1] Her inclusion in this concert of folksongs such as "L'Amour de moi", of Reynaldo Hahn's "Offrande", and the humorous aria "Air de la Femme-Médecin" from Gluck's *L'Ile de Merlin* showed how well she had thought out the programme without taxing her physique—"an eloquent demonstration that great singing can be done with hardly any voice at all," Winthrop Sargent found.[2] But Sargent was also amazed to witness the experienced craftsmanship with which she projected more vocally taxing items like "La Lettre" from Massenet's *Werther*: "Miss Teyte's peculiar art lies in immaculate musical taste, a vast range of inflection and color, a wonderful sense of the

---

* She sang to Peter Wadland some Reynaldo Hahn—"Il pleut des pétales des fleurs" —when she was eighty-four, remarking, "I don't call that singing."

dramatic content of a song, and a very rare personal quality that seems to make everything she sings a form of intimate communication with the people who are listening to her."

While she was still receiving these rapturous plaudits in New York, in London the BBC had decided she was too old to sing for them. Even though the GOSO (General Overseas Service Organizer) had written confidentially to the HOM (Head of Music) in 1950, "I can say from my own knowledge that she is very highly regarded indeed in the United States . . . invariably praised as a great singer," and, with perfect, totally inaccurate, British disdain for British artistic achievement, "She has also been in some operatic production at the Metropolitan Opera House recently—I cannot remember what it was—and was, I think, a big success . . ."—the opera production being her City Center début as Mélisande—HOM's assessment of her "present value to broadcasting" dropped, nay crumbled, to 30 guineas: less than half what she had been receiving previously. The AM (Artist Manager) did just about manage to concede she still made a "lovely sound".

In response to all this Maggie kept her price as high as her pride, may even have increased it; so the BBC, having shamefully attempted to get an inimitable veteran to sing for them on the cheap, stopped hiring her. Thus ended a collaboration, a virtual career in itself, a career within a career which had lasted three decades.

Her farewell to opera, in 1951, had been more fitting and honourable: in an outbuilding of his St John's Wood home, Bernard Miles was opening his first tiny Mermaid Theatre with Purcell's *Dido and Aeneas*. Kirsten Flagstad was to sing Dido. She had become friends with the Miles family after hearing Bernard Miles do his famous plodding bandsman's turn of "Tristan and Isolde and the Love Lotion" at a party, laughing so much that she signed with a kiss the light-hearted contract for Dido whereby the management undertook to supply her with two pints of oatmeal stout *per diem*, and "plenty of little surprises, presents of flowers, fruit, fish and fresh foliage, to recite poems to her . . . and to take every opportunity of making her laugh." That had been all. No money.

These were intimate, almost *salon* conditions of performance, such as those in which Maggie had often performed *La Damoiselle élue*. So when asked to sing Belinda, she had been deeply flattered and accepted with delight. The small audience was chic and well turned out, not at all as she saw the Covent Garden audience, "like peasants' wives in their antimacassars," there was royalty to be presented to—in the person of Marina, Duchess of Kent—and above all there was the delicious amateurism of the staging. Bernard Miles himself designed ingenious contraptions with mirrors so the singers could receive cues from the conductor, who was the celebrated harpsichordist Geraint Jones, positioned on a fragile balcony above, with his orchestra in wigs and period costumes. Both ladies, Flagstad fifty-six, Teyte sixty-three, were beyond the years at which divas normally retire and they had loved the experience. "Perfect harmony," warbled Teyte, while for Flagstad the whole thing was "almost indescribable . . . lovely, and sweet, and right."[3]

"What a voice"—Maggie was lost for superlatives—"the most marvellous machine I have ever been up against. When I did Belinda I was practically on her lap, so I could feel how the machine worked, it was like a band of steel." One night when Flagstad was singing "When I am laid in earth", Maggie's eyes filled with tears. Flagstad saw her and, very touched, said afterwards, "Oh Maggie dear, I'm not *that* good!" Later, reminded of the incident, Maggie avowed simply that Flagstad's voice was the greatest she had ever heard.[4]* The Mermaid production was later recorded and issued by EMI, except that Maggie was somewhat grotesquely replaced by Elisabeth Schwartzkopf as Belinda.

The American prima donna, Lillian Nordica, or "Yankee Diva" as she was affectionately labelled, affirmed movingly how a great woman singer dies no less than three times: first go her looks, that is death one; then her voice, the second; and finally the death these rare and unearthly creatures share with the rest of us. Short-circuiting this agony, Flagstad more bluntly averred: "I might as well be dead when I finally retire from opera and concert work."

Maggie's second "death", no less or more than that of any other singer, did affect her deeply; it was heightened by a sense of isolation and the loneliness of old age coming on. "I'm going to divest myself of everything. I don't want anything around me but gin," she kidded a friend much later. "I'm eighty-one—I'm not used to being old!"[5] But in her sixties still, retired, she did at first drink heavily. The famous Teyte cocktail served her all evening: two-thirds of a tumbler of gin, one-third tinned grapefruit juice (some students and visitors would leave their drinks

---

* But Melba always remained her vocal ideal and she was proud, as Philip Hope-Wallace wrote in the *Guardian* (17 April 1968), to have her Mimi likened to Melba's. Melba's voice, she thought, was really heaven-sent in its even, silver purity.

untouched on the mantelpiece for fear of losing their balance). Later, she switched to whisky and milk, "brown cow". She did not sleep well either, in this part of her life, and took sleeping pills.

She was growing emotional too, and more outspoken. Gerald Moore, normally the equable and affable accompanist who often said there was no other soprano in England who could thrill you like Maggie Teyte, was practising with her one day, and one of Maggie's students had been given permission to be present. Maggie stopped, and said to him: "Gerald, your tempo is too slow here." She then turned to her pupil with, "If ever your accompanist drags, you want to hit him on the head with a coke hammer!" Moore was furious, rose from the piano, and rushed out. Maggie repented at once, and raced after him; she was in tears. "I didn't mean it," she called. "Come back, Gerald."

Moore played for her at most of her late concerts and during one, at the Cowdray Hall, she suddenly pulled him up: "I'm not going to sing any more! You play for ten minutes." Moore dutifully filled the gap. Maggie hid as best she could and all the audience could see was her legs under the piano. "Oh," she said, "they like it." She overcame her resistance at last, and continued.

Sometimes stricken by inadequacy, at other times filled with confidence, how long could she continue? A pupil of hers came one day to the Dinely Studios in Marylebone, where she gave lessons, and stood outside her studio, listening. She was all alone, singing to herself. Her previous lesson, with Adèle Leigh, had finished. The student waited till she stopped. It had been beautiful. When he went in he found her in floods of tears. "I know each time I sing like that," she told him simply, "may be the last."

Her "last but one" concert, given at the Festival Hall in 1955, did turn out to be her last. It was the forty-ninth year of her professional life, she reckoned, counting from her unpaid début at Reynaldo Hahn's Mozart Festival in 1906; but if one counted from her very first appearance in public, at the church in Maiden Lane, fifty-two years had passed. Though the figure that greeted the eye on that long walk out to the platform of the Festival Hall was a more solidly built one, there was much of the same girlish stillness of manner, the demure reticence of look. There was still something very ungrown-up about her. She wore a white dress, with a floating red chiffon scarf, sustaining that capacity for looking beautiful before the public which she had never once lost. She was neat, tidy, well preserved, well rested, as ever she had been. She had not drunk anything. She had eaten her prescribed foods, and had not spoken to anyone for twenty-four hours. "If you have music in your life, you will never be lonely." She was making her offering of perfection for the last time on the high altar of art. In Hugo Wolf's "Kennst du das Land", with which she began the concert—just afterwards suffering a momentary lapse of memory—she "treated us to a display of vocal and interpretive mastery that was not only astonishing but often touching," wrote Desmond Shawe-Taylor.[6] Her elevation of the host, her communion and climax was nothing less than Mélisande's last scene with Pelléas, which she sang with a baritone pupil, David Bell. Pelléas is killed and Mélisande retreats once more into the shadows. Symbol and reality were one, fused for ever:

Pelléas: Oh! Oh! Toutes les étoiles tombent!
Mélisande: Sur moi aussi! sur moi aussi!
Pelléas: Encore! Encore! Donne . . .
Mélisande: Toute! . . .
                toute, toute! . . .
Pelléas: . . . donne, donne
                (*Golaud runs forward and strikes down Pelléas with his sword.*)
Mélisande: Oh! Oh! Je n'ai pas de courage! Je n'ai pas de courage! Ah!

She looked acute, intelligent: she listened. She loved the Festival Hall—one of the few places where to her, if to no other, a voice came back to a singer at the end of a phrase, at the end of a line, in echo. She could therefore almost evaluate her performance as it went along, and she decided it was good enough, to leave it there, and not perform the following year. A convenient accident, a fall, gave her the chance to withdraw, yet as Sartre has written, "Il n'y a pas d'accidents"—"there are no accidents": this was certainly true where Teyte and singing were concerned.

She thrilled herself, on that fine sunny afternoon in April, as she thrilled her audience who once again felt joined to this unique tradition and individual musical craftsmanship by someone who had lived intimately with the closest possible understanding of it. For the last time they witnessed a singer who now was, in Virgil Thomson's words, both "miracle" and "monument". For Shawe-Taylor, a world of pathos was contained in her delivery of that single line, "Oh! Oh! Je n'ai pas de courage! Ah!", arousing "nostalgia in those who had seen her stage impersonation, and envy in those who had not."*

Recognition of her achievement as a singer was delayed for Teyte. Largely through the efforts of Tony Mayer, the much-admired member of the French cultural services of the Forties and Fifties, who had with Felix Aprahamian planned the Free French concerts, in 1957 she was created a Chevalier of the Légion d'honneur, for her unique contribution to French music. This was, she said, "the only honour I have ever wanted." The English, ever slow to accord their own musical artists greatness but not wishing, as it were, to be left out—it is, as André Maurois has pointed out, the state which reaps the true benefit from the artist's acceptance of an honour, for the artist is a decoration on the government's chest, and never the other way about—rushed in the following year to make her a DBE. "Don't call me Dame. I'm not going to be known as Dame. I'll tell you something—I wouldn't have accepted anything less than that. It's fifteen years too late," she spluttered to the press.7 "They always are in the arts. Nobody gets anything until they are in their seventies." She might have added, what use is a medal to a bohemian and a recluse at heart? However, a few days later she had generated a little pleasure and gratitude in the event. "No," she said firmly, "I am definitely not going to sing again. Who wants to listen to an old woman of seventy singing?" but conceded it was the crowning point of her career, or, rather, a "beautiful coda".8

In later years her fame, and the memory of her, grew rather than diminished, a curious phenomenon led by the BBC who, now that she was out of the way as a negotiable and fallible vocal quantity, seemed only

---

* "Her singing," wrote Shawe-Taylor (*New Statesman*, 23 April 1955), "did not sound like that of an old singer, but it was singing as the art was understood fifty years ago. It was technically solid. Except when the musical phrase called for a veiled or distant quality, Miss Teyte never sang à *demi-voix*; she did not hint at notes, flutter, swoon, or croon, as many of her juniors do; she firmly and distinctly sang. Her attack was exemplary. In the Wolf song, those phrases in the refrain which begin on the upper F and A flat were precisely struck. She can still float a soft high phrase, still charm us with her sudden descents into that haunting viola-like register around middle C. Moreover she links her notes together so that they make a true legato phrase, and does not step from one to another in the decadent modern style, leaving a tiny hole between. There were moments, though surprisingly few, when a tightness or hardness in the voice betrayed her years; even then the strong individuality of her timbre was unaffected." (Cf. Chapter 3 above, on Maggie's training with de Reszke, especially the part on the "gaps" or "transitions" between registers.)

Maggie Teyte in 1946 on board the *Queen Elizabeth I*, on one of her crossings from New York.

Rehearsing *Pelléas* at the City Center in New York, 1948: (seated, from left) Fernand Martel and Theodore Uppman, both of whom were to sing Pelléas; Norman Scott (Arkel); Maggie Teyte standing, with her understudy, Ann Ayars, at her left. (*Left*) With the "handsome brute" Stephen Spender, working on his libretto for a concert version of Gounod's *Faust*, at Stockbridge, Massachusetts, in 1949.

too eager to play her records, transmit her inimitable impressions of the great musical personalities she had known, tackle her on interpretive technicalities, record her *risqué* comments on her living *bêtes noires*, like Solti,* which they kept close, labelled "not to be broadcast", and even place her on a desert island, for which she took along her own "perfect" recording of a boy soprano singing the "Et incarnatus est" from the C minor Mass by Mozart—alas they would not let her play it, for the use of non-commercial recordings on desert islands was forbidden.† The BBC were mightily generous to her in her old age, did her royal justice, made sure she was not forgotten.

On a ten-year-old child a powerful character in the family makes such a strong impression that he bases his idea of what a "character" is on such a being—so much so sometimes, that he cannot really believe any other kind of "character" exists. This was the case with Maggie Teyte and myself, she being well into her sixties when I can first identify, for myself, some definite impression of her. Her transformation by then from all the phases and threads of personality which I have tried to suggest into an impressive *grande dame*—just as numerous small streams, broadening, in the end form a grand majestic river—was now more or less complete. Everyone, near and far, worshipped her. I saw none of the cracks, the ordinary vulnerabilities that made her seem more human, none of the untidy joins and gaps of sadness. She was a wonderful, vigorous, famous woman who looked as if she would—and did, from the point of view of a child of ten—go on living virtually for ever. My father's fortunes as a singer varied dramatically, plunging at times into the depths, but Maggie's were constant "as the northern star": she was like Caesar. "I've been lucky, I've had a marvellous life," she would say, the stress falling heavily on the first syllable of "marvellous": the whole impact very grand and theatrical. "I've always done exactly as I pleased"— the vowel sounds lengthened to eternity.

* Her main objection to Sir Georg Solti, stripped of its obscenities, was that he drove singers too hard at dress rehearsals. She singled out Sir Geraint Evans's difficulties in *Rigoletto*.[9]

† The boy was Anthony Bramall; she also arranged for him to sing the "Panis Angelicus" by César Franck. She considered the boy soprano the perfect voice, and she put immense energy into arranging all this—for her eightieth birthday.[10]

I believed her. Who wouldn't? To hear an honest avowal that life has turned out in every way for the very best did not, at that hour, have for me the blithe overtones of an optimism so full of unwitting and dangerous pride as to tempt fate to do her worst. Yet had I contradicted her, cautioned restraint, proposed—then or a few years later, when I had read or seen something of the tricks that fate can play—a Greek reticence, she would have countered, "Why not say it, if it's true?"

Her life must have seemed miraculous to her too, but the truth as I now see was often far from these lanceolate assertions. Apart from Gay Vernon, Maggie lost other friends at this time, in certain frenzies of middle-aged jealousy. Saddest of all perhaps was the way she fell out with Joe Brogan: he happened one day to say in an unguarded moment that he admired Jennie Tourel, and this hit Maggie on a very raw spot, as she had been furious with Jennie Tourel not only for detaching from her the accompanist George Reeves, but more, she claimed, for persuading Reeves to teach Tourel all Maggie's French repertoire—her tricks, her treasured secrets. And now Joe, no less, was stabbing her in the back:

> America cannot brook a double reign
> Of Jennie Tourel and Marguerita Teytarina . . .

She refused to speak to him; he was disconsolate, almost in tears. He came along to the Wigmore Hall after a recital and told Gerald Moore: "Maggie is displeased with me, and I am not displeased with her. Nothing can come between me and my admiration." These were Brogan's exit lines.

Queen Victoria combined mediocrity as a woman with the fundamental qualities of a queen. Maggie, by this definition, had much more; she had the fundamental qualities of a great singer, allied to queenship, and much more than mediocrity as a woman. She was a fascinating person, and hereafter modelling herself on the function she had to perform, she set about both consciously and unconsciously to establish her immortality —the quality Keats above all distinguished in the nightingale. She wanted to be remembered. "As what?" someone asked her in an interview. "As a singer?" "As anything!" she answered back with a laugh. The hunger was there. Love had disappointed her, men too, she had no succession—for she did not, Rita apart, accept the O'Connors as her family; she accepted no family as such.

How then to capture immortality? The first, most generous way to go about this was to pass on all she knew through her students. The problems here were great: how did one find the right students, students who showed a balance of talent, of temperament, of intelligence? And teaching well, for a teacher, is the supreme test of the limits of self-knowledge: in no other profession do the blind spots of a person's character come so quickly to the surface, in no other profession does one, in order to succeed, have so directly to face and wrestle with the demons of impatience.

As a teacher Maggie could be very cruel, very kind, very truthful—but she was, above all else, extremely impatient. More than this, she was, in a word, unpredictable. Young singers went in fear, older ones gathered their shattered pride outside the chilly Dinely Studios, where she taught, and fled. But then, on a good day, hundreds of spectators would sit awed and hushed in admiration as she conducted a formal master class at the Juilliard School in New York, in San Francisco, or at Dartington Hall in Devon.

She was not a steady teacher; she taught what de Reszke taught her, but not with the experience de Reszke had had of his voice failing him and his efforts to re-educate himself, not with his paternal authority, which held power both for men and women: as a teacher, he had been something of a genius, and she fell far short of this. She hadn't the tenacity of will to build up slowly, brick by brick, a whole vocal personality and technique.

But she was always colourful. Her revelations or judgement would suddenly illuminate a singer's work, or for a singer, a composer's *œuvre*, like a flash of lightning. But few pupils—though there were some, undeniably—found thunder and lightning, with passing patches of blue sky, the best conditions to work under. Maggie was often strangely confused, imagining brutality to be the only satisfactory expression of frankness: "Now I'm going to be brutal ..." "Now I'm going to tell you the truth and you won't like it"—these were often the form of address. She failed to see how adverse comment may be passed on graciously.

One pupil who did not mind the direct and blunt approach was the American soprano, Estelle Johnstone, a naturally fine and confident singer; indeed she held Maggie's whole approach to be terrific just because she was so very forthright. She was relieved when she began singing to find Maggie not too worried—in contrast with Gay, with whom Estelle had started studying—about payment. "You can pay me when you become famous." Maggie would take her along to sing with her at charity concerts—they sang at one for the blind. At first she found Maggie didn't spare herself and "gave all". "This is what I'm giving you. *I'm* giving it!" she would tell her.

But she had great difficulty in explaining exactly what she wanted, Estelle found. She would never write anything down, and if she had some ideas, she had to dictate them to someone else; the physical act of writing tired her and made her impatient. "It's like trying to explain God, or love," or, "Jean de Reszke could never say it." The latter statement was not strictly true, for de Reszke, while never laying down inflexible rules and sometimes giving contradictory instructions, showed himself a subtle commentator on voice and interpretation. As she did, sometimes, though impatient of more than snap judgements, however unerring. Perhaps the difference between them—and Maggie's disadvantage—was that she threw herself into teaching fifteen years later than de Reszke; he was fifty when his operatic career was terminated by bronchial catarrh (poetically just, perhaps, that he should be remembered as a cigarette brand). De Reszke found fulfilment in teaching in a way Maggie never did; for her it was more of a solace, a substitute performance, a studied self-perpetuation.

The debt to de Reszke was always acknowledged: "I didn't have much," she would aver to Estelle Johnstone, overmodestly. "I had some pathos in my voice—I owed everything to Jean de Reszke." But she sometimes made the mistake of trying to stretch a voice, not realizing that when de Reszke had pushed her voice up to extend its range she had been very young: it was easy at that time, the voice was malleable and her grasp was instinctive—what she had done was not necessarily good for others. She had been, too, Estelle thought, such a completely fastidious performer—as many said, she hardly sang a wrong note throughout her career—that she could not quite appreciate the mentality of a singer not on such a tightrope as she had been. She never worked well with men singers, and though Terrence O'Rourke and Charles O'Byrne took lessons with her, and she thought highly of both, she never felt much sympathy with male singers as a whole. The conceit customary in her profession outraged her and she commented all too frequently and derogatorily on the self-love of certain tenor colleagues, while de Reszke had taken all such temperament in his *grand seigneur* stride. She had been, above all, unself-conscious when very young, while de Reszke's self-consciousness had exposed him very early to self-analysis. "I never had any nerves"—they came later, and with a vengeance; in the Forties she was even sick before a Wigmore Hall concert. But by that time she was becoming terrified that her memory, which had always been faultless, had begun occasionally to fail her.

From the standpoint of a teacher, the main problem Estelle Johnstone presented was that she married, had one child—and then went on having more. "Wonderful," Magggie told her at first. "Have them when you're young." Her pupil had three, and when she came to the fourth—another son—Maggie changed her tune. "Estelle, you've got a wonderful husband and four sons—don't ask for too much!" she said bluntly.* And she wrote ominously to a singing teacher in New York: "I saw Estelle's big boy last week—he's going to be a handful."[13]

But how could a woman teach well whose early life had, in its diamond tiaraed way, put such pressure on her—with her obligations to de Reszke, the Rubens family, to Plumon, then to the Cottingham family whose captive, in a financial sense, she still was? For the tolerance of a great teacher comes from being able to let himself go, as Estelle Johnstone rightly appreciated, and this Maggie was never really able to do. In spite of being energetic and uninhibited, she remained on her guard, never relaxed a moment, never made a student feel she was exposing to him her inner being—except, that is, when she was in full vocal flight, filling the last few words of "Si mes vers avaient des ailes" with such exquisitely naked feeling: "Comme . . . l'amour."

Another former pupil who remained, like Estelle, a loyal friend for the last twenty-five years of Teyte's life, was the antique dealer, David Tron. To him she gave a "scholarship", two years' free lessons. Teyte, Tron found, if presented with a singing problem, would not go round and round it, thinking it over, feeling her way into a solution; if a solution did not suddenly present itself, and work with a bang, she rejected it. One day he was singing the *Dichterliebe* of Schumann, and she stopped him, asking furiously: "David, have you ever heard a choir of nightingales?"

---

* Maggie said of Estelle Johnstone, "a wonderful voice, fascinating woman, charming, with four sons . . . They can't do anything with children running around." She seemed to think one child was enough for a singer. Melba had one. So did Flagstad. Sutherland ("I was at her début as Lucia. She made me cry, first time since Melba . . . I didn't care about her pronunciation")[11] had one. Clara Butt, an exception, had two sons, but both pre-deceased her, one on the Eton cricket field. Louise Homer had six, including twins, but no nerves.[12]

"No, Maggie." "When I was a young girl, a lover took me into the Bois de Boulogne, and I heard a choir of nightingales—and that's why you'll *never* be able to sing this as it *should* be sung!" She may, as Tron conceded generously, have been right, but it was hardly the thing to say to inspire confidence in a twenty-year-old pupil.

Another time a well-known singer who had been a pupil was rehearsing with Gerald Moore in the empty Wigmore Hall. She was stopped dead in her tracks by Maggie, who had entered the balcony unseen and un-announced, rising like a phoenix in the dark house, "——, your singing is too German!" she pronounced in oracular fashion. The singer, stifled, could not resume. Another pupil was reliably reported to Maggie as singing out of tune: Maggie wrote at once, to order her own name, as the singer's teacher, to be taken off the programme.

Her example counted for more than the sum of what she said, for all agreed she was the epitome of hard work and true professionalism. Never was there anything sloppy or ill-considered in her approach and she hated short-cut effects. Adèle Leigh, whose lessons with her took place over fifteen years, was one day singing an aria, using the great swoops down on to notes which were fashionable at the time, when Maggie suddenly slammed shut the piano: "Cheap spaghetti! cheap spaghetti!" she cried, then said not a word for fifteen minutes, furiously pacing the room. Leigh was not put off, and found her teacher indispensable for interpretation.

Others found her resilience and advice a help to them in bearing their own griefs during World War Two: Megan Foster, a soprano whose career had been temporarily in suspension when her husband, Rear-Admiral E. J. Spooner, D.S.O., naval commander at Singapore, was reported missing, remained sunk in grief until, under Maggie's close encouragement, she began singing again. "The acts of God," Maggie told her, "are easier to bear than the acts of man." For Martha Deatherage, a teacher from Texas who first met Maggie when she was seventy-six, her example and dynamic personality illuminated her technical assessments:

She was so petite and blonde. She stomped in and grabbed my arm like a teenager. Bawdy sense of humour, quicksilver mind. Abrupt loud manner and loud laugh. Completely alive at every second, although I was aware she rested and took good care of herself in order to be that way. She said high C was felt between the eyes, open sinuses. One must choose in each song, which came first, words or music. I said how do you tell which one, and she said, Ah that's the hard test. Her secret is in using absolute control discipline in her thought. Talent is then free to act. She does not sit around theorizing. Absolutely practical. Immediate sense and feel for the words. No introspection . . . Viennese Mozart style always show head voice about D (octave above middle C). She told me that I was luscious in looks and should therefore sing "like marble". "I don't want any tuppenny-ha'penny emotion." Once on an "Oh" vowel she told me I sounded like a drowning duck in the rain. She recommended two conductors—Prêtre and Colin Brown. Said best she ever sang was "Connais-tu le pays" (*Mignon*) by Liszt. She wanted to sound like Melba. Avoid too much noise in a high voice. Pig has smallest chords—loudest voice due to his big nose . . . I was "ready" and eager to learn . . . Beautiful information simply poured out of her and I had not been given so much before, by any of several fine teachers, including Lotte Lehmann. Correction: I have never been given so much by any person in my life. I felt as though I had known her always and loved her instantly.

Passing on what she knew by teaching was one way to be remembered; a second, even stronger, claim on immortality, was to write a book. But here hunger was awoken but not wholly satisfied. She had met publishers in New York and London, dining out with them, delighting them with her gift for mimicry, the sharpness of her comments and her ubiquitous charm. Theodore Purdy, of G. P. Putnam in New York, had been responsible for a number of singers' memoirs and other books on opera and music in America, and wondered whether Maggie should not try to write her autobiography. He approached Roger Lubbock, head of Putnam in London, who agreed on a joint venture. Lubbock sought a "ghost": Purdy, after investing a thousand dollars in the project, then let the trial-and-error tactics of author and ghost take their course. The book took six years to produce and in the end, though the book was published in 1958 by Putnam in London, Purdy did not exercise his option. He was dissatisfied with its bitty nature, its slightness, its lack of proper chronological sequence; also Maggie's image in the States had faded by this time.

The "ghost", Cedric Wallace, and Maggie had just about managed to keep together, but Maggie, a constant reviser, would change chapter after chapter, trying to find, as she put it, exactly her own "tone of voice". The resulting effort was exceedingly guarded and rather stilted, though some of her personality does come through—her no-nonsense, down-to-earth approach to singing is there, and good advice on choosing a recital programme. In this, at least, she did realize her intention to produce something different from the usual run-of-the-mill memoir with its flamboyant tissue of half-truths, compulsive name-dropping, and flurries of self-congratulatory comment.* But for the most part Maggie's design to deliver a down beat "anti-memoir"—best summed up by the book's original title, *Twinkle, Twinkle, Little Star*, from the deflating rhyme, she found, one day when she was touring with the Boston Opera Company, smeared in red lipstick on her mirror:

> Twinkle, twinkle, little star,
> Who the hell do you think you are?

—was not sustained. The book came to be called, meaninglessly, *Star on the Door*, and though it includes a chapter on her failures—largely imagined ones, like Eva in *Die Meistersinger*, which was far from being a real failure—the rest of the book is hardly full of misgivings. Her main difficulty in literary endeavour was an impatience with steadily applied effort; she changed her mind from day to day as to what she wanted to say and dozens of drafts of chapters circulated chaotically among Lubbock, her "ghost", and herself. "I remember Henry Wood gave me an immense work—in six volumes.† Beautifully bound, of course, but you couldn't read it. Only fit for the furnace." It should hardly come as a surprise that her greatest literary gift was for the epigram.

From *Star on the Door* great chunks of Maggie's career were omitted wholesale. Virtually all her work with the Boston Opera Company was left out, to which the chronicler of that Company, ruefully and rightfully, took exception.[14] But she had kept no records, and hardly remembered that time of her life at all. Every memento of her career was consigned to

* That Teyte avoided the pitfalls of *Mary Garden's Story* when writing her own book, was the generous appraisal of Andrew Porter, who in a personal letter to her of 4 April 1958 wrote: "I must tell you how enormously I have enjoyed reading *Star on the Door*. I have read scores of singers' autobiographies—and yours is the first to be really articulate about the art of interpretation. (How different from the Mary Garden Story!)"

† She may well have been referring to Henry Wood's *The Gentle Art of Singing* (1927–8), which in fact is in four volumes.

the dustbin. She kept in all perhaps half a dozen programmes, a completely random selection from her whole career, and these she chopped up to form a collage for the cover of her book, losing valuable dates and other details. From this collage we know, for instance, that she sang with Caruso, but not when or where. She kept no reviews of her performances either: one sheet on the Beecham 1910 season is about the sum of it. I suppose she knew that butter, eggs, salt, and herbs do not, in Lytton Strachey's phrase, by themselves make an omelette.

Could the Mélisande side of Maggie's character ever have written a good book? This was hardly possible for she was far too shy. She wrote most of *Star on the Door* to conceal the past, or to seal it down, rather than to reveal it. It shows mainly the didactic side of her nature: the rest she preferred to hide away and leave to others to dig out. In a radio interview with Alec Robertson in 1950 she demonstrated her disruptive tactics: "Alec, can I ask *you* a few questions?" she demanded. Robertson spluttered back, "Well, I'm supposed to be interviewing you!" She was a formidable match for NBC's silky-voiced Tex McCrary when he brought the eighteen-year-old Judy Garland and the sixty ("six-O!") -year-old Teyte together. She loved a fight. "And look at *your* Mr Petrillo," she said of the notorious union leader featured in the headlines at that time: "he has definitely stopped people getting music." "If you're becoming an American he's *your* Mr Petrillo too," quipped Tex in reply.[15]

The truth about Mélisande is that she has been brutally raped by Bluebeard. She is in a state of shock; for a short while, in her love for Pelléas, she becomes alive, restored to vitality and hope. But then Golaud's jealousy rears up, sending her back into the shadows, back into numbness and then death.

The truth about Maggie was that she had never been loved for herself, the common fate of the artistic prodigy. "But tell me," the boy Mozart was heard to say, this immaculately laundered, concert-platform gift to humanity, "do you *really* love me?" Maggie would have given up everything for love, did indeed try to give up everything for it. Tragically it all misfired, becoming an empty theatrical gesture with financial compensation. This was her greatest and her most endearing mistake, sapping her career when she was in her prime. Of this there is no mention at all in her book.

CHAPTER FOURTEEN

Technique in the Top Register

Sometimes he bent over the whirring, pulsating mechanism as over a
spray of lilac, wrapt in a cloud of sweet sound.

THOMAS MANN, *The Magic Mountain*

LIKE A PLAY within a play, or a miniature hung on a wall behind the
subject of a portrait, Teyte's recording life had a definite form. Indeed it
had, with Aristotelian definiteness, a beginning, a middle, and an end.

The beginning was dramatic enough. Twenty-three-year-old Miss
Teyte, the cocksure prima donna of Chicago, fresh from her success in
Cendrillon in the winter of 1911–12, coming face to face with a tall and
stocky, dishevelled man who fixed her with his strange, bluey fish-eyes,
and who had been in a laboratory for two whole days and a night without
a break: Thomas A. Edison, no less. His dirt was dirt enough to cause her
disgust. "No one could miss his hands—the nails were broken and eaten
away with some green acid."[1]

She had just recorded several songs for Edison in Newark, New Jersey,
in a huge warehouse piled from floor to ceiling with bales of merchandise.
They were not quite the first records she ever made, for she had recorded
earlier in Europe, but it was the moment at which her recording aspirations were first strongly stirred.* With her was her accompanist, her
husband Eugène, and her agent. They had been waiting for Edison a good
half-hour and wondered if he would appear. His forgetfulness was
legendary and he had no sense of time—even on his wedding night he
worked late, forgetting to return home to his bride.

When he did arrive she did not at first understand a word, as his talk,
mostly directed at his assistant, was highly technical, with words like
"evolutions", "vibrations", "oscillations" figuring largely in it, which
meant nothing to her. But apart from thanking her, he did later direct at
her one comment: "Be careful of the technique in the top register," he
told her. Teyte bristled: she was not prepared for such criticism.

He then invited her to listen to a recording he thought perfect: as she

* She also made, on 21 November 1911, a test for Victor, in Camden, New Jersey.

recalled, a "dreadful English contralto", unnamed, indeed unnameable. She could not for the life of her understand why he liked such a terribly pallid voice. For herself, she had been quite happy with what she had recorded; if anything it was her diction she felt had been imperfect, but she had been pleased with the head voice.

However, she never forgot Edison's remark, and sixty-two years later she suddenly realized what it was he had meant. The occasion was her eighty-fifth birthday, when the actor and record collector, Richard Bebb, was broadcasting a tribute to her: Bebb played a recording she had made of Duparc's "Extase", and she found herself straight away reminded of Edison's comment. Here was perfection in recording as he had sought it. "I'm sad Mr Edison is not alive. I would send him a copy of this record. And perhaps he would change his mind." She praised her own work so sparingly, that such an opinion voiced by her merits close consideration. This was how, she continued, "Edison taught me so much without telling me practically anything." It is these deeply lodged realizations forcing their way out in time that lend such strength to character. There was Teyte, turning over for virtually a life-span some ill-phrased, probably almost chance remark Edison had made, probing its significance. She was an obstinate seeker, and in the end found what she was looking for: inexpressible in words, perhaps, but roughly speaking, it was as follows:

What Edison was "after", and what she heard in "Extase", was a technically true emotionless voice, the result of air from the lungs striking the vocal cords with an absolutely consistent flow and in perfect purity, following the ancient law, as described by Aristotle, in *De Audibilibus*, that "all sounds, whether articulate or inarticulate, are produced by the meeting of bodies with other bodies, because . . . (the air) is set in motion in a way in which bodies are moved, whether by contraction or expansion or again when it clashes together by an impact from the breath." This is a sound which maturity, experience, emotion to a certain extent stifle, dim, or turn misty. The pristine sound of the English choirboy. The innocence of tone that Nellie Melba sustained until late in life. For if the air from the lungs striking the cords has small bumps in it, tiny pockets or lumps of air caused by emotions interfering with the regularity of the nervous system, by experience or, put another way, by "interpretation", then the technical perfection of sound could be marred. It was this impurity of sound, she concluded, that Edison as a scientist was trying to eliminate from his recording. She realized further that it was the same problem the great violinist Yehudi Menuhin had identified, during one of his lessons, when he said, as she quoted him, that "intepretation is the greatest enemy of technique".

The war, the tension between these two polarities, technique and interpretation, is present in all Teyte's best recordings, and possibly it is the tension between the two that is remarkable rather than any sacrifice or resolution of one in terms of the other. Let us say, rather, that it is the relationship of the two that gives Teyte's records their uniquely thrilling quality, the striving for an impersonal ideal of perfection whilst in the midst of feeling, or, conversely, a hunger for sensation and sentiment in the rarefied abstractions of sound.

Although several commentators have regretted that she recorded little when her voice was in its prime, in the Twenties and early Thirties, it was the storing up of her emotions experienced during these years which she was able to release in distilled form into her recordings of the late Thirties and Forties, which give some of these recordings an almost uncanny autobiographical clarity of feeling. They are local, personal, as well as universal in their appeal, and naturally the music best suited to this form of romantic expression at one remove—not direct emotional expression, but the emotions as if seen through a gauze, subtly refined, their colours delicately heightened—are the *mélodies* of Debussy and his contemporaries. The way she sang these songs, moving herself in private, others in public, before, during, and after the Second World War, has been vividly testified to by her accompanist for many of her recordings, who reported that it was not uncommon for them to end up weeping at rehearsal. "Performances in public", she told a friend, "are the echo, or reflection, of emotions, including grief, keenly felt in preparation." Another powerful testimony to the emotions Maggie carried within her during these years and which found individual release in her singing, comes from the string orchestra conductor Boyd Neel: "When she sang Chausson's 'Poème de l'amour et de la mer' with us, I don't think there was a dry eye on the platform at the end of it, and knowing the attitude of the average orchestral player to these things made it certainly an occasion to remember." A singer in the audience at that same concert, Megan Foster, found Teyte's singing of the Chausson had such a strong effect on her that she had to hold on to the chair in front in order not to put up her head and howl like a dog.

The contrast, indeed miracle, of the tough, in many ways imperious and utterly selfish woman Teyte became, and this pure vulnerability, the extraordinary youthfulness and tenderness of feeling she was able to offer her muse ("Muse demands all", she often said) can be heard in many recordings of this time, notably of Fauré's "L'Absent", "Soir", "Clair de lune", and "Après un réve", and the even more sensitive Duparc's "L'Invitation au voyage", and "Phidylé". There is only one description of the singing that fits, that it possesses a naked intimacy, almost embarrassingly private, even disturbingly so: it grabs you, as one woman unexpectedly said, "by the short hairs." Richard Bebb found the first time he ever heard Teyte's record of "Psyché" by Paladilhe, that "my hair was standing up on the nape of my neck—the communication of the singer was so direct, so personal. From the first words 'Je suis jaloux, Psyché,' I was lost in the art of one of those rare singers, who through sound alone could demand total attention."[2] Though there is nothing comparable in the voices except sometimes the unexpectedly warm mezzo notes, Teyte's capacity to shock and thrill without degrading feeling has in it something of Edith Piaf's defiant spirit (they were of similar build). It is a popular, an unusually earthy quality, the tradition of the *café chanteuse*, in which the despair, the seediness, the sensuality—and the beauty—as well as the defiance, the gaiety, all predominate by turns, and sometimes unite. Teyte's mastery of such profane *fin-de-siècle* feeling is most supremely shown in her recording of Debussy's setting of Pierre Louÿs's prose poems, *Chansons de Bilitis*, which she recorded in her inspired two-day session with Cortot in 1936. But, while she expresses feeling through the medium of the words and music, absolutely no liberties are taken with the dynamics of the form. Composer first, not Teyte. "The *Chansons de Bilitis*," she said, "are so much of the pure Debussy—Debussy the primitive, the sybarite—yet one who in his voluptuousness, knew *the art of concealment*."[3] In "La Chevelure" she gives "more weight to the enunciation of the words, than to the resonances of the notes," because that is how Debussy liked it; he knew his own mind and allowed no liberties to be taken with his music. Here the comparison of Teyte with Piaf falls down, however, because Piaf adapted her songs to suit her own distinctive style while Teyte subtly, with great precision, only exercised interpretive freedom within the limits allowed by the composer, and within the meaning and mood of the poem. Even so "La Chevelure"'s greatest and most potent effect is that it often approaches speech: the narrative is utterly haunting towards its close, with "peu à peu, il m'a semblé, tant nos membres étaient confondus". . . .

It should be asked, even if it cannot be fully answered, on what foundation did Teyte's interpretive skill become secure? First and foremost, her knowledge of the composers themselves made her see their compositions in a different light from the ordinary view afforded a dead composer's work. For she had met and known many of the composers whose songs she recorded so successfully twenty to thirty years later. Chausson, who died by losing control of his bicycle in Limay and riding into a stone wall, was one she did not know; the reticent Duparc, also, whose undue sensitivity grew so burdensome that he composed nothing for the last nearly fifty years of his life—these two were strangers to her. But the rest almost without exception she had encountered at one time or another, and more often than not sang in their company and gained confidence from their approval. Add to this the confidence that age and time brought to early knowledge, and the supreme authority is achieved; see the way the "petite"* sums up the revered Fauré, with fairness and masterful judgement:

Fauré, who fascinates me no end, is quite different from Debussy. He appeals to me through a sense of surprise; one always expects him to end quite differently. One is tempted to say something cold and austere about Fauré, but that is not quite fair, for Fauré speaks from the heart, only perhaps he lets his intellect control his emotions. He is less earthy than Debussy, more mental. In relation to the poem, his musical notation shows discrimination, a tempering of emotion with the intellect. Verlaine and Debussy blend like a perfect glove on the hand. Fauré and Verlaine are like the heat and the cold, never quite fusing— and yet the elegance and grace of Fauré's art cannot be dismissed, it has an intellectual appeal. My favourite song of his is "Clair de lune"; here his emotional reticence is beautifully calculated. His discretion in not permitting his emotions to run away with him is exemplified in his setting of Verlaine's "D'un Prison". How strongly he gives us the feeling of the prisoner trying to get out. Hahn has also made a lovely setting of this poem, a setting, however, which suggests resignation. The Fauré song is one that can be successfully sung in the concert hall; the Hahn should be reserved for an intimate gathering in a salon.[5]

* "Bravo ma petite!" had been Fauré's comment when she sang for him at the Princesse de Polignac's house.[4]

Her closeness to the variety of Debussy's output of songs is equally striking:

> He was, in my estimation, the designer of the most beautiful modern dresses, with a fine sense of the exotic. He put the most persuasively beautiful clothes on the poems he set to music. Take "Des fleurs", from *Proses lyriques*, for which Debussy wrote the text; it is a song that wears a musical dress which is sinuous and snake-like. If a modern dress designer were to evoke a similar creation it would be the costume of an exotic woman of great magnetism and beauty—perhaps the Cleopatra type. Take the group of songs Debussy called *Ariettes oubliées*; what a variety of changing dress we find here and how appropriate they all are—could anything be more Debussyan in harmony and emotion than "L'ombre des arbres"? And does not the elemental in Debussy stand revealed in "C'est l'extase langoureuse"?[6]

The fusion of voice and words is difficult to achieve and various authorities suggest various ways. Teyte was always quite definite that the balance between voice value and word value must be exact. She believed also, though other outstanding interpreters such as Pierre Bernac might well disagree, that French for singing is a different matter altogether from spoken French. "The great singers of French song are not the French," she once averred, wilfully ignoring such artists as Jane Bathori and Ninon Vallin. "They often make the mistake of taking the easy way out in singing their own language by putting too much into the nasal tone." This dulls the voice's expressive power, for "when we are tired and want to make a big noise, we go into the nasal tone."[7] But, such statements apart, Teyte's good fortune had been to assimilate so much at such an early age, learning from de Reszke and at the Opéra-Comique how to place the French language correctly in her mouth, that she never really needed to rationalize or systematize the exact pressures of her voice upon the syllables of the poem. Even so it is remarkable how often they coincide with the markings that Bernac sets out at length in his book, *The Interpretation of French Song*.

No one could argue that Teyte's French diction, particularly by 1952, was 100 per cent perfect—by then it was thirty-two years since she had given up her French nationality, thirty-seven since she left her French husband—but her insight was far deeper than what might, for example, in an English singer draw criticism for sounding too Yorkshire, or in a French one for sounding too Lyonnais; she continued to penetrate and project "la musique de la langue", and her tap-root remained firm in the unconscious resonances, the archetypal meanings and structures of expression. Who can say, as I suggested earlier, but what this perfect sympathy may have had something to do with the name Tate being derived from Tête (head), her ancestry thus being traced back a long way to a French Huguenot?

As another means to interpretive power, Teyte stressed the value of learning *recitativo* singing in order to master the exact balance between words and music which was exemplified in particular in the title role of Gluck's *Orphée*. She cites Debussy's "Lettre de Geneviève" from *Pelléas et Mélisande* as a perfect example of more modern recitative. Fortunately we also have her recording of this, one of the two fragments of *Pelléas* she ever recorded, to exemplify this.

Most of Teyte's recordings are in French or in English, in both of which word value largely governs the musical shape. Her command of phrasing in both languages stems from an unrivalled faculty for thinking ahead to the end of each phrase. She never penetrated the German language in the way she did French, and although she has useful advice on German *Lieder* in her chapter on recitals in *Star on the Door*, her own recordings of *Lieder* (in particular Brahms's "Die Mainacht", "An die Nachtigall", "Meine Liebe ist grün", and Schumann's "Der Nussbaum" and "Aufträge") demonstrate no great sympathy with the corresponding German "musique de la langue". But to be fair, there is great spirit and colour in her singing of "Aufträge". Her statements about German song were often rash and ill-considered, such as that "in *Lieder* the singer can get away with a tolerable interpretation without fully understanding the words he or she is singing,"[8] though this may be explained by her lack of response to many German lyrics (an exception is Hugo Wolf's "Kennst du das Land"). The tradition of *Lieder* was at any rate more closely related to the popular folk song, and therefore more romantically direct in feeling: by nature she was less suited to this than to the more seductively oblique, hidden, and individual *mélodie* with its myriad forms of nuance, and its need for a voice to irradiate the words from within.

Reynaldo Hahn is often undervalued in the canon of French *mélodie*, but Maggie remained a firm admirer of his songs. Hahn was in no way pedantic about their interpretation. Once, shortly before his death, at tea with the wife of the British Ambassador in Paris, Teyte remembered telling Hahn that he played "Ce n'était pas la même chose" from *Ciboulette* rather quicker than she thought it should be played. "Ma chère," he told her, "any way you sing it will always be right." Her own favourite songs of Hahn were "L'Heure exquise" and "Offrande", both settings of Verlaine, and her most frequent encore, *cheval de bataille* as she dubbed it, which she recorded at least twice, was "Si mes vers avaient des ailes", to a lyric by Victor Hugo. One critic wrote that we ought to recoil at its "swoops, its total disdain for straightforward rhythmic flow, its final sentimental caress like a blown kiss," but that we cannot, "because she had it in her to create a level of beauty no less equal to the song itself."*

Technical perfection, no less than interpretive perfection, lies at the very heart of the Teyte–Cortot Debussy recordings. Both artists spared no effort to get the effect exactly right. "Debussy's very thought finds an echo in the voice of his faithful interpreter," wrote Cortot of these sessions. The *Fêtes galantes* show to perhaps best advantage the flexibility and delicacy in exact interpretive and technical balance. In the fifth, "Le Faune", Cortot achieved a compelling *tambour illusoire* effect—

> Jusqu'à cette heure dont la fuite
> Tournoie au son des tambourins

by inserting a sheet of paper in the piano, between string and hammers, in the appropriate register.

Teyte made further Debussy recordings in complete *rapport* with Gerald Moore, after the Cortot set, but her most perfect recording with Moore was of Ravel's "Le Martin-pêcheur" (The Kingfisher), to a Jules Renard poem (from *Histoires naturelles*) which tells enchantingly of the little kingfisher alighting on a boy's fishing rod, thinking it is a twig. The stillness of the wild little bird, scenting something strange in its plight, is perfectly mirrored in the music. It was, Teyte thought, the most difficult record she ever attempted to make, and the result conveys the musical intricacy of Ravel's score, the breathless, hush-hush quality of the boy's reaction—"Gerald is marvellous," she said of this—the thin and

---

* The review, by Alan Rich in *High Fidelity* (May 1965), refers to the Teyte–Reeves recording made in London in 1932. She made a later recording with Gerald Moore in 1941, which was re-issued on LP in 1976.

light rod, and the brilliant plumage of the bird: a wonderful example of "holding the mirror up to nature". Another Ravel recording, "D'Anne jouant de l'espinette", is hardly less perfect.

Ravel's *Shéhérazade* was her last great recording. Although she had met Ravel earlier on in Paris, *Shéhérazade* had not been part of her repertoire until 1931, when Sir Henry Wood introduced her to it, and she sang it at a Queen's Hall symphony concert. The song cycle had thrilled Felix Aprahamian at the time, but she had to wait until 1948 to record it, and she was by then sixty. Even so, Irving Kolodin wrote in reviewing it, "Her 'Asie' is still a cry of the heart rather than merely the beginning of a song," and "in view of the number of singers who have taken unto themselves so much of what she pioneered, it is remarkable how much remains inimitable."[9]

The singing in *Shéhérazade* preserves possibly better than any other recording a sense of the lasting technical soundness which de Reszke's teaching had secured for her early on in life. Other recordings with orchestral accompaniment which are available are "Absence" and "Le Spectre de la rose" by Berlioz (from *Nuits d'été*); those she is not able to encompass without a break in register in some of the phrases—she did not have as retentive a breath as other larger and more powerful singers— but it matters little in the sheer urgency and haunting beauty she infuses into the Gautier poems. Indeed one of the fascinations of the last big re-issue of several sets, the four-record "L'Exquise Maggie Teyte" (EMI RLS 716), is that it enables a listener to chart her vocal development over more than forty years, since her first record reportedly made in 1908, "Because" (d'Hardelot).*

In this album, the voice, while maintaining its unmistakable timbre (even when she had to sing into a horn), progresses into a lush ease, a brightness in the operetta numbers she recorded, before deepening to oboe by about 1940, when the scale of the voice is also reduced slightly in quantity. One of the most perfect early recordings, though light in quality, is Offenbach's "Tu n'es pas riche, tu n'est pas beau", from *La Périchole*, which is full of roguish and teasing charm; Romberg's "Deep in my Heart", from *The Student Prince*, supplies the finest high note she recorded,

---

* To be precise, "Because" was recorded in 1907, when she was in Paris, and still using the name Tate—at least for signature purposes. It was then that she signed her first recording contract, for ten records spread over three years, for which she was paid 150 guineas.[10]

in her own estimation: a top B natural.[11] Her sense of parody is finely conveyed in "Sweet Mistress Prue"—"Sweet Mistress Prooo, how do you doo"—and her singing of "Oft in the Stilly Night", as well as of a sentimental ballad she recorded with John McCormack, "Still as the Night", show her more in the vein of her non-stop variety appearances at the Victoria Palace, or on BBC "Workers' Playtime".

In the recordings mentioned above Teyte's art can still be savoured. There are other examples, not currently available: an unreleased and tantalizingly incomplete version of Massenet's *Manon*, sung in English and recorded for the BBC, with Heddle Nash; some ten jewels of eighteenth-century opera by Grétry, Monsigny, Méhul, Pergolesi, and others, with orchestral accompaniment by Jean Morel, recorded by RCA Victor, which cry out for re-release on LP. There are pirated recordings of operatic arias taken from the Bell Telephone Hour broadcasts in 1946, a wonderful "Voi che sapete" from *Le Nozze di Figaro*, as well as two arias from *La Bohème* which open magic casements on her early career. They remain prized collectors' items for the present.

While it is true that the art of Maggie Teyte has been salvaged from certain loss through the gramophone,* it is also undeniable that she was an artist for whom the gramophone was a perfect invention, which she herself was quick to realize. At heart reclusive and mysterious, she gained through recording that much-sought-after distance from her public, was freed from the disadvantages of close personal contact to which she did not naturally respond. It provided a sort of screening process which enabled her to reveal much more of herself, her moods and emotions, than she could through opera in her mature years—opera having been more of an adventure in stardom which belonged to her youth. Most of all her performing temperament was of a singular kind: she liked to do a thing really well only once, and repetition of it was onerous to her.

There is a kind of greatness in the constant reproduction of well-established effects with freshness, testified to by the hundreds of performances in a single role by such great artists as Flagstad; but for Teyte each performance was a unique experience. This is why she gave so few, and why, probably, those who saw one of the few she gave found it so unforgettable. The roles she went on singing she developed considerably,

---

* In three months of 1977, over 3,200 of her records were sold, although the majority of these were miscellany records such as "HMV Treasury", "Great British Sopranos", and "Stars of the Old Vic and Sadler's Wells".

but when she felt she had no more to offer, she gave them up. This unique approach was perfectly suited to the French *mélodie*.

She once told a friend in Hamilton Terrace, Lois West-Russell, that her voice was like a large pearl, but often the smallest pearls can be better trained and grow into rarer jewels. Possibly she was speaking indirectly of herself: her early voice was a fair-sized pearl, not one of the largest by any means, but large enough to fill most auditoria, and very penetrating in quality. But it was the smaller quantity of sound that she cunningly worked on later to fashion these recording masterpieces of rare and lasting quality.

The final answer as to what made Teyte a great interpretive artist must be that no matter what happened to her, she remained throughout a child of nature, instinctive and elemental in thought and feeling. Herein ultimately is the cause of her inability to interpret Schoenberg's *Pierrot Lunaire*, for it appealed too much to theory and the intellect to register fully with her. For Teyte, music had to awaken and elicit elemental responses, be they of joy, of sorrow, of awe or fear, of love or of loneliness.

CHAPTER FIFTEEN

An Expensive Way To Die
(1960–1976)

Arkel: Il n'arrive pas d'événements inutiles.
Pelléas et Mélisande

As a child Maggie had no sympathy with her family, kept no records of them, pushed them away from her whenever she could; as a middle-aged woman she would not come near what was now a different family; as an old woman she hid herself away, even long before the end when her health had got worse. She thrived on mystery to the very end, and in the end the mystery even deepened. She never wanted anyone to have the whole picture: "Don't give them the last chapter," she would say, "till they've got through the whole book."

This, then, is the last chapter.

She had come to depend emotionally, as much as she had depended on anyone in her life, on her niece Rita, whom she brought up after a fashion, paying liberally for her to go through school and college while not exactly giving her a home. Rita at last took on the role of mother to her: she would fetch and carry for her, reply to her letters, answer her summonses to appear, her pathetic and childish pleas for attention. The child who had outgrown and passed way beyond the appeal for protectiveness shown in the delicate, sensitive roles she created, was herself calling at the end to be mothered. And why should she have turned to Rita? Perhaps because Rita had given up her singing career, was herself a mother, something Maggie had never been. As an artist she may have been perfect and exemplary, but as a human being she was often incomplete, selfish, and spoilt, incapable of compassion. But she was willing to learn up to the last moment.

In her early seventies, from 1960 onwards, she saw much of her "walking telephone" friend, so called from her manner of receiving and relaying gossip: this was Josephine Wray, a hugely fat, delightfully ebullient lady with red hair and arthritic fingers. "Looks like a whorehouse keeper yet lives in a £25 a week flat," Teyte said of her. Josephine had sung much at Covent Garden in the Thirties and had been the mistress of Sir Eric Geddes, a prominent City businessman. Maggie and she made an odd pair going about together—"Puck and the Valkyrie", which tickled Maggie. Another friend was Ursula Guinness, widow of Colonel Blois, formerly the administrator of Covent Garden.

Teyte had now grown very outspoken about fellow artists but was often electrifyingly shrewd. Of Joan Sutherland, whose ability to stand up to great suffering she admired, if not her crimson-dyed hair: "She shouldn't call attention to her face. . . . I hate gossip, you know, but if people started gossiping over me I should feel finished!" Of Maria Callas: "Callas is so ugly—she has that great trench of green make-up under her eyes; it makes her look like the witch in *Snow White and the Seven Dwarfs*." (But, of the moment she loved most in a performance: Callas's first entrance in *Medea*.) Of Elena Suliotis: "Short, fat, three double chins," but "where Callas has kept her wonderful musicianship, Suliotis looks and sings like a common peasant; I heard the other day she has money in the bank from a Greek shipping Co!!! so that's the reason for the press propaganda."[1] Of Joseph Hislop, with whom she had sung *Bohème* at Covent Garden: "His face . . . It's quite paralysed into a rigid expression." Of Lina Pagliughi (a pupil of Tetrazzini): "Marvellous . . . a deformity— a bottom like a table; she did beautiful *pianissimos*—the voice is enriched by internal fat." Of Tom Burke: "Like all tenors he got so bum of himself." Of Dietrich Fischer-Dieskau: "Why, this man is nothing more than a German policeman." Elisabeth Schwartzkopf she admired, but couldn't resist saying, "She gave singing lessons between acts in her dressing room . . . but with Walter Legge around it's not surprising." Of Victoria de los Angeles: A "very good Butterfly; she was nice and small." Of Adèle Leigh: "A very good Manon."

She now had too much time for thoughts of death, of love, and sex. Old age meant for her letting her imagination run wild. One afternoon, perhaps one of the first I ever spent alone with her, she showed me a folder containing a large quantity of miscellaneous material, newspaper cuttings, letters of appreciation, scraps of paper on which, she said, she had tried— not very successfully, she confessed—to jot down what she thought. "This I am going to hand over to you. When I am dead you can, if you want or think . . . (you know—'interesting', 'readable', a . . . 'book'—

that kind of thing . . .)." I was tempted but I never got the folder. It was like her ancient and trusty Wolseley, which she promised me when she could no longer drive—she still at this date drove fast and dangerously about the streets of London, slamming her high-heeled shoe down on accelerator or clutch, usually with her head well down below the level of the dashboard but shooting up now and again to see if anything was coming: she had forgotten the promise when it came to carrying it out. Once, Rita recalled, she took the Wolseley into the West End, parked it there and then, quite unaware she had left it, picked up a taxi to take her home. Later in Hamilton Terrace it suddenly struck her: "Oh my God, where's my car?" After she was dead I did receive a diminished and paltry pile of letters and papers, but I fear she had already weeded them out, burying as many traces as she could of her former life. She must have known what remained would be tantalizing, the excitement of discovery so much greater than the boredom of sifting.

In the course of conversation she turned to probing her young grand-nephew's sexuality. "I was thinking about you," she said one day; "I was thinking a lot about you this morning." "Were they nice thoughts?" I asked innocently, clearly no match for her. "No, they were not nice thoughts, to be frank." We left it at that.

She now seemed to fit perfectly into the role of eccentric great-aunt, sometimes on an epic scale. Her view of politics was simple but accurate: "It's all a matter of geography." For one who spent her formative years criss-crossing not only France, Europe as far as Russia, and the Atlantic, it was no surprise she should come up with the view that "The Russians are only trying to get into the sun." Subsequent events proved her accuracy.* Other predictions were more dour: "There will be war— and I *hope* there will be war." She liked Anthony Eden, knew his short-comings; the trouble was that he was too human: "a man of principle." She hated Eisenhower, saying prophetically (in the light of his protégé Nixon's future career), "He's an opportunist, a Nazi, a careerist." If only I could have warned the world of my great-aunt's potent premonitions; but I was far too young to be able to.

She had met dozens of the famous about whom she reminisced. Hitler: her idea of Mephistopheles. In Paris she had encountered Youssoupoff,

* In her last thirty years she showed similar prescience in checking meticulously, even obsessively, her cholesterol count—a practice which only became fashionable towards the end of her life.

one of Rasputin's killers; she found him captivating and was entranced by his beautiful wife, the daugher of Grand Duke Serge. Lord Russell: "I hated Russell till I heard he loved England." Lord Beaverbrook: "He summoned me to look me over. When I was leaving, at the door, he stopped me. 'Know something?' he said to me, 'You're bowlegged.'" (She was not).

For someone born in the last quarter of the nineteenth century in Enoch Powell's former constituency, she had kept a remarkable continuity with the contemporary white phobias of her birth-town. When a psychiatrist living next door to her in Hamilton Terrace sold his house to a black man, she was furious, stalking up and down, watching out of her windows for days on end. The psychiatrist, she declared, was a red: "I bet you he sold his house to the blacks on purpose. He had the most extraordinary behaviour—for a psychiatrist. One morning his car wouldn't start, so he lost his temper—and you know what? He punched it"—and she showed how, with a Kabuki shout—"Ah!! Like that! He broke the glass of his headlight. And that glass is damned thick!"

So Hamilton Terrace was going downhill too, like everything else. She looked out of the window; black children were trying to catch fruit that fell off a pear tree in her garden into the garden next door. "My dear," she once had said, "Hamilton Terrace is the most snob area in London—there's even a special way to make love in Hamilton Terrace," and now it was becoming the playground of black monkeys. Mind you, Alfred Cave, the violinist against whom she still bore a special grudge over Grace, also looked like a monkey, an orang-utan to be precise. We knew that already. But now Fischer-Dieskau, her latest symbol of a rival voice, had long arms "like an orang-utan". And even Debussy became an octoroon in her deteriorating fantasy, his final vibration one of darkness. Life was reducing itself to phobias. She showed how Alfred Cave moved with Neanderthal strides and loose arms. "And, my dear, he is so lazy and BORING. And conceited. He has no life at all." The old jealousy was really stirred.

Then the bottle-green eyes lit up as she recalled a macabre encounter with Beecham, not long after the death of Vaughan Williams. She had asked after Beecham's second wife, Lady Betty Humby Beecham, and he had replied, "She's gone on tour," adding, as an ominous afterthought, "with Dr Vaughan Williams."

But she still loved England: "There's only one place on this planet."

Then one day she took a last bus ride on the now brutal London buses: "I had a little *contretemps* on a bus—at least the bus had a little *contretemps* with a car, and the sudden brakes gave me a broken rib for my fourpenny ride." She was beginning to hate the outside world, a hate which was to intensify as she grew very old.

I told her I once knew a beautiful Abyssinian girl, but she dismissed this with the social prejudices of Edwardian society. "But that is so *different*, my dear!" Then perhaps fragments of the past would be washed up: a lover in Chicago, "So frightening, so *imprudent*." Someone she met in an *auberge* at Boulogne, with whom she went to a casino: "Je vous jouerais pour une nuit d'amour," he told her. A time during a performance of *Tristan und Isolde* when she had sex with the conductor in the entr'-acte. (But had she ever sung in *Tristan*?) Then there was someone who had tried to take her to bed only five months before: a "bugger", she said, delivering the word with relish, for she never minced such matters.

Indeed she averred she never became friends with a man (though it was difficult to believe her here) unless she had been to bed with him; but the gin was so strong that evening, or afternoon, that she even talked of the female organs. Ahead of the now suffocatingly prevalent fashion, she identified the clitoris as all-important: "The periwinkle coming out of the shell, the chink in the female armour, the apparatus of making love." And then she went on: "Sexuality is so much more interesting than love." Was she merely endeavouring to impress an extremely impressionable young man, her own sexuality now no longer active and her enjoyment being to talk about it with huge frankness, shock her listeners, above all if they were young, and then to dissolve into high peals or low crumples of laughter? If so she had caught the flavour of the Sixties as she had of most other decades in her life. The expression of her thoughts was uninhibited, not coarse, and there was still that clipped Anglo-French hauteur in her voice.

Early, brutally, she had identified strong selfish thoughts she herself had put to the test: "Genius has no imagination, has no talent. Just single-minded—or narrow-minded if you like." Who else again was in her thoughts but Debussy, the orchid man, her Prince of Darkness?

She had no health problems, though in August 1961 she fractured her left wrist. She still taught at Dinely Studios, having set up with her accountant a new organization called The Teyte School—dropping the

Vernon part. Her pupils still very much intrigued and stimulated her. To her doctor she wrote about one of them, "I would be very interested if you could find out what happens to the vocal cords of a pupil of mine, an American girl who studied in New York with somebody who, apparently, has a method to break a voice before they can sing!!! I don't understand it, but there you are . . . a very beautiful voice, but when she arrived here, three notes were missing in the top register!" The doctor set to work to correct this alarming deficiency. In November 1962 she addressed herself to her accountant with her usual bluntness and command: "Dear Jack, are you still alive? . . . If so," she went on, "you can drop in for a 'wee drop of scotch'."

She herself was still very much alive. She lost her purse just before Christmas of that year and made a huge fuss with the insurance company until she received compensation for a treasured diamond brooch. After all, she would often say, what is *The Ring* about but money? The following year in April she took three guests, American friends, to the Grill Room at the Ritz, sending ahead of her a cheque for £10. The bill came to £10 and 2/-, a remarkably accurate prediction. The Ritz sent her a bill for the extra 2/-.

In 1963 she gave a master class at Dartington Hall. In January 1964 Decca began a series of long-playing reissues with some of her pre-war recordings from operetta, songs by Fauré and Hahn, together with the 1937 BBC recital, and this was followed by EMI with the Debussy album. So she decided to expand physically upwards at Hamilton Terrace, to build an extension, with the idea of having someone living in with her, a female helper or companion. She waited a year and a half to obtain planning permission to do this; in the meantime going on teaching as before.

She had made a will in March 1961; in March 1965 she made another. There was nothing much to leave besides the lease of the house in Hamilton Terrace and her record royalties, for her income from the W. S. Cottingham Estate would cease absolutely on her death. She was determined and specific in the will that none of the capital or income from her estate should fall into Cavan O'Connor's hands—a remnant of her old jealousy over her niece, though they no longer picked fights with each other as they had in the late Fifties, over gin and on the subject of singing. She was always exhorting Cavan to sing well: "Sing well," she wrote to him in 1967, "and never practise without a nosegay!!" My elder brother,

Maggie's godson, was struck off the will as executor: he had become more bohemian and grown his hair long. She now hated long hair and very dark men and Michael could not grow one without turning into the other. She also left £1,000 to the Haydn Mozart Society for an annual prize to a young singer: the one string attached was that the bequest be used to preserve the traditions of Mozart, Haydn, and Gluck.

In 1966 she decided she was too old to teach and the affairs of The Teyte School were wound up. As the extension in Hamilton Terrace had become an impossible idea, her estate agents were asked to see if they could "secure" for her a flat in a new block in Grove End Road, round the corner from her cottage. They were successful, and offered her a flat on a 98-year lease, at such-and-such a ground rent, for a purchase price of £9,500. But with the offer came a curious request: that in consideration of letting her have a chance at one of these flats in advance of their being offered to the general public, the owners should be allowed to announce publicly "that one of the units had been disposed of to Dame Maggie Teyte". Apparently they felt that such an announcement would help to attract "purchasers of similar calibre".

What had they in mind? Dame Eva Turner? Kirsten Flagstad? Mary Garden or Patti? Melba? Fascinating as it would have been to found such a co-operative, one wonders whether the flimsy new fabric of the development would have stood up under the strain of a colony of prima donnas. In any case Maggie agreed and in September 1966 put down a deposit of £100; in the following April she caught shingles of the face, possibly the outward sign of an inner crisis over her unmotivated and rash move away from Hamilton Terrace into Century Court. Anyone who had seen her at this time, tottering along the pavement in Hamilton Terrace, would have been quite shocked by the sudden change in her appearance after the attack of shingles. She was no longer the sturdy, sure-footed "Meg", but an alien, frail, and physically timid—though not in will—old lady. She might take her visitor to see the new flat, extremely dull and modest after her charming den at No. 42, with its aura of pink gin and parapsychology; though the staircase in the cottage was narrow and treacherous, threatening sudden falls—the nightmare of the elderly—and its rooms tiny. Arranging such a move near her seventy-ninth birthday was a huge folly, even if she was born under the obstinate sign of the Ram. Was she imitating her father in his late move from Wolverhampton?

The cottage in Hamilton Terrace fetched a handsome £11,700 and the sale went through in July 1967. But—in true British fashion—the new flat was not ready, and so while committed to moving out of Hamilton Terrace, and still recovering from shingles, she had to go into a temporary flat rented from the Peachey Property Corporation. As those faithful furies the Inland Revenue buzzed again on her trail she recovered a bit of her old humour, writing to her accountant:

> Flat 570 Park West,
> Edgware Road,
> W.2.

Mon cher Monsieur,
    Voici le chèque pour le Inland Revenue et mon adresse pour le présent.

> M.T.

In the last nine years of her life she was to move—or, by the end, to be moved—no less than six times, with financial stability growing more and more precarious as her health deteriorated.

Completion of the flat in Century Court proved even slower than the agents' most pessimistic forecast. It was 6 April 1968, ten days before her eightieth birthday, before Maggie, tenant number one, moved into her flat on the seventeenth floor. There were telegrams and flowers—her accountant sent her button roses and Felix Aprahamian a floral basket—and she was clearly delighted with her new address, and even more that no phone had been installed. She would be sorry when it did come, and wrote to Aprahamian that she had been "Out of circulation for a little while as I banged my nose running round the place like a silly goat! I am not quite presentable yet, and the swelling has not quite disappeared! Please be discreet, and do not mention it to anyone. . . ."

Then she had another fall. A few days later she was taken off by Rita to the Hospital of St John and St Elizabeth in St John's Wood, her face streaming with blood. She was stitched up by a black doctor, who found no fracture, but it was some time before she recovered her balance. She had been well versed in negotiating the narrow stairs at Hamilton Terrace, even in her dangerously high heels secured with straps over her trousers, while in the new block, with its smooth surfaces and silent lifts, she fell about all the time.

In her eightieth year, she had recorded Gounod's "Ave Maria", almost stopping during it ("I'm getting cramp," she said) but reaching the top B.[2] On her eightieth birthday the BBC broadcast a generous commemorative programme, and by early the following year she was fully recovered and able to give an amusing talk at Holborn Library Hall, with Aprahamian and Grenville Eves questioning her.

About this time she was negotiating with the Cottingham Trust, from which she received an income for her lifetime, about the release of funds to purchase an annuity. There was talk of a cash settlement of £20,000, but in the end it was considered that Vera, now Mrs Hue-Williams, would not be sympathetic to making over such a large sum. So Maggie's income, now £2,500 tax free, remained unchanged.

After living only a very short time in Century Court, Maggie decided to move again. Tired of being suspended on her luxury shelf in the sky over Lord's cricket ground, she put her flat up for sale and moved into a ground floor room in a private nursing home in Brunswick Gardens, W.8: "I was getting feeble and old—and I couldn't stand it—so all sudden-like I turned my back on the world," she told Madeau Stewart in a letter, "came here where they are very kind and look after me like a broken piece of china." Since her fall she was determined she was going to die within a year, like her mother Maria Tate, who had gone to bed saying she would die in six months and had done exactly that. Strikingly, Maggie's decision seemed to echo what Pelléas said of his friend: "Il dit qu'il sait exactement le jour où la mort doit venir." So she put a PRIVATE notice on her door, decided she hated the world, turned her back on all offers to be taken out—the blossom that year was in abundance—and switched on the radio. She did not listen much to music, but kept well up with current events. And there she waited for death.

But death did not come. She reported she had had a stroke but the evidence was slight. An examination at the Nuffield Hospital in 1970 showed nothing wrong with her. She looked the picture of health, so it was little wonder she could not die. The only serious danger threatening her were the high-colonic irrigations she insisted on taking.* She could still walk. Still eat. Still talk. Still write. She had given away her books,

---

* She shared with Kirsten Flagstad a belief in this treatment of dubious medical value. The latter had been asked to remove her stays when she had the treatment, and when she at last agreed, so Maggie related with great relish, she "literally fell apart". The wicked laugh was still intact.

her small but valuable collection on Debussy, priceless scores, one the green-bound *Pelléas** with pencil marks in the composer's hand, her mink coats—she had four—her fine collection of Dutch silver. She even threw out some records: one was Mary Garden singing to Debussy's accompaniment. Such things had no value for her. From this time on she withdrew steadily and mysteriously.

At first her balance became a problem. Then she did have a series of small strokes, her imagination having been forerunner to the event. Her aggression, her will to live, her jealousy, her love, her power—all, at this moment, evaporated. The rest is a sorry tale. She wanted the curtain to come down, but in the descent it stuck fast, leaving her naked deterioration for all to see.

Most of all the vultures of inflation enjoy the spectacle of old people dying and feast off the declining value of their money. In 1972 she finally managed to sell her Century Court flat, for £12,000, to a Mr Agran. Her furniture, except for some choice carpets and a grandmother clock which she gave to her niece, she put into a Harrods' auction. In 1973 she was still receiving royalties from the gramophone companies and income from the BBC, held shares in Rolls-Royce, which had gone bankrupt, and ICI, which had not. She had acquired over the years the oddest collection of infinitesimal quantities of stock—sixteen 10/- shares in De La Rue, thirteen 5/- shares in Desoutter, £6 worth of Radio Rental, thirty 5/- shares of Unigate and eleven shares in the Zenith Carburettor Company†—which were now sold. She invested the capital from the sale of her flat in an annuity to cease on her death, and all was set for the final run. "It is so expensive to die!!!" she complained to more than one friend. But the tax-free sum of £50 a week she received from Sherwin's estate, which for forty years had remained strong in purchasing power, was now to be totally eroded; and because of various blunders over property, she was at the mercy of rapidly rising fees at the nursing homes. Yet she refused Rita's offer to come and live with her and Cavan in their Victorian flat in Olympia, where there was ample room for her to withdraw from the world—even to remain in it—which would have been a sensible family arrangement. No, the aged prima donna had again, as at so many times in her life, to go it alone. Fate, destiny, dictated so.

* She was superstitious about the colour green but overlooked it in the case of this score, which had brought the very reverse of bad luck.

† She also had £90 invested in Israel.

In the summer of 1972, Cavan and Rita visited her in Brunswick Gardens. Maggie was sitting up in bed. She looked delighted to see them but very concerned over some business she had summoned Cavan for. This was largely how she related to people she cared for: she asked them to do something for her. It was her own way.

Her eyes were as bright as ever, her voice with still that rich and humorous tone—a slight element of wickedness in it. She had undoubtedly aged heavily, the line in her neck was tauter, but the physical immobility apart, she still strained to maintain a momentum in her relationships. She turned first to business. She wanted Cavan to collect some share certificates to send to her solicitor, and they managed to raise some small dispute over the year of the certificates.

Suddenly Meg turned sharply: "There's a smell of mothballs or something!" Such outbursts and phobias could be put down to the ageing process. Yet there undoubtedly was a smell: Cavan had redeemed a shirt from mothballs that very afternoon, and Meg's acute nostrils picked it up. She turned to Cavan, due to sing next week up north: "Will you do something for me, Cavan?" He looked dubious. "I want you to end a song, one of the songs you sing, on a high note. A beautiful high note. Just for me. One of those beautiful *pianissimo* notes you do so well."

Cavan's eye moistened. But it had been instilled into him in his Nottingham working-class youth that giving way to emotion was cissy, so he passed it off roughly. But he said he would do it.

"How are your boys?" Maggie asked Rita. Rita told her. The "boys" were all grown men now. Rita and she chatted a few minutes in stilted French, Maggie bright as a button, alert in mind, launching into an attack on record pirates who had released the hitherto unknown record she and John McCormack had made together.

Then, abruptly, she was tired out, told Rita and Cavan to go. She sank back on her pillows, *épuisée*. Cavan, too, seemed exhausted. But in some ways she had become a sweet old lady, though the smouldering fire remained.

"I heard a very good radio programme on you," he said before parting. "In the morning?"

He nodded. "Martin Cooper. He was very nice."

"Surprising after all the things I said about him, he was so nice about me."

But who now was she? She seemed to have lost contact with the past, with her own childhood. Suspended by will, career centred, her early years were still a complete mystery. She had wanted to arrive on the stage of life as Mélisande arrived, with her mystery totally unexplained, something dark, something fascinating behind her. Her whole career was suspended in the light of performance, but there were no wings to relax in and no outside world. Again, in her old age, there was no outside world. "This raping world," she called it, "this copulating world: I don't want to have anything to do with it. We had the best of it: 1919. 1920. We had a wonderful time."[3]

Visitors would be discouraged from calling on her, cousins by marriage from America would be turned away, visiting colleagues told she could not see them. Even now she kept some control over her fate, but only within this pathetically diminished world, controlled by exacting small favours from friends and relations, shrinking, in no torment, but in terms of that extraordinary gaiety and vitality her life had shown, in hell. The helplessness without pain, the very lack of frustration or hostility, showed in some distorted way her egotism and her fulfilment. Hers not the glorious conclusion of Eleanora Duse, snuffed out fighting till the very last to act and to overcome poverty. Maggie had overcome poverty, she had been rich all her life, she had adopted her own epitaph—

> When Death comes by,
>   O Muse, Goddess of Art,
> Allow me in one small part
> Of your magic robe to lie![4]

—and now she lingered on, wrapped up, in the word she used of Debussy, "like a cocoon."

Power of attorney had first been conferred temporarily on Rita as far back as 1969, when she had handed to her some nine chequebooks for four different accounts—some in the name of Dame Margaret Cottingham, some in the name of Teyte, and one in the name of Maggie Teyte DBE, which Maggie refused to use. When Rita and Cavan set off in 1974 on a singing tour of South Africa and New Zealand, the power was passed wholly to Perman, her devoted accountant. While Cavan and Rita were away Maggie was moved out of the Brunswick Gardens home, which was closing down, to a nursing home in south-west London which was inadequate in every way, and was being done up. The cost was enormous, some £70 a week, and Maggie was desperately unhappy there.

With Maria Callas in the Crush Bar at Covent Garden, and (*right*) after receiving the DBE in 1958.

Maggie Teyte in her seventies: photographed by the author in 1966, with the score of *Pelléas et Mélisande*.

With Rita out of reach, she had a terrible lapse, struggled with a nurse, and fell, fracturing her left humerus. Telegrams flew back and forth between London and New Zealand, the gist of which was that Maggie thought everyone was trying to kill her. But, wrote her accountant, "It is a little difficult to know precisely what Maggie's feelings are because she fluctuates somewhat."

Did anyone ever know what her true feelings were? Or was she not at last showing them in her very fluctuations? Her great gift had been to picture the shades of feeling in her voice, just as it had been Debussy's to create them, but gone now was the precise nuance.

night

alone in a sky darker, gloomy
Roamed night the silent thieving prowler.
Around his head a sliver of gold
Moon r stars attached to his feet
Ever seeking a silver silver
To mingle with gold upon his head

one night he roamed . far in the sky
attracted by Earths wondrous light.
Valleys deep with silver streams
Mighty oceans, bluish— —green
'This indeed' is a jewel rare . "
It must be mine it shall be mine!"

A draft of Maggie's poem of 1974; see p. 167.

see p. 167.

Certainly she had grown morbid. In September 1970 she had given Rita written instructions, in her now pedantic way: "I am going to be cremated—nobody must be there except the family, if they wish—and you are not to see the coffin being burnt. Someone in the nursing home told me that they [the undertakers] charge a lot of money for a beautiful coffin, and then they put the body in an old wooden one—to put in the fire—I am not to have any flowers—and nobody is to know I am dead until after the cremation." She wanted to retain the element of surprise, of theatrical revelation, even in her going, as well as keeping expenses down.

Then she developed more sophisticated ideas of self-disposal: "Dear Dr Janvrin," she wrote to her doctor, "I wish to leave my body to a hospital for transplants, if they want it; my kidney machine is in very good order and I have had no trouble during my lifetime, with my heart; if they want my eyes, they can have them, if they think they are good enough; why don't they do something about deafness?"

She had been alone too much even though from her own choice. But she was still remembered: a publisher in Mainz wrote with an entry they were putting into their dictionary; the American impresario Kenneth Allen conveyed the intention of coming to see her—he had recently retired. Patrick Mahony, the Hollywood writer, and step-brother of the late Sir Arthur Bliss, visited her. So did her old friends in the BBC like Madeau Stewart and Barrie Hall; her boon companion David Tron; the distinguished music critics Desmond Shawe-Taylor and Felix Aprahamian also called by.

There was another caller: "Guess who called me on the telephone," she said to Estelle Johnstone on her eighty-fifth birthday. "Who?" Estelle brightly enquired. "G – A – Y . . ." The name came out with painful slowness . . . "G – a – y . . . V – e – r – n – o – n." "What did she ring about?" Estelle knew of the bitter break-up of their friendship. "I put down the receiver . . . I'm . . . not . . . going . . . to . . . speak . . . to . . . her. . . ." So passed the chance of reconciliation, for there was no wavering in her unforgiving nature.

After the disaster at the second nursing home, John O'Connor and Estelle Johnstone, still in Rita's absence, arranged another in Finchley, which lasted a few months. But there the nurses (who always left after a few weeks, especially if they were nice), beauticians, and colonic irrigators all began to find Maggie was becoming generous in an extraordinary and alarming way. Her grandnephew John was summoned after helping her move from the previous place. "Here, take a pen," she told him. "Write the following—'Dear Jack [the accountant], pay John O'Connor the sum of £100 for helping me move.'" John wrote it down but felt very embarrassed about taking it along to Perman. What if he thought John talked her into it? She then said in true Teyte fashion,

"Let's get drunk," and from the locker pulled out a bottle of Wincarnis.*

Although incapacitated, she could not give up her old patrician manner which at some level kept self-respect intact. Soon she was giving away £10 notes to the nursing staff. She was now frankly having to buy attention, as she sought the style of those old houses in which she had lived, Dunstall House, the Grange and Hall at Woolley, like some strange distorted caricature of Sherwin Cottingham drunkenly giving away gold and notes to his retainers, and all for love, all for good opinion.

From the home in Finchley, she was moved by Rita, on her return from New Zealand, back to W.8, to Pitt Street. Deeply concerned about the money Maggie was giving away, Rita managed to fix gratuities to the staff in the new place to £5 notes, which she took to Maggie herself. Then she began to send strange missives dictated to nurses. One to Perman, dated 31 July 1974, ran: "Dear Jack, as this world is made by the laws of man, why must he be the first to suffer? So bang goes my Christmas lists and you go with it. There will not be any gifts this year of 1974. I shall give a cash present of £2 to all the nurses and Matron so between now and Christmas I hope to have saved enough money so I will not have to borrow from you." On 22 August, returning to her obsession, Maggie gave Rita a list of Christmas presents to buy—a little, as Rita remarked to Perman, on the early side. The two of them decided to limit her to £7 a week for distributing. Then Maggie wrote to say she wished to spend every bit of spare cash there was "in the kitty", as she was going to die— for the second time—before Christmas. The end of money for her was the end of life.

She had always made a distinction between love of money and money itself; the first she thought a great evil, and while she did not love money itself she rightly saw, and had seen early on, its use as a means to power. She had bribed, paid for, people all her life, and even now in her own mind, was dominating the nurses. Miss Murphy, a favourite, left to marry, and received £100 as a wedding present, not a bad tip for a couple of months. Maggie considered she was paying for all these people, not by indirect means through the nursing home but actually handing it to them; and with the prospect of her cash drying up shortly (though of course her income from the Cottingham estate would continue), the power would be at an end. Now, in her old and befuddled mind, possibilities of other kinds of relationships hardly seemed to exist: people were greedy, selfish, out

* A tonic, fortified with alcohol.

for what they could get; affection, generosity of spirit, hardly entered into it—though strangely enough, as often with powerful autocratic figures, she never lacked people devoted to her in a completely disinterested way. By now her voice was slurred and came heavily and slowly; she could not walk, though as a curious development of her obsession with money, she instructed Rita in September 1974 to give her £10 to walk again—she would hire extra staff to help her. But she forgot about this in October, went back to Wincarnis, and felt more settled.

She was happier in Pitt Street than at any other nursing home she had been in. She had a quiet room near the top of the house, where the tranquil if bare atmosphere made her feel at home. But her mood varied enormously. In September 1974 she decided to give up her "little", as she called it, competition, blaming inflation, however, not her own carelessness about money. Even so, the prize was awarded for that year.* In line with her desire to be rid of all her money by the end of 1974 she requested Perman to purchase a further annuity from Hill Samuel, to cease with her death.

The next year, 1975, was altogether more calm. Maggie was safely caught on a last peaceful shelf before death, and was not going to fall off or even go too near the edge. The last flickering of her will power, the desire to give away money, had now died down, though she still succeeded in giving plenty away: £5 notes, given her in an envelope, were disappearing at the rate of six a month in early 1976 on the rapidly changing staff. Her consumption of Wincarnis rose, to more than four bottles a week, and Rita had to ask her to go steady.

In August 1975 Maggie heard that EMI were going to publish their four-record set the next year.† Bryan Crimp, who compiled the set with loving devotion, visited her several times and told her of progress. This was a great stimulus and she talked with more connectedness of thought than she had to anyone for some time.

* In 1975 the money from the prize fund was returned to her. Appropriately, it consisted entirely of shares in the Distillers' Company. The London Mozart Players had charged £50 a year for administering the fund, and indeed, the costs of handing out money to striving artists were far in excess of the annual prize: in the competition for 1974, £184 was spent to give away prizes worth £100. Even the Royal College of Music, under whose auspices the prize was given, charged £17.64 for the hire of a room. After her death a successful appeal was made to relaunch the prize, and it was awarded in 1978 and 1979.

† The set appeared posthumously, in 1976.

About this time I made a visit to her. "Who are you?" she asked after a very long lack of recognition. Long pauses, too, between words. She was very bent now, half curled on her side in a foetal position, sucking and clawing the air, appalling to look at. I was with my brother John who had often visited her. Her head moved from one of us to the other and back. We were of similar build. "John?" she asked. I gave my name. She repeated it. She looked quizzical. She said it again. It meant nothing to her. Long pause. We tried to make conversation. We said it was a nice room. About my own activities: I was going to Edinburgh. I was having a play performed. About John's painting: he was publishing some prints. Then there was another long pause. Then she repeated my name. Following this she remarked suddenly and oddly, "Are you still as conceited as you used to be?" I jumped. A *coup de tonnerre* of vintage Teyte. She always liked to catch you out. John grinned. I smiled although I was irritated. "I have never been thought of as conceited." You had to stand up for yourself. She respected that.

She retracted a little; perhaps on reflection she had overstepped the mark. Perhaps she had been trying to find in me something of herself. She then said, retreating painfully and slowly, "My older sister always called me stuck-up . . . S T U C K - U P" she repeated, the words agonizingly slow, like a tape-recorder at half speed. "Do they still have that expression nowadays?" Yes, we do, I said. Conversation stumbled on a little but it was hard going. It was only too easy to sense her feeling of embarrassment at her old age, and embarrassment for us. It was the spur for our swift banishment in the next few moments. She said to Estelle Johnstone at this time, the words coming with the same infinite and painful difficulty, "I . . . am . . . having . . . to . . . learn . . . patience. . . ." While this, above all else, was for Maggie Teyte not easy to learn, it was astonishing that in all these trials she should still seek knowledge and a moral self-advancement she had been all too reluctant to value.

Then the pressure of higher charges began to mount dangerously. In December 1975 the Pitt Street nursing home put the price of her room up to £70 a week, to which nursing fees averaging £40 a week had to be added. Rita and Perman were aghast. It was quite possible Maggie might go on living for another ten years. There was nothing wrong with her heart; apart from a general physical decline caused by withdrawal her body functioned normally. The crisis was met by moving her to a higher and cheaper room, but still the devil inflation blasted away on his apocalyptic trumpet. In May 1976 Perman wrote Rita that the balance on Maggie's deposit account was down to a few pounds. Her yearly income remained high and constant, a total of £4,234, £2,713 from the Cottingham estate, still under the terms of the covenant dated November 1933, and £1,056 from the annuity into which she had put the capital from the sale of her flat. Even so, approaching death, listening to the radio, doing nothing except sometimes asking Rita to jot down a thought,⁵ she had outgrown her means.* As the next annuity payment was not due till August, they would have, Perman wrote to Rita, to think about applying to the Musicians' Benevolent Society: "It is obvious that in a few months' time we shall have to seek financial aid for Maggie and the question is whether we should do it now or whether we should leave it until the last possible moment." But Teyte, who before the First World War had frequently earned more than $3,000 a week, and $3,000 a broadcast after the Second, with some acute inner ear must have heard the distant approach of penury. Her condition, as if by magic, began to worsen. She became deaf, then blind.

On or about 25 May, in her eighty-ninth year, she lapsed into a coma. Two nights later, around ten o'clock, Rita had a strong premonition and called in at the Pitt Street home unsummoned. Maggie died peacefully in her arms. This was Rita's reward for looking after her all these years. A peaceful death. The immediate cause, as certified, was a cerebral haemorrhage and atherosclerosis.

The transformation of Maggie Teyte's appearance in death was remarkable. Her strong jaw was restored as if by magic. Her hair was dazzlingly white and fine. She carried again in death the characteristically truculent expression she had worn when alive, but which she had not shown these last years. The face had a slightly mauve tint, the mouth pushed forward, the skin round it dead, puckered. The nostrils were slightly off square. The body perfectly reposed. It bore great dignity.

At the nursing home my brother wore a tie, something he rarely does, and muttered Latin over her. He was the deeply religious member of the family. "I have not lived like a Catholic," she had said, "but I hope I shall

---

* The last shares she held were in Rolls-Royce. When the notice of a general meeting of shareholders in December 1976 arrived, the company was in voluntary liquidation, and she was dead.

die like one." She did. John saw to that. I found myself thinking more of martyrdom to art. Of Mélisande. Of the tresses of golden hair; of the crown in the water, and her leaning forward to pluck the lily stem. Of the ring that was lost. Of love. And of mystery.

That afternoon the *Evening Standard* had telephoned Rita and asked if it was true Teyte had died in poverty. Rita was fiercely indignant at the question: Maggie had been spending at least £150 a week. Cavan's comment, untransmitted to the press, was typical of his cynicism mingled with deep regard: "Her money", he observed, "was about to run out!"

So the body left the nursing home with its friendly Irish ladies. The air smelled fresh with the May blossom, for her that was all over. It was the first time in his life John had viewed a corpse and he could not sleep all night. Maggie's last appearance retained for him the troubling quality of a vision.

Teyte's more morbid demands for her eyes and kidneys to be donated were not respected. Her wish to be cremated was. Low mass was sung at the Carmelite Church in Kensington High Street on Tuesday, 1 June 1976 at 10.30. It was a fine fresh morning. The priest, a Father Joseph from the west coast of Ireland and like Maggie one of a large family, gave a moving and impressive sermon. He extolled Teyte for the way she used her God-given voice, and she would no doubt have agreed that it was from God that it came. It was a full communion mass, joyful and celebrative. While the tall candles burned, Father Joseph, with a cheerful smile on his face, sprinkled the wax-polished oak coffin—lined inside with domett, silk and flannel sheets, of which Maggie would certainly not have approved, for in her imagination it was to be whisked away before the fire by thievish undertakers, and plain boxwood substituted—with holy water and incense. On her express wishes no one had "put on special clothes" and the congregation smiled and chatted amicably with one another at this last but one gathering of her extended family. The priest, the organist, and the undertaker's men then repaired to the cremation parlour with Rita, her husband, and her sons. Only the immediate family—"if they wish"—Teyte had stipulated, should come to the interment. The ashes were buried and a rose tree planted over them.

Afterwards the family went for a drink in a pub. They were not so much celebrating her death as toasting her immortality and their own relief that a difficult phase in their lives had passed. They raised their glasses to her. There was no doubt she would have approved, and would even have had a rich and thoroughly distinctive chuckle at the thought. "Good!!!" she would have said, lengthening the vowels: "g o o d ! ! !" And then more sharply, in that crisp and decisive way, "What a good idea!!!"

The memorial service, held five months later at St James's Church, Spanish Place, was a more solemn act of homage. The requiem priest was a somewhat dry and crusty celebrant, though Felix Aprahamian spoke a warm and thoughtfully exact valedictory. At the end of the service they played Teyte's recording of Berlioz's "Absence". On hearing the unearthly purity of the first few phrases, many of those present felt a weak and overpowering desire to cry. The sudden mellowness breathed into the last refrain—

> La fleur de ma vie est fermée
> Loin de ton sourire vermeil

—conveyed such vulnerability, so very unexpected and so human, it pierced an otherwise sombre occasion.

NOTES ON SOURCES

APPENDICES

DISCOGRAPHY

INDEX

Notes on Sources

MT = Maggie Teyte

The following sources, cited frequently, are referred to by title only: Maggie Teyte, *Star on the Door* (1958); Olga Lynn, *Oggie* (1955); Mary Garden and Louis Biancolli, *Mary Garden's Story* (1952). Material from interviews taped by Peter Wadland (1969–72) and by Madeau Stewart (BBC, 7 March 1968) is cited by the interviewer's name only.

Chapter 1   *Good God, Why Wolverhampton?*

[1] Peter Wadland tapes.
[2] Annette Hullah, *Theodor Leschetizky* (1906), pp. 72–3.
[3] *Wolverhampton Antiquary*, vol. I (1933), no. 9.
[4] Conversation with author, 1973.

Chapter 2   *The Church of Corpus Christi*

[1] *Star on the Door*, p. 15.
[2] Harold Nicolson, *Some People* (1927), p. 82.
[3] E. F. Benson, *As We Were: a Victorian Peepshow* (1930), p. 186.
[4] ibid., pp. 185–6.

Chapter 3   *Last Rays of Opera's Golden Age*

[1] *Oggie*, pp. 12–18.
[2] Talk with Madeau Stewart.
[3] Quoted in MT's publicity booklet, "Third American Season 1913–1914, Prima Donna Soprano of the Philadelphia–Chicago Opera Company". Incidentally, Teyte is not mentioned in the standard biography of de Reszke by Clara Leiser (1933).
[4] Quoted by Clara Leiser in *Jean de Reszke*, p. 32.
[5] Lord Wittenham, letter to *The Times*, 6 April 1925.
[6] MT on tape in Rita O'Connor's possession.
[7] Notes, unused, for a broadcast (lent by Catherine Salkeld).
[8] Conversation with Cavan O'Connor, who once sang with Melba; they discussed de Reszke.
[9] *Oggie*, p. 37.

[10] *M.A.P.*, 4 Dec. 1909.

[11] Artur Rubinstein, *My Young Years* (1973), p. 156.

[12] Unused notes for broadcast.

[13] *Star on the Door*, p. 20.

[14] Talk with Madeau Stewart.

[15] Lilli Lehmann, *How to Sing* (1902), p. 239.

[16] W. Johnstone Douglas, "Jean de Reszke's Principles of Singing", *Music and Letters*, July 1925.

[17] Talk with Madeau Stewart.

[18] *Oggie*, p. 26.

[19] ibid., p. 27.

[20] Recalled with Madeau Stewart. The date of the performance, according to Clara Leiser, op. cit., was May 1907.

[21] *Oggie*, p. 24.

[22] ibid., p. 23.

Chapter 4   *A Setting of Limits*

[1] Talk MT gave, with Felix Aprahamian and Grenville Eves, Holborn Central Library, 1968. Talk with Madeau Stewart.

[2] Talk with Madeau Stewart.

[3] W. Johnstone Douglas, "Jean de Reszke's Principles of Singing", op. cit., p. 23.

[4] Article by "W.", *Music and Letters*, July 1925, p. 210.

[5] *Oggie*, p. 24.

[6] *Star on the Door*, pp. 29–30.

[7] B. Gavoty, *Reynaldo Hahn* (Paris, 1976), p. 27. The lines were Stéphane Mallarmé's.

[8] ibid., p. 121.

[9] *Oggie*, p. 48.

[10] Quoted in B. Gavoty, op. cit., p. 93.

[11] Talk with Madeau Stewart.

[12] B. Gavoty, op. cit., p. 90.

[13] ibid., p. 122.

[14] Interview with Alec Robertson, BBC, 29 Oct. 1959.

[15] The relevant pages of this diary later came into MT's possession.

[16] L. Schneider, *Offenbach* (Paris, 1923), p. 135n.

[17] T. G. Walsh, *Monte Carlo Opera* (1975), pp. 211–12, 214, 217.

[18] B. Gavoty, op. cit., p. 58.

[19] *Le Théâtre*, May 1907.

[20] *Mary Garden's Story*, p. 95.

[21] Published by Editura de Stat. Pentru Literature si Arta (Bucarest, 1956).

22 Peter Wadland tapes.
23 Georges Enesco, *Souvenirs*, ed. B. Gavoty (Paris, 1955), p. 71.
24 Peter Wadland tapes.
25 Lily McCormack, *I Hear You Calling Me* (1949), p. 48.

Chapter 5   *Partners in* Pelléas

1 Ford Madox Ford, *Mirror to France* (1926), Introduction.
2 Alfred Cobban, *A History of Modern France* (1965), vol. I, p. 71.
3 Recalled by MT, Peter Wadland tapes.
4 *Star on the Door*, p. 185.
5 Patrick Mahony, *Magic of Maeterlinck* (1951), p. 62.
6 Georgette Leblanc, *My Life with Maeterlinck* (1932), p. 111.
7 Edwin Evans excellently summarized Debussy's dislike in the *Radio Times*, 26 Oct. 1928.
8 ibid.
9 MT, talking to Frank Granville Barker, *Music and Musicians*, August 1962.
10 Georgette Leblanc, op. cit., p. 110.
11 Peter Wadland tapes.
12 Edward Lockspeiser, *Debussy: His Life and Mind* (1962), vol. II, p. 188.
13 *Mary Garden's Story*, p. 70.
14 ibid., p. 57.
15 Patrick J. Smith, *The Tenth Muse* (1971), p. 121.

Chapter 6   *Stars in Opposition*

1 *Mary Garden's Story*, p. 57.
2 William Boosey, *Fifty Years of Music* (1931), p. 42.
3 Peter Wadland tapes.
4 BBC talk, 13 Sept. 1948.
5 Claude Debussy, letter from St Petersburg, 28 Nov. 1913.
6 Richard Fletcher, letter to Desmond Shawe-Taylor, 1976, and Maurice Emmanuel, *Pelléas et Mélisande* (Paris, 1926), pp. 64–73.
7 Compiled from broadcasts, MT's talk with Madeau Stewart, taped sources (Peter Wadland), conversations with author.
8 Conversation with author.
9 Claude Debussy, letter to Jacques Durand, 18 May 1909.
10 François Lesure, "Claude Debussy after his Centenary", *Musical Quarterly*, July 1963, p. 283.

Chapter 7   *English, and a Tiny Thing*

1 MT recalled these incidents more than sixty-five years later (Peter Wadland tapes).
2 Francis Haskell, *Patrons and Painters* (1963), p. 180.

3 Edward Moore, *Forty Years of Opera in Chicago* (1930), p. 139.

4 *Oggie*, p. 50.

5 Holborn Central Library talk, 1968.

6 Victor Gollancz, *Journey Towards Music* (1964), p. 120.

7 Nigel Nicolson, *Portrait of a Marriage* (1973), p. 49.

8 Conversation of the late Benedict Nicolson with author, and letter from Nigel Nicolson to author, 1977.

9 Quaintance Eaton, *The Boston Opera Company* (1965), p. 249.

10 Quoted in ibid., p. 249.

11 Ronald Davis, *Opera in Chicago* (1966), p. 87.

12 *San Francisco Chronicle*, 15 March 1915.

13 Henry Lahee, *The Grand Opera Singers of Today* (1922), p. 432.

14 Ronald Davis, op. cit., p. 97.

15 Edward Moore, op. cit., p. 90.

16 ibid., p. 92.

17 *Variety*, 1 May 1912.

18 *American Record Guide*, November 1945.

19 Edward Moore, op. cit., p. 109.

20 See "Loose Leaves", Appendix A.

21 Peter Wadland tapes.

22 Edward Moore, op. cit., p. 116.

23 *The Boston Opera Company*, p. 249.

24 *Star on the Door*, p. 122.

25 Quaintance Eaton, op. cit., p. 273.

26 For a lovingly detailed account of the effect of this performance on someone hitherto unfamiliar with Debussy's opera, see Victor Gollancz, op. cit., pp. 121–4.

27 Harold Rosenthal, *Two Centuries of Opera at Covent Garden* (1958), p. 387.

28 *Daily Mail*, 10 May 1914.

29 Mary Fitch Cushing (Watkins), *The Rainbow Bridge* (1954), p. 34.

30 Extrait des Minutes du Secrétariat-Greffe du Tribunal de Grande Instance de Paris, 10 Nov. 1915.

31 *Star on the Door*, p. 124.

32 *Daily Telegraph*, 18 Feb. 1916.

33 Letter to the author, 1977.

34 Interview with Walter Anthony in *San Francisco Chronicle*, 21 Oct. 1917.

35 Richard Aldrich, *Concert Life in New York, 1902–23* (1941), pp. 340–1.

Chapter 8   *The Nightingale of Maidenhead Thicket*

1 Conversation with Bryan Crimp, tape, 1975.

2 Henry E. Bannard, *The History of Littlewick* (n.d.), p. 12.

3 Desert Island Discs, BBC, 15 April 1968.
4 Claude Debussy, *Monsieur Croche, the Dilettante Hater*, trans. B. N. Langdon Davies (1928), p. 167.
5 *The Times*, 21 April 1919.
6 The song "Philomel" was recorded, and issued in the EMI boxed set, 1976. See Discography.
7 D. Jeffrey Farnol, *Portrait of a Gentleman in Colours* (1935).
8 Quoted in *The Chameleon* (magazine of the Sherwin-Williams Paint Company, Cleveland, Ohio), May 1930.
9 Rita Odoli-Tate heard these rumours as a girl, and they were confirmed—as rumours—in conversation with Mrs R. Wheeler, the wife of Sherwin Cottingham's chauffeur.
10 *Southern Electricity Board House Magazine*, April 1977, p. 19.
11 ibid., p. 24.
12 MT told Estelle Johnstone this.
13 Louis MacNeice, *Astrology* (1964), p. 196.
14 *Star on the Door*, p. 129.
15 William Boosey, op. cit., p. 40.
16 A letter dated 9 Jan. 1973 to MT from Kenneth Allen, a son of one of Sherwin Cottingham's sisters, speaks of a Cottingham relation having been institutionalized in Florida.
17 William Boosey, op. cit., p. 170.
18 *Liverpool Echo*, 12 March 1921.
19 *The Pall Mall and Globe*, 12 March 1921.
20 ibid.
21 *Liverpool Echo*, 15 March 1921.
22 *Daily Graphic*, 14 March 1921.
23 MT told this some years later to Ivor Newton, who in 1977 recalled it in conversation with the author.
24 C. N. Elvin, *Mottoes Revised* (1971), p. 117.
25 *Daily Telegraph*, 28 June 1975.
26 Ivor Newton, *At the Piano* (1966), p. 215, and conversation with the author, 1977.
27 *Star on the Door*, p. 130.
28 Mr S. F. Smith, in conversation with the author, 1977.
29 *Star on the Door*, p. 130.
30 *Evening Standard*, 6 May 1931.
31 MT gave the telegram to Gay Vernon, who related the gist of it to Richard Bebb.
32 Extrait des Minutes des Actes de Naissance, XVIème Arrondissement, Paris, 5 Oct. 1977.

33 Mrs Howlett's account.

34 Peter Wadland tapes.

35 Noted in conversation (1977) between the author and Mrs Howlett, who was eighty-one. The way Mrs Howlett's account of the Cottinghams, remembered over forty years, fell into place with other servants' memories— these various people not knowing of each other's continuing existence—and with what he knew from other sources, the author found quite uncanny. Indeed one of his interlocutors did claim that MT was talking to her "from the beyond".

Chapter 9   *Breaking the Ice with Red-hot Irons*

1 Harold Rosenthal, op. cit., p. 413.

2 Henry Wood, *My Life in Music* (1938), p. 337.

3 *Daily Express*, 2 April 1930.

4 Andrew Porter, *High Fidelity*, May 1977.

5 *Star on the Door*, p. 111.

6 *New English Weekly*, 8 July 1937.

7 Letter from René Lambert to Angus Morrison, 29 Dec. 1938.

8 Interview with Derek Parker, BBC, 7 Jan. 1967.

9 Berta Geissmar, *The Baton and the Jackboot* (1945), p. 236.

10 John O'Connor to the author.

11 Berta Geissmar, op. cit., p. 297.

12 *Star on the Door*, p. 124.

13 BBC interview, 1959, in answer to John Bowen.

14 *Star on the Door*, p. 168.

15 Walter Legge, letter to the author, 1977.

16 Berta Geissmar, op. cit., p. 91.

Chapter 10   *Cows and Concert Artists*

1 Boyd Neel, letter to the author, 1977.

2 *Star on the Door*, p. 163. Grace Vernon wrote this chapter.

3 Quoted in *American Record Guide*, November 1945.

4 Thomas Russell, *Philharmonic Decade* (1945), p. 97.

5 Felix Aprahamian, "Maggie Teyte and French Music", published in booklet to the LP recording COLH 138, December 1964.

6 Thomas Russell, op. cit., p. 92.

7 Berta Geissmar, op. cit., p. 391.

8 Felix Aprahamian, op. cit.

9 ibid.

[10] Another but mistaken report in the *Daily Telegraph* spoke of the award being given in the Pinafore Room at the Savoy Hotel, and the host as M. Cassin.

[11] Peter Wadland tapes.

[12] *American Record Guide*, op. cit.

[13] Philip Hope-Wallace, writing in the *Guardian*, 17 April 1968.

Chapter 11   *Park Avenue to Mélisande's Tower*

[1] *Star on the Door*, p. 183.

[2] Quoted in *Current Biography* (1945), p. 603.

[3] *American Record Guide*, November 1945.

[4] Estelle Johnstone, a New York pupil of MT now living in London, recounted this.

[5] Theodore Uppman, letter to the author, 1978.

[6] Undated letter from the Waldorf-Astoria.

[7] Theodore Uppman, letter to the author, 1978.

[8] Conversation with Madeau Stewart.

[9] *New York Times*, 28 May 1976.

[10] ibid., 27 March 1948.

[11] BBC memo of 5 Dec. 1947.

[12] Interview in the *Wolverhampton Chronicle*, 19 Aug. 1949.

[13] Letter of 17 June 1949.

[14] Letter of 11 Feb. 1949.

[15] *Oggie*, p. 145.

[16] Letter of 17 June 1949.

[17] *Newsweek*, 15 Aug. 1949.

[18] So said *Time*, 15 Aug. 1949.

Chapter 12   *Girls Eternal*

[1] Peter Wadland tapes.

[2] Josephine O'Donnell, *Among the Covent Garden Stars* (1936), pp. 204-5.

[3] *Star on the Door*, p. 175.

[4] Claude Debussy, *Monsieur Croche*, p. 7.

Chapter 13   *Last Performances and Immortal Longings*

[1] *Saturday Review*, 8 May 1954.

[2] *The New Yorker*, 1 May 1954.

[3] Louis Biancolli, *The Flagstad Manuscript* (1952), p. 183.

[4] Barbara Fischer-Williams, "Ginger Beer with Mélisande", *Opera News*, 21 March 1970.

5 Said to Martha Deatherage, of Austin, Texas.

6 *New Statesman*, 23 April 1955.

7 *Daily Mail*, 12 June 1958.

8 *Sunday Times*, 21 June 1958.

9 Interview with Madeau Stewart.

10 So the boy's mother, Lady Bramall, informed the author in 1977.

11 Peter Wadland tapes.

12 Mary Fitch Cushing (Watkins), op. cit., p. 172.

13 Letter to Thelma Halverson, 4 March 1964.

14 Quaintance Eaton, op. cit., p. 249.

15 "Hi Jinx" programme, broadcast 31 Aug. 1949.

Chapter 14 *Technique in the Top Register*

1 Tape, 1975, in Rita O'Connor's possession.

2 Richard Bebb, booklet for EMI recording "L'Exquise Maggie Teyte".

3 Quoted in *American Record Guide*, November 1945.

4 *Star on the Door*, p. 59.

5 *American Record Guide*, op. cit.

6 ibid.

7 Interview with John Amis, BBC, 27 Sept. 1966.

8 *Star on the Door*, p. 55.

9 *Saturday Review*, 27 Feb. 1965.

10 From EMI archives.

11 Peter Wadland tapes.

Chapter 15 *An Expensive Way to Die*

1 Letter to Thelma Halverson, 8 Jan. 1962.

2 Tape, with Nina Walker, piano, in possession of Rita O'Connor.

3 Peter Wadland tapes.

4 *Star on the Door*, p. 187.

5 See Appendix A.

A Collection of Loose Leaves with Hints for Vocal Students

by

MAGGIE TEYTE*

And I thank my niece Rita O'Connor for her valuable assistance.

MAGGIE TEYTE

SUCCESS IN MUSIC AND HOW IT IS WON.
H. T. FINCK

The essence of art lies deep beneath the surface, and the notes on a manuscript piece of paper do not tell you what lies between or behind them.

The pupils must study well the poem, if they wish to be successful in their repertoire.

It is because they do not reach the roots of their art, that so many musicians fail, and after a brief season of bloom, or none at all, they disappear for ever.

TRADITION

In this year of 1970, the word tradition is like a red rag to a bull.

Musical traditions are a technical way of interpreting compositions that have stood the test of time.

If we can trace tradition back thru time, and find that it still stands up, and teaches us to do better, then we accept it.

What is musical Tradition? It can only be obtained by how it is handed down, so that the good had been separated from the bad.

* Jotted down by MT, with Rita O'Connor's assistance, between 1970 and 1973, on separate sheets of paper. MT's spelling and punctuation have been retained.

Many people will regret losing the bad, as it denotes for them an emotional outlet.

There are academic teachers of tradition, who will not exercise imagination of any kind, and the vandals who imagine they are doing Mozart a service by stripping him of all his charming ornaments and embellishments.

Does a composer when writing his composition instil into it the traditional interpretation?

Tradition can be a great friend in the hour of need, as when one is feverish and has the beginning of a cold and must appear before the public. I used to call upon the teachings of de Reszke to help me thru the evening . . . such as no portamentos where they should not be, also clean attack.

I advise you all to sing Mozart, for only in singing the works of Mozart, you learn his tradition. It won't come at once.

In repetition—Mozart forces his own will upon the student, and after a certain amount of study, you begin to realise he is a whole education in himself.

Beginners sometimes make the mistake of practising long hours, thinking it will help them in the development of their vocal power. This should come with the daily repetition of exercises and scales which should not exceed one hour.

SCALES

No method of singing is complete without a thorough study of scales, not just as exercises, they should also be learnt to interpret the text of the aria in which they are written.

Scales should be studied for laughter, tenderness, and sadness.

Scales with de Reszke never varied, only the tessitura was changed by a tone or two, as the case maybe for sopranos, mezzos and contraltos.

The scale exercises as they were done by him seemed to cure all faults, and restored tired and frayed chords to their former glory, as the exercises consisted of eighteen scales starting on middle C with two variations going up in semitones to F.

I was present at Covent Garden when Tettrazini made her début in "La Traviata". Her success was overwhelming. Melba was also present at this performance.

A few days later Melba was at a cocktail party, where praise was loud for Tettrazini's brilliant performance.

Melba was heard to say, "Yes, wonderful technique, but ask her to sing me a slow scale".

But, only singers and wind instrument players will know what this entails!

Have any of you sung, "Have you seen but a whyte Lily grow" with the measured scale on the word "grow"? It has to be executed with the precision of a mechanical instrument, combined with grace and charm.

There is another scale that comes to my mind, this time for accompanists. It is in the opening bars of "La Flûte de Pan" (Debussy).

In the Artists' room before a recital many accompanists tried out different speeds of this scale, even Cortot was not satisfied with himself.

Pay attention to your scales, as once they are mastered, they become a joy to sing, and who knows? You may be as successful as the famous coloratura soprano Adelina Patti, who left over three million dollars in America alone.

VOCAL RANGE

Don't be misled by your vocal range. Singers are born with more notes than the repertoire calls for. If you can sing a low G it doesn't mean you are a contralto . . . or a top E, a coloratura.

Somewhere along the line, confusion has been caused by sopranos and mezzos who overlap in their music repertoire.

In these days we are not allowed to encroach into other singers' territory.

Right up to the beginning of this century, sopranos more than any other singers were taught to use the full range of their vocal chords, and the two artists that come to mind, and that I actually heard were Lilli Lehmann, and Emma

Calvé. Lehmann became the great dramatic soprano, started her career by singing the Queen of the Night, and ended it with the Wagnerian repertoire.*

Emma Calvé also sang the lyric repertoire of sopranos and ended with "Carmen", which we consider in this year of 1970 to belong to mezzos and contraltos, but, if this tendency continues, the teachers of tomorrow will have their work cut out to know what operas their pupils should learn!†

TRANSLATIONS

Sometimes we are forced to sing songs with translations of the poem, which means a little extra work for the student. To me translations are like a glass door, between artist, composer, and poet.

Translation is also like looking thru a shop window at a beautiful dress model, the allover aspect is beautiful, but one cannot see any detail, and it has to be studied very carefully for timing and the rhythm between composer and poet so that you can transfer the interpretation without disturbing the melodic line.

If you do come up against bad translation then ask yourself one question? Are you a singer or an actress? If a singer then you must put aside your acting ability to do justice to the composer and his composition.

MODERN MUSIC

I think singers make a mistake in learning a modern piece of music as tho it belonged to a new cult.

They are trying to create a new register that doesn't exist.

The modernity lies in the form of the composition, not in your vocal chords.

I was very anxious to sing "Pierrot Lunaire", by Schoenberg, but when I read the directions I did not understand them, and the following is a quotation, taken from the fly-leaf of "Pierrot Lunaire".

* Not strictly true. Lehmann's great days as a Wagnerian singer were in the middle of her career but she was still singing *Traviata* in her sixties and giving *Lieder* recitals in her seventies.

† "There is no doubt Calvé sang *Carmen* in the soprano key through all the early years of her career: for instance for her first attempt at recording, in 1902, the Seguidilla she chose the upward transposition—but having fluffed the top note and exclaimed 'Oh mon dieu!' she immediately remade the aria in score pitch." (Richard Bebb to author, 1978.)

"The difference between the usual way of speaking and one which assists a musical form has to be made clear, but it ought never to remind us of singing!"

I met Fritz Kreisler, who also disliked the modern idiom, for this is what he said. "Arnold Schoenberg and I were close friends when we were young men in Berlin. When he was a young composer he wrote beautiful music. I remember when he showed me the manuscript of 'Verklärte Nacht' . . .

"A little later he wrote the 'Gurrelieder'. It reminded me of 'Parsifal'. It is a fine work.

"Then he started to do different things, and I must say I could not understand what he was driving at . . . or why.

"We saw little of each other for some years, and then one day I noticed there was an entire program of his latest music.

"I went to hear it. In that whole program there was only one song that meant anything to me. After the concert I met Arnold, and told him what I thought. I told him there was one song that I liked.

"He could be sharp-tongued too. He said, 'Have I fallen so low in my art, that Fritz Kreisler likes any part of it.' "

There was also Ernest Newman who wrote the following, "My own desire from the beginning has been to hear the music without having to submit to the annoyance of having to listen to something that is neither song or speech."

I as a singer cannot bring myself to admire the new modern idiom, altho I have sung Debussy all my life.

Having been brought up on the classics I find the modern idiom has no form, and no melodic line, therefore I experience no pleasure in listening to it.

So to make a success of this modern singing you must bring forth all your vocal knowledge of *Bel Canto*, of its classical repertoire, and technical application.

SLOGANS

Students can teach themselves a great deal by knowing the dividing line between quality and quantity.

Good conductors put musicians on their feet, but bad ones give them feet of clay.

Don't let success turn into conceit.

Bad artists use "Sexy" behaviour to hide the gaps in their artistic temperament.

The standard of singing in any country, rises and falls with their teachers.

Voices of exceptional quality can be found in every country, like the diamond which needs men of experience for cutting and polishing, the students of singing also need expert teachers to give them the necessary finish.

Singing in public. An artist should start a recital, with a classical song which shows the quality, and musicianship, and straightforward singing, such as "Caro mio ben", by Giordano.

When you have established this, then you can use your musical temperament to your heart's content, and as the poet's tales unfold, your public will judge your powers of interpretation.

VIGNETTE

Lucien Fugère, the leading baritone of the Opéra Comique was appearing as Falstaff in a very old provincial theatre, where the stage was practically enclosed except for one or two narrow fire doors, giving access to the stage. Fugère, hearing his musical cue, prepared for his entrance on to the stage, but alas the fire door was not quite big enough, stage hands came to the rescue . . . they pulled and they pushed, but they couldn't get him thru. All this time half of the top gallery who were in full view were adding their advice in no uncertain manner, but it was no use, he had to undress outside, get rid of his Falstaff framework, come thru the door in his under-pants and dress on the stage.

SLOGANS

Never make a friend in the Opera House, until you have made your name.

Singing is a natural function, but natural singing does not always earn us a living. We have to study to preserve and strengthen the natural beauty of the voice against the strain of a professional career.

The demand for first class Opera singers in particular, is very much greater than the supply.

Fritz Busch.

To achieve the technique of a difficult *aria* learn one that is more difficult.

BLENDING THE WORDS WITH VOCAL PRODUCTION

You must learn to irradiate the word from within. This makes the artist's singing so subtle, and yet so communicative. Recitative also is the foundation of all good diction, and good diction the foundation of good interpretation. Pupils who wish to be supreme in this branch of vocal art, should study two schools.

Recitatives of Mozart and Gluck.

The former has been based mainly on Italian comedy, and is "thrown away", as it is called in the theatre, but not those of Gluck, which are based on Greek plays and dramas, which demand the full knowledge of vocal technique with diaphragm support. Legato singing is also obtained by blending the words with vocal production on a steady flow of air and should never be interrupted by stressing any part of the poem or melodic line.

VACCAJ

Jean de Reszke always insisted that all his regular pupils should learn Vaccaj by heart. I know of no other exercises which perform the exact blending of words with the voice, the singing of the words being very difficult.

Vaccaj is written to Italian words and he well knew that this is the best language for beginners.

When I was feverish and starting a cold, and had to sing in public, I used to call upon the teachings of de Reszke to help me thru the strenuous programme. I remember a recital in Boston (Mass.), when I did have a cold, I didn't know how I was going to get thru the evening. I went back to the straight and narrow path, to the technique of my student days, and was so very surprised when George Reeves who was my accompanist said to me after leaving the platform, "I never heard you sing better".

De Reszke taught me the French language in his little theatre as it should be sung, because every language has a weakness in it, which your professor of singing should know how to correct. Every language came into this category. and all arias were sung in their original language. But de Reszke taught me French in such a way that I never had any difficulties to overcome. There's no doubt that he loved languages, and this is why . . . around 1895 Mr Camille Bellaigue, the veteran critic of the "Revue des deux Mondes" wrote the following.

That the French language had never been pronounced and accented with such accuracy and force, or if it need be with such charm & tenderness, as in the mouth of this foreigner Jean de Reszke.

VIGNETTE

In a famous European opera house, that possessed the usual narrow passages, from one side to another under the stage, two leading sopranos met, and they both waited for the other to give way, till one of them said, "Let me pass, don't you know who I am? I am the wife of the director, Madame T." Whereupon the other replied, "O, don't be funny, I was Madame T long before you."

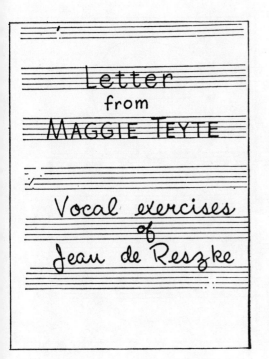

These vocal exercises, all from Jean de Reszke's teaching and written out originally in MT's own hand, were sent to Grace Vernon for her pupils.

These should be
practised daily.

Very legato, steady, no chest

From D♯ we begin to open
more & more. "oar" is the
transitional sound between "u" &
"Ah" so a high soprano
singing the following exercise
will start on "Ah"

The markings on the next exercise for
scales must be applied correctly - the C
in chest, then pass into head, where it
remains for the rest of the scale, in spite
of the diaphragm work for the crescendo.
Some singers have a habit when using
the diaphragm of pulling the sound
downwards that results in bad
tone - Basses & Contraltos have
this weakness -
We stress the second note of the scale
to give a "kick-off" so to speak -

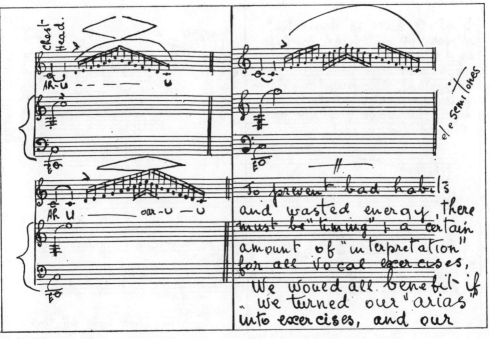

To prevent bad habits
and wasted energy, there
must be "timing" + a certain
amount of "interpretation"
for all vocal exercises,
We would all benefit if
we turned our "arias"
into exercises, and our

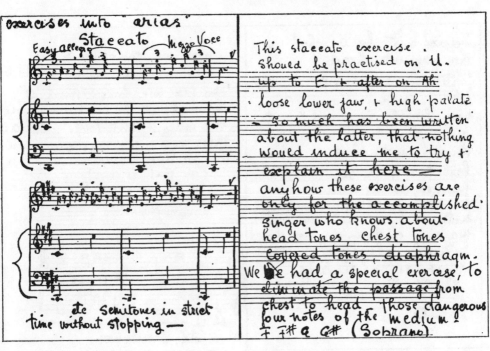

exercises into "arias"

etc. semitones in strict
time without stopping —

This staccato exercise
Should be practised on U.
up to E + after on Ah
loose lower jaw, + high palate
— So much has been written
about the latter, that nothing
would induce me to try +
explain it here —
anyhow these exercises are
only for the accomplished
singer who knows about
head tones, chest tones
covered tones, diaphragm.
We've had a special exercise, to
eliminate the passage from
chest to head those dangerous
four notes of the medium!
+ F# a G# (Soprano)

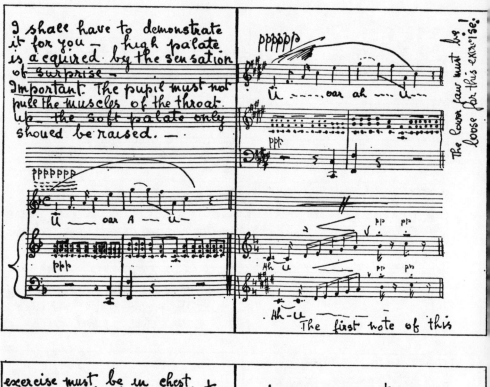

I shall have to demonstrate it for you — high palate is acquired by the sensation of surprise —

Important: The pupil must not pull the muscles of the throat up — the soft palate only should be raised. —

The lower jaw must be loose for this exercise!

The first note of this

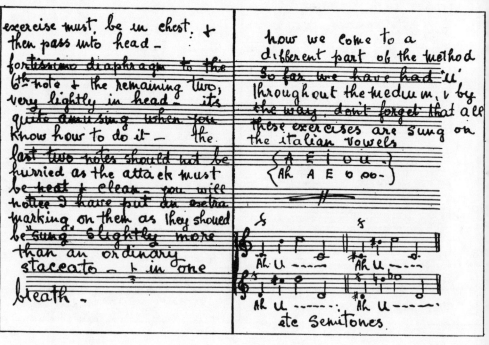

exercise must be in chest + then pass into head —

fortissimo diaphragm to the 6th note + the remaining two, very lightly in head — its quite amusing when you know how to do it — the last two notes should not be hurried as the attack must be neat + clean. you will notice I have put an extra marking on them as they should be "sung" slightly more than an ordinary staccato — + in one breath —

now we come to a different part of the method. So far we have had "u" throughout the medium, + by the way, don't forget that all these exercises are sung on the italian vowels

(A E i o u)

(Ah A E o oo—)

etc Semitones

This is what some singers call a covered tone but still. Jean made us open our mouths on F♭ upwards. The high soprano, + "soprano lyrique must watch out after G. as diaphragm plays the principal part in this exercise, which makes it dramatic —

The following example is a little easier —

Please take notice of stress marks — the grace notes are marked ƒƒ which means diaphragm work but the Bppp must be a head tone —
The same thing applies to the following —

Watch out after F.

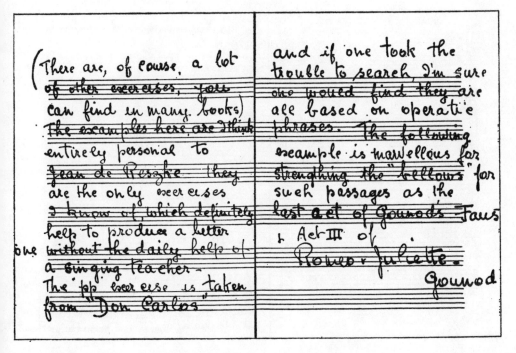

(There are, of course, a lot of other exercises, you can find in many books) The examples here are I think entirely personal to Jean de Reszke they are the only exercises I know of which definitely help to produce a better one without the daily help of a singing teacher. The "pp" exercise is taken from "Don Carlos" and if one took the trouble to search, I'm sure one would find they are all based on operatic phrases. The following example is marvellous for strengthing the "bellows" for such passages as the last act of Gounod's Faust & Act III of Romeo & Juliette.
Gounod

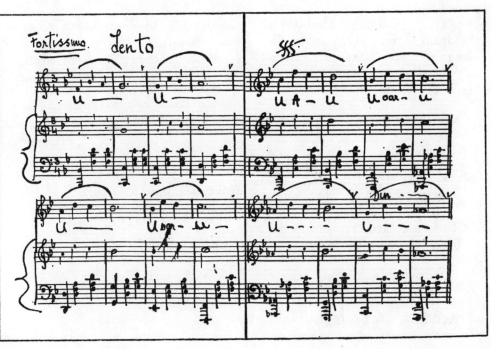

Fortissimo. Lento

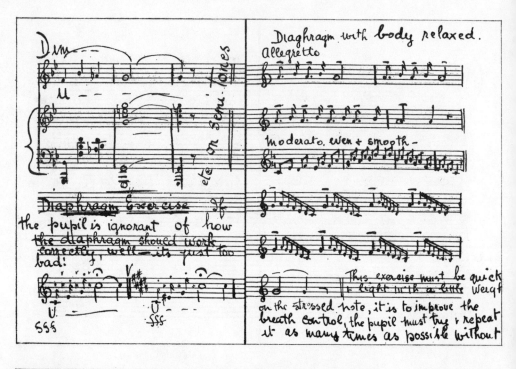

Dim - - -

etc. or semi tones

Diaphragm with body relaxed.
Allegretto

~~Diaphragm Exercise~~ If
the pupil is ignorant of how
~~the diaphragm should work~~
~~correctly, well — its just too~~
~~bad!~~

moderato, even & smooth -

This exercise must be quick
& light with a little weight
on the stressed note, it is to improve the
breath control, the pupil must try & repeat
it as many times as possible without

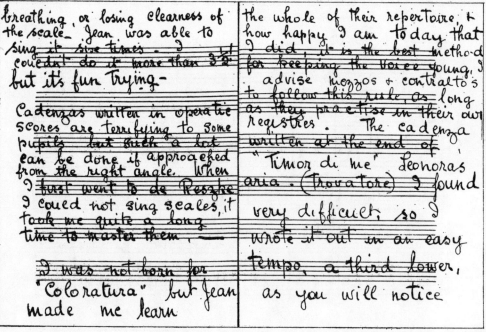

breathing, or losing clearness of
the scale — Jean was able to
~~sing it six times. I~~
~~couldn't do it more than 3½~~
but its fun Trying —

Cadenzas written in operatic
scores are terrifying to some
pupils ~~but such a lot~~
can be done if approached
from the right angle. When
~~I first went to de Reszke~~
~~I could not sing scales, it~~
~~took me quite a long~~
~~time to master them. —~~

~~I was not born for~~
"Coloratura" but Jean
made me learn

the whole of their repertoire, &
how happy I am today that
I did, it is the best method
for keeping the voice young. I
advise mezzos & contraltos
to follow this rule, as long
as they practise in their own
registers.   The cadenza
written at the end of
"Timor di me" Leonoras
aria. (Trovatore) I found
very difficult, so I
wrote it out in an easy
tempo, a third lower,
as you will notice

and it becomes quite easy.

There is nothing more killing for a voice than practising or singing outside of its natural registre

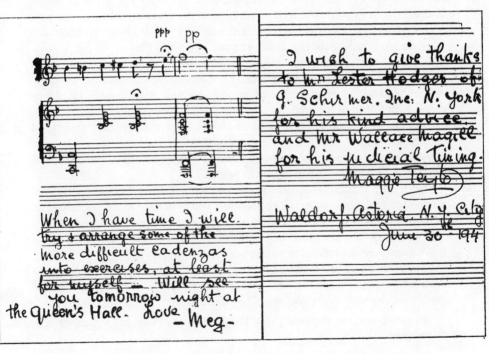

ppp   pp

I wish to give thanks to Mr Lester Hodges of G. Schirmer. Inc: N. York for his kind advice. and Mr Wallace Magill for his judicial Timing. Maggie Teyte

Waldorf. Astoria. N. Y. City
June 30ᵗʰ 194_

When I have time I will try & arrange some of the more difficult cadenzas into exercises, at least for myself — Will see you tomorrow night at the Queen's Hall. Love —Meg-

Bearding the Lion*

by

MAGGIE TEYTE

To the world in general, Claude Debussy is not very well known as a conversationalist. He almost never talks for publication. The inherent brilliancy of his mind has been inferred from the nature of his music, rather than from any direct proofs afforded by his daily life. Yet Debussy, in the friendly atmosphere of his own home, is a brilliant talker and a brilliant thinker. Like all Frenchmen, he has very decided ideas on all subjects which his mind has had time to analyze. And like most Frenchmen, he possesses the ability to express his ideas, when he pleases, in a pithy and sententious fashion which makes his conversation a delight to the listener. Unfortunately, however, this conversation is usually limited to a very close circle of intimate friends, all of whom are in honor bound to keep their knowledge a secret as far as the general public is concerned.

But last summer, in the course of a flying visit to the Debussys, I actually succeeded in bearding the lion in his den, and persuaded him to talk for publication. He had been even more scintillating than usual. Reporters and hawkers of publicity had left him in peace for some time, and he was in a thoroughly good humor. As the bubbling stream of his conversation rippled gaily on, I was seized with a sudden inspiration.

"You must let me publish some of these things that you are saying," I exclaimed. "This is something that the world should know!"

To my great surprise he assented readily. "Do as you like," he answered, pleasantly. "I have no secrets from the world."

I am not a journalist by profession, but a singer somehow becomes fairly well acquainted with the way in which reporters work, so the task of publishing an "exclusive interview" with Mr Debussy did not daunt me. And while I have no knowledge of shorthand, my memory is fairly reliable, as a rule, and I think I can trust it in the present instance.

The first point of real interest cropped up when I asked Mr Debussy what he intended to produce in the near future. His reply was astonishing. "*I shall produce nothing more of the kind that I have been writing,*" he said, calmly.

* Published in *Opera Magazine* (New York), May 1914, with MT's photograph of the composer.

"You mean that your style of music is not sufficiently appreciated?" I gasped.

"Not at all," he answered, smiling. "It *is* appreciated among the cognoscenti. And about the rest of the world I care little. You will find that in ten years *everyone* will be singing and playing my music. The general intelligence of the public will have caught up with me by that time. No, it is not a question of appreciation."

"What is it, then?" I urged.

"It is simply that I have reached the limit of the idiom in which I have chosen to write. There is a limit to all things. We try all possible variations, and after that, we fall back on wearisome repetition. The greater part of the world's music today consists of endless repetition of what has already been finally expressed without possibility of improvement."

"But is your form of expression really so limited?" I asked, incredulously.

"Yes," he answered, simply. "It is that which makes it so distinctly different. It is not a system that I deliberately invented. It is a necessity which has forced itself upon me. Now that I have reached its limits, I am forced to give it up, and turn to something else."

"But you are not ashamed of anything you have done, so far?"

"By no means. I think I have escaped the repetition of myself, so far. But imitation on the part of others had made much of my work seem uninspired and monotonous. The plagiarisms of other composers are the things that have hurt me. They do not know what I am trying to express. They only know that I am different. And by being different themselves, they hope to equal my reputation. Really, they are only harming me without helping themselves. I refuse to accept any responsibility for the so-called Debussyisms of modern composers."

"But how do you know that you have reached your limit?" I insisted.

"In two ways," he answered, readily. "First, through the fact that I have several times of late begun a composition which I quickly realized would be a plagiarizing of myself, as a consequence of which I have invariably given it up. In the second place, I have found it impossible to express certain new thoughts of mine in the idiom to which I have become accustomed, and have, therefore, decided that I must find a new language or stop composing altogether."

"Are you then dissatisfied with the form of expression which you have used in the past?"

"Not at all. It has very definite limits, and once it has been used in all its variations it refuses to re-create itself. But it is a natural form and a real one, and it has been revolutionary in its effect. If I forced this medium of expression into further activity the result would be what you call in English 'platitudes.' Did you ever stop to reflect that before anything can become a platitude it must embody a great truth? I prefer to leave my work at the stage when it is recognized as a great truth, and let other composers write the platitudes."

"You are not impressed, then, with the originality of the modern school of music?" I asked.

"Not deeply. In France it is largely superficial. In Italy they are still bound fast by traditions. In Germany there is not a single composer of original genius."

"What of Richard Strauss?" I demanded with some surprise.

"He is a marvellous technician, nothing else. In his early songs and minor compositions he showed some talent which might have developed into real greatness. But he chose to concentrate on his genius for orchestration and to become a musical scholar instead of an original creator. His 'Heldenleben' is a remarkable example of the laborious production of tremendous orchestral effects with absolutely no musical foundation. The themes of that composition, when taken by themselves, are puerile in their footless banality. By introducing them now and then on a single instrument in contrast with the preceding crash of a full orchestra, he almost makes his audience believe that they have real musical value. No, Strauss is merely a scholar, not a creative genius."

"And there is no one else?" I inquired tentatively.

"There is no one else," answered Debussy shortly. "The rest are not even worth mentioning."

"Possibly you are prejudiced against the German type of music," I suggested. "What do you think of Wagner, for instance?"

"Wagner was a great literary and dramatic genius," answered the composer, "but no musician. He had revolutionary ideas of form and of the realistic possibilities of opera, and he carried them out with splendid courage and vigor. But his music consists chiefly of new combinations of old material. You will find most of Wagner's themes in the musical literature of earlier times. On the whole Verdi was a more original composer."

This was too much, even for me, and to avoid a heated argument I hastened to change the subject.

"Since you have reached the limit of the form of expression which you have used thus far," I said gently, "may I ask whether you have found the *new* idiom as yet, and whether you have decided on any definite composition for the future?"

"Naturally you wish to know that," he began. But here my report of the conversation must stop, for Mr Debussy insists that what followed is *not* for publication.

The Wrong Note*

With my memory still keenly alive to her superb and unsurpassed interpretations of the roles of the Jongleur, Thaïs, Mélisande, Monna Vanna and other heroines of opera, I am a little bewildered by *Mary Garden's Story* which recounts the life of that gifted Scottish soprano, equally and justly famous in France and America. I cannot reconcile the wonderful illusions she gave us before the scenery with what, Miss Garden would have us believe, happened behind it. Her story seeks to give the impression that hard work had little to do with her performances, or that it consisted only in learning musical notation.

There is a continual reference to "living" a role on the stage as if this were something entirely due to inspiration and not the result of painstaking effort. Miss Garden insists that she stepped "into and out of" her roles as if they were dresses. It would be strange if a singer did not automatically step out of a role such as Salomé. I, for one, can hardly visualize Miss Garden returning to the Blackstone Hotel on Michigan Avenue with seven veils floating above her—a feature, apparently, of her stage performance—as though she were doing the Indian rope trick. When self-assurance, that necessary quality for a public career, becomes self-praise one is suspicious of the original incentive for artistic achievement.

For students and the prima donnas of tomorrow, the book contains some good and sound advice. It covers such points as the Italian language, the placing of the word, and the length of daily practice; but I sincerely hope that students will not take Miss Garden's account of her method of projecting a role too literally.

Maggie Teyte

* MT's review of *Mary Garden's Story*, by Mary Garden and Louis Biancolli, published in the *Sunday Times*, 2 March 1952.

Teyte's Roles in Opera & Light Opera (1907–1951)

With place and date of first performance, when known*

Tyrcis, *Miriame et Daphné* (Clairville and Cordier–Offenbach), Monte Carlo, 7 February 1907.

Zerlina, *Don Giovanni* (da Ponte–Mozart), Monte Carlo, 17 February 1907.

Rosa, *Le Timbre d'argent* (Barbier and Carré–Saint-Saëns), Monte Carlo, 26 February 1907.

Glycère, *Circé* (Haraucourt–P. and L. Hillemacher), Paris, 17 April 1907.

Mallika, *Lakmé* (Gondinet and Gille–Delibes), Paris, 13 May 1907.

Rhodis, *Aphrodite* (Louÿs–Erlanger), Paris, 26 February 1908.

Mélisande, *Pelléas et Mélisande* (Maeterlinck–Debussy), Paris, 13 June 1908.

Violette, *La Reine fiammette* (Mendès–Leroux), Paris, 8 February 1910.

2nd Boy, *La Flûte enchantée* (Schikaneder–Mozart), Paris, 31 May 1909.

Hansel, *Hansel et Gretel* (Wette–Humperdinck), Paris (open air), *c.* 1910.

Cio-Cio-San, *Madama Butterfly* (Giocosa and Illica–Puccini), Berlin (Imperial Opera), *c.* 1910.

Melka, *Muguette* (Ouida–Missa), London, 26 May 1910.

Antonia, *Tales of Hoffmann* (Barbier–Offenbach), London, 1 June 1910.

Blonde, *Die Entführung aus dem Serail* (Stephanie–Mozart), London, 20 June 1910.

Cherubino, *Le Nozze di Figaro* (da Ponte–Mozart), London, 22 June 1910.

Nuri, *Tiefland* (Lothar–d'Albert), London, 5 October 1910.

Marguérite, *Faust* (Barbier and Carré–Gounod), London, 1 November 1910.

Cendrillon, *Cendrillon* (Cain–Massenet), Chicago, 27 November 1911.

Lygia, *Quo Vadis* (Cain–Nouguès), Chicago, 19 December 1911.

Dot, *The Cricket on the Hearth* (Willner–Goldmark), Philadelphia, 7 November 1912.

Mignon, *Mignon* (Barbier and Carré–Thomas), Chicago, 23 December 1912.

Mimi, *La Bohème* (Giacosa and Illica–Puccini), Chicago, 15 January 1913 (poss. earlier—Berlin?).

Manon, *Manon* (Meilhac and Gille–Massenet), Cannes, 23 March 1913.

Oscar, *Un Ballo in maschera* (Somma–Verdi), Paris, 16 May 1914.

* The list is as complete as possible, but by no means definitive.

Countess Gil, *Il Segreto di Susanna* (Golisciani–Wolf-Ferrari), Paris, 23 May 1914.

Desdemona, *Otello* (Boito–Verdi), Boston tour, *c.* 1915?

Nedda, *I Pagliacci* (Leoncavallo), Boston, 20 November 1915.

Gretel, *Hänsel und Gretel* (Willner–Humperdinck), Boston, 11 December 1915.

Gilda, *Rigoletto* (Piave–Verdi), Boston or Pittsburgh, *c.* 1916?

Fiora, *L'Amore dei tre re* (Benelli–Montemezzi), U.S. tour, *c.* 1916.

Lady Mary Carlisle, *Monsieur Beaucaire* (Ross–Messager), London (Birmingham prior to that date), 19 April 1919.

Princess Julia, *A Little Dutch Girl* (Graham–Kalman), London, December 1919.

Princess, *The Perfect Fool* (Holst), London, 14 May 1923.

Georgine, *The Lilac Domino* (H. B. and R. B. Smith–Cuvillier), BBC, London, 30 January 1928.

Sylva, *The Gypsy Princess* (Miller and Stanley–Kalman), BBC, London, 8 March 1928.

Colette, *La Basoche* (Carré–Messager), BBC, London, 26 May 1930.

Lady Ann Gallop, *Tantivy Towers* (Herbert–Dunhill), London, 6 June 1935.

Euridice, *Orphée et Euridice* (Calzabigi–Gluck), London, 17 June 1937.

Eva, *Die Meistersinger von Nürnberg* (Wagner), Liverpool, 4 November 1938.

Belinda, *Dido and Aeneas* (Tate–Purcell), London, 9 September 1951.

The Tempo of a Career

Teyte's most important engagements in North America and
Europe in the 1912–13 season

1912

November	7	Dot in *The Cricket on the Hearth*, Metropolitan Opera House, Philadelphia.
	8	Soloist, New York Symphony Orchestra, New York City.
	10	Soloist, New York Symphony Orchestra, New York City.
	13	*The Cricket on the Hearth*, Metropolitan Opera House, Philadelphia.
	18	Title role in *Mignon*, Metropolitan Opera House, Philadelphia.
	22	*Mignon*, Chicago Grand Opera Company, Baltimore, Md.
	30	Title role in *Cendrillon*, Auditorium, Chicago.
December	7	*The Cricket on the Hearth*, Auditorium, Chicago.
	8	Concert, Auditorium, Chicago.
	13	Concert, Fine Arts Society, Pittsburgh, Pa.
	15	Concert with Tita Ruffo, Hippodrome, New York City.
	16	Recital, Aeolian Hall, New York City.
	19	Private engagement, Boston, Mass.
	23	*Mignon*, Auditorium, Chicago.
	25	*The Cricket on the Hearth*, Auditorium, Chicago.
	27	*Mignon*, Chicago Grand Opera Company, Milwaukee, Wis.
	31	Private engagement, Washington, D.C.

1913

January	1	*The Cricket on the Hearth*, Auditorium, Chicago.
	3	Private engagement, Chicago.
	6	Amateur Musical Club, Chicago.
	9	*Cendrillon*, Auditorium, Chicago.
	11	*Mignon*, Auditorium, Chicago.
	14	*The Cricket on the Hearth*, Auditorium, Chicago.
	15	Recital (afternoon), Chicago.
	15	Mimi in *La Bohème*, Auditorium, Chicago.
	16	Recital, Union League Club, Chicago.
	18	*Mignon*, Auditorium, Chicago.

20 *La Bohème*, Auditorium, Chicago.
22 Morning recital, Syracuse, N.Y.
24 Soloist, Boston Symphony Orchestra, Boston, Mass.
30 Costume recital, Aeolian Hall, New York City.
31 Recital, Jordan Hall, Boston, Mass.

February 3 Recital, Wellesley College, Wellesley, Mass.
6 Recital, St Paul, Minn.
7 Recital, Minneapolis, Minn.
9 Private engagement, New York City.
10 Recital, New York City.
11 Private engagement, Boston, Mass.
14 Costume recital, Aeolian Hall, New York City.
16 Recital, Symphony Hall, Boston, Mass.
17 *La Bohème*, Metropolitan Opera House, Philadelphia.
18 Private engagement, New York City.
20 Farewell recital, Aeolian Hall, New York City.

A partial list of her engagements after leaving America, 22 February 1913:

March 3 Birmingham
4 Manchester
5 Liverpool
6 Newcastle   Tour with the Queen's Hall Orchestra,
7 Glasgow   conductor Sir Henry Wood
8 Edinburgh
9 London

10 Recital at Salle Gaveau, Paris.
11 Recital, Amsterdam.
13 *Mignon*, Cannes.
14 Concert, Cannes.
15 *Mignon*, Menton.
17 *La Bohème*, Cannes
19 Marguérite in *Faust*, Cannes.
23 Title role in *Manon*, Cannes.
24 *La Bohème*, Menton.
25 Concert, Nice.

April 5 Recital, Berlin.
9 Recital, Vienna.
14 Recital, Berlin.

May 17 Recital at Queen's Hall, London.
20 Recital at Salle Gaveau, Paris.
21 Second recital at Queen's Hall, London.

Maggie Teyte

Compiled by J. F. Perkins (G & T, HMV, EMI, Columbia), W. R. Moran (U.S. recordings), and G. O'C.

Acknowledgements to W. Bryant, Leah Burt, the BBC, EMI, BIRS, Bryan Crimp, David Tron, and Raymond Wyle.

Bold-face numbers indicate the take used, when known; catalogue numbers are those of the first issue.

Matrix no.		Catalogue no.
	28 September 1907, Paris: G & T	
7406 o	Because (Teschemacher–d'Hardelot)	
7407 o	Because (Teschemacher–d'Hardelot)	3729
7408 o	A Memory (Goring Thomas)	3730*
7409 o	Goodbye (Whyte-Melville–Tosti)	3731*
	26 November 1913, New York: Columbia	
36829–1	Parted (Wetherly–Tosti)	
39114–1	Down in the Forest (Simpson–Ronald)	
39115–1	*Le Nozze di Figaro*: Voi che sapete (Mozart)	
39116–**1**/–2	When Love is Kind (Moore)	A 1472
39117–1	Obstination (Coppée–Fontenailles)	
39118–**1**	Obstination (Coppée–Fontenailles)	A 1471
39119–1	The Birth of Morn (Dunbar–Leoni)	
39120–**1**	Mifanwy (Weatherley–Forster)	A 1490
39121–1	L'Heure exquise (Verlaine–Hahn)	A 1490
39122–**1**	An Open Secret (Anon.–Huntingdon Woodman)	A 1471
	28 November 1913, New York: Columbia	
39123–**1**	*The Marriage Market*: Little Grey Home in the West (Wilmot–Löhr)	A 1472
	10 March 1914, New York: Columbia	
39114–2/–**3**	Down in the Forest (Simpson–Ronald)	A 1555
39123–2/–3/–4	*The Marriage Market*: Little Grey Home in the West (Wilmot–Löhr)	
39271–1/–**2**	Believe me, if all those endearing young charms (Moore–Trad.)	A 1555

* Issue number assigned, but thought to be unpublished.

Matrix no.		*Catalogue no.*

1914 or 1915, London: Columbia

29164	The Homes They Leave Behind (Walter Rubens)	2467
29165	Your King and Country Want You (Paul Rubens)	2467
6424	The Homes They Leave Behind (Walter Rubens)	496
6425	Your King and Country Want You (Paul Rubens)	496

19 November 1915, New York: Columbia

39123–**5**	*The Marriage Market*: Little Grey Home in the West (Wilmot–Löhr)	A 1938
46209–1/–2/–3/–**4**	A Little Love, a Little Kiss (Ross–Silésu)	A 1957
46210–1/–2/–3/–4/–**5** Just You (Miller–Burleigh)		A 1957
46211–1/–2/–3/–**4**	Until (Teschemacher–Sanderson)	A 1938

6 June 1916, New York: Columbia

46812–1/–2/–3	My Heart is Sair for Somebody (Burns–Trad.)	
48813–**1**	Oft in the Stilly Night (Moore–Trad.)	A 5834 5031–M
48814–**1**	Home Sweet Home (Payne–Bishop)	A 5834 5031–M

8 June 1916, New York: Columbia

46819–1/–2	The Little Silver Ring (Gérard–Chaminade)	

14 June 1916, New York: Columbia

48820–1	Keep the Home Fires Burning (Ford–Novello)	
46837–1/–2	Comin' thro' the Rye (Burns–Trad.)	

30 June 1916, New York: Columbia

48849–1	Down in the Forest (Simpson–Ronald)	
48924–1	(a) Lullaby (unknown); (b) The Birth of Morn (Dunbar–Leoni)	
48925–1	(a) The Year's at the Spring (Browning–Beach); (b) The Fairy Pipers (Weatherly–Brewer)	
48851–1	Laddie in Khaki (Novello)	

20 January 1919, New York: Edison★

6573–A/–B	*Mignon*: Dost thou know (Thomas)	
6574–A/–**B**	My Ain Folk (Mills–Lemon)	82163

★ Teyte was paid $200 per title by Edison.

Matrix no.   *Catalogue no.*

30 January 1919, New York: Edison
6596–A/–**B**   All Through the Night (Trad. Welsh)
6597–A/–**B**   Believe me, if all those endearing young
                    charms (Moore–Trad.)   82163

3 February 1919, New York: Edison
6603–A/–B/–**C**   I'se Gwine Back to Dixie (White), with
                    Lyric Quartet   82159
6604–A/–**B**/–C   Kashmiri Song (W. Findon–Lehmann)   82205

5 and 6 February 1919, New York: Edison

6608–A/–B/–**C**   Ma Curly-Headed Baby (Clutsam)   82159
6609–**A**/–B/–C   Dreams (Porteus–Streletzki)   82331
6613–A/–**B**/–C   Happy Days (Streletzki)   82331
6573–F/–G   *Mignon*: Dost thou know (Thomas)

April 1919,* London: Columbia
Monsieur Beaucaire (Ross–Messager)
76461   Philomel   L 1310
76462   I do not know (with Chorus)   L 1311
76463   Lightly, lightly (with Marion Green)   L 1312
76464   Say no more (with M. Green)   L 1313
76473   Finale, Act I (with M. Green)   L 1314
76474   What are names (with M. Green)   L 1315
76475   Finale, Act II (with M. Green and Robert
                    Parker)   L 1316

25 May 1932, London: Decca†
GB 4517   Christine's Lament (Dvořák, arr. Creyke)
GB 4518   Si mes vers avaient des ailes (Hugo–Hahn)

20 September 1932, London: Decca
With George Reeves (Piano)
GB 4907   Songs My Mother Taught Me (Heyduk–
                    Dvořák)   M 444
GB 4908   Après un rêve (Bussine–Fauré)   F 40300‡ LXT 6126
GB 4909   Si mes vers avaient des ailes (Hugo–Hahn)   F 40300 LXT 6126
GB 4910   Christina's Lament (Dvořák, arr. Creyke)   M 444

* Precise date unknown, but the waxes were cut before *Monsieur Beaucaire* opened—
so sure were they that it would be a success.

† Two Decca master pressing tests have recently come to light: PRL4-595-2DJ,
La Flûte de Pan (Louÿs–Debussy) and PRL8, Slumber Song (composer unknown).

‡ Issue number assigned, but thought to be unpublished.

Matrix no.		*Catalogue no.*
	22 September 1932, London: Decca	
	With orchestra	
GB 4929	*The Lilac Domino*: What is done, you never can undo (Smith–Cuvillier)	M 425
GB 4930	*The Student Prince*: Deep in my heart dear (Donnelly–Romberg)	M 425
FGA 4931	*Véronique*: Petite dinde, ah quel outrage/ Ma foi pour venir de Provence (Vanloo and Duval–Messager)	T 201
FGA 4932	*La Périchole*: Tu n es pas beau . . . Je t'adore brigand (Meilhac and Halévy–Offenbach)	T 201

	28 November 1932, London: Decca	
	With orchestra	
GB 5258	*Sir Roger de Coverley*: Sweet Mistress Prue (Legh–Gibson)	M 430
GB 5259	*Sir Roger de Coverley*: Care Free (Legh–Gibson)	M 430
TB 1120	*Conversation Piece*: I'll Follow my Secret Heart (Coward)	F 3919
TB 1121	*Conversation Piece*: Nevermore (Coward)	F 3919

	October 1934, Abbey Road, London: The Gramophone Co.	
	With orchestra conducted by Kennedy-Russell	
OEA 861–1/–2 Transfers OEA 861–3/–4/–5/–6	*By Appointment*: White roses (Stanley–Kennedy-Russell)	B 8242
OEA 862–1/–2/–3 Transfers OEA 862–4/–5/–6/–7	*By Appointment*: Hold me in your heart (Stanley–Kennedy-Russell), with Charles Mayhew	B 8242

	12 March 1936, Abbey Road, London: The Gramophone Co.	
	With Alfred Cortot (piano)	
	Fêtes galantes: Set 1 (Verlaine–Debussy)	
OEA 3146–1/–2	Clair de lune	DA 1472
OEA 3147–1	En sourdine	DA 1471
OEA 3148–1/–2/–3	Fantoches	DA 1471
	Fêtes galantes: Set 2 (Verlaine–Debussy)	
OEA 3149–1/–2	Les Ingénus	DA 1472
OEA 3150–1/–2	Le Faune	DA 1473
OEA 3151–1/–2	Colloque sentimental	DA 1473

Matrix no.   *Catalogue no.*

Trois Chansons de Bilitis (Louÿs–Debussy)

OEA 3152–**1**/–2	La Flûte de Pan	DA 1474
OEA 3153–**1**/–2	La Chevelure	DA 1474
OEA 3154–**1**/–2	Le Tombeau des Naïades	DA 1475

13 March 1936, Abbey Road, London: The Gramophone Co.
With Alfred Cortot (piano)
Le Promenoir des deux amants (Tristan l'Hermite–Debussy)

OEA 3155–**1**/–2/–**3**	Auprès de cette grotte sombre	DA 1475
OEA 3156–**1**/–2	Crois mon conseil, chère Climène	DA 1476
OEA 3157–**1**/–2	Je tremble en voyant ton visage	DA 1476
OEA 3158–**1**/–2/–3	Ballades des femmes de Paris (Villon–Debussy)	DA 1477
OEA 3159–**1**/–2/–3	Proses lyriques No. 2: De grève (Debussy)	DA 1477

15 August 1937, London: BBC Recital
With Rita Mackay (piano), later issued by Decca

BBC Tape:	Die Mainacht (Hölty–Brahms)	LXT 6126
T 27844	An die Nachtigall (Hölty–Brahms)	LXT 6126
	Meine Liebe ist grün (Schumann–Brahms)	LXT 6126
	Der Nussbaum (J. Mosen–Schumann)	LXT 6126
	Aufträge (L'Egru–Schumann)	LXT 6126
	Now Sleeps the Crimson Petal (Tennyson–Quilter)	LXT 6126
	Indian Love Song (Shelley–Delius)	LXT 6126
	The Fields Are Full (Armstrong–Gibbs)	EJS 478★
	E'en as a Lovely Flower (Kroeke–Bridge)	LXT 6126
	The Nightingale sings to his mate in the trees (Webber)	LXT 6126
	Wander–thirst (Gould–Peel)	LXT 6126

17 February 1939, London: BBC
With Heddle Nash, Dennis Noble, Orchestra conducted by Stanford Robinson.
In English

BBC Tape:	*Manon* (Meilhac and Gille–Massenet) Acts I,	
T 34689	III (Acts II, IV, and V recorded but	
	incomplete.)	UORC–208★

★ Unauthorized private issue in U.S.A.

Matrix no.   *Catalogue no.*

31 July 1940, London: EMI Columbia for The Gramophone Shop, New York
With London Symphony Orchestra conducted by Leslie Heward

CTPX 11583-**1**	*Nuits d'été*: No. 2, Le Spectre de la rose (Gautier–Berlioz)	JG 177
CTPX 11584–**1**	*Nuits d'été*: No. 4, Absence (Gautier–Berlioz)	JG 177
CTPX 11585–**1**	L'Invitation au voyage (Baudelaire–Duparc)	JG 178
CTPX 11586–**1**	Phidylé (Coppée–Duparc)	JG 178
CTPX 11587		

14 August 1940, London: EMI Columbia for The Gramophone Shop, New York
With Gerald Moore (piano)

CTPX 11588–1		
CTPX 11589–**1**	*Proses lyriques*: No. 3, De fleurs (Debussy)	JG 179
CTPX 11590–**2**	*Proses lyriques*: No. 1, De rêve (Debussy)	JG 179
CTPX 11591–**2**	*Proses lyriques*: No. 4, De soir (Debussy)	JG 180
CTPX 11592–**2**	Le Jet d'eau (Baudelaire–Debussy)	JG 180

20 February 1941, Abbey Road, London★
With Gerald Moore (piano)

OEA 9094–1/–2	Ave Maria (sung in Latin) (Bach–Gounod)	
OEA 9095–1	(a) The Bayley beareth the bell away (Anon.–Warlock)	RLS 716
	(b) Lullaby, My little sweet darling (Anon.–16th cent.–Warlock)	RLS 716
OEA 9096–1/–2	Old Sir Faulk (Sitwell–Walton)	

19 March 1941, Abbey Road, London
With Gerald Moore (piano)

OEA 9213–1/–2/–3	Old Sir Faulk (Sitwell–Walton)	
OEA 9214–1/–2	Daphne (Sitwell–Walton)	
OEA 9215–1/–2	Through gilded trellises (Sitwell–Walton)	

26 March 1941, Abbey Road, London
With Gerald Moore (piano)

OEA 9221–1/–2	Après un rêve (Bussine–Fauré)	DA 1777
OEA 9222–1/–2	Si mes vers avaient des ailes (Hugo–Hahn)	DA 1777
OEA 9223–**1**	Psyché (Corneille–Paladilhe)	DA 1779

17 April 1941, Abbey Road, London
With Gerald Moore (piano)

OEA 9244–1/–2	Chanson triste (Lahor–Duparc)	DA 1779
OEA 9245–1/–2	Offrande (Verlaine–Hahn)	DA 1821

★ Unless otherwise stated, all further recordings made at Abbey Road, London, were for The Gramophone Co., issued under HMV labels.

Matrix no.		Catalogue no.
OEA 9246-**1**	*Ariettes oubliées*: No. 5, Aquarelles-green	
	(Verlaine–Debussy)	DA 1893
OEA 9247-**1**/–2	L'Heure exquise (Verlaine–Hahn)	DA 1821

18 July 1941, Abbey Road, London
With Gerald Moore (piano)

OEA 9339–1/–2	*King Arthur*: Fairest isle (Dryden–Purcell)	
OEA 9340–1/–2	*The Libertine*: Nymphs and shepherds (Purcell)	
2 EA 9393–1/–2	Clair de lune (Verlaine–Szulc)	

1 August 1941, Abbey Road, London
With Gerald Moore (piano)

OEA 9339-**3**/–4	*King Arthur*: Fairest isle (Dryden–Purcell)	DA 1790
OEA 9340–**3**/–4	*The Libertine*: Nymphs and shepherds (Purcell)	DA 1790
2EA 9394-**1**	Extase (Lahor–Duparc)	DB 5937

22 August 1941, Abbey Road, London

OEA 9505-**1**/–2	En sourdine (Verlaine–Hahn)	DA 1830
2EA 9393-**3**/–4	Clair de lune (Verlaine–Szulc)	DB 5937

3 October 1941

OEA 9524-**1**/–2	Oft in the Stilly Night (Moore–Trad.)	DA 1804
OEA 9525-**1**/–2	Comin' thro' the rye (Burns–Trad.)	DA 1804

25 November 1941, Abbey Road, London
With John McCormack. Piano acc. Gerald Moore

OEA 9651-**1**/–2	Night Hymn at Sea (Hemans–Goring Thomas)	
2EA 9652–**1**	Still as the Night (Lockwood–Götze)	RLS 716
Transfers 2EA		
9652–2/–3/–4	(24 December 1947).	

5 December 1941, Abbey Road, London
With Gerald Moore (piano)

OEA 9660-**1**/–2	Pleading (Salmon–Elgar)	
OEA 9661-**1**/–2	Now Sleeps the Crimson Petal (Tennyson–	
	Quilter)	
OEA 9662-**1**/–2	La Lune blanche luit dans les bois (Verlaine–	
	Fauré)	
OEA 9663-**1**/–2	Le Secret (Silvester–Fauré)	DA 1876

23 December 1941, Abbey Road, London
With Gerald Moore (piano)

OEA 9660-3/-4	Pleading (Salmon–Elgar)	DA 1807
OEA 9661-3/-4	Now Sleeps the Crimson Petal (Tennyson–Quilter)	DA 1807
OEA 9675-1	Dans les ruines d'une abbaye (Hugo–Fauré)	
OEA 9676-1	Soir (Samain–Fauré)	

6 January 1942, Abbey Road, London
With Gerald Moore (piano)

OEA 9694-1/-2	Clair de lune (Verlaine–Fauré)	DA 1876
OEA 9695-1/-2	Ici-bas (Prud'homme–Fauré)	DA 1830

16 January 1942, Abbey Road, London
With Gerald Moore (piano)

OEA 9675-2/-3	Dans les ruines d'une abbaye (Hugo–Fauré)	DA 1810
OEA 9676-2/-3	Soir (Samain–Fauré)	DA 1819
OEA 9687-1/-2	Plaisir d'amour (Florian–Martini)	DA 1810

28 May 1942, Abbey Road, London
With Gerald Moore (piano)

OEA 9875-1/-2	*La Bonne Chanson*: No. 9, L'hiver a cessé (Verlaine–Fauré)	DA 1693
OEA 9876-1/-2	Les Roses d'Ispahan (de Lisle-Fauré)	DA 1819
OEA 9877-1/-2	L'Absent (Hugo–Fauré)	RLS 716

10 February 1943, Abbey Road, London
With Gerald Moore (piano)

OEA 9971-1/-2	Lydia (de Lisle–Fauré)	DA 1831
OEA 9972-1/-2	Nell (de Lisle–Fauré)	DA 1831

7 June 1943, Abbey Road, London

OEA 10004-1/-2	Chanson d'Avril (Bouilhet–Bizet)	DA 1833
OEA 10005-1/-2	Le Colibri (de Lisle–Chausson)	DA 1833

2 September 1943, Abbey Road, London
With the Blech String Quartet and Gerald Moore (piano)

2EA 10049-1/-2/-3	Chanson perpétuelle (Cros–Chausson) Part 1	DB 6159
2EA 10050-1/-2/-3	Chanson perpétuelle (Cross–Chausson) Part 2	DB 6159

10 February 1944, Abbey Road, London
With Gerald Moore (piano)

OEA 10140	Romance (Bourget–Debussy)	DA 1838
OEA 10141	Beau Soir (Bourget–Debussy)	DA 1838

Matrix no.   *Catalogue no.*

13 March 1944, Abbey Road, London
With Gerald Moore (piano)

OEA 10161–**1**/–2   *Deux épigrammes*: D'Anne jouant de
                            l'espinette (Marot–Ravel)   (DA 1839)* RLS 716
OEA 10162–**1**/–2   D'Anne qui me jecta de la neige   (DA 1839) RLS 716

3 April 1944, Abbey Road, London
With Gerald Moore (piano)

OEA 10176–**1**/–2   Pastorale (Régnard–Bizet)   DA 1840
OEA 10177–1/–**2**   Chanson d'Estelle (Florian–Godard)   DA 1840

20 July 1944, Abbey Road, London
With James Whitehead (cello) and Gerald Moore (piano)

OEA 10257–**1**   Elégie (Gallet–Massenet)   DA 1847
OEA 10258–**1**   Obstination (Coppée–Fontenailles)   DA 1847

15 November 1944, Abbey Road, London
With Gerald Moore (piano)

2EA 10316–1/–**2**   Le Temps des lilas (Boucher–Chausson) with
                           James Whitehead (cello)   (DB 6179)† RLS 716
2EA 10317–1/–**2**/–3 Les Papillons Op. 2 No. 7 (de Lisle–
                           Chausson)   (DB 6179) RLS 716

20 August 1945, New York: Bell Telephone Hour
With orchestra or piano

Nuits d'été: Absence (Gautier–Berlioz)   ANNA 1007
Chanson d'Avril (Bouilhet–Bizet)   ANNA 1007‡
Oft in the Stilly Night (Moore–Trad.)   ANNA 1007
Le Nozze di Figaro: Voi che sapete (Mozart)   ESJ 478

17 September 1945, New York: Bell Telephone Hour
With orchestra or piano

Caro mio ben (Giordano)   ANNA 1007
Do not go my love (Tagore–Hageman)   ANNA 1007
Phydilé (Coppée–Duparc)   ANNA 1007
Si mes vers avaient des ailes (Hugo–Hahn)   ANNA 1007

* Issue number assigned, but thought to be unpublished.

† Issue number assigned, but thought to be unpublished. Both titles published by BIRS on HMB 15.

‡ Unauthorized private issue in USA.

25 February 1946, New York: Bell Telephone Hour
With orchestra or piano

L'Heure exquise (Verlaine–Hahn)
La Bohème: Mi chiamano Mimi (Puccini)   EJS 478
Plaisir d'amour (Florian–Martini)
La Périchole: Tu n'est pas beau (Meilhac and
Halévy–Offenbach)

20 May 1946, Abbey Road, London
With Gerald Moore (piano)

OEA 9675–4/–5   Dans les ruines d'une abbaye (Hugo–Fauré)
OEA 11016–1/–2   (a) L'Adieu du matin (Roche–Pessard)
(b) La Matinée champêtre (Ert–A. Webber)
OEA 11017–1/–2   *Ciboulette*: Ce n'était pas la même chose (des
Fleurs and de Croissat–Hahn)   HLM 7033

7 June 1946, Abbey Road, London
With orchestra cond. Leighton Lucas

Poème de l'amour et de la mer (Boucher–
Chausson):
2EA 11052–1   La Fleur des eaux Part 1   RLS 716
2EA 11053–1   La Fleur des eaux Part 2   RLS 716
2EA 11054–1   La Mort de l'amour Part 1   RLS 716
2EA 11055–1   La Mort de l'amour Part 2 (Le Temps des
lilas) with James Whitehead (cello)   RLS 716

26 August 1946, New York: Bell Telephone Hour
With orchestra or piano

Manon: Adieu notre petite table (Massenet)   EJS 478
Conversation Piece: I'll follow my secret
heart (Coward)   ANNA 1007
Le Temps des lilas (Boucher–Chausson)   ANNA 1007

21 September 1946, Lotos Club, New York
RCA Victor Orchestra, cond. Jean Paul Morel

D6–RB2867–1/
1A/–2/–2A   (a) *Le Trésor supposé*: N'avoir qu'une pensée
(Méhul)
(b) *Le Roi et le fermier*: Il regardait mon
bouquet (Monsigny)

Matrix no.		*Catalogue no.*

D6–RB 2868–1/
  1A/–2/–2A   *Le Tableau parlant*: Vous étiez ce que vous
                  n'êtes plus (Grétry)   10–1371
D6–RB 2869–1/
  –1A/–2/–2A   (a) Dans le printemps de mes années (Garat)
               (b) *L'Amant statue*: Jeunes fillettes (Dalayrac)
D6 RB 2870–1/–1A *La Servante maîtresse*: Air de Zerbina (Pergolesi) 10–1369

23 September 1946, Lotos Club, New York
RCA Victor Orchestra, cond. J. P. Morel

D6 RB 2875–1/–1A *Rose et Colas*: La Sagesse est un trésor
                  (Monsigny)   10–1369
D6 RB 2876–1/–1A *Zémire et Azor*: Rose chérie (Grétry)   10–1370
D6 RB 2877–1/–1A *Les Oies de Frère Philippe*: Je sais attacher des
                  rubans (Dourlen)   10–1370
D6 RB 2878–1/
  –1A/–2/–2A   *Le Déserteur*: Adieu, chère Louise (Monsigny) 10–1371

4 November 1946, New York: Bell Telephone Hour
En sourdine (Verlaine–Fauré)
Obstination (Coppée–Fontenailles)
La Bohème: Donde lieta (Puccini)   EJS 478
Monsieur Beaucaire: Philomel (Ross–Messager)

7 April 1947, New York: Bell Telephone Hour
In the Silence of the Night (Rachmaninoff)
L'Invitation au voyage (Baudelaire–Duparc)
Valse de Chopin (J. Marx)

30 June 1947, New York: Bell Telephone Hour
Jeanne d'Arc: Adieu forêts (Tchaikovsky)   EJS 478
La Bonne Chanson: La Lune blanche luit dans
  les bois (Verlaine–Fauré)
Oft in the Stilly Night (Moore–Trad.)

11 August 1947, New York: Bell Telephone Hour
Absence (Gautier–Berlioz)
Si mes vers avaient des ailes (Hugo–Hahn)
La Périchole: Tu n'es pas beau (Meilhac and
  Halévy–Offenbach)
Vieille Chanson de chasse (arr. Manning)

5 October 1947, Abbey Road London: The Gramophone Co.
for The Gramophone Shop, New York
With Gerald Moore (piano)

2EA 12375–1/–2	*La Bonne Chanson*: No. 3, La Lune blanche luit dans les bois (Verlaine–Fauré)	
	La Bonne Chanson: No. 5, J'ai presque peur en vérité (Verlaine–Fauré)	GSC 22
2EA 12376–1/–2	*Pelléas et Mélisande*: Voici ce qu'il écrit à son frère (Maeterlinck–Debussy)	GSC 21
2EA 12377–1/–2	(a) *Histoires naturelles*: No. 4, Le Martin-pêcheur (Renard–Ravel)	
	(b) *Deux épigrammes*: Anne jouant de l'espinette (Marot–Ravel)	GSC 22

11 October 1947, Abbey Road, London: The Gramophone Co.
for The Gramophone Shop, New York
With Gerald Moore (piano)

2EA 12409–1/–2	*Mozart*: Act I, Etre adoré (Guitry–Hahn)	GSC 23
2EA 12410–1/–2	*Mozart*: Act III, Air des adieux	GSC 23

26 October 1947, Abbey Road, London: The Gramophone Co.
for The Gramophone Shop, New York
With Gerald Moore (piano)

2EA 12453–1/–2	O quand je dors (Hugo–Liszt)	GSC 24
2EA 12454–1/–2/–3	Les Larmes (Blanchotte–Tchaikovsky)	GSC 24
2EA 12455–1/–2	*Pelléas et Mélisande*: Voici ce qu'il écrit à son frère (Maeterlinck–Debussy)	GSC 21

11 January 1948, New York: Bell Telephone Hour
La Bohème: Donde lieta (Puccini)
Sir John in Love: Greensleeves (Trad., arr. Vaughan Williams)
Les Larmes (Tchaikovsky)
Le Nozze di Figaro: Voi che sapete (Mozart)

26 April 1948, New York: Bell Telephone Hour
Christina's Lament (Dvořák, arr. Creyke)
L'Invitation au voyage (Baudelaire–Duparc)
La Bohème: Mi chiamano Mimi (Puccini)
Obstination (Coppée–Fontenailles)

12 and 13 July 1948, Abbey Road, London
Royal Opera House Orchestra, Covent Garden, cond. Hugo Rignold

2EA 13214–1/–**2**	*Shéhérazade*: Asie, Part 1 (Klingsor–Ravel)	DB 6843
2EA 13215–1/–2/–**3**		
/–4	*Shéhérazade*: Asie, Part 2 (Klingsor–Ravel)	DB 6843
2EA 13216–**1**/–2/–3	*Shéhérazade:* La Flûte enchantée (Klingsor–Ravel)	DB 6844
2EA 13217–**1**/–2	*Shéhérazade:* L'Indifférent	DB 6844

6 September 1948, Abbey Road, London
With Gerald Moore (piano)

OEA 13252–**1**/–2	Vieille Chanson de chasse (Trad., arr. Manning)	RLS 716
OEA 13253–1/–**2**	Heures d'été (Samain–Rhené-Baton)	RLS 716
OEA 13254–1/–2	Bonjour, Suzon (de Musset–Pessard)	
OEA 13255–**1**/–2	La Rosée sainte (Gorodetsky–Stravinsky)	RLS 716
OEA 13256–**1**/–2	Vieille chanson (Hugo–Webber)	RLS 716

8 September 1948, Abbey Road, London
With Gerald Moore (piano)

OEA 13257–**1**/–2	O thank me not, Op. 14, No. 1 (Widmung–Rückert, English trans. Oxenford–Franz). Violin obbligato by Alfred Cave	RLS 716
OEA 13258–1/–2★	*Jeanne d'Arc:* Adieu forêts (Tchaikovsky, arr. Spicker)	RLS 707
OEA 13259–1/–2★	*Sir John in Love:* Greensleeves (Trad., arr. Vaughan Williams)	RLS 716
OEA 13260–1/–**2**	Land of Heart's Desire (MacLeod–Kennedy-Frazer). Violin obbligato by Alfred Cave	RLS 716

11 November 1948, New York: Bell Telephone Hour
Land of Heart's Desire (Trad.)
Phidylé (Coppée–Duparc)

13 June 1949, New York: Bell Telephone Hour
Jubilee: Begin the Beguine (Porter)
Leezie Lindsay (arr. Lawson)
The Meeting of the Waters (Trad.)
Tristesse éternelle (Chopin)

★ Cannot be verified which tape was dubbed.

Matrix no.   *Catalogue no.*

2 June 1950, London: BBC
With Frederick Stone (piano)

BBC Tape: 15378   *Dido and Aeneas:* When I am laid in earth
(Tate–Purcell)   EJS 478

Dido and Aeneas: If music be the food of love
(Tate–Purcell)   EJS 478

Gentil Gallant de France (Wallis)   EJS 478

Vieille Chanson de chasse (Trad., arr.
Manning)   EJS 478

Heures d'été (Samain–Rhené–Baton)

Dein blaues Auge (Goethe–Wolf)   EJS 478

Psyché (Corneille–Paladilhe)   EJS 478

Si mes vers avaient des ailes (Hugo–Hahn)   EJS 478

7 October 1951, BBC Third Programme

Dido and Aeneas (complete Mermaid
production with Flagstad, Hemsley,
conductor Geraint Jones)   EJS 546*

25 November 1958, BBC

LP 24661   En sourdine (Verlaine–Hahn)†   EJS 478

Ciboulette: Ce n'était pas la même chose
(des Fleurs and de Croissat–Hahn)   EJS 171

BBC Talks and Interviews
13 September 1948

12257   Description of first meeting with Debussy

15 September 1950

16139–40   Personal View: Interview by Alec Robertson
on return from America

26 November 1958

LP 24661   As I Look Back: Reminiscences about her
fifty years as a singer

29 October 1959

LP 25744   Frankly Speaking: Talks to John Bowen,
Robert Muller and Alec Robertson

* Unauthorized private issue in USA.
† Not broadcast, though issued on EJS label.

17 January 1967

LP 30599   Interview: Reminiscences of Sir Thomas
                Beecham

7 March 1968

LP 32406   Interview by Madeau Stewart on Debussy
LP 32416–7   Interview by Madeau Stewart on her life and
                art

22 March 1968

LP 31834   Desert Island Discs: Interview on her career,
                and choice of records

1 November 1978
Desmar Records, New York

"Maggie Teyte at Town Hall, 1948"
  with John Ranck (piano)   GHP 4003
includes:
Les Illuminations (Rimbaud–Britten)
Excerpts from *Pelléas et Mélisande*
  (Maeterlinck–Debussy)

Index

GARRY O'CONNOR

GARRY O'CONNOR was educated at St Albans School and King's College, Cambridge. He studied mime at the Jacques Lecoq School in Paris before joining the Royal Shakespeare Company in 1962. He has reviewed theatre and films for *The Times* and the *Financial Times,* has directed plays at various theatres, and since 1967 has had five of his own plays produced, among them *The Musicians, Semmelweis,* and most recently, *Dialogue Between Friends* (London, 1976). His first book, *French Theatre Today,* was published in 1976.

Little Teyte had no such captivating powers. There was to be no throwing of kisses to win her public, no camping it up for the press corps. She was far more prepared to turn her back on them than open up her front. She would win through, if ever she was going to win through, on the quality of her technique. After all, as she so often thought and often said, who gave a damn about Melba's personality? It was the voice which mattered. When Teyte made headlines, Quaintance Eaton wrote, it was usually on behalf of righteousness; a stage manager was bullying a female member of the chorus in Philadelphia and she "threatened to have him horsewhipped" (actually, she said, she remonstrated forcibly). Another time she skilfully ensnared the leader of the Philadelphia claque, a sinister *bonhomme* by the name of Nathan Arlack who demanded $500 to ensure she would not be hissed, into repeating his demand so it could be heard by opera-house officials and press men in an adjoining room. The press burst in, the villain was unmasked.

Her American début was as Cherubino with the Chicago-Philadelphia Opera Company on 4 November 1911, at the Philadelphia Metropolitan Opera House. Otherwise the cast was Gustave Huberdeau, who sang Figaro; Alice Zeppilli as Susanna, Carolina White as the Countess, Louise Bérat as Marcellina, and Mario Sammarco as the Count. Campanini conducted. "The elements were a little racially diverse for a well-blended performance."[15] On 25 November in Chicago, opposite Mary Garden as Prince Charming, she sang the role of Cinderella at the American première of Massenet's *Cendrillon*. This was so successful she repeated it the next season, with Helen Stanley in the travesty role. Maggie wore her size $3\frac{1}{2}$ glass slippers—hardly a journalist missed picking this up—and looked utterly unearthly at the ball: there is to this day in the Art Institute in Chicago, on the fifth-floor landing, a painting of her in her spectacular jewel-studded and brocaded gown. According to the *Chicago Tribune* the scenic display was the most "attractive" and "pretentious" ever shown in Chicago, but the lighting left much to be desired: they never learnt the trick of handling it during the transformation scene.[16]

Andreas Dippel's Chicago-Philadelphia Company also produced, in Maggie's first season, Jean Nouguès's five-act opera *Quo Vadis*, in which she sang Lygia: this was based on the Sienkiewicz novel and was already showing its cinematographic potential, for several miles of painted scenery were needed. As was tartly pointed out, the conflagration scene would scarcely have warmed anyone's hands; however, on a reciprocal arrange-